THE EMOTIONAL DYNAMICS OF LAW
AND LEGAL DISCOURSE

In his seminal work, *Emotional Intelligence*, Daniel Goleman suggests that the common view of human intelligence is far too narrow and that emotions play a much greater role in thought, decision-making and individual success than is commonly acknowledged. The importance of emotion to human experience cannot be denied, yet the relationship between law and emotion is one that has largely been ignored until recent years. However, the last two decades have seen a rapidly expanding interest among scholars of all disciplines into the way in which law and the emotions interact, including the law's response to emotion and the extent to which emotions pervade the practice of the law. In *The Emotional Dynamics of Law and Legal Discourse* a group of leading scholars from both sides of the Atlantic explore these issues across key areas of private law, public law, criminal justice and dispute resolution, illustrating how emotion infuses all areas of legal thought. The collection argues for a more positive view of the role of emotion in the context of legal discourse and demonstrates ways in which the law could, in the words of Goleman, become more emotionally intelligent.

The Emotional Dynamics of Law and Legal Discourse

Edited by
Heather Conway and John Stannard

•HART•
OXFORD • LONDON • NEW YORK • NEW DELHI • SYDNEY

HART PUBLISHING
Bloomsbury Publishing Plc
Kemp House, Chawley Park, Cumnor Hill, Oxford, OX2 9PH, UK

HART PUBLISHING, the Hart/Stag logo, BLOOMSBURY and the Diana logo are
trademarks of Bloomsbury Publishing Plc
First published in Great Britain 2016

First published in hardback, 2016
Paperback edition, 2019

A catalogue record for this book is available from the British Library.

Library of Congress Cataloging-in-Publication Data

Names: Conway, Heather (Law teacher), editor. | Stannard, John E., editor.

Title: The emotional dynamics of law and legal discourse / edited by Heather Conway and John Stannard.

Description: Oxford [UK] ; Portland, Oregon : Hart Publishing, 2016. | Includes bibliographical references
and index.

Identifiers: LCCN 2016034319 (print) | LCCN 2016034946 (ebook) | ISBN 9781849467872
(hardback) | ISBN 9781509902477 (Epub)

Subjects: LCSH: Law—Psychological aspects. | Jurisprudence—Psychological aspects. | Emotions
(Philosophy) | Intentionality (Philosophy) | Empathy.

Classification: LCC K346 .E46 2016 (print) | LCC K346 (ebook) | DDC 340/.19—dc23

LC record available at https://lccn.loc.gov/2016034319

ISBN: HBK: 978-1-84946-787-2
PB: 978-1-50992-889-7
ePDF: 978-1-50990-246-0
ePub: 978-1-50990-247-7

Typeset by Compuscript Ltd, Shannon

To find out more about our authors and books visit www.hartpublishing.co.uk. Here you will find
extracts, author information, details of forthcoming events and the option to sign up for our
newsletters.

PREFACE

In March 2013, the School of Law at Queen's University Belfast hosted a two-day colloquium entitled 'The Emotional Dynamics of Law and Legal Discourse'. One of the first specialist conferences on law and emotion to be held in the UK, participants were treated to a range of thought-provoking papers from legal academics, a high court judge, a clinical psychologist and a professor of psychology. Our thinking behind the colloquium was fairly straightforward: to bring together a diverse range of people working in the area of law and emotion, and to stimulate further research collaboration. The current edited collection is the first of what we hope will be many by-products of that gathering.

The authors owe a huge debt of gratitude to all those who were instrumental in bringing the collection to fruition. The School of Law at Queen's University provided the funding for the initial colloquium, which ultimately allowed us to invite speakers from England, Scotland, Europe and the United States, and to bring them to Belfast—in some instances for the first time.[1] Thanks also to each of the contributors involved in the collection for producing such a diverse and insightful array of scholarship, and for putting up with our numerous emails when we were probably driving them to the proverbial point of distraction. Every paper in this collection has been subject to a triple peer-review process, with individual chapters reviewed by the co-editors, another contributor to the collection and by an anonymous referee. The editors are extremely grateful to all those individuals who gave their valuable time and expertise to this, and who enhanced the collection as a result.

On the publishing side, thanks to Richard Hart for encouraging the submission of this proposal, and to Hart Publishing for agreeing to publish the book and for their professionalism and endless patience along the way. In particular, we are grateful to Annie Mirza who advised us and reassured at all stages of the submission process, even when it was yet another request for more time! Thanks also to everyone involved in the production process, and especially to Tom Adams as Production Manager.

Heather Conway and John Stannard
School of Law, Queen's University Belfast
March 2016

---

[1] Though neither the colloquium organisers nor the School of Law can take credit for the heavy snowfall which greeted everyone on arrival, and prompted a very distinctive emotional response from Professor Kathy Abrams who travelled from the University of California at Berkeley and had never seen real snow before!

EDITORS AND CONTRIBUTORS

Editors

Dr Heather Conway is a Senior Lecturer in the School of Law at Queen's University Belfast. She has written a number of articles on emotion in selected aspects of property law, and in the areas of property law and succession law more generally. Her main research interest is in the law governing the fate of the recently dead and associated decision-making responsibilities, with particular emphasis on the laws around the post-mortem treatment of bodies, corpse disposal and disputes within families over their dead (including funeral disputes, and family tensions around exhumation and commemoration). She has presented and published extensively in this area, and is the author of *The Law and the Dead* (Routledge, 2016).

Dr John Stannard is a Senior Lecturer in the School of Law at Queen's University Belfast where he has worked since 1977. His interest in law and emotion dates back to a conference paper written in 1992, and since then he has published on the subject in a range of journals, including the *Journal of Criminal Law*, the *Northern Ireland Legal Quarterly* and the *University of New South Wales Law Journal*. He has also delivered papers at numerous conferences, including the Society of Legal Scholars, the Irish Association of Law Teachers, the Association for the Study of Law, Culture and the Humanities, the International Association for Law and Mental Health, and the Multisensory Law Colloquium. In 2009 he was a Visiting Scholar at the Center for Law and Society in Berkeley, California, and he is keen on encouraging contacts between different groups of scholars working in the field of law and emotion on both sides of the Atlantic.

Contributors

Professor Kathryn Abrams is Herma Hill Kay Distinguished Professor of Law at the University of California-Berkeley School of Law. She holds a JD from Yale Law School, and previously taught at Boston University and Cornell University. Her early scholarship on statutory civil rights led to a focus on social movements that aim to secure greater equality under law. Her work on feminist jurisprudence analysed the use of experiential story-telling to produce feminist legal change, and the resistance to the expression or evocation of emotion in legal discourse. These interests led to her work with Professor Hila Keren on the cultivation of emotion through law, 'Law in the Cultivation of Hope' (*California Law Review*, 2007), and on the foundations and normative trajectory of law and emotions scholarship, 'Who's Afraid of Law and the Emotions?' (*Minnesota Law Review*, 2009). More recently she has become interested in the role of emotion in rights claiming and social movement mobilisation, 'Emotions in the Mobilization of Rights' (*Harvard Civil Rights–Civil Liberties Law Review*, 2011). Her current research project is an empirical study of the immigrant justice movement in the State of Arizona.

Laurel Farrington is a mediator with Mediation Hertfordshire. She has had a long career in local government and the voluntary sector in social work and management and in a wide range of settings across every client group. Originally trained and experienced in workplace mediation, over the past six years, she has focused on mediation and conflict coaching with housing association tenants. She is currently a PhD student at the University of Strathclyde, researching the role of empathy in mediation, with particular regard to 'difficult' clients.

Dr Jane Herlihy is a Chartered Clinical Psychologist based in London. She worked briefly at the Medical Foundation for the Care of Victims of Torture (now Freedom from Torture) and then at the Refugee Service of the Traumatic Stress Clinic, a centre for asylum seekers and refugees experiencing difficulties following traumatic experiences. She is now Executive Director of the Centre for the Study of Emotion and Law, writing and conducting research into decision-making in refugee status claims. She has presented widely to clinicians, lawyers and judges, both on the clinical treatment of asylum seekers and refugees following traumatic experiences, and on the psychological aspects of refugee status decision-making. She also has a clinical practice at the Trauma Clinic in London. Dr Herlihy is an associate member of the International Association for Refugee Law Judges (IARLJ) and an Honorary Lecturer at University College, London.

Professor Clare Huntington is Professor of Law and the Associate Dean for research at Fordham Law School. She is an expert in the fields of family law and poverty law. Her major writings include *Failure to Flourish: How Law Undermines Family Relationships*, published by Oxford University Press in 2014. She has also published articles and review essays in leading law reviews, including the *Stanford Law Review, New York University Law Review, Duke Law Journal, Michigan Law Review* and the *University of California at Los Angeles Law Review*. Professor Huntington's legal experience includes serving as an Attorney Advisor in the Justice Department's Office of Legal Counsel as well as clerking for Justice Harry A Blackmun and Justice Stephen Breyer of the US Supreme Court, Judge Merrick B Garland of the US Court of Appeals for the District of Columbia Circuit, and Judge Denise Cote of the US District Court of the Southern District of New York. Prior to joining the Fordham faculty in 2011, Professor Huntington was an Associate Professor at the University of Colorado Law School for seven years. Professor Huntington earned her JD from Columbia Law School and her BA from Oberlin College.

Charlie Irvine is Senior Teaching Fellow at the University of Strathclyde where he leads the LLM/MSc in Mediation and Conflict Resolution. An experienced mediator, he is also Director of Scotland's first Mediation Clinic. His academic work is concerned with the role of mediation in the justice system and the physical and psychological dimensions of conflict resolution. He is currently a PhD candidate at Queen Margaret University, Edinburgh.

Professor Terry A Maroney is Professor of Law and Professor of Medicine, Health and Society at Vanderbilt University. She is a *summa cum laude* graduate of New York University School of Law and has been named a Fellow of the Center for Advanced Study in the Behavioral Sciences at Stanford University for the 2016–17 academic term. Her research focuses on the role of emotion in law, with a particular focus on judicial decision-making; she frequently presents on these topics to judicial gatherings, both in the United States and abroad.

Professor Anne-Marie McAlinden is Professor of Law at Queen's University Belfast having previously held positions as Lecturer in Law and Lecturer in Criminology at the University of Ulster. Her main research interests lie in the areas of the management of violent and sexual offenders, institutional child abuse, and restorative justice where she has published widely. She has acted as a consultant to government on a number of projects including 'Public Attitudes to Sex Offenders in Northern Ireland' (Belfast, NISOSMC 2007) and 'Employment Opportunities and Community Reintegration of Sex Offenders in Northern Ireland' (NIO Statistical and Research Series Report No 20, Belfast, NIO, 2009). Her first book *The Shaming of Sexual Offenders: Risk, Retribution and Reintegration* (Oxford, Hart Publishing, 2007) was awarded the British Society of Criminology Book Prize 2008 for the best first sole-authored book published in the discipline in the previous year. Her second sole-authored monograph, *'Grooming' and the Sexual Abuse of Children: Institutional, Internet, and Familial Dimensions* was published in December 2012 by Oxford University Press as part of the prestigious Clarendon Series in Criminology. The primary research for this book was funded by a small research grant awarded by the British Academy.

Dr Mary Neal is Senior Lecturer in Law at the University of Strathclyde, where she teaches and researches in the fields of Healthcare Law and Bioethics, Property Law Theory, and Jurisprudence. She holds degrees from the Universities of Glasgow (LLB Honours, LLM) and Cardiff (PhD). Her research focuses on beginning and end-of-life issues, and in particular, on meta-disciplinary concepts such as dignity, sanctity, love, and vulnerability. Her most recent publications have addressed the conceptual structure and content of dignity, and rights of conscience in the healthcare context. Her current projects include articles on: assisted dying; conscience rights; and the role of dignity in human rights discourse. She is currently writing a monograph (for Routledge) on pregnancy, property, and personhood.

Professor Dr Antony Pemberton is Professor of Victimology and Deputy Director of the International Victimology Institute Tilburg (INTERVICT) at Tilburg Law School. He is a political scientist and a criminologist. His research interests concern the broad topic of 'Victims and Society', including victims' perspectives on justice, societal reactions to victims and processes of victimisation, cultural victimology, narrative victimology and the ethics of victimology.

Dr Timothy D Ritchie joined the Department of Psychology at Saint Xavier University as Chairperson in 2014. From 2009 to 2014, he earned tenure at the Department of Psychology, University of Limerick; and, from 2007 to 2009, he was a Research and Teaching Fellow at the Centre for Research on Self and Identity, School of Psychology, University of Southampton. In 2006, he earned a PhD in Social and Industrial-Organisational Psychology from Northern Illinois University; a MA in Clinical Psychology from Roosevelt University Chicago (1999); and a BS in Psychology with a Philosophy minor from Loyola University Chicago (1997). Dr Ritchie collaborates with scholars locally and internationally. He is a peer reviewer for over 30 scientific journals, an action editor for three journals, a lead author and a co-author on more than 40 peer-reviewed journal articles, encyclopaedia entries and book chapters; he frequently presents at conferences, colloquia and as a guest lecturer. He promotes students and colleagues to endeavour research, teaching and service that span multiple academic, scientific and applied disciplines across cultures, languages and geographical locations.

Dr Eimear Spain is Senior Lecturer in Health Law in the University of Limerick. Eimear's research interests lie in health, criminal and constitutional law. One of her key interest areas is in the field of law and emotions. She has published numerous books, book chapters and articles both nationally and internationally, including a monograph entitled *The Role of Emotions in Criminal Law Defences: Duress, Necessity and Lesser Evils* with Cambridge University Press (2011). Much of her research is interdisciplinary in nature and she has secured grant funding with colleagues in obstetrics, midwifery, educational psychology and social psychology. She is a founding member and Co-Director of the Centre for the Understanding of Emotions in Society at the University of Limerick.

Dr Stuart Turner is a Consultant Psychiatrist, practising in London. He has an extensive background in the field of traumatic stress, having led a national treatment service, having been past president of both European and International Societies for Traumatic Stress Studies, having co-founded the Centre for the Study of Emotion and Law, and in 2015 being the recipient of the Wolter de Loos award for Distinguished Contribution to Psychotraumatology in Europe.

TABLE OF CONTENTS

1

Contextualising Law and Emotion: Past Narratives and Future Directions

HEATHER CONWAY AND JOHN STANNARD[*]

I. Introduction

In his seminal work, *Emotional Intelligence*, the psychologist Daniel Goleman suggests that the common view of human intelligence is far too narrow, and that emotions play a far greater and more positive role in thought, decision-making and individual success than is commonly acknowledged.[1] But what has emotion got to do with the law? Very little, according to the traditional view of the matter which decrees that law is, first and foremost, the province of reason. As Maroney pointed out in 2006, the law has tended to operate on the assumption that there is a world of difference between reason and emotion; that the sphere of law admits only of reason; and that, in this sphere, it is essential to keep emotional factors out of the picture.[2] Though the law has always had to take account of human emotion,[3] the conventional explanation has given it a very restricted scope;[4] and, while judges and lawyers may have emotions, one of the key skills that they are expected to exercise is setting those emotions aside, to ensure that emotion does not intrude on reason as the true preserve of law.[5]

---

[*] School of Law, Queen's University Belfast.
[1] D Goleman, *Emotional Intelligence* (New York, Bantam Books, 1995).
[2] TA Maroney, 'Law and Emotion: A Proposed Taxonomy of an Emerging Field' (2006) 30 *Law and Human Behavior* 119. See also ML Nelkin, 'Negotiation and Psychoanalysis: If I'd Wanted to Learn About Feelings, I Wouldn't Have Gone to Law School' (1996) 46 *Journal of Legal Education* 420; DM Kahan and MC Nussbaum, 'Two Conceptions of Emotion in Criminal Law' (1996) 96 *Columbia Law Review* 269; and J Schweppe and JE Stannard, 'What is So "Special" About Law and Emotions?' (2013) 64 *Northern Ireland Legal Quarterly* 1.
[3] Various examples are noted below.
[4] SA Bandes (ed), *The Passions of Law* (New York, New York University Press, 1999) 2.
[5] Ibid.

II. The Philosophical Tradition

The perception of law and emotion as essentially mutually exclusive realms has its roots in a broader philosophical tradition whereby, in the words of Robert Solomon, reason and emotion stand in what is essentially a master–slave relationship, the implications being that reason and emotion are essentially distinct; emotion is inferior to reason; and it is the function of reason to keep emotion under control.[6] For the Greek philosopher Democritus, one of the functions of wisdom was to free the soul from emotions;[7] for the Epicureans and Stoics, the extirpation of emotion was the key to the rational life.[8] As late as the seventeenth century, philosophers such as Descartes still held to a rigid distinction between passion and reason,[9] their goal being a model of philosophy based on the deductive method developed by Euclid.[10] However, others have questioned both the existence of a rigid distinction between emotion and reason, and the subordination of the former to the latter. For Aristotle emotions were not, in the words of Martha Nussbaum,[11] blind animal forces, but intelligent and discriminating parts of the personality, closely related to beliefs of a certain sort and therefore responsive to cognitive modification.[12] More recently, Oatley, Keltner and Jenkins have argued that emotions are rational in a number of respects; in particular, they are generally grounded in real events, they help individuals to function in a social world, and they inform and guide cognitive processes.[13] This 'cognitive' theory of emotion— picked up and developed throughout the second half of the twentieth century by a number of scholars[14]—has now spawned an extensive field of literature in its

---

[6] R Solomon, 'The Philosophy of Emotions' in M Lewis, JM Haviland-Jones and L Feldman Barrett (eds), *Handbook of Emotions*, 3rd edn (New York, Guilford Press, 2008).

[7] Cited by K Oatley, *Emotions: A Brief History* (Oxford, Blackwell Publishing, 2004) 42. See also R Sorabji, *Emotion and Peace of Mind: From Stoic Agitation to Christian Temptation* (Oxford, Oxford University Press, 2000).

[8] Oatley (n 7) 43. See also MC Nussbaum, *The Therapy of Desire: Theory and Practice in Hellenistic Ethics* (Princeton, NJ, Princeton University Press, 1994).

[9] Cited by Solomon (n 6) 6.

[10] J Haidt, 'The Emotional Dog and its Rational Tail: A Social Intuitionist Approach to Moral Judgment' (2001) 108 *Psychological Review* 814, 815. This distinction is well-illustrated in a myth (cited by Haidt) from Plato's dialogue *Timaeus*, in which the gods create human heads to house reason, but then have to supply emotional bodies to help the heads move around—ibid, 815.

[11] MC Nussbaum, 'Aristotle on Emotions and Rational Persuasion' in A Rorty (ed), *Essays on Aristotle's Rhetoric* (Berkeley, CA, University of California Press, 1996).

[12] Ibid, 303.

[13] K Oatley, D Keltner and JM Jenkins, *Understanding Emotions*, 2nd edn (Oxford, Blackwell Publishing, 2006) 259–60.

[14] See for example, MB Arnold and JA Gasson, 'Feelings and Emotions as Dynamic Factors in Personality Integration' in MB Arnold and JA Gasson (eds), *The Human Person: An Approach to an Integral Theory of Human Personality* (New York, Ronald Press Company, 1954) and cited by Oatley (n 7); HA Simon, 'Motivational and Emotional Controls over Cognition' (1967) 74 *Psychological Review* 29 and cited in Oatley, Keltner and Jenkins (n 13); and RS Lazarus, 'Thoughts on the Relations Between Emotion and Cognition' (1982) 37 *American Psychologist* 1019.

own right.[15] No longer are emotions seen as a hindrance to human behaviour and interaction; on the contrary, a person without emotion is now reviled in popular culture as a psychopath[16] rather than revered as a philosopher.

III. Emotion in Law

As in the realm of philosophy, the traditional neglect of emotion in law has not been consistent. In certain contexts, most notably that of criminal law, engaging with questions of emotion is unavoidable, and the same is true for other branches of the law. Emotions play a key role in family law disputes, for instance, and one of the main functions of the law of evidence is to avoid the risk of juries drawing conclusions which might be based on emotional prejudice. Meanwhile, practices such as restorative justice and therapeutic jurisprudence are designed to point the way towards the resolution of disputes in a manner so as to avoid leaving those concerned with a sense of grievance and injustice. Nor has emotion necessarily been regarded as something alien to the practice of law; the famous biblical account of the judgment of Solomon in the First Book of Kings[17] is a perfect example, and challenges the assertion that the exercise of emotional empathy has no place in the judicial function.[18]

Despite this, the actual relationship between law and emotion is one that has largely been ignored until recent years. There have always been those who have argued for a more nuanced view of the subject, ranging from members of the American realist movement, such as Jerome Frank, in the early part of the twentieth century,[19] to the advocates of therapeutic jurisprudence in the 1990s.[20] However, the last two decades have witnessed a growing interest in the relationship between law and emotion at a more general level. The agenda was set in 1999 with the publication of *The Passions of Law*,[21] an anthology of original essays

[15] For a general overview see Oatley, Keltner and Jenkins (n 13) ch 10. There is also a journal dedicated to the topic—*Cognition and Emotion* (Routledge), first published in 1987.

[16] See for instance, William Hirstein, 'What is a Psychopath?': www.psychologytoday.com/blog/mindmelding/201301/what-is-psychopath-0. Fans of the US television show *Dexter* (HBO, 2006–13), whose central character worked as a blood-splatter analyst for the Miami Police Department while moonlighting as a vigilante serial killer, will recall Dexter's ongoing struggle to simulate human emotions in order to create the appearance of being a 'normal' person.

[17] 1 Kings 3: 16–28.

[18] We return to this theme in the final chapter.

[19] Noted in TA Maroney, 'The Persistent Cultural Script of Judicial Dispassion' (2011) 99 *California Law Review* 629.

[20] DB Wexler and BJ Winick, *Essays in Therapeutic Jurisprudence* (Durham, NC, Carolina Academic Press, 1991); and DB Wexler and BJ Winick (eds), *Law in a Therapeutic Key: Developments in Therapeutic Jurisprudence* (Durham, NC, Carolina Academic Press, 1996). See also C Slobogin, 'Therapeutic Jurisprudence: Five Dilemmas to Ponder' (1995) 1 *Psychology, Public Policy, and Law* 193; and D Rottman and P Casey, 'Therapeutic Jurisprudence and the Emergence of Problem-Solving Courts' (1999) 240 *National Institute of Justice Journal* 12.

[21] Bandes, *The Passions of Law* (n 4).

looking at the role that emotions play, do not play and ought to play in the practice and conception of law and justice. Edited by Susan Bandes, the collection opened with the same author's ringing declaration that 'emotion pervades the law'.[22] Since then, the relationship between the two has been developed further, and systematic attempts have been made to map out the role of emotion in the law and legal decision-making.[23] The relevant literature has also expanded in a variety of directions, with special journal collections[24] and other discrete publications, covering a range of diverse fields such as criminal law;[25] emotion in judging;[26] victims' rights;[27] refugee law;[28] hate crimes;[29] family law (most notably, divorce and child custody proceedings);[30] and aspects of property law.[31]

Yet, as Maroney herself pointed out a decade ago[32] there is still some way to go before law and emotion becomes established as a discipline in its own

---

[22] Ibid, 1.

[23] As well as the sources immediately below, see BH Bornstein and RL Wiener, *Emotion and the Law: Psychological Perspectives* (New York, Springer, 2010); and SA Bandes and JA Blumenthal, 'Emotion and the Law' (2012) 8 *Annual Review of Social Science* 161.

[24] See for example, the collection of articles published in 'Symposium: Law, Psychology and the Emotions' (2000) 74 *Chicago–Kent Law Review*; 'Special Issue on Emotion in Legal Judgment and Decision-Making' (2006) 30 *Law and Human Behavior*; J Schweppe and J Stannard (eds), 'Special Issue: Law and Emotions' (2013) 64 *Northern Ireland Legal Quarterly*; and TA Maroney and SA Bandes (eds), 'Special Section: Law and Emotion' (2016) 8 *Emotion Review*.

[25] Kahan and Nussbaum, 'Two Conceptions of Emotion in Criminal Law' (n 2) (revisited some 15 years later in DM Kahan, 'Two Conceptions of Two Conceptions of Emotion in Criminal Law: An Essay Inspired by Bill Stuntz' in M Klarman, D Skeel and C Steiker (eds), *The Political Heart of Criminal Procedure: Essays on the Themes of William J Stuntz* (New York, Cambridge University Press, 2011)); V Nourse, 'Passion's Progress: Modern Law Reform and the Provocation Defense (1997) 106 *Yale Law Journal* 1331; and E Spain, *The Role of Emotions in Criminal Law Defences: Duress, Necessity and Lesser Evils* (Cambridge, Cambridge University Press, 2011).

[26] Maroney has written extensively in this field—see for example, Maroney, 'The Persistent Cultural Script of Judicial Dispassion' (n 19); TA Maroney, 'Angry Judges' (2012) 65 *Vanderbilt Law Review* 1207; TA Maroney, 'Judges and their Emotions' (2013) 64 *Northern Ireland Legal Quarterly* 11; and TA Maroney and JJ Gross, 'The Ideal of the Dispassionate Judge: An Emotion Regulation Perspective' (2014) 6 *Emotion Review* 142.

[27] J Doak, *Victims' Rights, Human Rights and Criminal Justice: Reconceiving the Role of Third Parties* (Oxford, Hart Publishing, 2009); SA Bandes, 'Victims, "Closure", and the Sociology of Emotion' (2009) 72 *Law and Contemporary Problems* 1; and J Doak and L Taylor, 'Hearing the Voices of Victims and Offenders: The Role of Emotions in Criminal Sentencing' (2013) 64 *Northern Ireland Legal Quarterly* 25.

[28] See J Herlihy, 'The Psychology of Seeking Protection' (2009) 21 *International Journal of Refugee Law* 171; and J Herlihy and S Turner, 'What Do We Know So Far about Emotion and Refugee Law?' (2013) 64 *Northern Ireland Legal Quarterly* 47.

[29] K Abrams, 'The Progress of Passion' (2002) 100 *Michigan Law Review* 1602.

[30] See for example, S Moldonado, 'Cultivating Forgiveness: Reducing Hostility and Conflict after Divorce' (2008) 43 *Wake Forest Law Review* 441; and C Huntingdon, 'Repairing Family Law' (2008) 57 *Duke Law Journal* 1245.

[31] See H Conway and J Stannard, 'The Emotional Paradoxes of Adverse Possession' (2013) 64 *Northern Ireland Legal Quarterly* 75; and H Conway and J Stannard, 'Property and Emotions' (2016) 8 *Emotion Review* 38.

[32] Maroney, 'Law and Emotion' (n 2). See also SJ Morse, 'New Neuroscience, Old Problems' in B Garland (ed), *Neuroscience and the Law: Brain, Mind and the Scales of Justice* (New York, Dana Press, 2004); and K Abrams and H Keren, 'Who's Afraid of Law and the Emotions' (2009) 94 *Minnesota Law Review* 1997.

right,[33] and the current edited collection addresses some of the main gaps in the existing scholarship. A number of issues can be identified, the first of which is the somewhat disjointed nature of the work in this field, with different groups approaching the topic from different angles instead of taking a more holistic approach. Mention has already been made of the American realist and therapeutic jurisprudence movements; other groups are also interested in law and emotion from a range of perspectives such as multisensory law, the restorative justice movement, community justice and collaborative law, all operating independently and largely in ignorance of each other.[34] Second, though attempts have recently been made to look at the topic from a wider perspective, much of the earlier work on law and emotion tended to focus on criminal justice aspects,[35] as well as being somewhat speculative in nature.[36] Third, the study of law and emotion has historically been very much a North American phenomenon, and though there is now a growing interest amongst scholars elsewhere, few concerted efforts have been made to raise its profile to a wider audience. Last but not least, a lot more needs to be known about law and emotion in the context of legal discourse. Some work has been done in this area,[37] but this is still one of the major gaps in law and emotion scholarship, and an area which needs to be explored.

IV. The Current Collection

The Emotional Dynamics of Law and Legal Discourse addresses these issues in a number of ways, building on a colloquium hosted by the School of Law at Queen's University Belfast in March 2013 and attended by a number of international scholars who are also contributing here. The aim is to raise the profile of law and emotion outside North America, with a theoretically grounded collection of essays

---

[33] One underlying reason is the fact that there are so many ways in which the topic can be approached—something which we return to below.

[34] See for example, CR Brunschwig, 'Law Is Not or Must Not Be Just Verbal and Visual in the 21st Century: Toward Multisensory Law' (2010) *Internationalisation of Law in the Digital Information Society: Nordic Yearbook of Law and Informatics* 231; LR Spain, 'Collaborative Law: A Critical Reflection on Whether a Collaborative Orientation Can Be Ethically Incorporated into the Practice of Law' (2004) 56 *Baylor Law Review* 141; J Braithwaite, *Restorative Justice and Responsive Regulation* (Oxford, Oxford University Press, 2002); and G Bazemore and M Schiff, *Restorative Community Justice: Repairing Harm and Transforming Communities* (Abingdon, Routledge, 2015).

[35] A point made in Abrams (n 29) and again in K Abrams and H Keren, 'Law in the Cultivation of Hope' (2007) 95 *California Law Review* 319, 319–20.

[36] More recently, the point has been made that, for law and emotion to have any credibility it must—as with any other interdisciplinary field—have a proper theoretical grounding: Maroney, 'Law and Emotion' (n 2); and Schweppe and Stannard, 'What is So "Special" about Law and Emotions?' (n 2). Some of the challenges that this poses are discussed in JA Blumenthal, 'Law and the Emotions: The Problem of Affective Forecasting' (2005) 80 *Indiana Law Journal* 155.

[37] See for example, Abrams and Keren, 'Law in the Cultivation of Hope' (n 35) and Maroney, 'Angry Judges' (n 26).

which draws on a range of scholarship and takes the discipline to a wider audience. The collection looks at law and emotion in a much broader legal context, focusing on a range of discrete areas of law across the spectrum of private law, public law, criminal justice and dispute resolution, to show how emotion infuses all areas of legal thought while arguing for a more positive view of the role of emotion in the context of legal discourse. Emotions tend to be noticed in law when they are creating a problem—for example, in the context of crimes of passion, family disputes over the dead and damages for emotional distress.[38] However, emotions can also be a solution, and a common thread running through the collection is an acceptance of the way in which emotions can legitimately infuse and pervade the world of law.

So, how do we go about exploring these various themes? In an influential article published in 2006, Terry Maroney suggested at least six possible approaches to law and emotion:[39] (1) the 'doctrine-centered' approach (the ways in which emotions are or should be reflected in different areas of legal doctrine); (2) the 'emotion-centered' approach (the way in which the law responds to or reflects particular discrete emotions); (3) the 'actor-centered' approach (the way in which emotion can or should affect the work of particular legal actors such as judges, solicitors and barristers); (4) the 'emotional phenomenon' approach (describing particular emotional phenomena and analysing how these should be reflected in law); (5) the 'emotion-theory' approach (examining legal doctrines and practices in the light of particular theories of emotion); and (6) the 'theory-of-law' approach (analysing the emotional theories and presuppositions reflected in particular legal theories). Another way of looking at it is to divide the study of law and emotion into three broad, but interlinking, strands. The first looks at the law's response to emotion (moving beyond the traditional paradigm of a calm and dispassionate law having to deal with complex and unruly emotions coming before it); the second at the ways in which the law can create an emotional response in others (both participants in legal actions and the wider public); and the third at the role of emotion in the practice of the law. Obviously, the extent to which these emotional dynamics come into play will vary from case to case, as the individual chapters in this collection illustrate.

Drawing on these core themes, chapters two, three and four of the collection begin by looking at a number of issues within the private law setting, focusing on legal disputes which are driven by emotion and which require an emotionally-responsive approach. Huntington initiates the discussion in chapter two by looking at family law's response to emotion in disputes surrounding close personal

---

[38] See for example, J Horder, *Provocation and Responsibility* (Oxford, Clarendon Press, 1992); and H Conway and J Stannard, 'The Honours of Hades: Death, Emotion and the Law of Burial Disputes' (2011) 34 *University of New South Wales Law Journal* 860.

[39] Maroney, 'Law and Emotion' (n 2).

relationships and child welfare, and at attempts within the US legal system to move towards a more reparative model. In chapter three, Conway explores another type of emotionally-charged family conflict: that of adult siblings fighting over a dead parent's estate where assets are not divided equally, and the unique and inherently complex emotional matrix that this creates. Staying within the private law realm, Stannard uses chapter four to suggest how an understanding of the emotional dynamics of the relationships involved can help to illustrate and inform the law of undue influence, where it is claimed that one person has used a position of dominance to persuade another individual to enter into a disadvantageous legal transaction.

Chapter five sees a change in emphasis, as Neal unpacks the emotional context of end-of-life narratives in the field of healthcare law and ethics, focusing on the concept of dignity and how emotion-shaping language triggers certain reactions. Similar broad themes are explored in chapter six, as Pemberton examines victims' emotions in the criminal justice context, and the importance of empathy and narrative in shaping an appropriate legal response. McAlinden then focuses on a distinct aspect of contemporary criminal justice debates in chapter seven, exploring the complex relationships between emotions, cognition and appraisal and the 'degrees of emotion' evidenced in public responses to sex offenders against children. The role of emotion in legal decision-making assumes centre stage again in chapter eight, as Herlihy and Turner examine the role of emotion in UK asylum cases, using the examples of claims by survivors of torture and victims of sexual assault. Abrams explores another topical issue in chapter nine: how emotion functions and changes in the context of social justice movements, focusing on the US movement for immigrant rights and how existing laws and policies have also elicited a specific emotional response.

In chapters ten, eleven and twelve the emphasis shifts to emotions in the practice of law and the shared experiences of key personnel within the legal system. Irvine and Farrington begin by focusing on the role of the mediator in chapter ten, and the need for such persons to be 'emotionally literate' in dealing with emotions and displaying empathy in particular. In chapter eleven, Spain and Ritchie look at the emotions experienced by members of the legal profession, and the impact of emotional suppression and emotional dissonance on their health and wellbeing. Maroney then uses chapter twelve to examine the role of emotion in judging, challenging the traditional view that judges should not feel emotion or allow it to influence their judgments, and arguing that certain emotions should be embraced. Finally, reflecting on the collection overall, Stannard and Conway use chapter thirteen to sketch out ways in which the practice of emotional intelligence can help the law to be more receptive to emotions and their consequences, while positing ways in which this might be achieved.

V. Conclusion

Of course, *The Emotional Dynamics of Law and Legal Discourse* will not be the last word on the subject. Much remains to be done in terms of bringing together the different groups involved in the study of law and emotion, and aligning the often disparate literature on the topic. The various chapters in this collection have also signposted potential directions for future developments and interactions, which other works might explore.[40] Our goal in producing this collection, however, is to present a range of insights into what is still a relatively new and emerging field, but one which promises to bear much fruit as both legal scholarship and interdisciplinary research within the humanities and social sciences pursue more meaningful lines of enquiry. In 2007, Abrams and Keren acknowledged that '[l]egal thought has been slow to engage the emotions'.[41] Almost a decade later, things have certainly moved on as legal academics and those involved in the practice of law increasingly accept that the role of emotion can neither be avoided nor neglected. *The Emotional Dynamics of Law and Legal Discourse* is another attempt to counteract many of the negative assumptions which have attached to law and emotion scholarship in the past.[42] Winning over a sceptical audience is never easy, as those who have been writing in the area for years will testify; but in highlighting the ways in which emotions and their consequence can enrich both law and legal discourse, the collection ultimately points the way towards a more emotionally intelligent system of law.

---

[40] Other areas of future study have also been signposted elsewhere—see for example, Bandes and Blumenthal (n 23).

[41] Abrams and Keren, 'Law in the Cultivation of Hope' (n 35) 319.

[42] In particular, the distinction between emotions and reason, and the idea of a dispassionate law which must not yield to displays of emotion.

2

Affective Family Law

CLARE HUNTINGTON[*]

I. Introduction

A casual observer of the US legal system (or any legal system for that matter) might think that if any area of the law is attuned to emotion it would be family law. It does not take a degree in psychology to understand that divorcing spouses may feel anger and resentment; that children in foster care may experience abandonment and fear; and that parents who lose custody of a child to the state may suffer a deep loss. Despite this intuitive understanding, family law fails, for the most part, the emotional intelligence test. That is, the US family law system is not well attuned to the emotional needs of the litigants. Rather than recognising a range of emotions, and rather than trying to work with these emotions productively, too often family law embraces a thin understanding of the emotional lives of families and fails to cultivate positive emotions within families. This chapter explores these themes, demonstrating that the emotional valence of family relationships presents both challenges and opportunities for family law. There are subjects within family law, but this chapter chooses the creation and dissolution of legal ties—whether through marriage, divorce, separation, adoption, or the removal of a child from the home—to illustrate the value of a law-and-emotion analysis.

In examining the role of emotion in these areas of family law, this chapter does not argue that family law has a unique claim on emotion. As the other chapters in this volume demonstrate, emotion runs through nearly all legal disputes. But there are distinct considerations in family law—as evidenced by this chapter as well as Conway's chapter on siblings and inheritance[1]—that require attention to the role of emotion and make family law a fruitful site for exploring the themes in this collected volume. In particular, this chapter examines family law's response to existing emotions and the appropriate place for emotion in family law.

---

[*] This chapter draws on earlier work by the author, most notably C Huntington, 'Repairing Family Law' (2008) 57 *Duke Law Journal* 1245.
[1] See Conway, ch 3.

The chapter focuses on US law, but the broad lessons are applicable to other family law systems, especially countries that, like the US, rely on a court-based system of dispute resolution for family matters.

As elaborated below, the central argument of the chapter is that family law must be particularly careful not to introduce or exacerbate existing acrimony but that it also has an opportunity to cultivate more positive emotions in family members. Paying close attention to the emotional aspects of disputes within the family holds the potential for creating a more effective legal system that benefits both litigants and society more broadly. After establishing these principles, this chapter looks at one of the most important issues facing family law in the US: the treatment of non-marital families. These families present particular challenges for the family law system because parents often do not use the court system following the end of the relationship; thus, parents are left on their own to negotiate changes in their families. The chapter argues that a law-and-emotion analysis points to alternative strategies to help non-marital families restructure their families following the end of a relationship.

II. Family Law's Response to Emotion

A starting point for examining the role of emotion in family law is what Terry Maroney has called the 'emotion-theory approach'.[2] This takes a discipline, such as psychoanalysis or cognitive neuroscience, and then focuses on a theory within that discipline. Investigating one theory of emotion—here, the cyclical nature of emotion within relationships, particularly as articulated by psychoanalytic theorist Melanie Klein[3]—demonstrates the severe shortcomings of family law.

The current system of family law reflects a shallow and binary understanding of the affective family. Families are either solidaristic and altruistic, filled with love and care, or families are filled with anger and jealousy and prone to violence. This binary model of family law infuses the substance, process and practice of family law in contexts as far ranging as marriage, child welfare and adoption. Yet, it stands in stark contrast to the reality of dynamic, fluid familial relationships with a range of emotions felt across and fluctuating across time. Understanding Klein's theory of the cyclical nature of human emotions and the reparative drive offers powerful insights across the breadth of family law.

This chapter offers Klein's insights into human intimacy not as a scientific theory that can be empirically proven, but rather as a point of entry for thinking about the cyclical nature of emotions in familial relationships.

---

[2] TA Maroney, 'Law and Emotion: A Proposed Taxonomy of an Emerging Field' (2006) 30 *Law and Human Behavior* 119, 128.

[3] M Klein, Love, Guilt and Reparation: And Other Works 1921–1945 (New York, The Free Press, 1975).

A. The Dynamic Cycle of Intimacy

Klein, an early follower of Sigmund Freud and a pioneer in the field of child psychoanalysis, articulated an understanding of the cycle of intimacy.[4] At its broadest level of generality, the theory is that close human relationships move through a cycle of emotions. A person feels love for another. This is almost always followed by negative feelings (which Klein usually calls 'hate', but which is better captured for a modern reader in her other term for these negative feelings—'aggression'),[5] leading to a breach in the relationship. The person then feels guilty about the breach and so seeks to repair the relationship.

Klein developed this theory in the context of the relationship between mothers and infants, theorising that infants first experience love and hate in relation to their mothers. Infants love their mothers when their mothers are satisfying their needs, say during breastfeeding. But when their needs are not gratified, infants feel hatred and aggression towards their mothers.[6] This leads the infant to experience guilt about the negative feelings; the guilt, in turn, creates a powerful drive in the infant to repair the relationship and restore the feelings of love.[7]

This cycle—with feelings of love, then hatred and aggression giving birth to guilt and the reparative drive—is repeated throughout a lifetime, each time widening the scope of a person's ability to love and make reparations. Klein argued that wherever there is a feeling of love, the conflict between hate and love is aroused, which leads to feelings of guilt and then wishes to make good. Thus, according to Klein, making reparation is 'a fundamental element in love and in all human relationships'.[8] Klein concluded that 'these basic conflicts profoundly influence the course and the force of the emotional lives of grown-up individuals'.[9]

A key element of reparation is the acknowledgment of hate and aggression. As one of Klein's colleagues, Joan Riviere, wrote, 'we spend our lives in the task of attempting to keep a sort of balance between the life-bringing and the destructive elements in ourselves'—in other words, counterpoising love and hate.[10] Balancing these forces requires recognition of the universal force of hate. Without such recognition, hate and aggression are more likely to take extreme forms and the cycle of human intimacy is more likely to be forestalled. Recognising the negative emotions enables people to move to the guilt and reparation phases of intimacy.[11]

---

[4] M Klein and J Riviere, *Love, Hate and Reparation* (New York, WW Norton & Company, 1964). Each individual author wrote their own section of the book, but the theory used here is Klein's and is cited accordingly.
[5] Ibid, 58.
[6] Ibid, 61.
[7] Ibid, 117.
[8] Ibid, 68.
[9] Ibid, 62.
[10] Ibid, 45–46.
[11] Ibid.

Similarly, in Klein's view, guilt is a productive emotion, fuelling the reparative drive. Other scholars agree, noting that unlike empathy, which is a 'bystander emotion' experienced by someone who is not responsible for hurting another, guilt is the recognition that the person feeling it played a role in hurting another.[12] It thus becomes a signal to that person that a relationship is threatened and some action should be taken.[13] The reparation that follows can occur within a person's own internal, emotional landscape, but it takes its primary expression in a person's relationships with others and becomes a powerful force for constructive action in repairing those relationships.[14] Klein acknowledged that not everyone is able to realise the drive towards reparation, but she contended that it exists in everyone.[15]

Although Klein makes claims of innateness,[16] the reparative drive does not have to be universal to be relevant.[17] Instead, Klein's reparative theory is emblematic of a broader discourse on the importance of repair.[18] Moreover, the reparative drive is part of a larger group of relational instincts and motivations, such as tending[19] and altruism,[20] and parallels the enquiry of moral psychologists.[21]

In short, Klein articulated a cycle of intimacy, and argued that facilitating the flow from one phase to the next holds great potential both for individual development and wellbeing as well as for relationships between individuals. With Klein's theory in mind, the next section examines the implications of the theory for family law.

B. Stasis and Opposition in Family Law

Despite its fundamental importance to the relationships that family law regulates, the substance, process and practice of family law too often fail to account for

---

[12] See, eg HW Bierhoff, *Prosocial Behaviour* (East Sussex, Psychology Press, 2002) 139.

[13] Ibid, 144.

[14] RD Hinshelwood, *A Dictionary of Kleinian Thought* (London, Free Association Books, 1989) 399–400.

[15] Klein and Riviere (n 4) 82–87.

[16] Ibid, 65–66.

[17] Claims of universality are always fraught. See, eg AP Harris, 'Race and Essentialism in Feminist Legal Theory' (1990) 42 *Stanford Law Review* 581, 585–86 (arguing that categorical unity is an illusion obtained through the sacrifice of silenced voices).

[18] An extended discussion of the broader discourse can be found in C Huntington, 'Repairing Family Law' (2008) 57 *Duke Law Journal* 1245.

[19] The 'tending instinct', has been described as 'a fundamental truth about human nature: The brain and body are crafted to tend ... in order to attract, maintain, and nurture relationships with others across the life span'. SE Taylor, *The Tending Instinct: Women, Men, and the Biology of Relationships* (New York, Holt Paperbacks, 2002) 12.

[20] A partial survey of the robust literature on altruism can be found in RA Prentice, '"Law &" Gratuitous Promises' (2007) 3 *University of Illinois Law Review* 881, 884–90.

[21] L Kohlberg, *The Psychology of Moral Development: Essays on Moral Development*, vol 2 (San Francisco, Harper & Row, 1984) 174–76. See also L Kohlberg, 'Stage and Sequence: The Cognitive-Developmental Approach to Socialization' in DA Goslin (ed), *Handbook of Socialization Theory and Research* (Chicago, Rand McNally, 1969) 376; ML Hoffman, *Empathy and Moral Development: Implications for Caring and Justice* (Cambridge, Cambridge University Press, 2000) 3.

the cyclical nature of emotions in general and the reparative drive in particular. Family life is neither all about the positive (love, forgiveness, caring, altruism), nor all about the negative (anger, jealousy, envy). Rather, family life is a mixture of these emotions and many more. Perhaps most importantly, familial relationships are dynamic, cycling through emotions of love, anger, guilt and the drive to repair. And yet family law reflects a binary model of emotions—all positive or all negative—and does not reflect or encourage the reparative drive.

Beginning with substance, family law provides binary rules governing entry into and exit from close relationships. In the US, a couple is either married, with all the accompanying benefits and obligations, or unmarried, with very few of these obligations.[22] In the US child welfare system, parents must regain custody of their children or face termination of their parental rights.[23] In the adoption context, after giving birth, a biological parent either places the child for adoption, thus losing all parental rights, or retains custody of the child with parental rights completely intact.[24] Gestational surrogates and close intimates are either granted parental rights or not.[25] These binary rules are justified by the importance of certainty and stability for the child and the need to induce parents to undertake the difficult work of parenting,[26] but they admit of only two possibilities—deep connection or complete rupture.

This binary substance suffuses the process of family law. Courts seek to determine the 'truth' about a familial conflict by settling on a single account of a disputed incident or circumstance. Courts decide whether a parent abused or neglected a child, whether a putative father established a relationship with a child such that he should be entitled to full parental rights, and whether a gestational surrogate intended to relinquish the child upon birth. Although a court will hear evidence on contested facts representing multiple perspectives, the court will ultimately choose one set of facts to the exclusion of others. Once these Manichean narratives reach their conclusion, the family law system then discourages disputants from revisiting such judgments by establishing a higher standard for appealing the outcome.

More fundamentally, the process of family law pits one family member against another. As elaborated below, some procedural alternatives are developing in the

---

[22] AL Estin, 'Ordinary Cohabitation' (2001) 76 *Notre Dame Law Review* 1381, 1395. Of course, the position may be different in jurisdictions that embrace alternative mechanisms for recognising relationships, such as France's Pacte Civil de Solidarité. For a discussion, see, eg E Aloni, 'Registering Relationships' (2013) 87 *Tulane Law Review* 573.

[23] 42 USC s 671(a)(15) (2000).

[24] EJ Samuels, 'Time to Decide? The Laws Governing Mothers' Consents to the Adoption of Their Newborn Infants' (2005) 72 *Tennessee Law Review* 509, 513–18.

[25] *Johnson v Calvert* 851 P 2d 776, 782 (Cal 1993) (holding gestational surrogates do not have parental rights).

[26] J Goldstein et al, *Before the Best Interests of the Child* (New York, The Free Press, 1979); J Goldstein et al, *Beyond the Best Interests of the Child*, 2nd edn (New York, The Free Press, 1979); J Goldstein et al, *In the Best Interests of the Child* (New York, The Free Press, 1986); ES Scott and RE Scott, 'Parents as Fiduciaries' (1995) 81 *Virginia Law Review* 2401, 2440.

US, and mediation is widely used in the divorce context,[27] but the adversarial system remains at the centre of family law. Most marital dissolution actions are settled,[28] but the court remains an important force, with the parties aware that they cede control if the court decides the issues for them.[29] And alternative dispute resolution has barely entered the world of child welfare cases, which are largely decided in courtroom proceedings.

Finally, the practice of family law both embodies and can reinforce the oppositionalism that this substance and process generates. Although it is important not to overstate the case, family law practitioners are often criticised for fuelling their clients' winner-take-all mentality in familial disputes.[30] This is unsurprising in light of the legal training provided to family law practitioners. Family law courses typically are not structured as an interdisciplinary study of family systems, with great attention paid to the emotional dynamics of family relationships. When teaching divorce, for example, most family law courses will examine the legal rules governing child custody and property distribution. The course may acknowledge the emotional stakes in these issues, especially child custody, but the class will not usually teach future lawyers how to work productively with clients who are feeling bitter and resentful towards the other party. Similarly, when teaching students about the child welfare system, the course will focus on the legal rules governing the removal of a child from the home and the standard for terminating parental rights. But very few courses will engage in an in-depth study of family-systems theory, exploring how the parent's behaviour needs to be understood and evaluated in the larger context of the family as a whole, often across generations.

In short, the substance of family law provides only two options for family members—connection or rupture. The process of family law fuels negative emotions by pitting one family member against another in a win or lose battle. And the practice that flows from this substance and process reinforces the binary, adversarial approach. As the next section demonstrates, this approach to family law exacts a tremendous human cost.

C. Failings of the Binary Model

The law should not presume to interfere with private decisions about family relationships—such as whether to get divorced or give up a child for adoption—but the law does determine how those decisions are effectuated, and holds great

---

[27] JC Murphy and JH Singer, *Divorced From Reality: Rethinking Family Dispute Resolution* (New York, New York University Press, 2015) 32.

[28] Ibid.

[29] A Sarat and WF Felstiner, *Divorce Lawyers and Their Clients: Power & Meaning in the Legal Process* (Oxford, Oxford University Press, 1995) 120–26.

[30] RJ Gilson and RH Mnookin, 'Disputing Through Agents: Cooperation and Conflict Between Lawyers in Litigation' (1994) 94 *Columbia Law Review* 509, 541–50.

potential to either exacerbate or alleviate emotional harm. By giving legal force to rupture but providing no room for repair, the binary model short-circuits the cycle of intimacy, thwarting the reparative drive and freezing relationships at the moment of conflict.

i. Hallmarks of Familial Disputes

To understand the harm of the binary model, it helps to recognise how family law is different from other areas of law. There are three hallmarks that typify family law disputes: intense emotions; ongoing relationships; and the need for repair.

Intense emotions. Litigants in family disputes typically know one another at the deepest personal level and are likely to have complicated, emotional relationships with particular histories. Parties include spouses and other romantic partners, biological and adoptive parents, children, extended family members, birth parents, donors of eggs and sperm, gestational surrogates, and prospective parents. Their disputes generally involve intense, usually negative, emotions. Divorce, for example, is understood to be one of the greatest emotional upheavals in a lifetime. The emotional process typically is not linear but rather cyclical, with emotions moving back and forth between love, anger and sadness.[31]

In the child welfare context, the emotions accompanying abuse and neglect for the child victims are complex and can include fear, anger, anxiety, guilt, sadness and bewilderment. A child's emotional response to abuse is necessarily complex, and even though a child will almost certainly experience relief when away from the abuse or neglect, being removed from the home, even temporarily, can be deeply traumatising.[32] For parents who abuse or neglect their children, the emotions are similarly complex. Parents often experience guilt over the abuse, along with anger, denial and fear of losing a child permanently.[33]

Likewise, adoption can evoke complex and conflicting emotions—joy, guilt, loss, fear, anxiety and denial—for birth parents, adoptive parents and adopted children, both at the time of adoption and later.[34] A biological parent whose parental rights are terminated by a court may feel tremendous loss, grief and regret; and parents who voluntarily relinquish a child may feel ambivalent about the decision. During the adoption process, an adoptive parent is often on an emotional roller coaster, worried about the finality of the decision and unsure whether

---

[31] RE Emery, Renegotiating Family Relationships: Divorce, Child Custody, and Mediation (New York, Guilford Press, 1994) 42–48.

[32] See generally J Bowlby, *Separation: Anxiety and Anger* (New York, Basic Books, 1973) 13, 245–57; J Bowlby, *Loss: Sadness and Depression* (New York, Basic Books, 1980) 7–14, 397–411; J Bowlby, *Attachment*, 2nd edn (New York, Basic Books, 1982) 24–34; WL Haight et al, 'Parent–Child Interaction During Foster Care Visits' (2000) 46 *Social Work* 325, 337–38.

[33] CC Tower, *Understanding Child Abuse and Neglect*, 3rd edn (Boston, Allyn and Bacon, 1996) 255.

[34] AR Appell, 'The Endurance of Biological Connection: Heteronormativity, Same-Sex Parenting and the Lessons of Adoption' (2008) 22 *Brigham Young University Journal of Public Law* 289, 295–96.

the child will be returned to a birth parent. And adopted children can experience a range of emotions towards their birth and adoptive parents.

These underlying emotions can lead family members to engage in a range of self- and relationship-destructive behaviours, which, in turn, often affect the legal proceedings. A divorcing couple, for example, may find it exceedingly difficult to set aside their own anger, resentment and disappointment about the ending marriage. Such parties will be more inclined to find fault with each other, rather than recognise the need to work together as co-parents (if the couple had children).

Ongoing relationships. More often than not, the relationships in a family law dispute will continue, even after significant shifts in legal status. When the legal relationship between the parties ends, an emotional relationship or tie is likely to continue. A divorcing couple with minor children will relate to one another for years to come, even if only about the children. A parent in the child welfare system whose parental rights are terminated may well continue to see that child, especially if the child is placed with a relative, as so many older children are. And in the adoption context, only 20 to 30 per cent of domestic adoptions are of infants by unrelated individuals.[35] In all other cases, it is far more likely that the adopted child will maintain a relationship with the birth parent. Even in infant, non-relative adoptions, adopted children may either remain in touch with their birth parents if their adoptions were 'open' (that is, the adoption preserves some relationship between the birth parent and child, ranging from a simple exchange of information to ongoing visitation), or they may reconnect with their birth parents at some later point in their lives.[36]

Changing a legal status may be the right decision for a family. Some marriages should end. Finalising an adoption gives both the adoptive parents and the child peace of mind. And terminating parental rights in some cases is appropriate. But these legal changes do not mean that the underlying relationships are over.

The need to repair relationships. This ongoing contact means that it is critical to repair relationships. Although the romantic relationship between a divorcing couple may be finished, the children still need a relationship with each parent. For this to happen, the parents will need to get along well enough to facilitate these relationships and function as co-parents. In the child welfare context, for the children who eventually return home, it is essential to repair their relationships with their parents. Even when children do not return home, their parents often (although not always) remain an important influence in their lives, and therefore repair is needed. And in the adoption context, although the issues are complex and vary with each case, it is important to pay attention to a child's relationships with both birth and adoptive parents.

---

[35] JH Hollinger, *Adoption Law and Practice* (Danvers MA, Matthew Bender, 2015) s 1.05[2].
[36] NR Cahn and JH Hollinger, 'Adoption and Confidentiality' in NR Cahn and JH Hollinger (eds), *Families by Law: An Adoption Reader* (New York, New York University Press, 2004).

ii. A Fundamental Mismatch

The binary model works against these fundamental realities. The central harm of the model is that it reinforces rupture with no recognition of the need to repair relationships. In some family law cases—particularly those involving domestic violence or sexual abuse—a complete break is essential for the safety and well-being of the parties. Too often, however, family law takes a complete rupture approach and imposes it on all cases, rather than recognising that in many cases, relationships will and should continue even after a change in legal status.

By bringing legal relationships to what the legal system perceives to be closure, courts determine 'winners' and 'losers' and this can be internalised by the parties. Parents often share custody of a child, but the sense that the person with more time with the child has won persists.[37] Family law generally requires that marital assets are divided 'equitably', but parties often experience a sense of victory or defeat in this context as well.[38] There is little recognition in the legal system that 'winning' may create or further weaken a fragile relationship with an ex-spouse, who now is a co-parent and with whom the litigant must work out myriad issues. Instead, the binary model takes any instinct for reconciliation and compromise and directs it towards hard lines and conflict. Some practitioners try to help disputants reach amicable solutions, but in a fundamentally adversarial system, there are substantial constraints on the practice.

In short, the binary model thwarts the cycle of emotions in general and the reparative drive in particular. By recognising only love and transgression, family law freezes familial relationships at the moment of rupture. But because former family members so often continue to relate to one another, stopping at the moment of rupture hinders the ability of individuals to heal the rifts that initially led to the legal proceedings and engage in the reparative work necessary for the future.

D. Partial Reforms

Sometimes drawing on models from other countries, such as New Zealand and Australia, US family law is slowly developing new rules and procedures that are beginning to move the system beyond the binary model. These reforms seem intuitively to embody the reparative drive, but this central organising instinct has not been well recognised and remains underdeveloped.

---

[37] See, eg B Barlow, 'Divorce Child Custody Mediation: In Order to Form a More Perfect Disunion?' (2004) 52 *Cleveland State Law Review* 499, 510.
[38] KB Silbaugh, 'Money as Emotion in the Distribution of Property at Divorce' in RF Wilson (ed), *Reconceiving the Family: Critique on the American Law Institute's Principles of the Law of Family Dissolution* (Cambridge, Cambridge University Press, 2006) 234, 238–44.

Much of the innovation has occurred in the field of marital dissolutions.[39] States have adopted statutes encouraging shared parenting responsibility between parents after a divorce rather than awarding complete custody to one parent and only visitation rights to the other.[40] This sharing recognises the ongoing tie between a child and both parents, as well as the possibility that former spouses can co-parent after a divorce. Similarly, no-fault divorce, widely available since the 1970s in the US, is an attempt to acknowledge that relationships do not always persist and that couples can choose, amicably, to end their marriages.

Mediation has a well-established place in marital dissolution proceedings,[41] and studies have demonstrated its success, particularly in fostering a co-parenting relationship between the parents and an ongoing relationship between non-residential fathers and their children.[42] States are also experimenting with innovations focused on co-parenting after divorce. Many states, for example, have formal parenting co-ordinator programmes.[43] The parenting co-ordinator, typically a mental health professional paid by the hour by the parents (often on a sliding scale basis), helps parents work through issues related to the children. Although charged with decision-making responsibility, the co-ordinator more often helps the parents negotiate their own compromise. Another innovation is parenting programmes—education programmes, sometimes mandated by the court, designed to teach parents how to work together following a divorce or separation. In one study, a programme designed for non-custodial fathers showed that participants had a significant increase in co-parenting with a corresponding decrease in parental conflict after fathers participated in the programme.[44]

In another example of innovation in marital dissolutions, practitioners have led efforts to resolve disputes outside the adversarial system.[45] In the growing

[39] JB Singer, 'Dispute Resolution and the Postdivorce Family: Implications of a Paradigm Shift' (2009) 47 *Family Court Review* 263.

[40] For a discussion of this trend, see, eg JL Grossman and LM Friedman, *Inside the Castle: Law and the Family in 20th Century America* (Princeton NJ, Princeton University Press, 2011) 221–23.

[41] AL Milne et al, 'The Evolution of Divorce and Family Mediation: An Overview' in J Folberg et al (eds), *Divorce and Family Mediation: Models, Techniques and Applications* (New York, Guilford Press, 2004) 6.

[42] RE Emery et al, 'Child Custody Mediation and Litigation: Custody, Contact, and Co-parenting 12 Years After Initial Dispute Resolution' (2001) 69 *Journal of Consulting and Clinical Psychology* 323, 325–31. See also J Pearson and N Thoennes, 'Mediating and Litigating Custody Disputes: A Longitudinal Evaluation' (1984) 17 *Family Law Quarterly* 497.

[43] NL Tooher, 'Parenting Coordinators Help Divorced Couples Who Won't Stop Fighting' *Lawyers USA* (20 November 2006) 12. For an example of a state statute, see Colo Rev Stat s 14-10-128 (2013).

[44] JT Cookston, 'Effects of the Dads for Life Intervention on Interparental Conflict and Coparenting in the Two Years After Divorce' (2007) 46 *Family Process* 123, 132–35.

[45] eg, Charles Asher, a practitioner in Indiana, has been making both local and national efforts at reform and in particular has been attempting to help parents understand the impact of adversarial proceedings on children. In a website he designed, Asher asks parents to enter into commitments regarding their behaviour towards each other and their children. C Asher and B Asher, 'Up To Parents' (*UpToParents.org*): www.uptoparents.org.

field of collaborative law,[46] both the parties and their lawyers agree to negotiate divorce settlements without litigation. To this end, the lawyers and parties decide that the attorneys will represent the clients only during settlement negotiations and, if settlement fails, the attorneys will be disqualified from taking the case to trial. The parties contract for this representation through a limited retention agreement between each attorney and client. The attorneys and clients also often sign a 'four-way' agreement setting forth the intention of the representation and understanding of the process.[47] Collaborative coaches trained in the field of mental health help couples address emotional issues underlying the divorce, issues that may undermine the collaborative process.[48] Practitioners who use collaborative law contend that the process is appropriate for a broad range of individuals, leads to far more creative and responsive settlements between the parties, is generally less expensive than traditional adversarial litigation conducted by attorneys, and can be more satisfying for clients and attorneys.[49] Although collaborative law is best known for its use in marital dissolution proceedings, it is starting to be used in other settings, such as estate planning and probate, in which maintaining or repairing family relationships is at a premium and traditional litigation may threaten those relationships.

In the field of child welfare, the US has drawn from an innovative process used in New Zealand: family group conferencing. Part of the restorative justice movement, family group conferencing is a legal process designed to help families solve problems and avoid court proceedings.[50] After substantiating a report of child abuse or neglect, the state convenes a conference with immediate and extended family members and other important people in the child's life, such as teachers or religious leaders, to decide how to protect the child and support the parents. The participants, who include the parents and, if old enough, the child, identify the underlying problems and develop a plan for working on the challenges facing the family. Members of the family group conference and the state then work together to provide the needed supports to the family.

In the adoption field, birth parents and adoptive parents can have crafted agreements (often called open adoptions) to ensure ongoing contact between the child and birth parent. Some states make such agreements legally enforceable, but typically only in limited circumstances where there is likely to be ongoing contact

---

[46] PH Tesler, *Collaborative Law: Achieving Effective Resolution in Divorce Without Litigation* (Chicago IL, American Bar Association Publishing, 2001) xix, fn 1.

[47] PH Tesler and P Thompson, Collaborative Divorce: The Revolutionary New Way to Restructure Your Family, Resolve Legal Issues, and Move on with Your Life (New York, HarperCollins, 2006) 39–64.

[48] Ibid, 43–45.

[49] Tesler (n 46) xx–xxi, 14; Tesler and Thompson (n 47) 55–56.

[50] A more detailed description of family group conferencing can be found in C Huntington, 'Rights Myopia in Child Welfare' (2006) 53 *University of California Los Angeles Law Review* 637.

even without the agreement, such as adoptions from the child welfare system, adoptions among relatives, or adoptions by stepparents.[51]

As these reforms demonstrate, family law has begun to move beyond the binary model, but this movement lacks a larger theoretical framework to support these reforms and encourage others. Additionally, although these nascent developments are promising, some of these efforts have met considerable resistance. For example, the Ethics Committee of the Colorado Bar Association in 2007 declared the practice of collaborative law unethical.[52] The Committee found that the four-way agreement violated the rule of professional conduct that bars a lawyer from representing a client if that representation is materially limited by the lawyer's responsibility to a third party.[53] The American Bar Association quickly responded with an opinion of its own, sanctioning the use of collaborative law and thus giving support to collaborative law practitioners in other states,[54] but the Colorado opinion reflects a discomfort with placing the family law attorney in a new, more reparative role. Similarly, family group conferencing is still on the margins of the child welfare system in the US. States and localities have not implemented it on a widespread basis and, too often, have changed the model, taking decision-making power away from families and placing it in the hands of professionals.[55] In the adoption context, courts are often reluctant to uphold open adoption agreements—for example, when a birth parent seeks enforcement of a visitation agreement— precisely because they contravene the idea of clean lines in the law, raising concerns about who, exactly, is the parent of the child, and because an open adoption goes against the tradition in adoption law of transferring all legal rights from a birth parent to an adoptive parent.[56]

These examples are far from the only evidence that a more complete move away from the binary model is needed, on both the theoretical and practical level. As the next section argues, it is possible for the legal system to be much more emotionally attuned to the reality of family life and the needs of family members.

---

[51] United States Department of Health and Human Services et al, 'Postadoption Contact Agreements Between Birth and Adoptive Families: Summary of State Law' (Washington DC, Child Welfare Information Gateway, 2005) 2–4.

[52] Colorado Bar Association, 'Ethics Opinion 115: Ethical Considerations in the Collaborative and Cooperative Law Contexts' (24 February 2007): www.cobar.org/repository/Ethics/FormalEthicsOpion/ FormalEthicsOpinion_115_2011.pdf.

[53] Ibid.

[54] American Bar Association Standing Committee on Ethics and Professional Responsibility, 'Formal Opinion 07-447: Ethical Considerations in Collaborative Law Practice' (9 August 2007) 3–5.

[55] Huntington, 'Rights Myopia in Child Welfare' (n 50) 680.

[56] JH Hollinger, 'The Uniform Adoption Act: Reporter's Ruminations' (1996) 30 *Family Law Quarterly* 345, 373.

III. The Appropriate Place for Emotion

Rather than hinder the cycle of intimacy, family law should facilitate and nurture it. With the reforms just described, family law is moving in a more reparative direction, particularly in the field of marital dissolutions, but much work remains to be done. A comprehensive and clear theoretical framework would undergird these reforms and point to additional and more far-reaching changes that could be made in all areas of family law. In particular, family law should replace the binary model of family law with a reparative model. This new model would acknowledge a range of emotions in familial relationships and incorporate them into the substance, procedure and practice of family law.

A. A Reparative Model of Family Law

Instead of reflecting only love and transgression, the law should embrace the full cycle of intimacy as its framework. This would mean that even when the legal system is facilitating the resolution of conflicts—with divorce, termination of parental rights, or adoption—it would also allow for the possibility of the relationship continuing in some new and perhaps unfamiliar way.

Consider each phase of the cycle of intimacy, beginning with the transgression. Family law must not gloss over harms or negative feelings but instead must acknowledge them fully. In recognising the negative emotions and pain that led to the legal conflict, however, it is important not to prolong those emotions. As psychologist Robert Emery has explained, divorcing spouses often use anger to remain connected with each other and to protect themselves from more painful emotions, such as grief over the loss of the relationship.[57] And, he argues, family law abets this defence mechanism by giving the divorcing spouses a means for fighting.[58] Instead of allowing families to remain mired in negative feelings, it is important to view negative emotions as a tool that helps open the door to the emotion of guilt.

Turning to guilt, the idea is to use this emotion to fuel the reparative drive. Thus, for adults, the goal is not to identify a wrongdoer but instead to acknowledge mutual responsibility for wrongdoing, at least in some instances. As elaborated below, there are some cases, particularly those involving domestic violence, where emphasising mutual responsibility could reinforce a victim's tendency towards

---

[57] RE Emery, The Truth About Children and Divorce: Dealing with the Emotions So You and Your Children Can Thrive (New York, Penguin Group, 2004) 29–34, 160–61.

[58] Ibid, 69, 139–40.

self-blame and a perpetrator's tendency to deny responsibility. But in non-abusive relationships, it may be useful for all adult family members to consider how they contributed to the rupture. In parent–child relationships, the idea of guilt is to recognise that most parents want to seek amends. In the typical child abuse or neglect case, then, the idea is to help the parent see the harm he or she has inflicted, and then work with that parent to repair the relationship.

Finally, reparation is the heart of the new approach. This does not mean a pro forma reparation, which would do little to change the family dynamic. For example, some states still require courts to attempt to reconcile a couple filing for divorce.[59] This type of law is a superficial attempt to 'repair' the relationship. Instead, the focus for the repair should be on the functional relationship of the couple as co-parents. This means helping the ex-spouses understand that theirs will continue to be a joint enterprise, built on a shared love for the children, rather than a shared love for each other.

In the adoption context, repairing relationships means helping the parties understand that a child, particularly an older child, will likely have emotional ties to both the birth family and the adoptive family. Allowing a child to maintain contact with a birth parent would recognise the reality that some adoptive children have multiple ties with different adults, in both birth and adoptive families. This is particularly important when a child is, as so many are, adopted by an extended family member or a stepparent. And in the child welfare context, attending to the relationship between the parent and the child means recognising that a child often will have an emotional tie even to an abusive or neglectful parent. It is easy to think that children in foster care do not want to return home to far-from-perfect parents, but this is often not the case.

There are many reasons why the reparative model will fall short of nurturing reparations-like behaviour. Some litigants may be unwilling to compromise; some parties may not be able to or want to move beyond a sense of being wronged; serious mental illness may make a person unable to engage in a reparative process; and some parties may just want more time before seeking reparations.

---

[59] See, eg Neb Rev Stat s 42-360 (2012); SC Code Ann s 20-3-90 (2006). In addition, some states require their courts to determine whether reconciliation is possible, or continue the proceeding for a certain amount of time, if a spouse or minor child's attorney petitions the court, or if the court believes that the marriage is not irretrievably broken. See, eg Ariz Rev Stat Ann ss 25-316, -329, -381.09 (2012); Cal Fam Code s 2334 (West 2004); Colo Rev Stat s 14-10-110 (2013); Conn Gen Stat Ann s 46b-53 (West 2009); Haw Rev Stat Ann s 580-42 (West 2008); Iowa Code Ann s 598.16 (West 2014); Ky Rev Stat Ann s 403.170 (LexisNexis 2005); Mo Ann Stat s 452.320 (West 2011); NH Rev Stat Ann s 458:7-b (2012); SD Codified Laws s 25-4-17.2 (1998); Vt Stat Ann tit 15, s 552 (West 2015); Wash Rev Code Ann s 26.09.030 (West 2008). Other states permit their courts to order some kind of conciliation counselling upon petition of one or both of the parties, or if the court believes the marriage may be reconcilable. See, eg Idaho Code Ann s 32-716 (West 2010); 750 Ill Comp Stat Ann 5/404 (West 2015); Me Rev Stat Ann tit 19-a, s 902 (2006); Mont Code Ann ss 40-3-121, -124 (West 2009); Ohio Rev Code Ann s 3105.091 (West 2013); Or Rev Stat Ann s 107.540 (West 2003); Tenn Code Ann s 36-4-126 (West 2000); Tex Fam Code Ann s 6.505 (West 2010); Utah Code Ann s 30-3-16.2 (West 2015); Wis Stat Ann s 767.323 (West 2007).

But no model will solve all problems, and despite these limitations, the reparative model holds much greater potential to repair family relationships than the existing binary model.

B. Applying the Model

Having described the reparative model as a conceptual matter, the challenge is to identify the tools and procedures that family law should adopt as a practical matter to further the goals of the model. The proposed changes to the substance, procedure and practice of family law set forth below are intended to begin a conversation—they hardly exhaust the reparative model's potential.

Substance. The reparative model could lead to significant changes in the substance of family law. For example, the reparative model would encourage further adoption of predictable rules governing custody. The American Law Institute has proposed a custody principle that would award physical custody in an approximation of the time each parent spent with the child during the marriage.[60] The goal is to decrease litigation by establishing a settled rule that is fairly easy to apply and that parents could know in advance of the litigation.[61] By contrast, unpredictable rules encourage parties to litigate emotional issues through a custody dispute, thus prolonging the rupture phase and hindering the movement to guilt and reparation.

Another reform is the development of a new legal status for family members who are no longer legally related but who, nonetheless, retain emotional connections. When a couple divorces, for example, if the marriage produced a child and if, as in almost all such marriages, both parents retain at least some legal right to maintain a relationship with the child, the divorcing adults could receive something like a 'co-parent' designation.[62] This legal status would recognise that the parents will almost certainly continue to relate to one another and would reflect that reality, instead of adhering to the legal fiction that their own relationship has completely ended. In the child welfare and adoption contexts, after birth parents' rights are terminated, they could receive the legal status of 'former legal parent' or 'birth parent'. This proposal would better reflect the reality of complex family lives. Rather than imposing a complete break, the new legal status acknowledges the ongoing connection that exists and thus conceives of a place beyond rupture.

---

[60] American Law Institute, *Principles of the Law of Family Dissolution: Analysis and Recommendations* (Philadelphia PA, American Law Institute, 2002) ss 2.08, 2.09.

[61] ES Scott, 'Pluralism, Parental Preference, and Child Custody' (1992) 80 *California Law Review* 615, 617 (first proposing this standard).

[62] Legal scholar Merle Weiner has proposed such a status that would attach at the birth of the shared child: MH Weiner, *The Parent–Partner Status in American Family Law* (Cambridge, Cambridge University Press, 2015). I have also explored this concept, especially as it relates to non-marital families, see C Huntington, 'Postmarital Family Law: A Legal Structure for Nonmarital Families' (2015) 67 *Stanford Law Review* 167.

Whether these designations would lead to legally enforceable rights and responsibilities is a tricky question beyond the scope of this chapter,[63] but at the very
least the designation would recognise and reflect the ongoing connection between
family members.

Other formal changes along these lines could help encourage the reparative
drive. Legal terms can affect the perception of what is at stake, with increasing numbers of states abandoning the win/lose terminology of 'custody' and
'visitation'.[64] In 1999, for example, Colorado changed the legal term to 'parental
responsibilities'.[65] Parental responsibilities are then broken down into 'parenting
time' and 'decision-making authority'.[66] Parenting time is the actual time the child
spends with each parent, and decision-making authority is the ability to make
major life decisions for the child, such as where the child should attend school and
whether the child should be brought up in a religious tradition. Colorado changed
the terminology to recognise the important place of both parents in a child's life
after a divorce.[67] The new terms also help focus the parents on what matters: not
winning or losing custody but instead taking care of children and making important decisions.

Procedure. In many ways, procedural innovations such as collaborative law and
family group conferencing (as well as mediation, which has been in existence
longer) have made it easier to envision a new approach to resolving family law disputes under the reparative model. These efforts all intuitively seek to move away
from the binary model and help family members work towards individualised
solutions. Clients using these alternative processes report high rates of satisfaction
with the process.[68]

More importantly, there is evidence that these alternative processes facilitate the
reparative drive, leading to better relationships in the long term. For example, in
a study that randomly assigned divorce cases either to mediation or litigation, the
parties in the two groups reached relatively similar agreements. But 12 years later,
the fathers in the mediation cases had much more contact with their children and
the parents had a better co-parenting relationship.[69] The researchers in the study

---

[63] A preliminary discussion of the kinds of legal rights that could attach to the co-parent designation can be found in Huntington, 'Postmarital Family Law' (n 622).
[64] See, eg Ariz Rev Stat Ann s 25-403 (2012) ('legal decision-making' and 'parenting time');
Minn Stat s 518.175 (2012) ('parenting time'); Neb Rev Stat s 43-2923 (2012) ('parenting arrange-
ment'); NH Rev Stat Ann s 461-A:6 (2012) ('parental rights and responsibilities'); ND Cent Code
s 14-09-06.2 (2011) ('parental rights and responsibilities'); Ohio Rev Code Ann s 3109.04 (West 2013)
('allocation of parental rights and responsibilities' and 'shared parenting'). See also AE Skove,
'Parenting Time' (Williamsburg, National Center for State Courts, 2000): cdm16501.contentdm.oclc.
org/cdm/ref/collection/famct/id/231.
[65] Colo Rev Stat s 14-10-103 (2013).
[66] Ibid.
[67] Skove (n 64).
[68] See, eg JJ Alfini et al, *Mediation Theory and Practice*, 2nd edn (Danvers MA, LexisNexis, 2006)
555–62.
[69] Emery et al, 'Child Custody Mediation and Litigation' (n 42).

hypothesised that one of the benefits of mediation is that it allows for greater recognition of emotion. In particular, parents in mediation would express anger, but once the mediator probed the anger, it quickly transformed into grief and hurt.[70] This research on mediation supports the need for the reparative model. It could be argued that even in the binary model, former family members will, with the passage of time, heal their rifts. This may be true in some cases, but the research on mediation provides compelling evidence that the law can help families down a reparative path.

Practice. Finally, the reparative model suggests fundamental changes to the practice of family law. The mindset with which attorneys approach their cases has a tremendous impact on the experience of clients, particularly in family law cases.[71] Thus, the goal is for family law attorneys to work with family law clients in a different manner, helping clients think more broadly about disputes and consider whether a legal strategy is furthering a rupture or helping the family repair.

Asking an attorney to help move a client from anger and on towards guilt and reparation raises interesting ethical questions for the lawyer. Some clients may not be ready to move on and instead may insist that the attorney act in a way that entrenches the rupture. The question is whether the attorney should act according to the client's stated wishes or help the client understand that doing so will not serve the client in the long run because it will hinder reparation. In the case of collaborative law, the clients themselves have chosen the alternative process, but whether a reparative mindset can be imposed on an unwilling client, and whether doing so is paternalistic or possibly unethical, are important questions.

There are at least two ways to address these issues. First, attorneys could simply try to persuade their clients of the benefits of following a reparative path. The attorney could try to explain that reparation would further other interests valued by the client, notably a healthy relationship with the child or the child's wellbeing in general. Further, an attorney could model reparative behaviour by not adopting a win/lose attitude to the case. This counselling function is analogous to the role of attorneys representing children in abuse and neglect proceedings under a direct representation model. There, the attorney is supposed to advocate for the expressed wishes of the child client, rather than the best interests of the child.[72] Experienced attorneys acknowledge, however, that even within a direct representation model there is an inevitable counselling role for the attorney to play.[73]

---

[70] RE Emery et al, 'Divorce Mediation: Research and Reflections' (2005) 43 *Family Court Review* 22, 33.

[71] CM Meadow, 'The Lawyer as Problem Solver and Third-Party Neutral: Creativity and Non-partisanship in Lawyering' (1999) 72 *Temple Law Review* 785, 791–92. See also KE Maxwell, 'Preventive Lawyering Strategies to Mitigate the Detrimental Effects of Clients' Divorces on Their Children' (1998) 67 *Revista Juridica Universidad de Puerto Rico* 137, 137, 155–58.

[72] E Buss, '"You're My What?" The Problem of Children's Misperceptions of Their Lawyers' Roles' (1996) 64 *Fordham Law Review* 1699, 1700–01.

[73] Ibid, 1721–25.

Second, and much more fundamentally, we could reconceive the role of the family law attorney in the code of professional conduct. A new approach would require an attorney to provide holistic advice rather than merely advocating for the stated interests of a client. This would not require the attorney to counsel a divorcing couple to reconcile, but rather would require the attorney to resist taking steps that would further harm the relationship. The attorney should not pursue an amicable relationship to the exclusion of all other interests, but rather the attorney would at least consider the interests of the client in the broader context of the family, and attempt to find a way forward that accommodated potentially divergent interests.

This reparative standard of practice could be reinforced by sanctions for those who clearly violate the standard.[74] For example, a sanction could be imposed when an attorney files for sole custody in a case in which there clearly is no basis for it, such as when both parents have been equally sharing the caregiving before the divorce. This raises difficult questions about an attorney's obligation to follow the wishes of the client, and the interest in repair should be balanced against other interests, such as client autonomy. But it is at least worth thinking about reconceiving the role of the family law attorney to reinforce the notion that in family law, a particular kind of practice is needed and expected.

Making these changes to the practice of family law would begin with changes to the family law curriculum in law school.[75] Family law courses would need to train students in the reparative method. This would involve teaching students to have greater emotional competence in the typical emotions surrounding divorce, child welfare cases and adoptions, but also training students to recognise the limits of their own emotional competence.[76] There are necessarily constraints on the lawyer as a locus of reparation, and a legal education should explore these limits, but the skills needed to focus on reparation are taught in other professional institutions, such as social work schools. It is a question of making the time for these kinds of courses and skills training, not our ability to teach the skills. These kinds of skills might be best taught in an interdisciplinary setting, with law faculty teaming up with faculty from other disciplines.

The training in reparative work would continue throughout a career. Professional bar associations, for example, could offer continuing legal education classes (which lawyers are required to take), perhaps culminating in a certification, representing a rigorous course of reparative training. Lawyers could then represent to clients that they have the necessary background and mindset to work with the family in a different manner.

---

[74] One starting point for such a standard would be a close examination of the aspirational standards written by the American Academy of Matrimonial Lawyers in 1992. R Aronson (ed), *The Bounds of Advocacy: Standards of Conduct* (Chicago IL, American Academy of Matrimonial Lawyers, 1992).

[75] ME O'Connell and JH DiFonzo, 'The Family Law Education Reform Project: Final Report' (2006) 44 *Family Court Review* 524, 525.

[76] BG Fines and C Madsen, 'Caring Too Little, Caring Too Much: Competence and the Family Law Attorney' (2007) 75 *University of Missouri Kansas City Law Review* 965, 973–97.

C. Boundaries of the Model

The reparative model does not elevate repair above all other values. Domestic violence is perhaps the most important boundary to the reparative model. There is a strong argument that a battered partner should never be asked to repair a relationship with the batterer and that any ongoing contact, such as through shared custody, creates opportunities for ongoing abuse. Although it is true that family law must be attentive to abuse, in all forms, this does not necessarily mean a complete retreat to the binary model.

Some experts believe that a less adversarial approach to domestic violence can benefit survivors. A leading advocate of restorative justice has asserted that 'court processing of family violence cases actually tends to foster a culture of denial, while restorative justice fosters a culture of apology', and that apology, 'when communicated with ritual seriousness, is actually the most powerful cultural device for taking a problem seriously, while denial is a cultural device for dismissing it'.[77] To the extent that the reparative model better acknowledges the harm done by violence, rather than glossing over it, it might help overcome this denial.

A more fundamental issue is whether family law should encourage co-parenting between partners where there is a history of abuse. A useful place to begin is by acknowledging the debate among domestic violence researchers about typologies of violence between intimate partners. The sociologist Michael Johnson has argued that domestic violence is not a 'unitary phenomenon', and that instead there are four main categories of domestic violence among heterosexual partners: situational couple violence; intimate terrorism; violent resistance; and mutual violent control.[78] The categories are distinguished not by the type and severity of violence, but rather by the degree of control one partner exerts over the other.[79] Professor Johnson argues that in situational couple violence, although violence may be present, controlling behaviour is largely absent.[80] By contrast, in intimate terrorism, the defining characteristic is one partner controlling the other, often using violence as one method of exerting control.[81]

Professor Johnson's typology has been criticised, particularly with the argument that it is difficult to distinguish types of cases ex ante and that situational couple violence may over time escalate into intimate terrorism.[82] But if subsequent

---

[77] J Braithwaite, 'Restorative Justice and Social Justice' (2000) 63 *Saskatchewan Law Review* 185, 189. See also D Coker, 'Enhancing Autonomy for Battered Women: Lessons from Navajo Peacemaking' (1999) 47 *University of California Los Angeles Law Review* 1, 38–73 (describing the benefits of Navajo Peacemaking for victims of domestic violence).

[78] MP Johnson, 'Conflict and Control: Gender Symmetry and Asymmetry in Domestic Violence' (2006) 12 *Violence Against Women* 1003, 1005, 1010–12.

[79] Ibid, 1005–06.

[80] Ibid, 1006.

[81] Ibid.

[82] See, eg V Frye et al, 'The Distribution of and Factors Associated with Intimate Terrorism and Situational Couple Violence Among a Population-Based Sample of Urban Women in the United States' (2006) 21 *Journal of Interpersonal Violence* 1286, 1290–93, 1303–10.

research confirms his typology, it may be possible to treat situational couple violence differently from the other types of domestic violence for purposes of the reparative model. As Professor Johnson argues, the typical situational couple violence case involves far fewer incidents of violence, is less likely to escalate, is less likely to involve severe injury, and is initiated almost as frequently by a woman as by a man.[83] He contends that situational couple violence is probably a result of a conflict expressing itself in violence, rather than one partner controlling the other and using violence as one means of control.[84]

If different types of domestic violence could be predicted with reasonable accuracy, then the reparative model may be the appropriate theoretical framework to help some individuals engaged in situational couple violence move past the violence and be better able to co-parent. By contrast, for cases of intimate terrorism, encouraging reparation and co-parenting is likely a dangerous path to follow.[85] In some cases, complete rupture is necessary, and for these cases, the binary model should be retained. But this only underscores the point that a one-size-fits-all approach to family law misses the important differences between cases and the disparate needs of families.[86] Acknowledging differences among cases does not condone abuse or imply that one type of abusive relationship is less serious than another. Instead, differentiation acknowledges the varied needs of families and can lead to more effective intervention and policies.

As with domestic violence, differentiation in child welfare cases is important.[87] In cases of egregious child abuse and neglect, repairing the relationship likely is misguided. This is especially true in cases of sexual abuse, particularly where the abuser is unwilling to acknowledge the abuse. But for the remainder of cases, some repair may be both possible and desirable.

In all cases, even if personal contact between former family members should not continue, the individuals will need to heal the relationship internally. In this way, the legal system would not facilitate the cycle of intimacy through ongoing relationships, but instead by acknowledging the harm within the person. This recognition would provide an additional rationale for state funding of domestic violence and mental health services. Another potential concern with the reparative model is the need to ensure that family members are on an equal footing. For example, some scholars are concerned that mediation and other alternative

---

[83] Johnson (n 78) 1010.

[84] Ibid, 1005.

[85] *cf* PG Jaffe et al, 'Common Misconceptions in Addressing Domestic Violence in Child Custody Disputes' (Fall 2013) *Juvenile and Family Court Journal* 57, 57–65.

[86] BV Smith, 'Battering, Forgiveness, and Redemption: Alternative Models for Addressing Domestic Violence in Communities of Color' in NJ Solokoff and C Pratt (eds), *Domestic Violence at the Margins: Readings on Race, Class, Gender, and Culture* (Piscataway NJ, Rutgers University Press, 2005) 328–35. See also NV Steegh, 'Differentiating Types of Domestic Violence: Implications for Child Custody' (2005) 65 *Louisiana Law Review* 1379, 1379–80, 1427.

[87] P Schene, 'The Emergence of Differential Response' in *Protecting Children: Differential Response in Child Welfare* (Washington DC, American Human Society, 2005) 4–6.

processes can disadvantage women. Arguments have been made that mediation may require women to speak in inauthentic voices, such as a voice that suppresses anger, and, further, that mediation may disadvantage the party who places a premium on maintaining relationships, arguably the woman.[88] Although this concern should be taken seriously, there is also evidence, at least in some contexts, that women are not disadvantaged in alternative processes. A study of mediated custody agreements, for example, found that women still obtained custody in roughly the same numbers as women with litigated custody agreements.[89]

A final boundary concerns people who will not engage in reparations. When dealing with such participants, it may not be possible to seek reparation between individuals. For example, when a parent refuses to admit the sexual abuse of a child, and the child refuses to have a relationship with the parent absent such acknowledgment, seeking reparation would be misguided. To address the emotional needs of the survivor there may well be a role for third parties— attorneys, friends, other family members—to play in acknowledging the rupture and helping the survivor continue on with life.[90] This support would focus on repairing the harm to the victim, but not repairing the actual relationship with the abuser.

IV. A Case Study: Non-marital Families

A law-and-emotion analysis can be used in many areas of family law, and one of the most pressing issues facing US family law today is the rise of non-marital families.[91] In the US, the percentage of non-marital childbirths has sharply increased. In 2014, 40 per cent of all children were born to unmarried parents, and even higher levels in some demographic groups.[92] Patterns vary in different countries, but in the US, unmarried parents differ from married parents in important respects. They are generally younger, lower income, and have lower levels

---

[88] T Grillo, 'The Mediation Alternative: Process Dangers for Women' (1991) 100 *Yale Law Journal* 1545, 1576, 1600–07; PE Bryan, 'Killing Us Softly: Divorce Mediation and the Politics of Power' (1992) 40 *Buffalo Law Review* 441, 454–56; MF Brinig, 'Does Mediation Systematically Disadvantage Women?' (1995) 2 *William & Mary Journal of Women and the Law* 1, 33; A Sinden, '"Why Won't Mom Cooperate?": A Critique of Informality in Child Welfare Proceedings' (1999) 11 *Yale Journal of Law & Feminism* 339, 373–87.

[89] S Reynolds et al, 'Back to the Future: An Empirical Study of Child Custody Outcomes' (2007) 85 *North Carolina Law Review* 1629, 1631–35, 1658–75.

[90] W Ury, *The Third Side* (New York, Penguin Group, 2000) 114–96 (describing the myriad roles that third parties can play to resolve conflicts).

[91] For a full-length article discussing this issue, see Huntington, 'Postmarital Family Law' (n 62).

[92] BE Hamilton et al, 'Births: Preliminary Data for 2014' (2015) 64 *National Vital Statistics Reports* 1, 4. See also ibid 13 (showing in table 6 that 71.5% of all births to African American mothers were non-marital and 53.2% of all births to Hispanic women were non-marital).

of educational attainment than married parents.[93] Most unmarried parents are romantically involved when the child is born, but the relationship soon ends and many parents then go on to form new relationships and have additional children, creating what sociologists call 'complex' families.[94] After the parents end their relationship, children almost always stay with their mothers,[95] and unmarried fathers become much less involved, with many fathers seeing their children rarely, if at all.[96]

Family law—which is designed for, and largely used by, married families— has not adapted to this new reality of non-marital family life. One of the central problems is that the legal institutions created to oversee the family, particularly upon divorce, are designed for married families that have been formally recognised by the state. A married couple seeking a divorce must go to court to dissolve their legal relationship, but an unmarried couple's relationship was never recognised by the state and thus the couple does not need a court to end the relationship.

As discussed above, the court system presents many problems for married couples, but at least they have a process to help establish co-parenting structures for the couple's post-divorce family life. The court system is open to unmarried couples, but most do not go to court to formalise issues such as custody.[97] This means that unmarried parents are left without an effective institution to help them transition from a family based on a romantic relationship to a family based on co-parenting, and they do not have the benefit of clearly established expectations for their rights and responsibilities following the breakup. Left on their own to negotiate the difficult world of co-parenting, the typical pattern is for mothers to control fathers' access to shared children through maternal 'gatekeeping'.[98] Fathers, who generally do not have custody orders, see their children only if they are able to stay on good terms with the mothers of their children, which many are unable to do.[99] Unsurprisingly, many unmarried fathers see their children irregularly, and much less than divorced fathers.[100]

---

[93] SS McLanahan and I Garfinkel, 'Fragile Families: Debates, Facts, and Solutions' in M Garrison and ES Scott (eds), *Marriage at the Crossroads: Law, Policy, and the Brave New World of Twenty-First-Century Families* (Cambridge, Cambridge University Press, 2012) 146–47.

[94] Ibid, 145–47, 152, 155.

[95] S McLanahan and AN Beck, 'Parental Relationships in Fragile Families' (2010) 20 *The Future of Children* 17, 22–23 (describing father involvement after a relationship ends and not mentioning any fathers with custody).

[96] MJ Carlson et al, 'Coparenting and Nonresident Fathers' Involvement with Young Children After a Nonmarital Birth' (2008) 45 *Demography* 461, 473, 479, 480 (citing data from the ongoing Fragile Families and Child Wellbeing Study and finding that at the time the focal children were five years old, 37% of the non-residential fathers had not seen their children once in the previous two years).

[97] Office of Child Support Enforcement et al, 'Child Support and Parenting Time: Improving Coordination to Benefit Children' (July 2013): www.acf.hhs.gov/sites/default/files/programs/css/13_ child_support_and_parenting_time_final.pdf, 1–2.

[98] K Edin and TJ Nelson, *Doing the Best I Can: Fatherhood in the Inner City* (Los Angeles CA, University of California Press, 2013) 157, 169, 208, 214.

[99] Ibid, 169, 208.

[100] ME Scott et al, 'Postdivorce Father–Adolescent Closeness' (2007) 69 *Journal of Marriage and Family* 1194, 1195 (describing the contact between divorced fathers and their non-residential children).

Using law and emotion to think about this problem sheds some light on a new approach to non-marital families. The starting point is recognising that although we are increasingly witnessing the separation of *marriage* from parenthood, we cannot separate *relationships* from parenthood. As with married parents, it is essential to help unmarried parents learn to work together so that both parents are better able to provide their children with the relationships necessary for healthy child development.

A law-and-emotion analysis reveals that, as in other areas of family law, it is critical to pay close attention to the three hallmarks of family disputes: intense emotions; ongoing relationships; and the need for repair. Both parents are likely to have strong feelings about the other parent as well as the child; the parents need to maintain contact if both parents are to be involved in the child's life; and the parents need to repair their relationship, at least to the point of functioning as co-parents. The challenge for family law, then, is figuring out how to establish an effective system to help non-marital families forestall conflict and transition from romantic relationships to co-parenting. To this end, the US should learn from Australia and their creation in 2006 of Family Relationship Centres (FRCs).[101] The FRCs offer free, readily accessible mediation services in the community, not the courts, to help unmarried parents move into co-parenting relationships and get into the habit of co-operating. Built in centrally located areas such as shopping malls, the centres are designed to be easily accessible and in familiar places.[102] The centres focus on issues concerning children and offer relationship counselling to parents and also referrals to outside services for specific needs, such as addiction and anger management.[103] Plans negotiated at the FRCs are not legally binding, but the idea is that by forging an agreement for the first year or two after the romantic relationship ends, a couple will get into the habit of working together; then, as their lives inevitably change, they will be better positioned to adapt and continue their co-parenting. It is too soon to assess the long-term impact of the FRCs, but initial assessments have shown that they have reached families that would not otherwise have gone to court[104] and that most clients are satisfied with the services they received.[105]

One of the most intriguing ideas of these new institutions is that they are specifically designed to resolve issues at the relationship level rather than resorting to the legal system. Most alternative dispute resolution systems are still legal in nature, either issuing legally binding agreements or established as a part of the court system. Staffed by mediators, FRCs are a community-based approach to

[101] P Parkinson, *Family Law and the Indissolubility of Parenthood* (Cambridge, Cambridge University Press, 2011) 187.
[102] Ibid, 188.
[103] Ibid, 187–88.
[104] Ibid, 208–09.
[105] R Kaspiew et al, 'Evaluation of the 2006 Family Law Reforms' (Melbourne, Australian Institute of Family Studies, 2006) E2, 58–62.

family conflicts, not a court-based approach, and are designed to forestall court involvement. In the words of Patrick Parkinson, the Australian academic who was the driving force behind the FRCs, '[t]he concept behind the … FRCs is that when parents are having difficulty agreeing on the post-separation parenting arrangements, they have a relationship problem, not necessarily a legal one'.[106] The courts are available if the FRC cannot help with the problem, but courts are only a backup system.

These centres not only offer a completely different paradigm for addressing the conflicts between unmarried parents; they also embody the reparative model outlined in this chapter. FRCs focus on the emotional relationship between the parents, allowing the couple to move forward in different roles: as co-parents not romantic partners. By helping parents create a future where they have a functioning relationship, the centres open the door for repair. And by focusing on concrete, short-term issues, the centres keep expectations manageable and allow the parents to adjust to their new family structure.

In short, FRCs are an innovative approach to helping non-marital families transition into a co-parenting relationship and negotiate ongoing obligations. This is one way to address this problem, and there are surely others as well. The central point is that using law and emotion illuminates the importance of relationships. By appreciating the difficult dynamic between unmarried parents, and maternal gatekeeping in particular, we can see an alternative path forward. Thinking about the role of emotion in the law highlights the real problem facing non-marital families and also points in a new direction.

V. Conclusion

Family relationships entail a range of emotions, and the legal system inevitably intersects with these emotions when regulating relationships. The emotional aspects of family relationships present both challenges and opportunities for family law. Family law must be particularly careful not to introduce or exacerbate existing acrimony, but it also has an opportunity to cultivate more positive emotions in family members, and this chapter has presented a number of possibilities.

As the study of emotion and family law develops, there will be ample opportunity to explore numerous interesting and significant questions. For example, a better understanding of more negative emotions—including the desire for vengeance and the ambivalence individuals experience in marriages and parenting— will help inform family law's approach to familial regulation. Through additional

---

[106] Parkinson (n 101) 197.

research and debate, commentators can help move family law scholarship, and family law itself, away from a rudimentary understanding of familial emotions and towards a richer understanding of the complex and conflicting emotions individuals experience in families. This will surely benefit litigants and families more broadly. In the meantime, however, family law can and should embrace some of the reforms proposed in this chapter. There is no reason to wait.

3

Where There's a Will … : Law and Emotion in Sibling Inheritance Disputes

HEATHER CONWAY[*]

I. Introduction

Succession law affects all families at an emotionally vulnerable time. As the family unit struggles to adapt to the loss of a key figure, estate distributions are a frequent source of conflict within common law systems, where the core value of testamentary freedom allows an individual to bequeath property on death as they see fit.[1] One of the most bitter examples occurs between adult children, following the death of their sole surviving parent.[2] While children are regarded as the 'natural' recipients of parental assets and the majority of wills reflect this,[3] modern distributive patterns favour equal treatment—a socially constructed norm that emerged in the late-twentieth century in Britain and other Western countries.[4]

---

[*] Senior Lecturer, School of Law, Queen's University Belfast. I am grateful to Professor Clare Huntington and Professor Prue Vines for their insightful comments on an earlier draft of this chapter.

[1] In sharp contrast to fixed inheritance rights in civil law jurisdictions—see for example, AL Marquès, 'We Are Not Born Alone and We Do Not Die Alone: Protecting Intergenerational Solidarity and Refraining Cain-ism Through Forced Heirship' (2014) 4 *Oñati Socio-Legal Series*.

[2] In a typical two-parent family model, inheritance issues seldom arise on the death of the first parent since shared parental assets typically pass to the survivor; it is the death of the surviving parent that triggers the distribution of assets between children and the sort of estate contests that this chapter considers.

[3] See for example, G Douglas, H Woodward, A Humphrey, L Mills and G Morrell, 'Enduring Love? Attitudes to Family and Inheritance Law in England and Wales' (2011) 38 *Journal of Law and Society* 245.

[4] M Isaacs, 'Distributing Your Inheritance Fairly: Equity Theory and Will Power' (1998) *Eastern Psychological Association*: scholarworks.rit.edu/article/191. See also D Drake, 'The Will: Inheritance Distribution and Feuding Families' in M Mitchell (ed), *Remember Me: Constructing Immortality—Beliefs on Immortality, Life and Death* (Abingdon, Routledge, 2007) 97 citing research findings by RJ Simon, ML Fellows and W Rau, 'Public Opinion About Property Distribution at Death' (1982) 5 *Marriage & Family Review* 25; and J Finch, L Hayes, J Masson, J Mason and L Wallis, *Wills, Inheritance and Families* (Oxford, Clarendon, 1996). The social norm that children should be treated equally is

As a result, disputes invariably occur when one child receives a larger share of the net financial estate than another or (in a more extreme scenario) inherits everything to the exclusion of his/her siblings; the allocation of specific items of property creates a similar effect where one child is given the family home or other symbolic realty,[5] or parental possessions imbued with monetary or sentimental worth. The financial consequences of an uneven distribution can be severe, with comparatively high levels of personal wealth among the 'baby boomers'[6] creating larger estates to pass on.[7] However, the emotional consequences are just as serious; inheritance inequities (whether real or perceived) are a perfect breeding ground for acrimony and rancour which rupture family ties.

Of course emotions run through many legal disputes, and private law actions are no exception—even in the average tort, contract or property claim where the parties are transacting on an 'arm's length' basis. However, when private law litigants are related to each other, the emotional dynamics take on added significance. Family law disputes are typified by emotion, and, despite a comparatively slow start,[8] the area has assumed a more prominent role in law and emotions scholarship.[9] Within the current collection, Professor Huntingdon's chapter on domestic relations and the 'affective family'[10] makes another important contribution to this burgeoning literature. In contrast, succession law has been largely overlooked by law and emotions scholars, despite the centrality of the family in testamentary

---

clearly time-based. For example, inheritance laws in most common law (and civil law) jurisdictions favoured sons over daughters, and also prioritised the eldest son until relatively recently (though gender preference can still be apparent when parents are allocating specific items of property—see part III below). However, there is also a strong socio-cultural dimension, since not every modern society or culture sees equality as the norm; for example, gender inequalities still exist in parts of Africa and Latin America where males have preferential inheritance rights (see for example, CD Deere and M León, 'The Gender Asset Gap: Land in Latin America' (2003) 31 *World Development* 925), and also within certain systems of customary law (see for example, MF Radford, 'Inheritance Rights of Women Under Jewish and Islamic Law' (1999) 23 *Boston College International & Comparative Law Review* 135).

[5] For example, a family farm or business; an old family vacation property.

[6] See generally, J Hills, F Bastagli, F Cowell, H Glennerster, E Karagiannaki and A McKnight, *Wealth in the UK: Distribution, Accumulation and Policy* (Oxford, Oxford University Press, 2013).

[7] This is still an important fiscal event, despite well-documented changes in the intergenerational transfer of wealth. A significant part occurs while parents are still alive and providing ongoing financial support to adult children (for example, paying university fees, financing a business venture and assisting with house purchases), while increased longevity also means that baby boomers are consuming more of their own capital post-retirement; both result in fewer assets to pass on—see JH Langbein, 'The Twentieth Century Revolution in Family Wealth' (1988) 86 *Michigan Law Review* 722; and C Sappideen, 'Families and Intergenerational Transfers: Changing the Old Order?' (2008) 31 *University of New South Wales Law Journal* 738.

[8] See K Abrams, 'Barriers and Boundaries: Exploring Emotion in the Law of the Family' (2009) 16 *Virginia Journal of Social Policy & the Law* 301, 307.

[9] See the various sources cited in Abrams (n 8), as well as S Moldonado, 'Cultivating Forgiveness: Reducing Hostility and Conflict after Divorce' (2008) 43 *Wake Forest Law Review* 441; C Huntingdon, 'Repairing Family Law' (2008) 57 *Duke Law Journal* 1245; and C Huntingdon, 'Family Law' (2010) 59 *Emory Law Journal* 10.

[10] See Huntington, ch 2.

giving and the crucial role that emotions play in inheritance disputes—especially those involving adult children following the testate death of a parent.[11]

Sibling relationships can be fraught; these tensions can carry on for years and often come to a head when a parent dies. A will, and especially one that gives children unequal shares of the estate, can trigger a lifetime of negative feelings and drive the disappointed sibling to litigation.[12] As we shall see, a number of features make these particular contests so inherently emotional: the fact that they centre on the two most formative and enduring family relationships (parent–child, and sibling–sibling), both coloured by years of history and personal interactions; the symbolic qualities of inherited wealth, along with attachments to specific items of property; parental intent, and the significance of the will as a conscious expression of someone's last wishes; and the personal, familial and social connotations of an uneven inheritance.

This chapter unpacks the underlying emotional narrative, identifying the complex sentiments that create and fuel inheritance disputes between adult siblings. Drawing primarily on a mix of legal, psychological and sociological literature which attributes many of these to unresolved childhood issues, it argues that estate conflicts have a distinctive contextual backdrop which exacerbates these negative feelings and ups the emotional ante even further. In keeping with the overall themes of the collection, the chapter goes on to look at how these emotions are reflected in legal processes and by legal actors. For example, while Anglo-American jurisprudence suggests a more nuanced emotional response to estate contests than in other areas of legal decision-making, the fact that judges often intervene when presented with an uneven estate distribution can indirectly reveal what they feel about sibling (or more usually) parental behaviour here. The chapter concludes by considering how the emotional fallout could be lessened, by will-makers, lawyers and the legal system being more cognisant of the underlying psychological and emotional dynamics.

II. Death and Discord: The Perfect Emotional Storm

Emotions are intrinsic to family relationships. While siblings experience a range of emotions—both positive and negative—throughout their collective lives, the death of a parent takes them into unchartered territory. Kennedy describes

---

[11] While intestacy distributions are also based on established kinship networks, the emphasis here is on will-making because the will-maker's freedom of choice and how this is perceived by his/her survivors makes it more amenable to a law and emotion analysis than a legislatively mandated universal scheme.

[12] The following contextual caveat is important, and will be revisited later in the chapter: leaving an estate unevenly does not actually mean that the parent favours one child over another; the underlying reasons vary (see pp 46–47), even if the excluded or marginalised child is likely to interpret the parent's actions in a negative way.

parental death as a 'shattering experience', which floods individuals with 'powerful forces' as the 'boundaries of [their] world are torn away'.[13] In many ways, this experience is not unique to siblings; the loss of any loved one is a traumatic experience as intimate bonds and personal relationships are irrevocably altered by death's seismic forces.[14] Yet, in some respects, it is more pronounced. Adult children, regardless of their age, feel anchorless and cast adrift as they mourn the loss of a lifelong relationship; the fact that death is in the natural order of things is irrelevant, as they confront an altered reality without the parent's comforting, constant presence.[15] Parental death also precipitates unprecedented change,[16] forcing siblings to navigate unchartered relational territory while finding a new emotional equilibrium—both as individuals and as a group.[17] Strong sibling bonds can be a source of comfort during this time, with Milvesky highlighting their compensatory value following the loss of a parent.[18] Yet, while we instinctively assume that death brings families together, the reality can be very different.

Death produces a range of complex and disorientating emotions, which manifest themselves through the grieving process.[19] For example, Lindemann famously identified grief as a syndrome comprising five key elements: somatic disturbance, preoccupation with the image of the deceased, guilt, hostility and disorganised behaviour.[20] In similar vein, Bowlby and others have analysed it as involving numbness and disbelief, anxiety and anger, depression and despair.[21] Despite subtle variances in the overall mode of expression, psychologists concede that anger and aggression are common features of the grieving process. The inevitable and inescapable sense of change for those who are left behind results in

---

[13] A Kennedy, *Losing a Parent: Passage to a New Way of Living* (New York, HarperOne, 1991) 2.

[14] See for instance, K Charmaz, *The Social Reality of Death: Death in Contemporary America* (Reading, MA, Addison-Wesley Publishing Co, 1980); and F Walsh and M McGoldrick (eds), *Living Beyond Loss: Death in the Family* (New York, WW Norton & Company, 1991).

[15] See generally, D Umberson, *Death of a Parent: Transition to a New Adult Identity* (Cambridge, Cambridge University Press, 2006); and R Abrams, *When Parents Die: Learning to Live with the Loss of a Parent*, 3rd edn (Abingdon, Routledge, 2012).

[16] Natural realignments and adjustments are inevitable, adding to the sense of posthumous disarray—CI Murray, K Toth and S Clinkenbeard, 'Death, Dying and Grief in Families' in P McKenry and S Price (eds), *Families and Change: Coping with Stressful Life Events*, 3rd edn (Thousand Oaks, CA, Sage, 2005) 75.

[17] The death of a parent also causes the children to confront their own mortality, since (assuming a natural order of events) the children are now next in line to die. This can trigger negative emotions, as well as worries about their own future and financial security which were not present before.

[18] A Milvesky, *Sibling Relationship in Childhood and Adolescence: Predictors and Outcomes* (New York, Columbia University Press, 2011).

[19] E Lindemann, 'Symtomatology and Management of Acute Grief' (1944) 101 *American Journal of Psychiatry* 797; J Bowlby, 'The Process of Mourning' (1961) 42 *International Journal of Psycho-Analysis* 331; J Bowlby and C Parkes, 'Separation and Loss within the Family' in CJ Antony and C Koupernick (eds), *The Child and his Family* (London, Wiley, 1970) 197; and CM Parkes, *Bereavement: Studies of Grief in Adult Life* (London, Tavistock Press, 1972).

[20] Lindemann (n 19).

[21] Bowlby and Parkes (n 19). See also J Archer, *The Nature of Grief: The Evolution and Psychology of Reactions to Loss* (London, Routledge, 1999) 24–26; and A Levy, *The Orphaned Adult* (Reading, MA, Perseus Books, 1999) 23.

post-mortem stress, a sense of 'sheer pressure [which] bereavement places upon the body and mind as an integrated whole'.[22] Past grievances often resurface following the death of a loved one. Emotions are running high; and where families are prone to conflict, bereavement acts as a 'stress amplifier',[23] putting additional strain on already fragile relationships.[24] However, sibling dynamics take this to another level, as unresolved childhood issues come to the fore.

Sibling bonds can last for a lifetime, making this one of the most enduring relationships that individuals can develop and foster.[25] Of course, few families conform to a utopian behavioural ideal, and siblings are no different. While part of a family unit, they are also unique individuals with distinct character traits, making them just as prone to personality clashes as other interpersonal relationships. At a more basic level, Brody notes that sibling relationships are 'rarely characterized by very high levels of support along with low levels of rivalry and aggression';[26] conflict is much more common. Sibling rivalry is one of the oldest emotional experiences within families, and its destructive and divisive nature has been well-documented throughout human history.[27] Underpinned by jealous struggles for parental attention from an early age, sibling rivalry exudes a range of feelings such as anger, anxiety, distress, resentment and worthlessness—though jealousy often predominates.[28] Jealousy itself is a self-critical and complex social emotion, invariably triggered by a third-party threat (whether real or apparent) to a key relationship.[29] In the sibling context, it represents 'the most powerful jealousy of youth' as the presence of a sibling rival threatens the parent–child dynamic that is the 'most important and formative relationship of a young child's early

---

[22] DJ Davies, *Death, Ritual and Belief*, 2nd edn (London, Continuum, 2002) 59.

[23] Levy (n 21) 90. See also B Raphael and M Dobson, 'Bereavement' in JH Harvey and ED Miller (eds), *Loss and Trauma: General and Close Relationship Perspectives* (Philadelphia, PA, Brunner-Routledge, 2000) 50–53.

[24] ES Traylor, B Hayslip, PL Kaminski and C York, 'Relationships between Grief and Family System Characteristics' (2003) 27 *Death Studies* 575. The American drama film *August: Osage County*, Smokehouse Pictures (2013) which reunites three siblings, their acerbic mother and the wider family circle at the father's funeral, illustrates this perfectly.

[25] Milvesky (n 18) ix citing VG Cicirelli, 'Sibling Influence Throughout the Lifespan' in ME Lamb and B Sutton-Smith (eds), *Sibling Relationships: Their Nature and Significance Across the Lifespan* (New York, Lawrence Erlbaum Associates, 1982) 267–84.

[26] GH Brody, 'Sibling Relationship Quality: Its Causes and Consequences' (1998) 49 *Annual Review of Psychology* 1, 19.

[27] For example, it is a recurring theme throughout the Bible—Cain's slaying of his brother Abel in the Book of Genesis (Genesis 4: 1–16) and the parable of the prodigal son in the Gospel of Luke (Luke 15: 11–32). More recent examples on this side of the Atlantic include the infamous spat between Noel and Liam Gallagher which prompted the 2009 split of Britpop band Oasis, and the 2010 Labour Party leadership contest between David and Ed Miliband when the younger sibling stood against and ultimately defeated his older brother.

[28] For a psychological analysis, see D Rowe, *My Dearest Enemy, My Dangerous Friend: Making and Breaking Sibling Bonds* (Hove, Routledge, 2007); and J Safer, *Cain's Legacy: Liberating Siblings from a Lifetime of Rage, Shame, Secrecy and Regret* (New York, Basic Books, 2012).

[29] See generally, P Salovey (ed), *The Psychology of Jealousy and Envy* (New York, Guilford Press, 1992).

life'.[30] Parents 'cannot attend and respond to ... [all of their] children's needs at all times',[31] and siblings invariably compete with each other for parental attention from an early age.[32] As a result, undercurrents of sibling rivalry probably infuse everyday transactions between brothers and sisters, especially when growing up together in the same household. Yet sometimes sibling strife develops into something more, straining relationships or causing them to break down completely, and generating patterns of behaviour which siblings replicate at key stages throughout their adult lives.[33]

The death of a parent is an obvious trigger, and as siblings come together—perhaps returning to their old family home, itself a 'deeply symbolic repository of memories and grievances'[34]—latent traits re-emerge. In the initial post-mortem period, preoccupation with funeral arrangements and fulfilling basic social and legal requirements (obtaining a death certificate, liaising with the funeral director, receiving visitors) can prevent simmering tensions from spilling over.[35] However, discovering the contents of a dead parent's will often puts 'the final nail in the coffin of ... a moribund sibling connection'[36] as unequal (or ostensibly unjust) distributions reignite 'old issues of sibling rivalry and dominance'.[37] The value of specific bequests and objects is not always important; it is the fact that the chosen estate distribution determines 'each beneficiary's relative importance and position in the family'[38] and, with adult children, is perceived as a measure of parental love and approval—regardless of the will-maker's underlying intent.[39] As Safer points

---

[30] BL Volling, NL McElwain and AL Miller, 'Emotion Regulation in Context: The Jealously Complex Between Young Siblings and Its Relations with Child and Family Characteristics' (2002) 73 *Child Development* 581, 583.

[31] Ibid, 584. See also LA Keister, 'Sharing the Wealth: The Effect of Siblings on Adults' Wealth Ownership' (2003) 40 *Demography* 521, 522: '[p]arents have finite material and non-material resources, and additional siblings dilute the amount that can be devoted to each child'.

[32] Studies suggest that infants can exhibit jealousy from as early as six months, if maternal attention is channelled elsewhere—see S Hart and H Carrington, 'Jealousy in Six-Month-Old Infants' (2002) 3 *Infancy* 395.

[33] '[P]roblems with siblings *are* childhood experiences in contemporary guise. Rivalry, competition, and anxiety about [their] place in [their] parents' affections underlie these problems, breeding rancor that haunts siblings all their lives and recurs in each phase of adulthood—work, marriage, parenthood, caring for aging parents, and eventually, settling that perpetual minefield, the estate'—Safer (n 28) 3.

[34] Safer (n 28) 181.

[35] This is not always the case. For example, disputes over funeral arrangements can be an immediate source of contention—see H Conway and J Stannard, 'The Honours of Hades: Death, Emotion and the Law of Burial Disputes' (2011) 34 *University of New South Wales Law Journal* 860.

[36] Safer (n 28) 157.

[37] J Folberg, 'Mediating Family Property and Estate Conflicts' (2009) 23 *Probate & Property* 8, 9.

[38] PM Accettura, *Blood & Money: Why Families Fight Over Inheritance and What To Do About It* (Michigan, Collinwood Press, 2011) 2. See also JG McMullen, 'Keeping Peace in the Family While You Are Resting in Peace' (2006) 8 *Marquette Elder's Advisor* 61, 81 (an inheritance 'may represent the approval or love of the benefactor-relative').

[39] Again, there are positive reasons why parents divide property unevenly between their children—see pp 46–47.

out, notions of parental favouritism, and who was loved more, are reinforced and perpetuated here:

> Money = Love is a very old equation, one that is played out with a vengeance in siblings' fights over the terms of their parents' will and the distributions of their possessions. The compulsion to demonstrate, in court if necessary, that you really were your parents' favourite (or to compensate for the fact that you were not) underlies these battles as much as greed does, and blinds people to the consequences, which will almost always include the permanent loss of their siblings' goodwill.[40]

As far as the children are concerned, any disparities in the estate distribution marks one child out as a 'loser' in what has been described as the 'parental-love competition',[41] with seemingly minor issues about the distribution of parental effects becoming symbolic battlefields for resolving claims on parental affection.[42] In many ways, estate contests are as much about deflected anger towards the dead parent as towards the other siblings,[43] as parental resentments resurface and are reconstituted by patterns of wealth distribution. An unequal inheritance disrupts (and in more extreme examples, destroys) what the disappointed beneficiary thought was a secure attachment relationship with their parent, developed and nurtured from childhood. The emotional needs of the child can also transcend the death of the parent, as the former craves parental validation which will now never materialise because the estate has been divided unequally, and the marginalised or excluded child has apparently been identified as less 'worthy' than their siblings.

What we have here is a toxic mix of negative emotions. Some of these (anger, hostility, sadness) are already lurking in the background as natural by-products of the grieving process; in the event of an uneven estate distribution, these are amplified and joined by other harmful sentiments (jealously, hurt, bitterness, disappointment and rejection, to list a few). Sibling inheritance disputes are 'so emotionally charged that they can easily escalate'.[44] Brothers and sisters refuse to back down in their quest to negate the emotional consequences of an uneven estate distribution, and prove themselves as an equally loved and equally worthy parental heir. The underlying feelings are not only complex and all-consuming; they can also cause the disappointed sibling to engage in seemingly irrational behaviour, with disastrous consequences.[45] Destroying or dissipating estate property so that no one gets anything (what Accettura describes as the 'scorched earth'

---

[40] Safer (n 28) 180–181.

[41] Ibid, 51.

[42] Levy (n 21) 110.

[43] 'Receiving less preferential treatment is particularly significant to a child because of the potent implications it carries ... Children's recognition of the inequality in their relationships with their parents is hypothesized to occasion emotional dysregulation, leading to anger that is displaced onto the favored brother or sister'—Brody (n 26) 12.

[44] T Mayersak, 'Examining the Use of Arbitration and Dealing with Decedent's Wishes in Wills, Trusts and Estates' (2010) 12 *European Journal of Law Reform* 404, 406.

[45] The fact that emotions can override rational thought and cause the parties to do things that appear 'nonsensical and counterintuitive' has been documented in the family law context—J Weinstein

approach)[46] is a classic example—and in February 2013, one brother took this to extremes when he destroyed a £300,000 family home in Cardiff, Wales with a sledgehammer after falling out with his siblings following a seven-year row over inheritance.[47] Of course, exorcising the ghosts of sibling rivalry and parental favouritism does not usually have such extreme consequences. However, one brother or sister's relentless march towards litigation is not just something which impacts on siblings; as members of an 'interactive, independent network in which behaviour in one individual or subsystem affects the others,'[48] a ripple effect spreads across the entire family system. Other relatives are drawn into the estate contest (even if they do not want to be involved), creating an existential emotional crisis which threatens broader family harmony and stability.

III. Emotional Attachments to Property

Inherited wealth is highly symbolic for siblings, and not just because it connotes parental love and approval. Different types of property are imbued with meaning, and generate strong emotional attachments, as well as creating their own distinct inheritance expectations.

Most wills focus on real estate and financial assets, as high value items. The family home is a good example;[49] since the property is not divisible in a practical sense, and adult children who have long since moved away are unlikely to return, a parent's will might direct that the home be sold and the proceeds divided equally between the children. Although consistent with social norms around the post-mortem allocation of wealth,[50] such directions can be problematic for the

---

and R Weinstein, '"I Know Better Than That": The Role of Emotions and the Brain in Family Law Disputes' (2005) 7 *Journal of Law and Family Studies* 351, 352 (discussing child custody disputes in particular). See also PH Huang, 'Reasons Within Passions: Emotions and Intentions in Property Rights Bargaining' (2000) 79 *Oregon Law Review* 435, 439 ('emotions such as fear and anger disrupt normal rational thought and reasoning capabilities'); and G Lowenstein, 'Out of Control: Visceral Influences on Behavior' (1996) 65 *Organizational Behavior and Human Decision Processes* 272.

[46] Accettura (n 38) 3.

[47] Tony McGuire had been living in the family home (originally owned by his father) with his wife and six children; however, his father's will left the property to Tony and his two other siblings who were trying to evict their brother before he took a sledgehammer to the property and reduced most of it to rubble. Mr McGuire was given a two-year suspended sentence for what the court described as an 'appalling act of spite'—'Sledgehammer House Attack: Tony McGuire Given Suspended Sentence', BBC News Online, 26 June 2013: www.bbc.co.uk/news/uk-wales-south-east-wales-23059344. Ironically, it was equal division of the parental estate that caused the problem here.

[48] Brody (n 26) 2.

[49] Increasing rates of home ownership from the latter half of the twentieth century onwards mean that home ownership 'is no longer for the relatively affluent' but is 'now normal experience for "ordinary families" who have not accumulated land or vast sums of wealth through the generations'— J Finch and J Mason, *Passing On: Kinship and Inheritance in England* (London, Routledge, 2000) 3.

[50] And the law's mantra to 'sell and divide' as the typical default stance where an asset of material value cannot be apportioned.

child who is not keen on selling because of their own emotional attachment to the property[51]—including the sense of both individual and family identity tied up in the home.[52] In the context of the present chapter, significant issues can arise where the parent decides to leave the family home to a particular child (often one who resided there with the parent, up until the latter's death);[53] this removes a valuable legacy from the parent's estate, and can generate anger, hurt and resentment on the part of the other siblings, regardless of the parent's intent. Family farms are also valuable items of real property which generate strong emotional attachments, yet attract very different inheritance perceptions. Here, it is not simply a question of whether to divide the land or leave it intact;[54] farms tend to be passed down through generations,[55] traditionally to (eldest) sons.[56] Social convention allows equality to be sacrificed here, but can still generate bitterness and ill-feeling on the part of the non-farming siblings.[57] Moving on to financial resources, money and cash convertible assets such as stocks and shares can be divided in whatever way a parent sees fit—more so than any of the other types of property being looked at here. Yet, siblings will still contest any resultant economic disparity, not because of particularly strong emotional attachments to the money itself,[58] but because of what the unequal distribution symbolises and the feelings that this generates.[59]

Personal possessions, in contrast, are often omitted from the distributive contents of a dead parent's will;[60] and while real estate and money are more

---

[51] Affective connections to the home have been well documented—see for example, H Easthope, 'A Place Called Home' (2004) 21 *Housing, Theory and Society* 128; and DB Barros, 'Home as a Legal Concept' (2006) 46 *Santa Clara Law Review* 255. For a more critical approach, see SM Stern, 'Residential Protectionism and the Legal Mythology of Home' (2009) 107 *Michigan Law Review* 1093.

[52] Similar issues can arise where the home is simply bequeathed to children jointly, and one person is not keen to sell (because of the emotional attachments just mentioned) yet the other siblings are. Constructs of fairness and equality can still create problems here—a situation which also frequently arises with old family cottages and vacation properties which parents (acting with the noblest of intentions) often leave to their children as shared owners. All too often, the result is discord when one sibling insists on keeping the property to recreate their own childhood idylls and another resents having their inheritance tied up in a place which they now only value as a cash asset—see SJ Hollander, DS Fry and R Hollander, *Saving the Family Cottage: A Guide to Succession Planning for Your Cottage, Cabin, Camp or Vacation Home* (Chicago, IL, Nolo, 2013).

[53] The same child may have cared for ageing parents, and have no home of their own.

[54] Though a farm may need to stay intact to remain a profitable enterprise—CS Olsen and T Osborn, 'Inheritance: "A Tale of Two Perceptions"' (2006) 1 *Online Journal of Rural Research & Policy*.

[55] The emphasis here is on 'intergenerational family farm continuity'—ibid, 6.

[56] When it comes to inheriting farmland, a 'gender bias ... seems far more frequent and acceptable than is the case for the distribution of money'—JJ Goodnow and JA Lawrence, 'Inheritance Norms for Distributions of Money, Land, and Things in Families' (2010) 1 *Family Science* 73, 76.

[57] Even with the compensatory gift of a cash settlement or a plot of land on the farm so they can build their own home.

[58] These would differ significantly from the type of affective connections a son or daughter had, for example, to their old family home or a dead parent's personal possessions.

[59] Though Goodnow and Lawrence suggest that bequests of money have 'personal meanings' attached and are 'often seen as a sign of relationship quality'—Goodnow and Lawrence (n 56) 75.

[60] Finch and Mason (n 49) 145 suggest that many lawyers discourage their clients from distributing items of personal property. And even where a will contains a direction to divide personal property

likely to trigger the sort of litigation discussed later in this chapter, disputes over who gets items of personal property (for example, a mother's wedding ring or a father's watch; photo albums; lovingly assembled collections of books, music or china; family mementoes such as Christmas ornaments and holiday souvenirs) can become just as embittered, even if they are less likely to end up in court. Any process of allocation is necessarily informal and sibling-led, but suffers from two main drawbacks. First, as items accumulated over a parent's lifetime (and sometimes across generations of the same family), they are imbued with personal meaning and have a sentimental value unrelated to their economic worth.[61] Because they symbolise the dead parent, personal possessions engender exceptionally high levels of emotional attachment;[62] on the death of a parent, these attachments are assumed and perpetuated by the child who claims it for him/ herself as an ongoing narrative of association with the deceased.[63] Second, the reality is that certain things (for example, a favourite painting or specific pieces of jewellery) cannot be divided, fuelling the sense of unfairness.[64] Stum highlights '[o]ngoing rivalries' and issues of 'power and control' among siblings as influenc- ing the transfer of personal possessions.[65] However, birth order and gender also have a role to play here—for example, a brother is more likely to claim a father's watch than his sisters, while a mother's wedding ring often ends up with the eldest daughter.[66]

IV. The Emotional Impact of Wills

Mayersak has argued that the 'emotional elements present in wills … disputes are not presented, or at least not as prevalent, as in other litigated matters'.[67]

---

evenly among the deceased's children, Stum argues that 'such vague and impossible directions provide little guidance for surviving family members'—MS Stum, 'Families and Inheritance Decisions: Examining Non-Titled Property Transfers' (2000) 21 *Journal of Family and Economic Issues* 177, 179.

[61] '[M]undane functional goods that were not necessarily singular or cherished can serve as potent material footprints of the departed'—D Turley and S O'Donohoe, 'The Sadness of Lives and the Comfort of Things' (2012) 28 *Journal of Marketing Management* 1331, 1342.

[62] For a detailed analysis see Stum (n 60) and Finch and Mason (n 49) ch 6. The latter note that the 'symbolic value of personal gifts and possessions is very high' (ibid, 140) and that 'keepsakes' and other reminders have a special status because the object *'carries the memory* of the person who owned it but who has now died' (ibid, 142).

[63] Such objects 'symbolize identities which may become the objects of reminiscences by survivors' (DR Unruh, 'Death and Personal History: Strategies of Identity Preservation' (1983) 30 *Social Prob- lems* 340, 344) and often 'continue to be thought of and named as belonging to former owners even though they are now worn by, used or in the possession of other people' (M Gibson, 'Death and the Transformation of Objects and Their Value' (2010) 103 *Thesis Eleven* 54, 55).

[64] Goodnow and Lawrence (n 56) 78.

[65] Stum (n 60) 194.

[66] See the general discussion in Drake (n 4) 98.

[67] Mayersak (n 44) 405. Mayersak exceptionalises wills in the trusts and estates context of her article. Of course, other litigated matters are deeply emotional, even if they do not raise exactly the same

While death, sibling strife and attachments to property are key contributors, the deceased's will is a highly emotive document—adding another layer of complexity.

Finch and others describe the will as a 'unique form of communication between the dead and the living'.[68] Imbued with a combination of legal and personal power,[69] wills do more than establish *what* the deceased valued in life; the distributional scheme indicates *who* was valued and the important role that certain individuals played in the deceased's personal narrative.[70] The final document 'gives permanent voice to the testator's wants',[71] articulating his/her thoughts and feelings on intensely private matters in what is ultimately a very public statement of intent. As financial legacies shade into affective ones, parental wills elicit a strong emotional response among grown-up children. Where the distributional scheme is more or less what the latter anticipated, the will can be a source of comfort and affirmation. Yet, where it creates an unexpected and seemingly unjust division, the will can elicit a hostile response, generating feelings of shock, outrage and disbelief.

Both the language used in the will, and the way in which the document is framed, are also important. The fact that wills are written in the present tense reinforces the idea that the parent is communicating directly with his/her children.[72] Yet, the parent's 'voice' may not be one that the children recognise, despite this being one of the most personal (and ultimately final) exchanges between them. Lawyers drafting wills for their clients adopt standard forms of legalise to ensure an operative, transactional document; the result is an emotionally sterile and depersonalised narrative, which speaks in an unfamiliar manner.[73] Recent commentaries have suggested that testators (aided and encouraged by lawyers) should include more expressive language in their wills, directly conveying their thoughts and feelings as part of the distributive process.[74] Glover highlights the therapeutic

---

emotional issues being discussed here (the family law arena is an obvious example, if we think about divorce decrees and orders terminating parental rights as two basic illustrations).

[68] Finch et al, *Wills, Inheritance and Families* (n 4) 1. See also P Vines, '"In the Name of God, Amen": Seeking the Testator's Authentic Voice in Research Using Wills' (2002) 6 *Law Text Culture* 63, 63: 'Wills are documents which have a unique power. No other document can communicate beyond the grave in the voice of the deceased with the same combination of legal and personal power'.

[69] Vines (n 68) 63.

[70] KJ Sneddon, 'The Will as Personal Narrative' (2012) 20 *Elder Law Journal* 355, 396–97.

[71] AA DiRusso, 'Testacy and Intestacy: The Dynamics of Wills and Demographic Status' (2009) 23 *Quinnipiac Probate Law Journal* 36, 61.

[72] Present tense drafting creates an overwhelming sense that the deceased 'is sharing his or her thoughts at the moment of probate'—Sneddon, 'The Will as Personal Narrative' (n 70) 387.

[73] See KJ Sneddon, 'Speaking for the Dead: Voice in Last Wills and Testaments' (2011) 5 *St John's Law Review* 683.

[74] Sneddon, 'Speaking for the Dead' (n 73) suggests that lawyers and others drafting wills should try to consciously craft a persona that injects the individual's voice into the will, while ensuring that the document continues to be legally effective. See also M Glover, 'A Therapeutic Jurisprudential Framework of Estate Planning' (2012) 35 *Seattle University Law Review* 427, 455–61 and the sources cited therein.

aspect of this approach, in allowing the testator to articulate both positive and negative emotions in the hope that doing so will 'ease family conflict during the administration of the estate'.[75] In the parent–child context, expressive statements may be useful where the testator wants to explain the reasoning behind seemingly inequitable bequests—for example, that benefiting one child more than another reflects the former's straitened financial circumstances, as opposed to being a reflection of unequal love. Of course, there is always an element of risk. Explanations do not always convey what they are intended to; and just as beauty lies in the eye of the beholder, meaningful interpretation (despite the testator's best efforts) lies in the mind of the disappointed child. English novelist Daisy Goodwin, whose mother died in 2013 and left a will giving most of her estate to Goodwin's siblings because they needed it more, still struggles with the feeling that this was because her mother loved her less:

> [W]hen a parent makes a will, they should be aware that although their children may be reasonable adults in every other respect, when it comes to inheritance, maturity dissolves into a puddle of childish resentments. Because when a beloved parent dies, what is being parcelled out may look like goods and chattels, but it feels a lot like love. A parent's will is not just a legal document; it is the last expression of their thoughts and feelings towards their children. It is a testament of love.[76]

V. Bequeathing an Appropriate Emotional Legacy: The Role of the Parent

Safer has noted that '[w]henever families gather, siblings notoriously take up their accustomed positions and reproduce their original dynamics, as though the roles were etched on their brains, ready to be magically reconstituted when the cast reassembles'.[77] That old resentments and rivalries should mysteriously resurface is hardly surprising. However, a key member of the cast is now missing: the dead parent, who mediated sibling disputes in the past, but is no longer there to prevent simmering tensions from spilling over.

While it would be easy to say that the deceased's absence exposes fault lines within sibling relationships, inheritance disputes are as much about the parent–child relationship as its sibling–sibling correlate. We instinctively assume that parents will divide their wealth equally among their offspring; studies tend to bear

---

[75] Glover (n 74) 460. See also TP O'Sullivan, 'Family Harmony: An All Too Frequent Casualty of the Estate Planning Process' (2007) 8 *Marquette Elder's Advisor* 253.

[76] D Goodwin, 'I Leave My Daughter Daisy Out Of My Estate' *Sunday Times* (7 December 2014).

[77] Safer (n 28) 59–60.

this out,[78] and any differential in treatment tends to be viewed as an overtly negative act of parental favouritism. Yet there are positive reasons why some parents
leave uneven bequests—for example, a child who lived with and looked after their
parent(s) may be rewarded more than one who was less attentive or assumed less
of the caregiving burden (thereby reflecting core notions of inter-family economic
exchange, and reparation for sacrifices rendered); the previous section raised the
possibility of a parent bequeathing a larger sum to a child with greater financial
need than his/her siblings.[79] As much as this generates resentment and anger
among the other children, it is not clear that unequal division is manifestly unfair
here or that it should be undone.[80]

Making a will is a poignant act, which forces an individual to confront their
own mortality, assess their life's achievements and contemplate their post-mortem
legacy.[81] If contemplating an uneven estate distribution, McMullen argues that
parents should think 'long and hard about the bitterness and fighting' that might
result among their children, especially when the parent is not there to 'explain or
defend' their actions, or to 'soothe hurt feelings and feelings of rejection'.[82] More
importantly perhaps, parents should be mindful of the old adage that 'honesty
is the best policy', and tell their children what they are contemplating well in
advance[83]—instead of leaving their grieving offspring to discover this for themselves when the contents of the will are revealed during what is already an emotionally fraught time (and when explanations written into the will itself might
not be enough, no matter how clear or well-meaning).[84] Adopting this approach

---

[78] Empirical studies around inheritance reveal that 'equal treatment of children is seen as the norm'
and 'reigns supreme when it comes to the division of major assets'—Finch and Mason, *Passing On* (n 49)
77. See also H Conway and L Glennon, '*To Give or Not To Give?': The Transmission of Wealth On Death by
Older Persons*, Report for the Changing Ageing Partnership, Institute of Governance, Queen's University
Belfast (October 2010) (interviews carried out with focus groups confirmed that the majority of
parents with more than one adult child intended to benefit them all equally). For a discussion of equivalent trends in the US, see Drake (n 4) 97; and TA Dunn and JW Phillips, *Do Parents Divide Resources
Equally Among Children?* Evidence from the AHEAD Survey, Centre for Policy Research, Maxwell
School of Citizenship and Public Affairs, Syracuse University (Aging Studies Programme, Paper No 5,
1997). However, studies have shown that unequal treatment is more common with lifetime gifts, with
parents taking account of their children's respective earning powers, financial needs and circumstances
when giving them different levels of monetary support—see Dunn and Phillips (ibid), as well as
M Lundholm and H Ohlsson, 'Post Mortem Reputation, Compensatory Gifts and Equal Bequests'
(2000) 68 *Economics Letters* 165.
[79] See generally, McMullen (n 38) 78–79; and JC Tate, 'Caregiving and the Case for Testamentary
Freedom' (2008) 42 *University of California Davis Law Review* 129.
[80] Equal distribution could be perceived as unfair or unjust by the caregiving or financially needy
child, precipitating family breakdown.
[81] Sneddon, 'The Will as Personal Narrative' (n 70) 359, describing this as a 'journey of self-discovery'.
[82] McMullen (n 38) 87.
[83] 'To avoid leaving a legacy of injured relationships, older parents do best to grapple realistically
with the power they hold, rather than avoid facing this truth'—W Lustbader, 'Conflict, Emotion and
Power Surrounding Legacy' (1996) *Generations* 54, 54.
[84] For example, Daisy Goodwin's mother included a line in her will to the effect that: 'I leave my
daughter Daisy out of the estate, not because I love her any the less but because I think she has less need
of it' (n 76). In spite of this, Goodwin still feels that her mother did not love her as much Goodwin's
other siblings.

would also give the children time to come to terms with the intended estate division, and to understand the parent's motivations, instead of the disappointed sibling simply seeing this as a final statement that their parent loved them less and the same parent's memory being tarnished by the contents of the will. Engaging in these conversations presents its own challenges, because of an ingrained reticence to discuss such a sensitive topic. As Isaacs explains:

> Discussion of death and aspects of death by children with their parents in our society is still a major taboo. Parents generally keep the provisions of their will secret, and those who stand to inherit generally do not inquire about the will or the specific provisions involved in it. This leaves the parents in a position to decide unilaterally on the division of their estate without the unpleasantness of having to explain to potential recipients why specific decisions were made.[85]

However, the last point highlights what can be a significant emotional barrier to open disclosure: parents may be reluctant to reveal a will's contents, fearful that their children will be hurt, withdraw care and support, or pressurise the parent into changing their mind.[86]

Of course, there is an uncomfortable reality that we may be reluctant to confront here: by favouring unequal division (and in some cases, disinheriting a child) parents *are* admitting a preference for a particular son or daughter. Society assumes that parents love all their children equally, and 'the norm of equal attachment' is perhaps one of the greatest 'social perceptions regulating parents' relations with their children'.[87] Parents, in turn, may feel constrained by societal constructs of fairness and equality—and how an unequal or seemingly inequitable estate distribution would be perceived, despite how they feel about each of their children. Take Faith, Goff and Tollinson's analysis of sibling rivalry traits in competition for intergenerational wealth transfers, the authors drawing on earlier studies carried out by Berheim and Severinov:

> Berheim and Severinov ... assume that children care about how much their parents love them relative to their siblings and use bequests as a signal of parental affection. They show that under certain conditions, altruistic parents, whether they in fact love their children equally or not, choose equal bequests so that their kids will not suffer from any perceived inequalities in parental affection. Thus equal division becomes the social norm.[88]

---

[85] Isaacs (n 4). Though this social-cultural reticence may reflect a particular generation; the baby boomers who have been more open about money, religion and sex than previous generations, may be more willing to disclose the contents of their wills to their children. I am grateful to Professor Vines for drawing this to my attention.

[86] There is also the possibility that, raising the issue in the hope of preventing bitterness and fighting between one's children at a later stage, simply runs the risk of bringing the dispute forward.

[87] J Aldous, E Klaus and DM Klein, 'The Understanding Heart: Aging Parents and Their Favorite Children' (1985) 56 *Child Development* 303, 303.

[88] RL Faith, BL Goff and RD Tollinson, 'Bequests, Sibling Rivalry and Rent Seeking' (2008) 136 *Public Choice* 397, 398. Lundholm and Ohlsson (n 78) also suggest that parents are aware of the public nature of bequests under wills, and want to avoid the post-mortem reputational damage they would 'suffer' if they left their children uneven amounts.

However, not all parents are thus inclined when it comes to estate distributions, and what precedes them. Overt acts of parental favouritism are perhaps more common than we think: consider the biblical example of the favourite son Joseph in the Book of Genesis,[89] and a recent anonymous English survey which suggested that parents (while not willing to admit it) do have a favourite child.[90] In legal jurisdictions where there is no principle of compulsory succession, parents can treat their children unequally when making an estate distribution—reflecting the fact that a particular child is 'the favourite', or that the parent does not, for example, have a close and loving relationship with one child or does not approve of that particular child's lifestyle choices etc. An unequal estate distribution may feel like an obvious choice in these circumstances; the dead parent may also 'lack inhibitions at death which tempered [their] … conduct during life',[91] and is 'exempt from the consequences'[92] of their actions. Disinheriting a child (or treating them less favourably than their siblings) is the ultimate parental sanction, a final and lasting signal of displeasure, disappointment and rejection.[93]

Brody has suggested that discrepancies in a parent's treatment of their children 'create negativity in the sibling relationship by inducing feelings of rivalry and anger'.[94] In the will-making context, this suggests that parents play a significant role in what materialises between their children following a parent's death. However, this is only part of the picture; it is ultimately the siblings themselves who are responsible for *perpetuating* old grievances and resentments which re-emerge here, particularly when they are adults. As Safer has remarked:

> Parents are responsible for converting sibling rivalry into sibling strife in the first place, but it is the siblings themselves who perpetuate it … Even when they are adults—even when their parents are dead—many siblings nurse memories of slights, recalling to their detriment who was preferred and who was overlooked.[95]

An unequal inheritance simply provides another excuse for keeping sibling feuds alive, long after the parent is dead.

---

[89] 'Now Israel loved Joseph more than all his children, because he was the son of his old age: and he made him a coat of many colours' (Genesis 37:3).

[90] One in 12 parents admitted to having a child they liked more than their other offspring, while 8% said they had a child who they treated differently because that child was their favourite—J Stevens, 'One in 12 Parents Admits to Having a Child They Love More Than the Rest' *Daily Mail* (21 February 2013): www.dailymail.co.uk/news/article-2281781/1-12-parents-admits-having-child-love-rest.html. See also J Kluger, *The Sibling Effect: What Bonds Among Brothers and Sisters Reveal About Us* (Riverhead Books, 2013), the author citing a study by researchers from the University of California which followed 384 sibling pairs and their parents for three years; its findings suggested that 65% of the mothers and 70% of the fathers exhibited a preference for one child.

[91] AJ Hirsch and WKS Lang, 'A Qualitative Theory of the Dead Hand' (1992) 68 *Indiana Law Journal* 1, 13.

[92] McMullen (n 38) 87.

[93] 'To be disinherited by a parent is to be disowned—to become an orphan retroactive to birth. Even to receive less than other beneficiaries who are similarly situated is exquisitely painful'—Accettura (n 38) 35. See also Lustbader (n 83) 56: 'Inflicting a hurt that can never be redressed, the most painful power a parent can wield is to punish from the grave'.

[94] Brody (n 26) 7.

[95] Safer (n 28) 58.

VI. The Law's Response to Contested Wills

When it comes to bequests from parents to children, equal treatment now tends to be viewed as the parental and social norm.[96] This means that non-conformist estate distributions often attract judicial scrutiny, if challenged by a marginalised or excluded child.

Although testamentary freedom is a foundational principle of common law legal systems, the idea is most firmly entrenched in American legal jurisprudence. Courts here cannot simply overturn an estate distribution, since they have no authority to vary the terms of an otherwise valid will. However, herein lies the problem: a judicial tendency to invalidate wills on slender evidence of non-compliance with the requisite formalities, where a testator has excluded their immediate family. Foster has noted that such wills raise 'judicial red flags' and are more susceptible to defeat on grounds of undue influence or lack of mental capacity,[97] sentiments echoed more recently by Johnson:

> Numerous commentators have noticed that testamentary plans that conform to social norms, such as providing for members of the decedent's family, are likely to be upheld; while wills that seek to dispose of a testator's property in a less conventional manner are often defeated on various grounds.[98]

What Leslie describes as 'covert manipulation'[99] of legal doctrine to invalidate non-traditional wills can also be invoked where parents exclude children completely or favour one child at the expense of the other(s).[100] The judicial tendency towards this produces an ironic result: people are encouraged to write wills where they 'desire a non-standard [estate] distribution',[101] but the resultant legal scheme is vulnerable if it seems inconsistent with prevailing socio-cultural norms.

---

[96] '[A]t least in the normal situation of a parent liking all the children, ignoring the values of rewarding a child who has helped the parent more … or the child in greater need of the money'—Isaacs (n 4).

[97] F Foster, 'The Family Paradigm of Inheritance Law' (2001) 80 *North Carolina Law Review* 199, 211.

[98] ID Johnson, 'There's a Will, But No Way: Whatever Happened to the Doctrine of Testamentary Freedom and What Can (Should) We Do to Restore It?' (2011) 4 *Estate Planning and Community Property Law Journal* 105, 106 and the sources listed in support. See also MB Leslie, 'The Myth of Testamentary Freedom' (1996) 38 *Arizona Law Review* 235, 236 ('[n]otwithstanding frequent declarations to the contrary, many courts are as committed to ensuring that testators devise their estates in accordance with prevailing normative views as they are to effectuating testamentary intent'); and R Madoff, 'Unmasking Undue Influence' (1997) 81 *Minnesota Law Review* 571, 576 ('the undue influence doctrine denies freedom of testation for people who deviate from judicially imposed testamentary norms').

[99] Leslie (n 98) 236.

[100] Though wills which favour one child may still be upheld where 'disinheritance of the other children was apparently based on their unworthiness relative to the child who was the primary beneficiary'—see Johnson (n 98) 116 and the various cases cited therein.

[101] Johnson (n 98) 110.

The property owner's ability to make free choices can be heavily circumscribed here, because of a judge's socially-conditioned, subjective disapproval of what the will-maker has done.

Similar trends can be seen on the other side of the Atlantic.[102] However, English law offers a more direct route for challenging wills where a deceased parent exhibits a clear preference between their offspring, or excludes a particular child. The Inheritance (Provision for Family and Dependants) Act 1975 governs what is known as 'family provision' in this country, allowing specific individuals to challenge a valid will[103] on the basis of relational or dependency ties to the deceased which transcend death.[104] If successful, financial provision can be made for the applicant from the deceased's estate, despite the fact that no such reward (or a substantially lower one) was contemplated under the deceased's will.[105] Adult children can apply,[106] on the basis that a deceased parent failed to make 'reasonable financial provision' for them.[107] Judges have consistently stressed that it is *not* their function to rewrite the deceased's will or pass moral judgment on the deceased's actions; in any application under the 1975 Act, courts cannot simply overturn what seem like blatant injustices or provide for someone who feels hard done by.[108] Yet, context is everything, and as Arden LJ pointed out in the first Court of Appeal judgment in *Ilott v Mitson*,[109] what constitutes reasonable

---

[102] For example, in *Sharp v Adam* [2005] EWHC 1806 (Ch) (upheld on appeal at [2006] EWCA 449) the testator was suffering from secondary progressive multiple sclerosis, and was paralysed and unable to speak when he made his final will. He left the bulk of his estate to two employees, along with a legacy for a carer, but excluded his two adult daughters who had previously been the primary beneficiaries. The judge held that the deceased lacked testamentary capacity, most likely because of a 'temporary poisoning of his natural affection for his daughters, or a perversion of his sense of right, which nobody could satisfactorily explain' ([2005] EWHC 1806 (Ch), [254]). The fact that the estate distribution favoured non-family members was undoubtedly the key factor here—for an overview of this and other similar cases, see J Aspen, 'Where Now for Testamentary Freedom?' *Barrister Magazine* (2010).

[103] Or intestacy distribution—though the emphasis here is on testate deaths.

[104] For an overview, see G Douglas, 'Family Provision and Family Practices—The Discretionary Regime of the Inheritance Act of England and Wales' (2014) 4 *Oñati Socio-Legal Series*.

[105] New Zealand was the first country to limit freedom of testation in this manner, under the Testator's Family Maintenance Act 1900. Similar statutory schemes were subsequently adopted by other common law jurisdictions—see L Englefeld, *Australian Family Provision Law* (Australia, Lawbook Company, 2011); and C Harvey and L Vincent, *The Law of Dependants' Relief in Canada*, 2nd edn (Toronto, Carswell, 2006). However, the US remains a notable exception.

[106] s 1(1) of the 1975 Act lists the eligible categories of claimant, and includes 'a child of the deceased' (s 1(1)(c)). There is no age restriction.

[107] 1975 Act, s 1(2). Failure to make reasonable financial provision underpins the legislation. However, with the exception of a surviving spouse or civil partner of the deceased, all other claims under the 1975 Act are restricted by a 'maintenance' threshold under s 1(2)(b)—in other words, reasonable financial provision is defined by what it would be reasonable for the applicant to receive for his/her maintenance. The concept of 'maintenance' is not defined in the statute, although the following dictum of Goff LJ in *Re Coventry* [1980] Ch 461, 485 is still regarded as authoritative: 'What is proper maintenance must ... depend on all the facts and circumstances of the particular case ... [I]t is not just enough to enable a person to get by, [but] on the other hand, it does not mean anything which may be regarded as reasonably desirable for [an applicant's] general benefit or welfare'.

[108] See for example, the comments of Oliver J at first instance in *Re Coventry* [1980] Ch 461, 475.

[109] *Ilott v Mitson* [2011] EWCA Civ 346.

financial provision must take account of 'current social conditions and values'.[110] More importantly, when deciding family provision claims, judges must,

> decide questions involving value judgments within four corners of the statutory framework and with the benefit of their own awareness and experience of society and social issues, and their own considered view of how such matters ought fairly to be decided in the society in which we live.[111]

The mere fact that an individual is a child of the deceased does not generate any automatic entitlement to an (increased) inheritance; the system is a discretionary one, with clear statutory parameters.[112] However, judicial decision-making appears, on occasion, to be influenced by prevailing socio-cultural norms around how parents should treat their children when passing on wealth.[113] In some instances, courts have not been inclined to rule in favour of an adult child who has been left nothing (or little) under a parent's will, deciding that financial need was not enough in itself and that a long-term rift between parent and child 'justifies' no inheritance provision.[114] In others, claims have been allowed based on inequalities in the respective life positions of siblings,[115] or a particular son or daughter's lack of earning capacity.[116] The long-running litigation in *Ilott v Mitson*,[117] where a mother excluded her only child from an estate worth close to £500,000, may also signal a more expansive approach. In July 2015, the Court of Appeal awarded the daughter £163,000, despite the fact that mother and child had been estranged for almost 40 years and the mother was clear in her intent to exclude the daughter from the will and had communicated this to her several years earlier.[118] *Mitson* not only reopens the issue of allowing courts to interfere

---

[110] Ibid, [67].

[111] Ibid, [68].

[112] Courts are instructed to take account of specific factors—for example, the financial resources and future needs of the applicant, those of the other estate beneficiaries, the size of the estate, and any mental or physical disability of the applicant to name but a few (1975 Act, s 3(1)). For applications by children, the court must also specifically look at the 'manner in which the applicant was being, or ... might expect to be, educated or trained' (s 3(3)).

[113] Though it is difficult to tease a clear jurisprudential thread from a highly fact-specific array of cases—see H Conway, 'Do Parents Always Know Best? Posthumous Provision and Adult Children' in W Barr (ed), *Modern Studies in Property Law: Volume 8* (Oxford, Hart Publishing, 2015) ch 7.

[114] See for example, *Re Garland* [2007] EWHC 2 (Ch).

[115] *Re Creeney* [1984] NI 397 (bulk of father's estate left to his financially secure daughter; deceased's son was not financially well off). Although this is a Northern Ireland case, the exact same statutory framework applies under the Inheritance (Provisions for Family and Dependants) (NI) Order 1979.

[116] *Re Hancock* [1998] 2 FLR 346 and *McKernan v McKernan* [2007] NICh 6. In the latter case, the daughter's claim succeeded, despite the court accepting that the deceased was 'quite clear in her mind that she did not want to leave a legacy to her only daughter' (ibid, [27]) and that she viewed her daughter as 'lazy' (ibid, [36]), as well as the court acknowledging that the mother 'was entitled to exercise a preference amongst her children' (ibid, [38]).

[117] [2009] EWHC 3114 (Fam); [2011] EWCA Civ 346; [2014] EWHC 542 (Fam); and [2015] EWCA Civ 797.

[118] The facts merit closer attention. In 1978, the 17-year-old daughter left home to live with a man of whom her mother disapproved; mother and daughter were not reconciled before the mother's death in July 2004. After executing her final will in April 2002, the mother informed her daughter in a letter that

with testamentary freedom, and a will-maker's 'right to spite'; it will encourage more independent adult children[119] to claim under the 1975 Act, regardless of the deceased's express wishes.[120]

Estate contests involving adult children require judges to resolve what are, effectively, emotional issues after a parent's death—dealing with overtly negative sentiments, complicated family histories and enduring estrangements, which the parties themselves could not resolve while the parent was still alive, and which may have been perpetuated for decades. Resorting to concepts such as non-compliance with formalities, duress or undue influence (the dominant models for invalidating wills in the US) or legislative constructs of 'reasonable financial provision' (under the English family provision system) allows judges to seek solace in established legal precepts and to place a veneer of objectivity on their decisions. There may also be therapeutic benefits for those involved in the dispute, as framing the outcome in this way reduces the amount of (additional) damage being inflicted on an emotionally vulnerable yet volatile family 'unit' which has already been pushed to breaking point. Yet, judges are seldom dispassionate and neutral observers,[121] and estate contests between adult siblings are no exception. The conclusions reached in some of these cases suggest that judges are, in many ways, 'passing judgment' on whether children should be treated equally; who was a good and dutiful child; who showed the dead parent proper love, respect and attention; and whether the deceased was 'justified' in treating his or her children differently or was simply being spiteful. These are all extremely difficult (and highly subjective) value-judgments for courts to make.

Of course, judges have their own intuitive sense of what is morally and emotionally acceptable, and not just because of the family scenario that unfolds

she would be excluded due to the pain which the daughter had inflicted on the mother. The daughter responded in another letter, indicating that she understood that she would receive nothing. When the mother died, her only child was aged 44 and had five children of her own, had not worked since the birth of her first child (the husband worked part-time) and was living in a 3 bedroomed house rented from a Housing Association; the mother's entire estate went to various animal welfare charities. The daughter argued under the 1975 Act that her mother had failed to make reasonable financial provision for her, and the district judge awarded her £50,000 from the estate. However, the daughter appealed on the basis that this amount was insufficient. Eleanor King J reversed the earlier decision—under the legislation, it was not a question of whether the mother had acted unreasonably; the parties' estrangement was 'profound and enduring' and while the daughter was in financial need this was the result of her own 'lifestyle choices'—[2009] EWHC 3114 (Fam), [61]. However, this decision was overturned by the Court of Appeal—[2011] EWCA Civ 346. The daughter's outstanding appeal was then remitted to the High Court which upheld the original award of £50,000 (despite the daughter seeking half the value of the estate)—[2014] EWHC 542 (Fam). Following a further appeal by the daughter, the Court of Appeal raised this amount to £163,000—[2015] EWCA Civ 797. At the time of writing, the charities had been given leave to appeal the decision on quantum to the Supreme Court.

[119] In other words, those who are economically self-sufficient (or, at least, capable of earning their own living), and who were not financially dependent on a deceased parent before death (even if in financial need).
[120] J Holland, 'Ilott v Mitson: A Lesson for Practitioners?' (2012) 2 *Elder Law Journal* 59.
[121] TA Maroney, 'The Persistent Script of Judicial Dispassion' (2011) 99 *California Law Review* 629. See also the same author's chapter in the current collection—Maroney, ch 12.

before them as both sides present their evidence. Perhaps we should not be too surprised if judges (who bring their own emotional instincts and cultural 'baggage' to the cases which come before them) may be tempted to correct parental disinheritance or unequal distribution between children in some way.[122] In many ways, the 'normative expectation that parents will leave their estate to their children create[s] a corresponding right of the children to receive'[123] and judges are using whatever legal tools they have at their disposal to achieve this. This creates its own problems; as Drake has pointed out, '[i]t is precisely the discretionary quality of inheritance giving that renders it powerfully symbolic of parental responsibility and affection'.[124]

VII. Limiting the Emotional Fallout

Most sibling inheritance disputes have their genesis in issues which are not solely related to the distribution of the dead parent's estate. Old family grievances masquerade as a quarrel over money, property and material possessions, with the parties hiding behind the institutional façade of the law to revisit past wrongs. As Folberg has pointed out:

> [F]amily property and financial disputes ... are matters of the heart and the law. They present challenges for how emotions and family dynamics are to be weighed against and balanced with legal rights and obligations.[125]

The question here is not whether emotions should be recognised in the law's response to sibling inheritance disputes; they are intrinsic and integral components of the legal matrix because these disputes are driven by and create emotion. And while lawyers and other legal actors already recognise this, more could be done to lessen the emotional fallout from an uneven estate distribution between children.

The role of the lawyer is an important one when the parent is making a will. It goes without saying that lawyers are obliged to reflect their client's wishes, and to ensure a legally binding document. However, the preoccupation with legalise and property arrangements often detracts from advising clients on the emotional legacy which the document will also generate. Noting that the estate planning process provides a unique opportunity for exploring someone's personal

---

[122] Though it is worth noting that, in family provision claims, courts have not substituted an equal division just because an adult child has been treated less favourably than their siblings—see for example, *Re Hancock* [1998] 2 FLR 346 and *Re Creeney* [1984] NI 397. In contrast, if a will is declared invalid in the US on any of the grounds mentioned (for example, non-compliance with formalities, duress), the estate would usually lapse into intestacy and the deceased's children would automatically inherit in equal shares.

[123] Drake (n 4) 96.

[124] Ibid.

[125] Folberg (n 37) 12.

legacy, Sneddon argues that an 'attorney draftsperson ... must be more than a mere transcribing device'.[126] Encouraging will-makers to appreciate the emotional ramifications of their choices if contemplating uneven bequests, and to discuss this sensitively with their children in advance, are important tools. Legal drafting can take account of emotions as well. Varying the language used in the will, to generate a more personal narrative and explain the parent's reasons for specific bequests, might also ensure that lawyers are the first stage in preventing family conflict.[127]

When sibling inheritance disputes end up in the legal arena, judges need to be cognisant both of the intense emotions at play but also of their limited ability to address these emotions in a judicial setting. By producing a certain result, judges can mitigate some of the hurt (both financial and emotional) inflicted by the dead parent. Invalidating a will on what might be minimal evidence of non-compliance with formalities is a classic example, as is the strategy of appeasement facilitated by the family provision system whereby judges can give the disadvantaged sibling something out of the estate. The big difficulty is that the doctrine of testamentary freedom is supposed to have some force, and overthrowing or changing the will undermines that. And while we might argue that judges should spend more time trying to discover a testator's underlying intent without judging his/her motives, Baron makes the point that 'empathy carries risks' because the 'finder of fact may be unable to cast aside his or her own beliefs in the attempt to grasp another's'.[128]

Another option would be to move away from a court-centric decision-making process, towards alternative dispute resolution. Of course, under the current regime, the actual litigation can be seen as a form of emotional catharsis; a sibling who feels excluded or marginalised by a parent's will is able to raise issues which have been festering for years, and to finally vent his/her feelings in public. However, the emotionally charged litigation route has obvious drawbacks. Sibling inheritance disputes (like any family dispute) involve ongoing relationships, yet an adversarial system 'affirms for the parties that the contest is about winning and losing'[129]—tapping into the same feelings which plagued the disenfranchised sibling throughout their childhood (though one could argue that everyone involved in these cases invariably feels hurt or angry). Court proceedings also dissipate the estate, and create further animosity between the siblings who, having just lost their sole, surviving parent, are now 'on the way to irrevocably losing each other'.[130] In exploring other options, legally mandated

---

[126] Sneddon, 'The Will as Personal Narrative' (n 70) 375–76.

[127] O'Sullivan (n 75) 25.

[128] JE Baron, 'Empathy, Subjectivity and Testamentary Capacity' (1987) 24 *San Diego Law Review* 1043, 1044.

[129] Weinstein and Weinstein (n 45) 375.

[130] LP Love, 'Mediation of Probate Matters: Leaving a Valuable Legacy' (2001) 1 *Pepperdine Dispute Resolution Law Journal* 255, 255.

mediation could offer a better alternative, and not just because it should be cheaper and more efficient; everyone involved could address the underlying emotional issues, develop a uniquely responsive solution within a private setting (since the dispute is not played out in a public form) and perhaps restore some measure of family harmony.[131] As with any solution, there are drawbacks. Mediation is not always effective, and research carried out in Australia suggests that it is more likely to fail in family provision disputes between siblings than in other categories of litigant:

> [A]necdotal comments from lawyers and mediators [suggest] that cases between siblings are the most bitterly fought of all. All other relationships seem more amenable to resolution through mediation. This is probably simply an expression of the fact that sibling rivalry is a lifelong psychological construct which is hardly likely to melt away with ease.[132]

Because siblings have already had longer (in reality, most of their lives) to get into their positions, there is no guarantee that mediation will succeed; and even if a solution can be reached, the resultant damage may be beyond repair so that siblings will be estranged from, or actively hostile towards, each other for years to come. Despite this, mediation should be encouraged, and given every chance to work. Resolving disputes without going to court not only allows everyone involved to retain some measure of control over the process. It also enables complex emotions to be expressed, acknowledged and recognised,[133] with a view to lessening the overall emotional harm and (ideally) paving the way for reparation—or, at the very least, inflicting less damage than adversarial litigation.

VIII. Conclusion

> Inheritance disputes are not so much about money. People fight over the love they feel they did not receive.[134]

Estate contests are not just about property and financial issues; they involve relational issues as well. The result is an inherently complex emotional dimension, something which is especially true in disputes between adult siblings over the

---

[131] Ibid, 256. Mayersak (n 44) also argues that arbitration offers a better chance of minimising conflict and preserving family relationships (though perhaps 'salvaging' what's left of family relationships would be a better descriptor).

[132] P Vines, *Bleak House Revisited: Disproportionality in Family Provision Estate Litigation in New South Wales and Victoria* (Australasian Institute of Judicial Administration, 2011) 32. The same report also found that the most disproportionate level of costs in family provision cases were in sibling disputes, well ahead of disputes between first families and later spouses—ibid, 14.

[133] Themes which Huntington also highlights in her chapter—Huntington, ch 2.

[134] Psychiatrist and author Reuvan Bar-Levav, quoted in Accettura (n 38) 1.

distribution of parental wealth. Most of these disputes are not simply driven by money (though that may be a factor as well); they are emotionally driven, because specific bequests are viewed as posthumous representations of 'love, validation, and importance'[135] between parent and child. Underpinning this are deep-seated feelings of sibling rivalry with all its negative traits, mixed with an equally toxic cocktail of grief emotions at a time of intense personal (and familial) upheaval.

Many people engage in destructive litigation; but sibling inheritance disputes take this to another level because of ongoing family relationships and the emotional backdrop to the litigation. These disputes become all-consuming. Each side 'demonises the other'[136] in what will usually be very public litigation over a very private issue (something of a paradox in itself). The impact of the dispute reverberates through the entire family, resulting in emotional wounds which, in more extreme scenarios, 'may be fatal or take generations to heal'.[137] In light of all this, there is much to be said for encouraging parents to be aware of the consequences of their actions from the outset, and for lawyers to be mindful of the role that they play in anticipating sibling disputes over parental wealth. By the time a dispute ends up in court, much of the emotional damage has already been done, and judges can only hope that their handling and resolution of the issues will not aggravate or perpetuate existing family tensions. Mediation is not a panacea, but offers one way of keeping these conflicts away from adversarial court proceedings in the interests of all concerned.

---

[135] Accettura (n 38) 2.
[136] Folberg (n 37) 9.
[137] Ibid, 9.

4

The Emotional Dynamics
of Undue Influence

JOHN STANNARD*

I. Introduction

Few people other than lawyers will have heard of the legal doctrine of undue
influence. However, more will be familiar with the novel of that name by Anita
Brookner.[1] There the 'undue influence' of the title relates to the efforts made by
the central character, Claire Pitt, to pursue the affections of Martin Gibson, an
intelligent and handsome but ineffectual man who wanders into the dusty old
bookshop where she is employed for a pittance by two elderly sisters. She imagines
him as a man who has always been subject to coercion, his weakness excites her,
and at the time of their meeting he is in thrall to the whims of a dominant and
invalid wife. This theme of unsatisfactory relationships, characterised by a selfish
dominance on one side and an excessively anxious desire to please on the other, is
repeated again and again throughout the book, ranging from Mrs Hilditch and her
son at the beginning of the book to the little girl Arabella and her grandmother at
the end. Yet in all these situations, unhappy though they be, there is an element of
choice—an element of advantage for both sides. Thus Claire speculates in relation
to her mother that it 'probably reassured her to be taken over by a will stronger
than her own'.[2] In his turn Martin, who has been weaned away from his academic
career by his overbearing wife Cynthia, 'exchanges the library for the sickroom and
servitude, and loyally makes that servitude his reason for living'.[3] Not for nothing
does Claire speculate as to whether she was witnessing 'one of those terrible relationships in which each party fed off the other'.[4]

* Senior Lecturer, School of Law, Queen's University Belfast. I am grateful to Eimear Spain and to
Roddy Cowie for their comments on the first draft.
[1] Anita Brookner, *Undue Influence* (New York, Vintage Contemporaries, 1999).
[2] Ibid, 18.
[3] Ibid, 115.
[4] Ibid, 60.

All of this may seem far from the arid technicalities of contract, equity and probate. Yet it is with the consequences of precisely this sort of relationship that these branches of the law in general, and the doctrine of undue influence in particular, often have to deal. The question for this chapter is to what extent, if at all, understanding the emotional dynamics of these relationships can help to illustrate and inform the law. To answer this question we need to explore the notion of undue influence in legal terms before turning to the insights of psychology and other disciplines.

II. The Law

Undue influence in legal terms is one of a family of related doctrines that allows a party to a transaction, or someone claiming on his or her behalf, to set that transaction aside on the grounds that it was procured by unfair means. Broadly speaking, these doctrines cover three situations. In the first situation, the party in question was misled in some way. In the second, the transaction was entered into as a result of coercion. In the third, the nature of the relationship between the parties, combined with the nature of the transaction itself, is said to call for a satisfactory explanation from the party who wishes to rely on the transaction; if this is not forthcoming, the transaction will be set aside. To a certain extent the legal concept of undue influence straddles all three of these situations, but the law is not easy to explain, not least because of the way in which it has developed. What is clear is that the doctrine operates in two distinct ways, depending on whether the impugned transaction was a will or some transaction made *inter vivos*—that is to say, between two living people. We shall begin with the second situation, as it is of far greater legal significance.

A. *Inter Vivos* Undue Influence

Where an *inter vivos* contract or gift[5] has been procured by undue influence, the basic rule in English law is clear: it can be set aside by the person on whom that influence has been exercised.[6] However, this picture is complicated by a number of factors, most notably the bringing into play of various 'presumptions' involving the existence of what is termed a 'relationship of trust and confidence' between

---

[5] As will be seen, the doctrine is generally discussed in the context of contract, but many of the cases on the topic concern gifts rather than contracts made for consideration.

[6] J Beatson, A Burrows and J Cartwright, *Anson's Law of Contract*, 29th edn (Oxford, Oxford University Press, 2010) (hereafter *Anson*) 359–72; MP Furmston, *Cheshire, Fifoot and Furmston's Law of Contract*, 16th edn (Oxford, Oxford University Press, 2012) (hereafter *Cheshire, Fifoot and Furmston*) 398–408; E Peel, *Treitel: The Law of Contract*, 13th edn (London, Sweet & Maxwell, 2011) (hereafter *Treitel*) paras 10-012–10-041.

the parties. Though there is currently some disagreement as to how precisely the cases should be classified,[7] the traditional approach is to divide them into two categories,[8] as can be seen from what has become the standard exposition of the law by Lord Nicholls of Birkenhead in *Royal Bank of Scotland v Etridge (No 2)*.[9] Having identified the rationale of the law as being to ensure that the influence of one person was not abused by unacceptable means of persuasion,[10] he went on to say that there were two ways recognised by the law in which this might be done.[11] The first of these comprised overt acts of pressure or coercion such as unlawful threats, whereas the second arose out of a relationship between two persons where one had acquired over the other a measure of influence, or ascendancy, of which the ascendant person then took unfair advantage.[12]

In the first category there need be no relationship of trust and confidence. These are sometimes called cases of 'actual' undue influence.[13] Here the essence of the complaint is that one party has been guilty of 'unfair and improper' conduct; such conduct can involve either deception,[14] or coercion,[15] or both.[16] In most cases this will have resulted in some advantage to the guilty party, but it seems that this is not an essential requirement.[17] We shall be discussing the emotional dynamics of this kind of situation more fully at a later stage, but it will already be obvious that cases of this sort do not necessarily involve any kind of attachment between the parties; if any kind of emotion is present, it is just as likely to be fear of the consequences that may ensue if agreement is not forthcoming to what is proposed by the guilty party.

In cases of the second sort the party who wishes to set the contract aside does so by proving not that undue influence was actually used, but rather: (1) that the relationship between the parties was such as to give rise to the risk of such influence being brought to bear; and (2) that the transaction is one which, while not

---

[7] In particular, doubts have been expressed about the existence of Lord Browne-Wilkinson's 'Class 2B' in *Barclays Bank Plc v O'Brien* (see below)—that is to say, a separate category of cases involving a relationship of trust and confidence outside one of the set categories: see *Royal Bank of Scotland v Etridge (No 2)* [2002] 2 AC 773, [107] (Lord Hobhouse) and [161] (Lord Scott).

[8] *Barclays Bank Plc v O'Brien* [1994] 1 AC 180, 189-190 (Lord Browne-Wilkinson); *Anson* (n 6) 360–61; *Cheshire, Fifoot and Furmston* (n 6) 399–400; *Treitel* (n 6) paras 10-14 and 10-17.

[9] *Royal Bank of Scotland v Etridge (No 2)* [2001] UKHL 44, [2002] 2 AC 773, [6]–[12]; see *Evans v Lloyd* [2013] EWHC 1725 (Ch), [2013] WTLR 1137, [56]; *Brown v Stephenson* [2013] EWHC 2351 (Ch), [2013] WTLR 1675, [127]; *Re Smith (decd): Kicks v Leigh* [2014] EWHC 3926 (Ch), [11]; *Birmingham City Council v Beech* [2014] EWCA Civ 830, [2014] HLR 38, [56]–[63]; *Crossfield v Jackson* [2014] EWCA Civ 1548; *Hart v Burbidge* [2014] EWCA Civ 992, [2015] 1 WTLR 1361, [33].

[10] *Royal Bank of Scotland v Etridge (No 2)* [2001] UKHL 44, [2002] 2 AC 773, [6]–[7]. For further discussion of the rationale of the doctrine, see below at nn 58–87

[11] Ibid, [8].

[12] Ibid.

[13] *Barclays Bank Plc v O'Brien* [1994] 1 AC 180, 189 (Lord Browne-Wilkinson) ('Class 1').

[14] As in *Lyon v Home* (1868) LR 6 Eq 655 (messages from the dead).

[15] As in *Williams v Bayley* (1866) LR 1 HL 200 (threat to prosecute son).

[16] As in *Morley v Loughnan* [1893] 1 Ch 736 (invalid donor subject to religious domination by carers).

[17] *CIBC Mortgages v Pitt* [1994] 1 AC 200.

necessarily manifestly disadvantageous to the weaker party, was such as to call for some explanation.[18] With regard to the first of these two requirements, the relationship is termed one of 'trust and confidence',[19] and it can be established in two ways, either by showing that it fell into one of a list of accepted categories where such trust and confidence can be presumed to exist, such as doctor and patient, solicitor and client, or religious leader and disciple,[20] or by showing that such a relationship existed on the facts.[21] It will be apparent that in cases of the former kind we have in effect a double presumption, one being that the relationship was one of trust and confidence in the first place, and the other being that it involved the exercise of undue influence on the weaker party.[22] In either case, however, the burden on the party wishing to uphold the contract will be the same; he or she must show that despite the existence of the impugned relationship, the other party entered into the contract after 'full, free and informed thought'.[23] Though the law does not prescribe as such how this should be done,[24] the best way of proving that this is the case is by demonstrating that the party concerned had independent legal advice.[25] Once again, we shall be discussing the emotional dynamics of this kind of case later, but clearly they will be very different from those involved in cases of actual undue influence; in particular, the focus will be on trust rather than on fear, and there is more likely to be some degree of emotional attachment between the parties.

B. Testamentary Undue Influence

The law of succession also allows for a will to be challenged on the ground of undue influence,[26] but this doctrine—generally known as 'testamentary' or 'probate' undue influence[27]—is much narrower in scope.[28] In particular, the notion of a relationship of trust and confidence has no part to play here; rather,

---

[18] *Royal Bank of Scotland v Etridge (No 2)* [2002] 2 AC 773, [14] (Lord Nicholls).

[19] *Barclays Bank Plc v O'Brien* [1994] 1 AC 180, 189 (Lord Browne-Wilkinson)

[20] Ibid ('Class 2A').

[21] Ibid ('Class 2B')

[22] However, as Treitel points out, the two presumptions are of different kinds, the first being a rule of law and the other a true presumption which may be rebutted on the evidence: *Treitel* (n 6) para 10-022.

[23] *Zamet v Hyman* [1961] 1 WLR 1442, 1461 (Lord Evershed MR).

[24] *Inche Noriah v Shaik Allie Bin Omar* [1929] AC 127, 135 (Lord Hailsham LC); *Lancashire Loans v Black* [1934] 1 KB 380, 413 (Lawrence LJ).

[25] *Allcard v Skinner* (1887) 36 Ch D 145, 190 (Bowen LJ).

[26] R Kerridge (assisted by AHR Brierley), *Parry and Kerridge: The Law of Succession*, 12th edn (London, Sweet & Maxwell, 2009) (hereafter *Parry and Kerridge*) para 5-14.

[27] P Ridge, 'Equitable Undue Influence and Wills' (2004) 120 *Law Quarterly Review* 617, 621.

[28] Indeed, it was argued as long ago as 1939 that the label 'undue influence' should be abandoned for this sort of case: see WHD Winder, 'Undue Influence and Coercion' (1939) 3 *Modern Law Review* 97. The reasons for the divergence between the two doctrines appears to be largely historical: M Tyson, 'An Analysis of the Differences Between the Doctrine of Undue Influence with Regard to Testamentary and Inter Vivos Dispositions' (1997) 5 *Australian Property Law Journal* 38.

the doctrine is restricted to cases of actual coercion, where it can be said, in the words of the then future Lord Penzance, that the testator has been 'driven' rather than 'led'.[29] However, this does not mean that a will cannot also be challenged on the basis of the sort of factors that we have been discussing above. On the contrary, there are several possibilities here; for instance, there may be a challenge on the basis of lack of testamentary capacity,[30] or fraud,[31] or lack of 'knowledge and approval'—that is to say that the testator knew the contents of the will and approved of them.[32] But none of these will help in a case where the testator knew full well what he or she was doing at the relevant time, but where the relationship between testator and beneficiary was such as to raise the suspicion that the former did not exercise 'full, free and informed thought'.

However, there is also another possibility, and that is to use what has been termed the 'suspicious circumstances' rule.[33] As with the *inter vivos* version of the undue influence doctrine, this works by way of a rebuttable presumption. Where it is shown that the testator had testamentary capacity and that the will was duly executed, the court will normally infer that he or she knew and approved of the contents of the will.[34] However where it can be shown that there was something suspicious about the circumstances in which the will was drawn up and executed, those who seek to uphold the will may be placed under the affirmative burden of showing that all was fair and above board.[35]

As the cases show, such circumstances may include the existence of a relationship of trust and confidence between the testator and the beneficiary.[36] However, though in many cases this rule may work in the same manner as the *inter vivos* doctrine of undue influence, the two are not identical in content. In particular, though the 'suspicious circumstances' rule may encompass cases where a relationship of trust and confidence exists, it is much wider in scope.[37] Moreover, the nature of the burden placed on the party seeking to benefit is not the same in the two cases. In the *inter vivos* context, as we have seen, the test is whether the other party entered into the transaction after 'full, free and informed thought'.[38]

---

[29] *Hall v Hall* (1868) LR 1 P & D 481, 482.

[30] According to the classic statement of the law by Cockburn CJ in *Banks v Goodfellow* (1870) LR 5 QB 549, 565 this requires proof that the testator understood three matters at the relevant time, namely: (1) the effect of the will; (2) the extent of the property disposed of under it; and (3) the nature of the claims that might be made on him or her (that is to say, by potential deserving beneficiaries). See also Mental Capacity Act 2005, ss 1(3) and 2 and *Parry and Kerridge* (n 26) para 5-04.

[31] *Parry and Kerridge* (n 26) para 5-15; *White v White & Cato* (1862) 2 Sw & Tr 504; *Riding v Hawkins* (1889) 14 PD 56.

[32] *Parry and Kerridge* (n 26) paras 5-17–5-25.

[33] Ibid, paras 5-26–5-38; *Wintle v Nye* [1959] 1 WLR 284; R Kerridge, 'Wills made in Suspicious Circumstances' (2000) 59 *Cambridge Law Journal* 310; Ridge (n 27) 622–25.

[34] Ridge (n 27) 622; *Barry v Butlin* (1838) 2 Moo 480.

[35] For how this may be done see below, nn 39–40.

[36] See for instance, *Barry v Butlin* (1838) 2 Moo PC 480 (doctor, solicitor and butler); *Re Stott* [1980] 1 All ER 259 (nursing home proprietor); cf *Re Walsh* (1892) 18 VLR 739 (priest).

[37] *Parry and Kerridge* (n 26) para 5-14.

[38] Above, n 23.

In relation to a will, the position is less clear; according to Lord Hatherley, any person who has been instrumental in drawing up a will under which he or she takes a benefit has the onus of showing 'the rightness of the transaction',[39] but others suggest that what has to be shown is merely 'knowledge and approval'.[40] Whichever test is correct, it is clear that the emotional dynamics of this kind of case may be very different from those which arise in cases of *inter vivos* undue influence.

C. Some Problems

Though the basic principles surrounding undue influence, whether in the testamentary context or *inter vivos*, are reasonably clear when seen, as it were, from a distance, numerous difficulties appear once the law is examined more closely. In particular, there are problems relating to the internal and external structure of the law, and as to its rationale. We shall now examine these more closely, with a view to considering later on in the chapter whether and to what extent an analysis in terms of emotional dynamics can point towards a solution to some or all of these.

i. The Internal Structure of the Law

As we have seen, testamentary undue influence is confined to cases of coercion, whereas *inter vivos* undue influence covers not only 'actual' undue influence (Class 1), but also cases where a so-called relationship of trust and confidence can either be presumed to exist (Class 2A) or proved on the facts (Class 2B). Class 1 and Class 2A are relatively straightforward, but the cases do not make it very clear where Class 2B fits into the picture, or even whether it exists at all as a separate category. The problem is that at the end of the day the claimant has to prove undue influence in Class 2B cases no less than in Class 1.[41] In the words of Lord Scott, the so-called 'presumption' in Class 2B cases is said to be doing

> no more than recognising that evidence of the relationship between the dominant and subservient parties, coupled with whatever other evidence is for the time being available, may be sufficient to justify a finding of undue influence on the balance of probabilities.[42]

The onus shifts to the defendant to counteract this by evidence, rather as in relation to the *res ipsa loquitur* principle in the context of the law of tort.[43] Another problem in relation to this presumption is *what* precisely has to be proved to bring a case within Class 2B. Traditionally this is expressed in terms of a relationship of

---

[39] *Fulton v Andrew* (1875) LR 7 HL 448, 471; *Parry and Kerridge* (n 26) para 5-35.
[40] Ridge (n 27) 622.
[41] *Treitel* (n 6) para 10-014.
[42] *Royal Bank of Scotland v Etridge (No 2)* [2002] 2 AC 773, [161]; see also Lord Hobhouse [107]; *Treitel* (n 6) para 10-024.
[43] *Treitel*, (n 6), para 10-24.

'trust and confidence', but what precisely does this mean? In 1985 Lord Scarman deprecated references to 'confidentiality' in this connection, pointing out that there were plenty of confidential relationships which did not give rise to any presumption of undue influence, such as husband and wife.[44] He went on to couch the doctrine in terms of 'victimisation' and dominance by one party over the other,[45] but this requirement too has been denied, on the grounds that it is enough to show that the party in whom the trust and confidence has been reposed is *in a position* to exert influence over the one who reposes it.[46] The trouble with this is that this can be said of almost any relationship of such a nature, for how can one person have trust and confidence in another without that other being in a position to exert at least *some* influence over him or her?

ii. External Structure

A closely related question is as to how undue influence relates to other legal doctrines of a similar nature. We have already seen that in the testamentary context the right to challenge a will on the grounds of undue influence is complemented by other doctrines, most notably the 'suspicious circumstances' rule.[47] In the same way, a contract or other transaction *inter vivos* can be rescinded not only for undue influence but also for misrepresentation (on the basis of a false statement of some kind),[48] or duress (as the result of an illegitimate threat),[49] or on the grounds that it constitutes an 'unconscionable bargain'.[50] Cases of misrepresentation clearly fall into a separate category, but how the others fit together is not at all clear.[51] Attempts have been made from time to time to discern an underlying principle, most notably by Lord Denning in a case in 1975 in which a charge executed by an

---

[44] *National Westminster Bank Plc v Morgan* [1985] AC 686, 702. Exactly the same could be said of the relationship that was in question in that case, namely that of banker and customer. For a historical discussion of the doctrine of undue influence in the broader context of fiduciary relationships, see LS Sealy, 'Fiduciary Relationships' [1962] *Cambridge Law Journal* 69.

[45] *National Westminster Bank Plc v Morgan* [1985] AC 686, 705 citing *Poosathurai v Kannappa Chettiar* (1919) LR 47 IA 1, 3 (Lord Shaw).

[46] *Goldsworthy v Brickell* [1987] Ch 378, 404 (Nourse LJ).

[47] Above at nn 33–35.

[48] *Anson* (n 6) ch 9; *Cheshire, Fifoot and Furmston* (n 6) ch 9; *Treitel* (n 6) ch 9.

[49] Such cases can be of three kinds: threats of unlawful violence or false imprisonment (*Barton v Armstrong* [1976] AC 104); extortion of money by the unlawful detention of goods (*Skeate v Beale* (1841) 11 A & E 983); and threats to break a contract or amounting to other illegitimate pressure (*Dimskal Shipping Co SA v International Transport Workers Federation (The Evia Luck) (No 2)* [1992] 2 AC 152; *Treitel* (n 6) paras 10-002–10-011.

[50] This is a relatively narrow doctrine defined in terms of cases where 'a purchase is made from a poor and ignorant man at a considerable undervalue, the vendor having no independent advice'; in such cases the Courts of Equity would set the contract aside: *Fry v Lane* (1888) 40 Ch D 312, 322 (Kay LJ).

[51] One problem is that the doctrines in question have different historical roots; thus for instance duress is a creature of the common law, testamentary undue influence a creature of the courts of Probate, and undue influence a creature of the courts of Equity. To make matters even more difficult, other common law systems adopt rather different structures: see SR Enman, 'Doctrines of Unconscionability in Canadian, English and Commonwealth Contract Law' (1987) 16 *Anglo-American Law Review* 191.

elderly man on his farm to support his son's failing business was set aside by the Court of Appeal on the grounds of undue influence from the bank.[52] In the course of his judgment Lord Denning conducted an exhaustive review of the cases[53] and came up with the following statement of principle:

> Gathering all together, I would suggest that through all these instances there runs a single thread. They rest on 'inequality of bargaining power'. By virtue of it, the English law gives relief to one who, without independent advice, enters into a contract upon terms which are very unfair or transfers property for a consideration which is grossly inadequate, when his bargaining power is grievously impaired by reason of his own needs or desires, or by his own ignorance or infirmity, coupled with undue influences or pressures brought to bear on him by or for the benefit of the other.[54]

However, the other members of the Court preferred to decide the case on the more traditional grounds of undue influence in its technical sense,[55] and Lord Denning's analysis was later deprecated in the House of Lords by Lord Scarman.[56] However, what is of interest is the way in which Lord Denning seeks to identify various key factors in cases of this sort, most notably: (1) the lack of independent advice; (2) what would be called the 'substantive' unfairness of the transaction;[57] and (3) the fact that at the relevant time the bargaining power of the party concerned was impaired in some way, in particular by what Lord Denning refers to as 'undue influences or pressures' brought to bear by or for the benefit of the other. This brings us on to a more fundamental problem, namely the rationale of the undue influence doctrine and the other related doctrines we have been considering. In other words, what is undue influence *for*?

iii. Rationale of the Doctrine

Given the importance of the doctrine of undue influence, there is a surprising lack of consensus among the standard texts as to the precise rationale of the doctrine. One textbook draws a threefold distinction between misrepresentation (one party misleading the other), duress (threats by one party to the other) and undue influence (one party improperly taking advantage of the other).[58] Another classifies undue influence, along with duress and the doctrine of unconscionable bargain,

---

[52] *Lloyd's Bank v Bundy* [1975] QB 326; C Carr, 'Inequality of Bargaining Power' (1975) 38 *Modern Law Review* 463; LS Sealy, 'Undue Influence and Inequality of Bargaining Power' [1975] *Cambridge Law Journal* 21.

[53] In particular, he considered five doctrines in this connection: (1) duress of goods; (2) unconscionable bargains; (3) undue influence; (4) what he termed 'undue pressure'; and (5) salvage agreements.

[54] *Lloyd's Bank v Bundy* [1975] QB 326, 339.

[55] Ibid, 340 (Sir Eric Sachs and Cairns LJ).

[56] *National Westminster Bank Plc v Morgan* [1985] AC 686, 708.

[57] In the sense that it was unfair in relation to its content rather than the way in was made: see AA Leff, 'Unconscionability and the Code: The Emperor's New Clause' (1967) 115 *Pennsylvania Law Review* 485.

[58] *Cheshire, Fifoot and Furmston* (n 6) 338.

as an instance of improper pressure.[59] Yet another speaks of these doctrines as involving improper conduct by one party, the vulnerability of the other, or a combination of the two.[60] In the same way the well-known twentieth-century contract scholar Patrick Atiyah framed the relevant law in terms of two duties, one being the duty to refrain from duress and undue influence, and the other the duty not to abuse a fiduciary position.[61] However another commentator, David Tiplady, saw *three* principles at work, all involving some element of deprivation of choice, the first being the abuse of confidentiality, the second the subversion of civic or moral duty for reasons of private advantage, and the third the abuse of monopoly power.[62] Despite these variations of emphasis a pattern can be discerned, in that some of these rationales focus on the need to protect the weaker party, while others are more concerned with the need to prevent wrongdoing by the stronger.[63]

The essence of the first approach, which is strongly associated with the late Peter Birks, has been described as 'claimant-sided';[64] his or her consent, if not actually negated by the circumstances of the transaction,[65] is nevertheless excessively impaired.[66] Whereas doctrines such as duress and unconscionable bargains are said to focus on the wrongful conduct of the stronger party in attempting to enforce or at least retain the benefit of the relevant transaction in circumstances where it is not consistent with equity and good conscience to do so, the essence of undue influence, it is argued, is the quality of the consent or assent of the weaker party.[67] This view gains support from a number of factors, most notably the absence of any requirement that the claimant prove bad faith or unconscionable conduct by the party seeking to uphold the transaction,[68] and the principle that a presumption

---

[59] *Treitel* (n 6) para 10-001.

[60] *Anson* (n 6) 350.

[61] PS Atiyah, *An Introduction to the Law of Contract*, 2nd edn (Oxford, Clarendon Press, 1971) chs XV and XVI.

[62] D Tiplady, 'Contractual Unfairness' (1983) 46 *Modern Law Review* 601.

[63] On this see generally, M Chen-Wishart, 'Undue Influence: Vindicating Relationships of Influence' (2006) 59 *Current Legal Problems* 231.

[64] Ibid, 236.

[65] Some of the older cases suggest this, but as was pointed out by Lord Wilberforce in the context of the criminal law defence of duress, a more accurate analysis is in terms of 'coactus volui'—'I willed it being compelled': *DPP for NI v Lynch* [1975] AC 653, 680; PS Atiyah, 'Economic Duress and the Overborne Will' (1982) 98 *Law Quarterly Review* 197. Indeed, it has been argued that the more extreme the pressure, the more genuine the consent: JP Dawson, 'Economic Duress—An Essay in Perspective' (1947) 45 *Michigan Law Review* 253, 267.

[66] P Birks and NY Chin, 'On the Nature of Undue Influence' in J Beatson and D Friedmann (eds), *Good Faith and Fault in Contract Law* (Oxford, Oxford University Press, 1995); R Bigwood, 'Undue Influence: "Impaired Consent" or "Wicked Exploitation"?' (1996) 16 *Oxford Journal of Legal Studies* 503; D Capper, 'Undue Influence and Unconscionability: A Rationalisation' (1998) 114 *Law Quarterly Review* 479.

[67] *Commercial Bank of Australia v Amadio* (1983) 151 CLR 447, 474 (Deane J); Bigwood (n 66).

[68] That is to say, short of the passive receipt of the benefits resulting from the transaction: see *Allcard v Skinner* (1887) 36 Ch D 145; *Tufton v Sperni* [1952] TLR 516; *Lloyd's Bank Ltd v Bundy* [1975] 1 QB 326; *Goldsworthy v Brickell* [1987] 1 Ch 378; *Simpson v Simpson* [1992] 1 FLR 601; *Hammond v Osborn* [2002] EWCA Civ 885, [2002] WTLR 1125; P Birks, 'Undue Influence as Wrongful Exploitation' (2004) 120 *Law Quarterly Review* 34; Capper (n 66) 493.

of undue influence can be rebutted by showing that the claimant entered into the transaction after 'full, free and informed thought'.[69] On this analysis cases of so-called 'actual' undue influence are shunted off into a separate category, while what remains is seen as akin to innocent misrepresentation, which can be a ground for setting a contract aside without necessarily providing any right of action on the part of the claimant.[70]

The second approach, by contrast, focuses on the conduct of the stronger party; in the words of an Australian judge, the law looks at the matter from the point of view of the person seeking to enforce the contract, and enquires whether, having regard to all the circumstances, it is consistent with equity and good conscience that he should be allowed to enforce it.[71] This approach, which is followed by Rick Bigwood and others, recognises the common historical roots of undue influence and unconscionability, and is reflected in the frequent reference in the cases to misconduct on the part of the stronger party.[72] Though this approach does not deny the issue of impaired consent, it sees it as no more than the context in which the exploitation takes place;[73] indeed, Bigwood argues that most if not all involuntary agreements, at least at first blush, involve objectionable forms of advantage-taking or exploitation.[74] In this context even where the stronger party was blameless at the time of the relevant transaction, he or she may still be guilty of unconscionable conduct in seeking to enforce it in the circumstances that now exist.

A radically different approach is taken by Mindy Chen-Wishart, who seeks to locate and explain undue influence in the context of what is termed 'relational autonomy'.[75] In this connection she points out that while the law quite correctly promotes and pursues the ideals of personal freedom and autonomy,[76] such autonomy is traditionally seen in unduly atomistic and individualistic terms.[77] Rather, the law should seek to recognise that what enables people to be autonomous is

---

[69] *Inche Noriah v Shaik Allie Bin Omar* [1929] AC 127, 135 (Lord Hailsham LC); *Zamet v Hyman* [1961] 1 WLR 1442, 1461 (Lord Evershed MR); Capper (n 66) 493.

[70] Birks (n 68) 36.

[71] *Blomley v Ryan* (1956) 99 CLR 362, 401–02 (Fullagar J), cited by Sir Anthony Mason in 'The Place of Equity and Equitable Remedies in the Common Law World' (1994) 110 *Law Quarterly Review* 238, 249; Bigwood (n 66) 503.

[72] Chen-Wishart (n 63) 237, citing such words as 'impropriety', 'abuse', betrayal', 'wrongdoing', 'stigma', 'reprehensible' and 'fault'.

[73] Bigwood (n 66) 507.

[74] Ibid. In this connection he cites Kronman's assertion that the problem of locating the necessary and sufficient conditions for involuntariness is equivalent to determining which of the many forms of advantage-taking possible in exchange relationships are compatible with the libertarian conceptions of individual freedom: A Kronman, 'Contract Law and Distributive Justice' (1980) 89 *Yale Law Journal* 473 at 480.

[75] Chen-Wishart (n 63) 241; C Mackenzie and N Stoljar (eds), *Relational Autonomy* (New York, Oxford University Press, 2000).

[76] Indeed, drawing on Rawls, she describes it as a 'fundamental feature of personhood', adding that respect for it is 'not just one value amongst many in human life, but an absolutely fundamental value which must always trump any other': Chen-Wishart (n 63) 239.

[77] Ibid, 240. In the present connection one is reminded of Atiyah's comment that our laws and institutions are based on the assumption that man is a rational being with particular characteristics,

not isolation but relationships with parents, teachers, friends and loved ones who provide support and guidance.[78] In this context, striving for connection with others is not inimical to autonomy; on the contrary, it is an essential prerequisite. However, such connections inevitably carry the risk of exploitation; unprotected commitment can be even more dangerous than unprotected sex.[79] So how can such protection be provided? It is here that the doctrine of undue influence comes in to play. Drawing on theorists such as Stewart Macaulay,[80] Sir Herbert Hart[81] and Joseph Raz,[82] the author then seeks to explain the doctrine in terms of the law's justifiable response to 'autonomy harms' in three distinct senses, the first being harm to autonomy-enhancing relationships of influence such as marriage, romance, family, care and friendship,[83] the second being harm to those legal institutions (contractual or otherwise) which support voluntary transfers,[84] and the third being harm to the claimant's personal autonomy when he or she makes a transaction that seriously jeopardises his or her chances of leading an autonomous life.[85] Though to a certain extent this approach incorporates insights from both of the previous two, it differs from them in its relational focus.[86] In this context, it is interesting to see that the author, while not writing in the law and emotion tradition, draws at one point on the insights of psychology and other disciplines.[87] It is to these insights that we can now turn.

III. The Emotional Dynamics

So much for the law; what of the emotional dynamics? In this section we shall outline five issues; (1) the nature of an emotion; (2) the relationship between

---

one of which is that he is presumed not to want or intend to give away his property without due reason: PS Atiyah, *Essays on Contract* (Oxford, Clarendon Press, 1986) 334. Chen-Wishart describes this in terms of 'Super-Detached Man'.

[78] Chen-Wishart (n 63) 242. She describes this in terms of 'Relational Man'.

[79] Ibid, 243.

[80] S Macaulay, 'The Real and the Paper Deal—Empirical Pictures of Relationships, Complexity and the Urge for Transparent Simple Rules' in D Campbell, H Collins and J Wightman (eds), *Implicit Dimensions of Contract: Discrete, Relational and Network Contracts* (Oxford, Hart Publishing, 2003). This is described by Chen-Wishart as analogous to Ian Macneil's 'relational' approach to determining contractual content: Chen-Wishart (n 63) 343.

[81] HLA Hart, 'The Ascription of Responsibility and Rights' (1948) 49 *Proceedings of the Aristotelian Society* 49; Chen-Wishart (n 63) 244.

[82] J Raz, *The Morality of Freedom* (Oxford, Clarendon Press, 1986); Chen-Wishart (n 63) 246–52.

[83] Chen-Wishart (n 63) 249.

[84] Ibid, 250.

[85] Ibid.

[86] To put it another way, if we consider a relationship as involving two parties, A and B, the essence of the approach is to focus not on A or B in isolation, or even A and B together, but also on the 'and'!

[87] Thus on p 241 she cites the findings of Harlow and Zimmermann in relation to the bonding of infant monkeys (HF Harlow and RR Zimmermann, 'Affectional Responses in the Infant Monkey'

emotion and reason; (3) the relationship between emotion and the will; (4) the emotions involved in undue influence; and (5) the way in which these map on to the traditional structure of undue influence law.

A. The Nature of Emotion

The concept of an emotion is one that is notoriously difficult to define;[88] indeed, it has been argued that the task is an impossible one owing to the heterogeneous nature of emotion.[89] Be that as it may, there are three key points worth noting in this context. The first is that whatever emotion is, it is certainly not to be equated with mere feeling or affect.[90] One key aspect that distinguishes emotion from feeling is the presence of 'intentionality';[91] whereas a feeling is no more than a feeling, an emotion is 'about' something[92]—or in the words of Robert C Solomon, 'a complex awareness of one's engagements in the world and one's tendencies to act on it'.[93] The second is the complex and multidimensional nature of emotion, including those of temporal duration,[94] intensity[95] and complexity.[96] Last but not

---

(1959) 130 *Science* 421), and locates these in the context of classical attachment theory, a theory which will form a key focus of our discussion in the pages which follow.

[88] K Oatley, D Keltner and JM Jenkins, *Understanding Emotions*, 2nd edn (Oxford, Blackwell Publishing, 2006) 28. A table given on that page lists no less than eight different definitions propounded by various leading theorists, and van Brakel identifies no less than 22 different senses of the term: J van Brakel, 'Emotions: A Cross-Cultural Perspective on Forms of Life' in WM Wentworth and J Ryan (eds), *Social Perspectives on Emotion*, Vol 2 (Bingley, Emerald Group Publishing, 1994).

[89] Oatley et al (n 88) 28.

[90] JV Brady, 'Emotion, Some Conceptual Problems and Psychophysiological Experiments' in M Arnold (ed), *Feelings and Emotions* (Cambridge, MA, Academic Press, 1970).

[91] P Goldie, *The Emotions* (Oxford, Oxford University Press, 2000) 16–28.

[92] In the words of Magda Arnold, 'emotion always focuses on the object, while feeling reveals my momentary state of mind': MB Arnold, *Emotion and Personality*, Vol 1 (New York, Columbia University Press, 1960) 21.

[93] R Solomon, 'The Philosophy of Emotions' in M Lewis, JM Haviland-Jones and L Feldman Barrett (eds), *Handbook of Emotions*, 3rd edn (New York, Guilford Press, 2008) 10.

[94] Thus one can have: (1) an emotional episode, which may only last for a few seconds; (2) a full-blown emotion, which may last for minutes or hours; (3) a mood, which may last for days, weeks, or months; and (4) a character or personality trait, which will last a lifetime: Oatley et al (n 88) 134.

[95] Thus for instance one can be mildly pleased or in an ecstasy of joy; apprehensive or terrified out of one's wits. In the same way, moods can be measured by an adjective checklist or by offering a list of statements and asking the subject to say which best describes his or her feelings at the time: Oatley et al (n 88) 125–26; DP Green, SL Goldman and P Salovey, 'Measurement Error Masks Bipolarity in Affect Ratings' (1993) 64 *Journal of Personality and Social Psychology* 1029.

[96] Thus there is all the difference, for instance, between being sexually attracted to someone (a relatively simple feeling which we share with the animals) and being in love with them. Note that the difference here is one of complexity rather than mere intensity. In the same way, Arieti postulates a three-level structure of emotion, the first of which is very basic and immediate, and requires a minimum level of cognitive input, the second of which is elicited by cognitive symbolic processes, and the third of which involves a greater role for language and a wider temporal representation, both past and future: S Arieti, 'Cognition and Feeling' in MB Arnold, *Emotion and Personality*, Vol 1 (New York, Columbia University Press, 1960) 135.

least, emotions do not exist in a vacuum, but can be seen to serve a purpose; in particular, they are said to help the individual maintain significant relationships with his or her environment, most notably the social environment.[97] Not for nothing have emotions been described as 'our fundamental mediators between inner and outer worlds'.[98]

B. Emotion and Reason

The traditional approach of the law has been to see emotion as an enemy of reason,[99] and this is reflected in the history of philosophy.[100] Thus, Plato's image of the emotions as wild horses which had to be kept under control by the charioteer of reason is one well known to all students of emotion, and the same theme can be seen in the philosophy of the Stoics and in the later writings of Spinoza and others.[101] In the words of the pioneering educational psychologist Lewis Terman, 'an individual is intelligent in proportion as he is able to carry on abstract thinking'.[102]

However, to others the divide between emotion and reason is not as watertight as some would suggest. In particular, much emphasis has been placed in recent years on the crucial role of cognition in the context of emotion, and it has been pointed out that the processes of appraisal and evaluation apply no less in the emotional sphere than they do in that of the rational.[103] Someone suddenly threatens me with a knife and I freeze in terror. Why do I do so? Because I perceive the threat, evaluate it as real and react accordingly. The fact that this, as we shall see, may happen instinctively rather than as a result of rational deliberation is neither here nor there. Needless to say, the relationship between cognition and emotion is not as simple as this suggests; it is a major topic in its own right,[104] with a vast body of literature to its credit.[105] However, it does offer us this key insight: in the

---

[97] Oatley et al (n 88) 28.

[98] T Dalgleish and MJ Power (eds), *Handbook of Cognition and Emotion* (Chichester, Wiley, 1999) xviii.

[99] In the words of Susan Bandes, emotion is given a narrowly circumscribed role in order to ensure that it does not encroach on the true preserve of law, which is reason: SA Bandes (ed), *The Passions of Law* (New York, New York University Press, 1999) 2.

[100] Solomon (n 93).

[101] W Lyons, 'The Philosophy of Cognition and Emotion' in T Dalgleish and MJ Power (eds), *Handbook of Cognition and Emotion* (Chichester, Wiley, 1999) 21–44.

[102] LM Terman (1921) 12 *Journal of Educational Psychology* 127, 128 and cited by P Salovey et al, 'Emotional Intelligence' in M Lewis, JM Haviland-Jones and L Feldman Barrett (eds), *Handbook of Emotions*, 3rd edn (New York, Guilford Press, 2008) 534.

[103] Oatley et al (n 88) ch 7; RS Lazarus, 'The Cognition-Emotion Debate: A Bit of History' in T Dalgleish and MJ Power (eds), *Handbook of Cognition and Emotion* (Chichester, Wiley, 1999).

[104] Lazarus (n 103).

[105] According to Lyons, even a superficial analysis of this would require several volumes: Lyons (n 101) 42 and fn 14.

words of William Lyons, it suggests that emotions are motives, and that emotional behaviour may sometimes be both rational and appropriate.[106] The importance of this in the context of undue influence is clear to see.

C. Emotions and the Will

One of the earliest cases on the topic of undue influence is *Huguenin v Baseley*,[107] where it was said that the law was concerned not only with the question whether a party intended to enter into a transaction, but also with the means by which such intention was brought into existence. In the words of Lord Eldon in that case:

> If the intention was produced by an unacceptable means, the law will not permit the transaction to stand. The means used is regarded as an exercise of improper or 'undue' influence, and hence unacceptable, whenever the consent thus procured ought not fairly to be treated as the expression of a person's free will.[108]

But what is the relationship between emotions and the will? In some cases emotions seem to bypass the will altogether, as where one instinctively flinches from a perceived attack,[109] or as in the case cited by William Miller of the soldier whose legs will not allow him to proceed into battle.[110] In other cases the will is not completely sidelined, but even here emotions can, in the words of Nico Frijda,[111] serve as 'action tendencies' which predispose a person to behave in one way rather than another, as where someone in a bad mood will tend to quarrel with others on the slightest provocation, or where someone who is nervous will tend to flee from a threatening situation. All in all, it has been said that emotion can make us ready to take certain courses, and that the greater the readiness the more likely we are to act in a certain way without a conscious exercise of will.[112] Again, the relevance of this to undue influence is clear to see.

---

[106] Ibid, 39. Needless to say, this may be true in the commercial and economic context no less than elsewhere: see S Rick and G Loewenstein, 'The Role of Emotion in Economic Behavior' in M Lewis, JM Haviland-Jones and L Feldman Barrett (eds), *Handbook of Emotions*, 3rd edn (New York, Guilford Press, 2008) ch 9.

[107] *Huguenin v Baseley* (1807) 14 Ves 273.

[108] Ibid, 300.

[109] J LeDoux, *The Emotional Brain* (New York, Simon & Schuster, 1996) 107–12. In such a case the action may even precede the affective state, as in James's famous example of the man who meets a bear and runs away; according to James, he does not run away because he is afraid, but is afraid because he is running away: W James, 'What is an Emotion?' (1884) 34 *Mind* 188.

[110] W Miller, 'Fear, Weak Legs and Running Away: A Soldier's Story' in SA Bandes (ed), *The Passions of Law* (New York, New York University Press, 1999) 247–49.

[111] N Frijda, 'Emotion, Cognitive Structure and Action Tendency' (1987) 1 *Cognition and Emotion* 115.

[112] I am grateful to my colleague Professor Roddy Cowie for this point.

D. The Emotions of Undue Influence

Though the jurisprudence of undue influence has little to say about emotion as such, even a cursory glance will reveal that emotional factors have an important part to play, especially in those cases involving close family relationships. The question as to *what* emotions are relevant is less easy to answer, not least because there is no standard taxonomy of emotions to which one can refer. The reason for this is that, as Roddy Cowie argues, the realm of emotion cannot be described in categorical terms; rather, the most emotion terms can do is to describe points of reference in a complex landscape defined by combinations of factors including appraisal, action tendency, feeling quality and visceral reaction.[113] As it is, the literature proffers numerous such taxonomies, ranging from Paul Ekman's six 'basic' emotions[114] to the multifaceted and complex classifications offered by W Gerrod Parrott[115] and others. However, a useful model in the present connection is the 'wheel' or 'flower' model drawn up by Robert Plutchik,[116] which is reproduced in Figure 1.

The crucial area of this for our purposes is between the east and north-east petals of the diagram. In the east we see terror, shading off into fear and apprehension; in the north-east, we see admiration, shading off into trust and acceptance. What is of particular interest is that in between these two petals we have the attitude of *submission*. This corresponds to a marked—indeed a remarkable—degree with the two traditional branches of undue influence we have been discussing above, that is to say Class 1 (based on coercion), and Class 2 (based on a confidential relationship between the parties). It is therefore worthwhile, without of course forgetting the problems of categorisation mentioned above, exploring these more closely: submission based on *fear*, and submission based on *trust*.

i. Fear

Fear has been categorised as a basic human emotion;[117] indeed, it is not confined to human beings, in that it is shared by large parts of the animal kingdom.[118] The

---

[113] R Cowie, 'Describing the Forms of Emotional Colouring in Everyday Life' in P Goldie (ed), *The Oxford Handbook of Philosophy of Emotion* (Oxford, Oxford University Press, 2010) 3.5.3. There he argues that the popular categorisation of emotions in terms of 'love', 'hate', 'fear' and so on can give rise to five misunderstandings, these being: (1) that the domain of specific emotions can be reduced to a fixed list; (2) that emotional life is composed of the states named by specific emotion terms; (3) that all states that can be described by the same specific emotion term are essentially similar; (4) that specific emotion terms describe internal states; and (5) that the categorical structure of emotion language reflects categorical structure in emotional life.

[114] That is to say anger, disgust, fear, happiness, sadness and surprise: P Ekman, 'An Argument for Basic Emotions' (1992) 6 *Cognition and Emotion* 169.

[115] WG Parrott, *Emotions in Social Psychology* (Philadelphia, PA, Psychology Press, 2001).

[116] R Plutchik, *The Emotions* (Lanham, MD, University Press of America, 1991).

[117] Ekman (n 114).

[118] JA Gray, *The Psychology of Fear and Stress*, 2nd edn (Cambridge, Cambridge University Press, 1987) 2. There the author points out that most of the research done in the area has had to be on animals

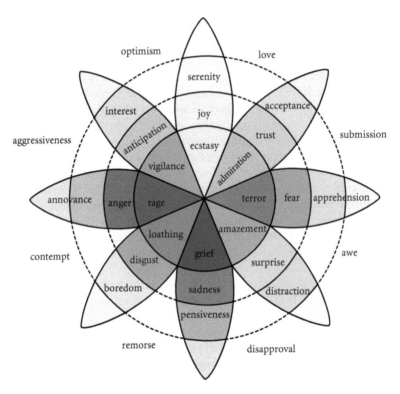

Figure 1: Plutchik's Wheel of Emotion

classic response to fear has been expressed in terms of the three F's—freeze, fight or flight.[119] However, there is clearly a difference between this basic level of fear and the sort of fear seen in a classic Class 1 undue influence situation; though fear involves the anticipation of pain for animals no less than human beings, it is a much more sophisticated notion, in that it can extend to consequences of a less immediate kind. As Ludwig Wittgenstein remarked, a dog may fear that its master is going to beat it, but it cannot fear that its master is going to beat it tomorrow.[120] For this reason Class 1 undue influence is perhaps better understood in terms of a classic 'choice of evils' situation, whereby the weaker party chooses to give in to the demand of the stronger rather than suffer the consequences.[121]

for ethical reasons, and even in that context there are limits beyond which the researcher cannot and should not go: see further, JB Overmeir, 'On the Study of Aversively Motivated Behavior' in MR Denny, *Fear, Avoidance and Phobias: A Fundamental Analysis* (Hillsdale, NJ, Erlbaum Associates, 1991) 1.

[119] Gray (n 118) 3.

[120] L Wittgenstein, *Philosophical Investigations* (trans GEM Anscombe, New York, Macmillan, 1953) 650.

[121] Compare the analysis of duress given in AP Simester et al, *Simester and Sullivan: Criminal Law: Theory and Doctrine*, 5th edn (Oxford, Hart Publishing, 2013) 739–40.

The fact that this need not necessarily involve 'fear' at all in the popular sense of being frightened—in the words of Andrew Ashworth, the person giving in to the demand may be as cool as a cucumber[122]—does not mean that the emotion of fear is not present. Rather, this is a situation where the fear manifests itself not so much as a feeling[123] as an 'action tendency' of the sort that we have been describing earlier.[124] In other words, the weaker party will be more likely to give in to the demands of the stronger where the process of rational calculation is supplemented by the emotion of fear, and to a certain extent this is recognised in other branches of the law.[125]

ii. Trust

The reasons for the law's readiness to strike down transactions based on fear are obvious, but those for striking down transactions based on trust are less so. After all, there is nothing inherently wrong with a relationship based on trust; indeed, as we have argued above, the ideals of relational autonomy demand that such relationships be positively encouraged. So why should the law intervene here? The answer lies in Chen-Wishart's observation quoted above to the effect that unprotected commitment can be even more dangerous than unprotected sex.[126] This is particularly so in cases where one party is unduly dependent in emotional terms on the other. At a popular level, such dependence is commonly described in terms of 'emotional dependency'. Emotional dependency has been defined as occurring when the ongoing presence and nurturing of another is believed to be necessary for personal security.[127] It is characterised by a number of factors, including over-possessiveness, excessive preoccupation with the other party's personality, problems and interests, and depending on him or her for one's sense of self-worth.[128] In psychological terms, this can go so far as to constitute what is termed 'dependent personality disorder', which is described as 'a pervasive and excessive need to be taken care of that leads to submissive and clinging behaviour and fears of

---

[122] A Ashworth, *Principles of Criminal Law*, 3rd edn (Oxford, Oxford University Press, 1999) cited by Simester and Sullivan (n 121).

[123] Feeling frightened would now often be described in terms of an 'emergent' emotion: see Cowie (n 113) 75.

[124] Above, n 111. This is sometimes described in terms of an 'attitude', but Cowie prefers to call it an 'established' emotion: Cowie (n 113) 75.

[125] For instance, by the criminal law principle that threats to a third party will only constitute duress if aimed at the defendant's immediate family, or to a person for whose safety the defendant would reasonably regard himself as responsible: *R v Hasan* [2005] UKHL 22, [2005] AC 467 (*sub nom R v Z*), [21] (Lord Bingham).

[126] Ibid, 243.

[127] L Rentzel, *Emotional Dependency* (Downers Grove, Ill, Intervarsity Press, 1990) 7.

[128] Ibid. RW Firestone, 'Emotional Hunger Vs Love' *Psychology Today* (2009): www.psychologytoday.com/blog/the-human-experience/200902/emotional-hunger-vs-love; R Weaver, 'Defining Emotional Dependency and the Top Five Ways to Become More Emotionally Independent': www.empowher.com/mental-health/content/defining-emotional-dependency-and-top-five-ways-become-more-emotionally-independent.

separation'.[129] Obviously cases of this are comparatively rare, but psychologists have identified two fundamental lower-order constructs in this connection, one being dependency or submissiveness, and the other attachment.[130]

In the psychological context the word 'dependency' can be used in a number of different ways,[131] but in this connection it connotes a tendency to comply with wishes and to obey orders given by others. In social settings this is said to be associated with suggestibility, conformity, affiliative behaviour and sensitivity to interpersonal cues, and also with a strong desire to maintain nurturant and supportive relationships.[132] In particular, it has been shown to be associated with a general tendency to be influenced by the opinions of others, to yield to others in interpersonal transactions and to comply with others' expectations and demands.[133] The relevance of this to undue influence is plain.

Attachment theory has its origins in the seminal work of John Bowlby,[134] who argued that human beings, in common with other primate species, had an innate orientation to social life.[135] This was shown in the tendency of children to exhibit certain patterns of behaviour towards the mother or primary caregiver.[136] These patterns of behaviour, which were termed 'attachment behaviors', included looking at the person concerned, following him or her around and trying to promote physical contact by clinging on to them.[137] Taken together, they were said to constitute what was described as the 'attachment behavioral system', the purpose of which was said to be to encourage physical and psychological proximity to a primary caregiver.[138] Though focused originally on children, this theory was soon seen to have wider ramifications,[139] and attachment theorists such as Cindy Hazan and Phillip Shaver began to apply it to adult relationships as well,[140] the

---

[129] WL Gore et al, 'A Five-Factor Measure of Dependent Personality' (2012) 94 *Journal of Personality Assessment* 488.

[130] Ibid. WJ Livesley ML Schroeder and DN Jackson, 'Dependent Personality Disorder' (1990) 4 *Journal of Personality Disorders* 131.

[131] Thus for instance it can be used in connection with addictions, and also to denote the theory whereby social dependency relationships were considered to have their origin in the need of the infant to have his or her basic physiological drives satisfied by the mother: MS Ainsworth, 'Attachment and Dependency: A Comparison' in JL Gewirtz, (ed), *Attachment and Dependency* (Washington, VH Winston, 1972) 97. No doubt this is why it was renamed: WJ Livesley and DN Jackson, *Manual for the Dimensional Assessment of Personality Pathology—Basic Questionnaire (DAPP)* (2002).

[132] RF Bornstein, 'The Dependent Personality: Developmental, Social and Clinical Perspectives' (1992) 112 *Psychological Bulletin* 3.

[133] Ibid.

[134] Most notably in his three volume work, J Bowlby, *Attachment and Loss* (New York, Basic Books) and first published between 1969 and 1980.

[135] WS Rholes and JA Simpson, *Adult Attachment: Theory, Research and Clinical Implications* (New York, Guilford Press, 2004) 5.

[136] Ibid.

[137] Ibid.

[138] Ibid.

[139] RC Fraley, 'A Brief Overview of Adult Attachment Theory and Research': internal.psychology. illinois.edu/~rcfraley/attachment.htm.

[140] See especially, C Hazan and P Shaver, 'Romantic love conceptualised as an attachment process' (1987) 52 *Journal of Personality and Social Psychology* 511.

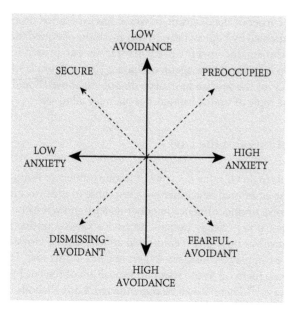

Figure 2: Dimensions of attachment

hypothesis being that attachment patterns in infancy would inevitably create a template for future intimate relationships, most notably marriage and other stable sexual partnerships.[141] In this way healthy attachment patterns in infancy provided the key to happy relationships in adulthood. However, subsequent research demonstrated that not all attachment patterns were equally healthy. In particular, whereas many people indicated that they found it relatively easy to get close to others and relate to them accordingly, some said that this made them uncomfortable and that they found it hard to trust others, while a third group thought that others were reluctant to get as close as they would like, and often worried that their partner did not love them and would not want to stay with them.[142] All of this was explained in terms of three patterns of attachment, the first being termed 'secure', the second 'avoidant' and the third 'anxious'.[143] This was later elaborated into the model given in Figure 2.[144]

In this model, the various patterns of attachment are delineated on the basis of the two variables depicted on the vertical and horizontal axes—that is to say avoidance and anxiety. Where both are low, one has a secure pattern of attachment. But where one or both is high, the attachment becomes less secure and the relationship more problematic. What is particularly significant for our purposes is

[141] Oatley et al (n 88) 232.
[142] Fraley (n 139).
[143] Ibid.
[144] Ibid.

the north-east corner of the diagram, in which low avoidance, or a desire for intimacy, is accompanied by high anxiety. In this situation—termed the 'preoccupied' pattern of attachment, the insecure party may feel that no price is too high to keep the relationship ongoing. Once again, we have a classic example of an emotional 'action tendency' of the sort we have been describing above,[145] and once again its relevance to the topic of undue influence is plain for all to see.

E. The Emotions and the Law

What has all this to do with the doctrine of undue influence? It must be confessed that not all close emotional attachments—even those of the insecure variety—will necessarily involve undue influence in either its legal or even its popular sense.[146] In the same way, it is perfectly possible to have a Class 2 undue influence relationship that involves little or no emotional attachment.[147] However, the factors discussed above can play a considerable part in cases of this sort. This can be seen if we try and map them on to the standard exposition of the law by Lord Nicholls in the *Etridge* case.[148] There, it will be remembered, Lord Nicholls referred to two classes of case, the first being where one party sought to gain the other's consent by 'overt acts of pressure or coercion such as unlawful threats'.[149] These 'Class 1' cases are reflected in the 'fear' situations discussed above, and nothing more need be said of them. When it comes to the second category, Lord Nicholls begins by referring to a 'relationship between two persons where one has acquired over another a measure of influence, or ascendancy, of which the ascendant person then takes unfair advantage';[150] in this sort of case 'the influence one person has over another provides scope for misuse without any specific overt acts of persuasion',[151] and 'the relationship between two individuals may be such that, without more, one of them is disposed to agree to a course of action proposed by the other'.[152] These 'Class 2' cases are reflected in the 'trust' situations; indeed, Lord Nicholls reinforces this conclusion when he goes on to say that 'typically this occurs when one person places trust in another to look after his affairs and interests, and the latter betrays

---

[145] Above at n 111.

[146] This is reflected in the observation by Lord Nicholls that in everyday life people constantly seek to influence the decisions of others, and that what the law does here is to set limits to the means properly employable for this end: *Royal Bank of Scotland Plc v Etridge (No 2)* [2001] UKHL 44, [2002] 2 AC 773, [6].

[147] Thus the relationship may relate purely to matters of business or finance, as with trustee and beneficiary. The old farmer in *Lloyd's Bank v Bundy* [1975] QB 326 may have implicitly relied on his bank manager for advice, but no one would say that there was any emotional attachment between them.

[148] *Royal Bank of Scotland v Etridge (No 2)* [2001] UKHL 44, [2002] 2 AC 773, [6]–[12]; see text accompanying n 4.

[149] *Royal Bank of Scotland v Etridge (No 2)* [2001] UKHL 44, [2002] 2 AC 773, [8].

[150] Ibid.

[151] Ibid, [9].

[152] Ibid.

this trust by preferring his own interests'.[153] Indeed, this is reinforced when he goes on to stress that the key question is not the type of relationship involved, but whether one party has reposed sufficient trust in the other.[154] At first sight Lord Nicholls would seem to qualify this to some extent when he says that 'the principle is not confined to cases of abuse of trust and confidence, but also extends to cases where a vulnerable person has been exploited',[155] but his subsequent reference to 'trust and confidence, reliance, dependence and vulnerability on the one hand and ascendancy, domination or control on the other',[156] combined with his previous characterisation of the relationship as being one where 'without more, one of them is disposed to agree a course of action proposed by the other'[157]—a classic description of an emotion in terms of an 'action-tendency'[158]—shows that he is not thinking of a separate category of cases here, but is merely anxious not to close off the categories of relationship to which the doctrine will apply. Not all cases of undue influence involve emotional attachment, or even 'trust and confidence' in the legal sense, but enough of them do for the factors we have been discussing to be of important significance in the present context.

IV. Conclusions

With this in mind, we can now return to the questions posed in the earlier part of this chapter. As will be remembered, these relate to the internal and external structure of undue influence law, and as to its rationale.

With regard to questions of structure, the key factor must surely be the distinction—a distinction suggested by Plutchik's analysis[159] and endorsed by Lord Nicholls[160]—between cases of coercion, which are based on fear, and the relationship cases, which are based on trust. This in turn suggests that Birks and Chin are right in discerning a significant distinction between 'Class 1' and 'Class 2' cases of undue influence.[161] In the light of this, Class 2B is clearly not a superfluous category; proving that the relationship exists, together with the other evidence, may indeed as Lord Scott suggests be enough to show that undue influence has taken place in Class 2B just as in Class 1,[162] but it is undue influence of a very different sort. In the same way, what has to be proved in Class 2B is very different

---

[153] Ibid.
[154] Ibid, citing Sir Guenter Treitel in *Treitel, The Law of Contract*, 10th edn (1999) 380–81.
[155] *Royal Bank of Scotland v Etridge (No 2)* [2001] UKHL 44, [2002] 2 AC 773, [11].
[156] Ibid.
[157] Ibid, [9].
[158] Above at n 111.
[159] Plutchik (n 116).
[160] Above at n 148.
[161] Birks and Chin (n 66).
[162] Above at n 42.

from what has to be proved in Class 1; in the latter case, the key factor is coercion, whereas in the former it is a relationship where, in the words of Lord Nicholls, one of the parties is 'without more ... disposed to agree to a course of action proposed by another'.[163] While this may or may not involve attachment in the emotional sense, the dynamics are of a different nature; whereas the former focuses on the conduct of the dominant party, it is the nature of the relationship itself that is the focus of the latter.[164]

The same considerations apply when we turn to the external structure of the law. On the one hand, the present distinctions between the doctrines of duress, unconscionable bargain, undue pressure and undue influence (in its testamentary and *inter vivos* forms) can only be understood in the light of history, and do no credit to the law. On the other hand, when one attempts to find a single principle to cover them all, one ends up either being too precise (in which case significant cases are left out) or too vague (in which the principle is too wide to be of any practical use). Indeed, though the label 'undue influence' is no doubt too hallowed to be abandoned at this late stage, one wonders whether it is even fit for purpose, at least in its *inter vivos* application.[165] In this connection there is a lot to be said for the suggestion of Birks and Chin that the so-called 'Class 1' cases be hived off into a category of their own, along with duress and the unconscionable bargain,[166] so leaving 'Class 2' to concentrate on the relational aspect. In this way the fear/trust distinction would be reflected right across the legal spectrum.

As far as the rationale of the law is concerned, Mindy Chen-Wishart is surely right in her conclusions: (1) that neither the 'claimant-centred' nor the 'exploitation' models are sufficient in themselves to explain the way the law works;[167] and (2) that at the end of the day they are no more than two sides of the same coin.[168] Though the law in this area clearly recognises the importance

---

[163] *Royal Bank of Scotland v Etridge (No 2)* [2001] UKHL 44, [2002] 2 AC 773, [9].

[164] That is not to say that both factors may not coincide—in the context of an abusive relationship there may be both coercion and a relationship of subservience. However, in such cases the existence of the latter will often render use of the former unnecessary.

[165] As we have seen (above at nn 26–40), the same does not apply in the testamentary context, where the doctrine is much more narrowly circumscribed. If one was starting from scratch, there would be a lot to be said for restricting the label 'undue influence' to cases of coercion in both testamentary and inter vivos contexts, and finding some new label to cover cases involving relationships. Given the importance of trust in this context, 'breach of confidence' would be a good label, if it had not been already appropriated for other purposes!

[166] Birks and Chin (n 66). This is recognised by Lord Nicholls, who concedes that there is now a considerable overlap between Class 1 cases of undue influence and the principle of duress as it has subsequently developed: *Royal Bank of Scotland v Etridge (No 2)* [2001] UKHL 44, [2002] 2 AC 773, [8].

[167] Chen-Wishart (n 63). Thus the claimant-centred view, though plausible at first sight, does not do justice to the historical roots of the doctrine, and requires one to find impaired consent in some cases where it is quite clear that the claimant had thought about the matter and went ahead in full awareness of the consequences. In the same way, the exploitation view can only be made to work by treating the other party's willingness to enforce the transaction as itself exploitative, which seems to beg the question.

[168] Ibid. In this connection, Bigwood's analogy of the 'Gestalt shift' is a telling one: Bigwood (n 66) 514.

of human emotion in the sense of taking it into account, its traditional attitude to emotion is to regard it with suspicion; as Cicero would say,[169] it is a *perturbatio* which stands in the way of reasoned thought, and has no place in legal discourse.[170] However, such a position is no longer tenable either from a philosophical or from a psychological point of view. What our study of the emotional dynamics shows is to confirm the importance of an approach that seeks to preserve and to promote the relational autonomy of the parties.[171] In demonstrating that all human beings have a fundamental need for social life, John Bowlby's theory of attachment confirms the insight of Chen-Wishart and others that striving for connection with others, so far from being inimical to autonomy, is the only context in which it can be properly exercised.[172] This in turn echoes the comments of Lord Nicholls to the effect that in everyday life people constantly seek to influence the decisions of others.[173] There is nothing wrong with that; the law is not there to guard against influence as such, but only *undue* influence. So what makes influence undue? Needless to say, there can be no single answer to this, not least because the question is intensely fact-specific. However, an analysis of the emotional dynamics involved suggests a range of factors, some of which relate to the stronger party, others to the weaker party and yet others to the quality of the relationship itself. In this way all three rationales discussed above have a key part to play.

What we have been doing in these pages is nothing new. Twenty years ago it was argued by Trent Thornley that the law of undue influence overemphasised the role of reason as a proper basis for decision-making, to the exclusion of other human faculties like emotion.[174] In particular, he argued that the law was far too much preoccupied with autonomy. In his own words:

> Autonomy theory conceives of society as the amalgamation of little pockets of individual self-rulers who are connected to one another only by means which do not compromise their self-ruling capacity ... One can draw an analogy to a honeycomb. Just as a honeycomb is the sum total of a myriad of individual beeswax cells, an autonomy perspective views society as the sum total of many self-ruling individuals. Like the honey inside each cell, each individual person is carefully secluded in her own little compartment, never to be inadvertently interfered with by others who are themselves in adjoining compartments. Each is separate and independent. Just as beeswax constitutes the walls around individual combs, so also do rights form the barriers around individual persons.[175]

---

[169] Cicero, *De Finibus* 3.10.35

[170] Indeed, it is not without significance that in this branch of the law rational consideration is equated with consulting a lawyer! (I am grateful to my colleague Roddy Cowie for bringing out this point.)

[171] Certainly this applies to the Class 2 type of case. Whether it is necessary to extend this approach to Class 1 is less clear, though see Chen-Wishart (n 63) 264.

[172] Above at nn 75–85.

[173] *Royal Bank of Scotland v Etridge (No 2)* [2001] UKHL 44, [2002] 2 AC 773, [6].

[174] T Thornley, 'The Caring Influence: Beyond Autonomy as the Foundation of Undue Influence' (1995) 71 *Indiana Law Journal* 513.

[175] Ibid, 526–27.

The missing dimension here, according to Thornley, was that of care. Rather than simply asking whether the weaker party's autonomy had been diminished or his or her will overborne, the law ought to ask in these situations whether or not this took place within the context of a caring relationship.[176] This is by no means the glib concept it might appear; on the contrary, much thought has been given by philosophers such as Carol Gilligan to formulating theories of care.[177] Such theories are based not on individual rights but on relationships, the essential features of a caring relationship being identification (becoming attentive to the needs of the other), disposition (making oneself responsible for those needs) and the mutual giving and receiving of caring activity.[178] According to care theorists, the processes involved are not entirely rational, nor entirely emotional, but form a convergence of the two.[179] All of this goes to show that this is a dimension which needs to be taken into account if we are to have an emotionally nuanced law of undue influence. The Book of Proverbs may tell us to guard our hearts,[180] but in the words of CS Lewis:

> Love anything and your heart will be wrung and possibly broken. If you want to make sure of keeping it intact you must give it to no one, not even an animal. Wrap it carefully round with hobbies and little luxuries; avoid all entanglements. Lock it up safe in the casket or coffin of your selfishness. But in that casket, safe, dark, motionless, airless, it will change. It will not be broken; it will become unbreakable, impenetrable, irredeemable. To love is to be vulnerable.[181]

[176] Ibid, 541.
[177] C Gilligan, *In a Different Voice: Psychological Theory and Women's Development* (Cambridge, MA, Harvard University Press, 1982).
[178] Thornley (n 174) 533–35.
[179] Ibid, 538–40.
[180] Proverbs 4:23.
[181] CS Lewis, *The Four Loves* (London, Fount Paperbacks, 1977) 111.

5

Discovering Dignity: Unpacking the Emotional Content of 'Killing Narratives'

MARY NEAL*

I. Introduction

It is now trite to observe that the term 'dignity' has a plurality of potential and actual uses, that its normative content and practical demands are difficult to pin down, and that all of this has led a number of academic commentators to deny that the term is normatively meaningful or that it can have anything other than a polemical value in ethical debates. Sceptical views of dignity seem particularly prevalent in the academic field of healthcare law and ethics (HCLE), and although some general critiques of the normative value of dignity exist,[1] the fiercest and most ill-tempered have been trained on the deployment of 'dignity' in the biomedical context.[2] Although the language of dignity is familiar in lay discourse about healthcare ethics—in debates about assisted suicide and euthanasia, for example, or when deploring the mistreatment of vulnerable patients—dignity-talk in HCLE scholarship has tended to be associated with scholars who are perceived

* The Law School, University of Strathclyde. I am grateful to two anonymous reviewers for helpful comments on an earlier draft of this chapter, and to the editors of this collection, Heather Conway and John Stannard, for their unstinting patience and generous advice. Any errors are my own.

[1] See, for example, M Bagaric and J Allan, 'The Vacuous Concept of Dignity' (2006) 5 *Journal of Human Rights* 257.

[2] The most infamous critiques are probably those by Pinker and Macklin: S Pinker, 'The Stupidity of Dignity' (2008) *The New Republic*: www.tnr.com/article/the-stupidity-dignity; and R Macklin, 'Dignity is a Useless Concept' (2003) 327 *British Medical Journal* 1419. Note that Pinker is generally sceptical about the value of 'bioethics'; however; he appears to believe it represents a harmful obstacle to biomedical research and should 'get out of the way', and he seems to object to ideas like 'social justice' as much as to 'dignity': S Pinker, 'The moral imperative for bioethics' *Boston Globe* (1 August 2015): www.bostonglobe.com/opinion/2015/07/31/the-moral-imperative-for-bioethics/JmEkoyzlTAu9oQV76JrK9N/story.htmlon. See also Ashcroft's robust response to Pinker's scepticism: R Ashcroft, 'On Not "Getting Out of the Way": A Reflection on Steven Pinker's Critique of Bioethics' *VELIM: A Blog for the Centre for Values, Ethics and the Law in Medicine*, 11 August 2015: velimblog.org/2015/08/11/on-not-getting-out-of-the-way-a-reflection-on-steven-pinkers-critique-of-bioethics/.

as writing from a religious/conservative perspective, and to be regarded critically and/or sceptically by others.[3]

This contrasts sharply with academic discourse about human rights law (HRL), which reflects a widespread acceptance of the idea that human dignity is the philosophical foundation of human rights. HRL scholars have begun in earnest to interrogate precisely *how* dignity is foundational to human rights,[4] and to investigate possible alternative (or additional) foundations for human rights, such as universal human interests, or desert.[5] Nevertheless, the view that human rights are—at least partially[6]—grounded in human dignity is very much mainstream, and it is commonplace to hear human dignity described, for example, as 'the main philosophical foundation of human rights'[7] or as the 'very essence' of the European Convention on Human Rights.[8]

What accounts for dignity's greater purchase in HRL than in HCLE? The answer will of course be complex, and cannot be explored fully here. One likely factor is that, whereas in HRL the language of dignity is the conventional vocabulary in which the importance and worth of human beings is discussed, HCLE scholars have a range of other terms at their disposal when they wish to discuss these things, some of which—'autonomy' and 'personhood', for example—can seem more precise than, and so preferable to, 'dignity'. Another possibility is that HRL scholars, because they are able to draw upon both an extensive jurisprudence which explores dignity directly or indirectly, *and* an authoritative and growing literature which takes dignity seriously, are simply more confident in working with the idea. They are bolstered (or hindered, depending on one's view) by a background reassurance that when they refer to dignity, they are at risk neither of being dismissed as religious/conservative, nor of being accused of simply talking nonsense. Moreover, a wealth of literature and case law can be brought to bear

---

[3] Some notable exceptions include D Beyleveld and R Brownsword, *Human Dignity in Bioethics and Biolaw* (Oxford, Oxford University Press, 2001); C Foster, *Human Dignity in Bioethics and Law* (Oxford, Hart Publishing, 2011); Roberto Andorno's work including R Andorno, 'The Dual Role of Human Dignity in Bioethics' (2013) 16 *Medicine, Health Care and Philosophy* 967; and the contributions to two 2010 special issues (volumes 21(3) and (4)) of the *International Journal of Bioethics.*

[4] See, for example, J Waldron, 'Is Dignity the Foundation of Human Rights?' (2013) New York University School of Law, Public Law Research Paper 12-73, as well as J Tasioulas, 'Human Dignity as a Foundation for Human Rights' in C McCrudden (ed), *Understanding Human Dignity* (Oxford, Oxford University Press/British Academy, 2013).

[5] See, for example, the papers contained in Part I of R Cruft, SM Liao and M Renzo (eds), *Philosophical Foundations of Human Rights* (Oxford, Oxford University Press, 2015).

[6] One influential proponent of a pluralistic approach to the foundations of human rights, John Tasioulas, considers that 'human dignity and universal human interests are equally fundamental grounds of human rights, characteristically bound together in their operation': J Tasioulas, 'On the Foundations of Human Rights' in R Cruft, SM Liao and M Renzo (eds), *Philosophical Foundations of Human Rights* (Oxford, Oxford University Press, 2015) 45, 53–54.

[7] M Nowak, 'Foreword' in P Kaufmann, H Kuch, C Neuhäuser and E Webster (eds), *Humiliation, Degradation, Dehumanization: Human Dignity Violated* (London, Springer, 2011) v.

[8] *Pretty v United Kingdom* [2002] ECHR 427, [65].

in ensuring that their discussions of dignity are anchored within a recognisable disciplinary framework. HCLE scholars, by contrast, have neither this sense of 'permission' nor any practical techniques for accessing and engaging with dignity as a value capable of clarifying HCLE controversies.

It is undoubtedly more challenging to try to 'get at' dignity in HCLE than in HRL. Although both contexts lack any agreed formula for defining dignity, HRL has the benefit of some guidance, consisting in (i) the general acceptance that dignity refers (albeit vaguely) to the 'intrinsic worth' of human beings, and (ii) the lists of particular rights that are said to be connected with dignity in some way (ie, to flow from it, protect it, etc). In the HCLE context, there is *neither* a vaguely agreed concept like 'intrinsic worth' *nor* a list of dignity's incidents/requirements to indicate a way forward. Neither, I have argued elsewhere, can we simply adopt what is decided about dignity in other contexts (including HRL) and transplant it into our deliberations about HCLE: dignity is not a single concept, but a range of concepts and we should expect the meaning (ie, the use) of 'dignity' to be different in different legal language games (such as HRL and HCLE).[9]

Nevertheless, what I will propose in this chapter is that it might be possible to unlock dignity as a useful value in HCLE *to some extent* by paying attention to the emotional content of end-of-life narratives. Drawing on Nussbaum's recent work, I will argue that, disagreement about the precise source and normative content of dignity notwithstanding, we can recognise some emotional responses as being compatible and others as being incompatible with respect for dignity. I will begin by noting Nussbaum's observation that respect for dignity is a matter of inclusion in the community of moral equals, and that conversely, denying dignity involves excluding individuals from the moral community. I will add to this her further insight that such inclusion/exclusion is accomplished in important part by 'emotion-shaping processes', which include narratives. I will focus on 'killing narratives', first by exploring some of the narratives that surround acts and practices of killing in non-healthcare contexts. Narratives that dehumanise and/or abjectify their subjects as a precursor to 'atrocity killings' (like genocide, for example) will be discussed as clear examples of negative emotion-shaping, since they promote emotional responses that are incompatible with a respect for equal human dignity. Finally, I will begin to apply the same analysis to end-of-life discourses in healthcare law, arguing that these can also be analysed as emotion-shaping narratives, and that undertaking such analysis may be able to help us to determine whether particular narratives are dignity-congruent or not. The value of this approach is that it may offer HCLE scholars a basis for discussing dignity's promotion or violation (at least in the context of end-of-life issues) in a way that can be the subject of meaningful exchange.

---

[9] M Neal, 'Dignity, Law, and Language-Games' (2012) 25 *International Journal for the Semiotics of Law–Revue internationale de Sémiotiquejuridique* 107.

II. Discovering Dignity: Nussbaum on Dignity and 'Emotion-Shaping Processes'

A significant strand of Martha Nussbaum's recent work has been concerned with the cultural and political importance of the emotions.[10] Most recently, in *Political Emotions: Why Love Matters for Justice*, Nussbaum has considered the role emotions play in civic life, and in particular, their role in shaping and constituting 'the decent society'. For Nussbaum, a 'decent society' is a liberal society which is committed to a strong conception of justice premised on the equal worth of all citizens; a 'political culture committed to a shared morality of human dignity'[11] which recognises 'the badness of various forms of discrimination and hierarchy'.[12]

'Sometimes', Nussbaum writes, 'people suppose that only fascist or aggressive societies are intensely emotional and that only such societies need to focus on the cultivation of emotions'.[13] In Nussbaum's view, however, it is 'both mistaken and dangerous'[14] to associate the cultivation of emotions only with 'bad' societies, since '[a]ll political principles, the good as well as the bad, need emotional support to ensure their stability over time, and all decent societies need to guard against division and hierarchy by cultivating appropriate sentiments of sympathy and love'.[15] According to Nussbaum, there are two tasks for the decent society with regard to emotion-shaping:

> One is to engender and sustain strong commitment to worthy projects ... The other related task for the cultivation of public emotion is to keep at bay forces that lurk in all societies and, ultimately, in all of us: tendencies to protect the fragile self by denigrating and subordinating others ... Disgust and envy, the desire to inflict shame on others.[16]

Thus, it seems clear that Nussbaum regards processes of emotion-shaping as fundamental to the constitution and maintenance of *all* societies, and as no less a feature of the 'decent', equal society than of fascist regimes. The critical difference is *which* emotions are being fostered and suppressed.

Nussbaum identifies compassion/sympathy/love—she appears to use these terms more or less interchangeably—as the main emotions that 'guard against

---

[10] See, for example, MC Nussbaum, 'Compassion: The Basic Social Emotion' (1996) 13 *Social Philosophy and Policy* 27; MC Nussbaum, *Upheavals of Thought: The Intelligence of Emotions* (Cambridge, Cambridge University Press, 2003); MC Nussbaum, *Hiding from Humanity: Disgust, Shame, and the Law* (Princeton, NJ, Princeton University Press, 2009); and MC Nussbaum, *Political Emotions: Why Love Matters for Justice* (Cambridge, MA, Harvard University Press, 2013).

[11] Nussbaum, *Political Emotions: Why Love Matters for Justice* (n 10) 140.

[12] Ibid, 7. Prima facie, Nussbaum's account of what constitutes a 'decent society' seems reasonable; however readers who prefer an alternative formulation need not endorse Nussbaum's particular account in order to accept the overall thrust of my argument here.

[13] Nussbaum, *Political Emotions: Why Love Matters for Justice* (n 10) 2.

[14] Ibid.

[15] Ibid, 2–3.

[16] Ibid, 3.

division and hierarchy'.[17] One of the main 'enemies' of these positive, dignity-congruent emotions is 'projective disgust': whereas 'primary disgust' serves a useful evolutionary purpose by directing us away from potentially harmful substances, creatures and environments, 'projective disgust' involves reacting in this way to other *people*:

> Projective disgust is disgust for a group of other humans who are segmented from the dominant group and classified as lower because of being (allegedly) more animal. Members of this group are thought to have the properties of disgust's primary objects: they are found dirty, smelly, slimy ... They are represented as quasi-animals, as occupying a border between the truly human (associated with transcendence of the body and its substances) and the utterly nonhuman.[18]

Projective disgust is obviously stigmatising. Nussbaum identifies it as '[a] key device of subordination',[19] inimical to equality (since it 'blocks equal respect')[20] and therefore to dignity; she claims 'it can be surmounted only by love'.[21]

Compassion's main enemies, besides projective disgust, are 'fear, envy, and shame'.[22] In shame, 'one acknowledges that one is something inferior, falling short of some desired ideal'.[23] In its purest form, it is a 'painful emotion directed at the self'[24] which provokes a 'natural reflex' of 'hiding'.[25] Humiliation is an extension of shame, 'the active public face of shame ... the hostile infliction of shame on others'.[26]

Thus, whereas a fascist or segregated society will cultivate negative, hostile emotions towards a section or sections of its population, a decent society will cultivate emotions such as compassion, sympathy and love. To put this another way, a decent society will cultivate an *emotional* (as opposed to a merely rational) appreciation of the equal worth and status of all its citizens. Simultaneously, such a society will endeavour to keep at bay those emotions—like projective disgust, envy, fear, shame and humiliation—which would undermine the positive side of the emotion-shaping project. One consequence of Nussbaum's argument (though she seems not to say this explicitly) appears to be that societies are 'bad' or 'decent'

---

[17] Ibid, 2–3. For a critical discussion of Nussbaum's philosophy of the emotions see, for example, L Hunt, 'Nussbaum and the Emotions' (2006) 116 *Ethics* 552 (reviewing Nussbaum's *Upheavals of Thought* (n 10) and *Hiding from Humanity* (n 10)). Note also that, although Nussbaum regards compassion as 'the basic social emotion', other commentators regard it as complex and ambivalent: see, for example, the essays collected in LG Berlant (ed), *Compassion: The Culture and Politics of an Emotion* (New York, Routledge, 2004) which explore compassion as a culturally-, historically- and even aesthetically-contingent phenomenon.

[18] Nussbaum, *Political Emotions: Why Love Matters for Justice* (n 10) 184.

[19] Ibid, 182.

[20] Ibid, 186.

[21] Ibid, 182.

[22] Ibid, 315.

[23] Ibid, 361.

[24] Ibid, 360.

[25] Ibid, 361.

[26] Ibid.

in significant part *precisely to the extent that* they successfully cultivate the 'right' emotions and keep the 'wrong' ones at bay.

Another feature of Nussbaum's analysis is that she explicitly links emotions with human dignity. She assumes that a normative commitment to 'equal human dignity'[27] will be one of the 'core values of a just society',[28] and she explicitly considers the role of the emotions, and of processes of 'emotion-shaping', in either cultivating/promoting dignity, or threatening/undermining it. Dignity, for Nussbaum, 'should be understood as a member of a family of conceptions'.[29] Like many scholars who write about dignity, Nussbaum makes the familiar association between 'equal human dignity ... [and] equal intrinsic worth and being objects of equal respect'.[30] Interestingly, however, she also associates dignity with 'both *striving* and *vulnerability*' (emphases added).[31] In this regard, there appears to be a symmetry between Nussbaum's understanding of dignity and the understanding I have begun to elaborate in my own recent work, at least insofar as both Nussbaum's understanding and my own emphasise dignity's groundedness in universal vulnerability, and insofar as both can be contrasted with accounts in which dignity is conflated with autonomy, 'personhood', or (only) 'intrinsic worth'.[32]

Nussbaum's analysis of 'political emotions' is incredibly rich, but the significant features of her account for present purposes are twofold: first, her observation that respect for dignity and its violation are, respectively, about inclusion and exclusion from the moral community; and second, that Nussbaum seems committed to insisting that a decent society will not only strive to cultivate those emotions which are congruent with (which affirm or promote) the 'core' value of equal human dignity, but will also endeavour to keep at bay emotions which tend to undermine or deny the value of equal dignity. For Nussbaum, in other words, emotion-shaping is crucial not only to the positive promotion and cultivation of dignity, but also to the task of resisting threats to dignity. These features, together with Nussbaum's insights regarding which emotions are dignity-affirming and which are dignity-denying, provide the substantive point of departure for the argument I will pursue here.

III. Killing and 'Killing Narratives'

Applying Nussbaum's insight about dignity and political emotions, if we want to establish whether a particular end-of-life practice is congruent with or inimical to a respect for equal human dignity, we ought to be attentive to its emotional

[27] Ibid, 120.
[28] Ibid, 118.
[29] Ibid, 120.
[30] Ibid.
[31] Ibid.
[32] See M Neal '"Not Gods But Animals": Human Dignity and Vulnerable Subjecthood' (2012) 33 *Liverpool Law Review* 177, where I have begun to enunciate my understanding of the nature of dignity.

context. Part of that context might include what I will call 'killing narratives': narratives that accompany, describe, explain and/or attempt to justify the end- ing of life.[33] Killing narratives are profoundly emotional discourses—they reflect and reveal (sometimes 'betray') emotional responses, but they also *shape* them; they are 'emotion-shaping processes', to use Nussbaum's phrase. The question we ought to be interested in from a dignity point of view is whether the emotions they reflect and shape are ones which tend to affirm dignity or to deny it: do they include people in, or exclude them from, the community of moral equals?

Sometimes killing narratives are provided explicitly and retrospectively, as part of a formal legal process. The criminal law of homicide is full of retrospective narratives of self-defence, provocation, temporary insanity and other narratives which attempt to explain or mitigate the act of killing. These are not 'exclusionary' killing narratives, since they seek to mitigate or excuse the act of killing not by excluding the victim from the community of moral equals, but rather by describ- ing the state of mind of the killer as threatened, provoked, or disordered. Killing narratives *can* be 'exclusionary', however. Before turning to the healthcare con- text specifically, I will discuss two distinct but related types of exclusionary killing narrative—narratives of *dehumanisation* and of *abjectification*—and explore how they reflect and shape emotion in order to exclude those who are killed from the community of equal human dignity.

A. Dehumanisation

Here, I adopt Sophie Oliver's definition of dehumanisation, which is that the word 'refers in the most basic terms to the denial, in part or whole, of the humanity of a person or group of persons'.[34] Dehumanisation, Oliver says, is '[a] process by which human beings are rendered so radically other that their lives count for nothing'.[35]

Although, in Oliver's words, dehumanisation involves a 'denial of humanity', contemporary dehumanisation obviously does not involve a literal denial of the biological or genetic humanness of the individual or group being dehumanised.[36]

---

[33] In this context, I am concerned only with the ending of *human* life, and I take 'the ending of life' to include cases where life is ended by an omission (for example, the withdrawal of life-sustaining treatment) as well as those where life is ended by a positive act of killing.

[34] S Oliver, 'Dehumanization: Perceiving the Body as (In)Human' in P Kaufmann, H Kuch, C Neuhäuser and E Webster (eds), *Humiliation, Degradation, Dehumanization: Human Dignity Violated* (London, Springer, 2011) 86.

[35] Ibid, 85.

[36] Such claims have been made in the past, by racist writers and 'scientists' in the 18th and 19th centuries. For example, the slave owner Edward Long in *The History of Jamaica* (published in 1774) espoused 'polygenesis', the claim that the different races were in fact different *species* with different evo- lutionary lineage. Proponents of this idea regarded only white people with European ancestry as truly human; those of other races were really members of other species, located somewhere between (white) humans and the other higher primates in a supposed hierarchy of races/species. Long's polygenism and its divergence from that of his contemporaries is discussed in S Seth, 'Materialism, Slavery and the History of Jamaica' (2014) 105 *Isis* 764. Inevitably, the subject matter is offensive.

Rather, it involves denying that the individual or group concerned shares in whatever it is that we regard as *uniquely important* about human beings; a denial, in other words, of precisely the status that the term 'human dignity' tries to capture. It is irrelevant for present purposes that different people have different views about what *is* uniquely important about humans, and so use the term 'human dignity' to signify different things. What matters here is simply that, absent an acknowledgment of and commitment to human dignity—ie, to the idea that there is *something* equally, distinctively and fundamentally important about human beings which demands to be respected by oneself and others—it can make no sense to speak of 'dehumanisation' at all. Dehumanisation just *is* the denial that a particular individual or group shares equally in the uniquely human value that attaches to the rest of us (however we describe that value).[37]

Oliver cites Kelman's description of dehumanisation as a violation of the two qualities that he says are key to perceiving someone as fully human: identity and community.[38] Both are stripped away in the process of dehumanisation. Identity is undermined by removing uniqueness—for example, by referring to people using numbers instead of their names, or by taking away physical uniqueness and making them all look the same. In pictures of concentration camp survivors immediately after liberation, for example, it is striking how the emaciated bodies, huddled together wearing uniforms and with heads shaven, all seem so similar. Oliver observes that '[identity is] among the most affectively devastating losses suffered by victims of dehumanization'.[39]

Victims of dehumanisation are also robbed of community. Oliver explains, quoting Kelman, that dehumanisation amounts to exclusion from the community of 'individuals who care for each other, who recognize each other's individuality and who respect each other's rights'.[40] This clearly intersects with Nussbaum's observation that the emotional content of political narratives works either to include or to exclude individuals from the community of equals. So too does Oliver's reflection, again following Kelman, that

> [t]o be dehumanized is to be excluded from [the] community. It is to be perceived by the in-group as outside the moral kinship or scope of justice ... By excluding a person or persons from our moral community, it becomes possible to act inhumanly towards them,

---

[37] Some philosophers deny, of course, that any unique value *does* attach equally to all human beings—Peter Singer is one who argues that claims of uniquely or distinctively *human* value are 'speciesist' (P Singer, *Practical Ethics*, 2nd edn (Cambridge, Cambridge University Press, 1993) 55–68. It is difficult to see how it could make sense to talk of 'dehumanisation' at all within the context of such a position, since the position itself 'dehumanises' all of us, deliberately. My own view is that while other species may well have their own (unique) dignities, there is a dignity which belongs specifically to humanity on the basis of *its* unique character (I argue that this consists in the union/balance between the finite and the transcendent which appears to be particular to humanity)—see Neal, '"Not Gods But Animals"' (n 32).

[38] Oliver (n 34) 87.

[39] Ibid.

[40] Ibid, quoting HC Kelman, 'Violence without Moral Restraint: Reflections on the Dehumanization of Victims and Victimizers' (1973) 29 *Journal of Social Issues* 25, 48.

or else to allow harm to be done to them by others, without invoking any sense of moral inhibition or self-reproach.[41]

Identity and community, for some philosophers, are so fundamentally bound up together that they are almost not conceptually distinct.[42] On this view, it would be impossible to attack identity *without* attacking community, and vice versa; the idea that dehumanisation involves a simultaneous denial both of identity and community has some intuitive appeal, therefore.

Between them, Margalit[43] and Haslam[44] describe the spectrum of dehumanising narrative quite comprehensively. Haslam identifies two main types of dehumanisation: 'animalistic' and 'mechanistic' (or 'object-like') dehumanisation, in which people are dehumanised by being treated like animals or objects/automata respectively.[45] Margalit recognises these two types,[46] but notes that dehumanisation can also take the form of 'demonisation' which portrays people as spreaders of disease, destruction or evil.[47] There is a degree of overlap between Margalit's 'demonisation' and Haslam's 'animalistic' dehumanisation; however 'demonisation' seems to play into subtly different fears on the part of the recipient of the narrative (fear of evil and *moral* harm, rather than mere physical disgust).[48] Presumably, more than one type of dehumanisation will often be discernible within a given narrative.

In some cases, dehumanising killing narratives have been officially promulgated and/or endorsed. Notoriously, Nazi propaganda dehumanised Jewish people in the animalistic sense, by explicitly comparing them to rats and parasites, and also demonised them as uncivilised, degenerate, manipulative, lascivious and unhygienic, all as a precursor to their mass extermination.[49] The demonising narratives which were deployed by the laws in many jurisdictions during early modern witch hunts provide another example of 'official' dehumanisation.[50] A more

---

[41] Oliver (n 34) 87.

[42] The seminal expression of the view of community as constitutive of self-identity is found in MJ Sandel, *Liberalism and the Limits of Justice* (Cambridge, Cambridge University Press, 1982).

[43] A Margalit, *The Decent Society* (Cambridge, MA, Harvard University Press, 1996).

[44] N Haslam, 'Dehumanization: An Integrative Review' (2006) 10 *Personality and Social Psychology Review* 252.

[45] Ibid.

[46] Margalit (n 43) 89.

[47] Ibid, 89–90.

[48] Margalit also claims that dehumanisation can involve treating people as 'subhuman'—(n 43) 89. However, the example he gives—of treating adults like children—is problematic, since although there is certainly an affront to dignity involved in such treatment, it seems improper to characterise it as 'dehumanisation', since children are clearly human, and are ordinarily valued highly as such.

[49] The anti-Semitic newspaper *Der Stürmer* and the 1940 Nazi propaganda film *Der Ewige Jude* (*The Eternal Jew*) dehumanised the Jewish population in all of these ways.

[50] For example, there are numerous references to the Devil, and to relationships between accused persons and the Devil, in the indictments collected in CL Ewen, *Witch Hunting and Witch Trials: The Indictments for Witchcraft from the Records of the 1373 Assizes Held from the Home Court 1559–1736 AD* (London, Routledge, 2013). See also J Sharpe, 'The Devil in East Anglia: The Matthew Hopkins Trials Reconsidered' in J Barry, M Hester and G Roberts (eds), *Witchcraft in Early Modern Europe: Studies in Culture and Belief* (Cambridge, Cambridge University Press, 1996) 237.

recent example is the dehumanising hate speech broadcast by some Rwandan media outlets before and during the 1994 genocide, inciting ethnic Hutus to kill their ethnic Tutsi neighbours. The radio station Radio Télévision Libre des Mille Collines (RTLM) (nicknamed 'Radio Machete' by the Rwandan public) regularly referred to Tutsis as 'cockroaches' and urged their complete annihilation (the station repeated the slogan 'the graves are not yet full' to incite Hutus to ever greater slaughter).[51] Animal-like dehumanisation is clearly visible in the references to 'cockroaches'; however note also Roméo Dallaire's observation that RTLM 'was created [in 1993] specifically as a tool of the *genocidaires* to *demonize* the Tutsi'.[52]

B. Abjectification

Whereas dehumanising killing narratives attribute animal-like, object-like, demon-like, or machine-like characteristics to individuals or groups in order to locate them outside the community of equal human dignity, *abjectifying* narratives threaten or undermine dignity in a subtly different way. Abjection is defined by Kristeva as a process of rendering someone negatively-Other, making her a site of horror or revulsion, with the effect that she is cast out, distanced from the moral community.[53] We could explain how abjectification differs from dehumanisation by saying that, rather than excluding people by *denying* their humanity, abjectifying narratives render their subjects '*abhuman*';[54] they cast them out to the *borders* of humanity, where they evoke the particular kind of horror or disgust that belongs to what Freud called the *uncanny*, the juxtaposition of the familiar with the unfamiliar, the human with the non-human. The abhuman subject exists liminally and interstitially, across and between categories, overlapping categories and challenging boundaries, simultaneously itself and Other. The landscape of gothic horror literature is populated with fictional abhumans (such as vampires, phantoms and Frankenstein's monster) which combine humanity and non-humanity to provoke emotional responses of horror, fear and revulsion, but also a terrible recognition and pity. Whereas in narratives of dehumanisation it is the *author* of the narrative who purports to place the subjects beyond the observer's sphere of moral concern, narratives of abjectification induce or invite the *observer* to perform the distancing for him or herself, to reject the subject as too challenging, too uncanny to embrace as an equal. Some real life examples will be discussed presently when I come to consider end-of-life narratives in the healthcare law context. Away from healthcare law, there are echoes of abjectification in Bartlett's

---

[51] A Jones, The Scourge of Genocide: Essays and Reflections (Abingdon, Routledge, 2013) 96.
[52] R Dallaire, 'The Media Dichotomy' in A Thomson (ed), *The Media and the Rwanda Genocide* (London, Pluto Press, 2007) 12, 16.
[53] J Kristeva, *Powers of Horror: An Essay on Abjection* (New York, Columbia University Press, 1982).
[54] K Hurley, The Gothic Body: Sexuality, Materialism and Degeneration at the Fin de Siècle (Cambridge, Cambridge University Press, 1996) 3–4.

analysis of cases of 'gay sexual homicide' (which he defines as sexual homicide involving male perpetrators and male victims).[55] Bartlett exposes narratives of hate, rage, disgust, fear, powerlessness and alienation: three of the perpetrators quoted in the article explicitly mention 'disgust' in their narratives, one of them also mentions 'nausea', and in a fourth narrative the perpetrator describes himself as having felt 'revolted'.[56]

I do not wish here to labour or overstate the distinction between abjectification and dehumanisation: they are clearly close relatives. Undoubtedly there is overlap between narratives that dehumanise and those that abjectify, and just as a combination of different forms of dehumanisation within a single narrative is possible, so too is a combination of dehumanising and abjectifying elements within a narrative. Moreover, it is important to emphasise two of the main things that dehumanisation and abjectification have in common. The first is that both operate to *exclude*: in dehumanisation, the dignity of community membership is denied outright, and in abjection the recipient of the narrative is incited to see the subject as existing at the margins of the community, or as defying categorisation such that the presumption of clear belonging is undermined. The second is that both perform exclusion by reflecting and shaping emotional responses; both dehumanisation and abjectification are profoundly emotional processes.

IV. The Function of Killing Narratives: 'Moral Disengagement'

Primo Levi wrote that 'before dying the victim must be degraded, so that the murderer will be less burdened with guilt'.[57] Albert Bandura has extensively researched 'mechanisms of moral disengagement', which he defines as 'psychosocial manoeuvres by which moral self-sanctions can be disengaged from inhumane conduct',[58] and found that:

> The strength of moral self-censure depends on how the perpetrators regard the people they mistreat. To perceive another as human activates empathetic reactions through perceived similarity ... It is difficult to mistreat humanised people without risking personal distress and self-condemnation. Self-censure for cruel conduct can be disengaged or blunted by stripping people of human qualities. Once dehumanised, they are no longer viewed as persons with feelings, hopes and concerns but as sub-human objects.[59]

---

[55] P Bartlett, 'Killing Gay Men 1976–2001' (2007) 47 *British Journal of Criminology* 573.

[56] Ibid.

[57] P Levi, *The Drowned and the Saved* (trans R Rosenthal, New York, Vintage, 1989) 126.

[58] A Bandura, 'Moral Disengagement in the Perpetration of Inhumanities' (1999) 3 *Personality and Social Psychology Review* 193, 193.

[59] A Bandura, 'Selective Moral Disengagement in the Exercise of Moral Agency' (2002) 31 *Journal of Moral Education* 101, 109.

In wartime, therefore, 'nations cast their enemies in the most dehumanised, demonic and bestial images to make it easier to kill them'[60] since '[t]he process of dehumanisation is an *essential ingredient* in the perpetration of inhumanities.'[61]

The organisation Genocide Watch identifies ten stages in the process of genocide, of which 'dehumanisation' is stage four. In other words, the dehumanising narrative(s) is acknowledged as *part* of the process of killing:

> One group denies the humanity of the other group. Members of it are equated with animals, vermin, insects or diseases. Dehumanization overcomes the normal human revulsion against murder. At this stage, hate propaganda in print and on hate radios is used to vilify the victim group. In combating this dehumanization, incitement to genocide should not be confused with protected speech. Genocidal societies lack constitutional protection for countervailing speech, and should be treated differently than democracies. Local and international leaders should condemn the use of hate speech and make it culturally unacceptable.[62]

The idea that narrative can sometimes form part of the process of killing is reinforced by the fact that some of those responsible for creating and disseminating killing narratives have been convicted for crimes of mass murder. Notable examples include Julius Streicher, the publisher of the anti-semitic newspaper *Der Stürmer* during the Nazi era, and those responsible for using media outlets to foment hatred during the Rwandan genocide.

What is crucial for present purposes is the *function* that Bandura, Levi and Genocide Watch all ascribe to dehumanising narratives: for these writers, as for Nussbaum, narratives of exclusion (dehumanisation and/or abjectification) are 'emotion-shaping' discourses, designed to create and foster some emotional responses, and to suppress and circumvent others. The emotions being circumvented or blocked in dehumanising or abjectifying killing narratives are emotions like compassion, empathy and love; those being promoted are fear, revulsion, disgust, horror, rejection. In other words, narratives of dehumanisation and abjectification function to *block* precisely those emotions that Nussbaum has identified as being prerequisites of dignity, and to *foster* emotions that are incompatible with dignity, and that point to its violation. Techniques of moral disengagement exist precisely because most of us have a strong aversion to hurting and harming others; as Bandura warns, however, '[g]iven appropriate social conditions, decent, ordinary people can do extraordinarily cruel things.'[63]

A final thing to note here is Bandura's acknowledgement that the kind of 'human estrangement that fosters dehumanisation' can occur unconsciously, in the absence of any deliberate *agenda* of disengagement; he notes that many of the conditions of modern social life tend to estrange us from one another: '[b]ureaucratisation,

---

[60] Ibid.

[61] Ibid (emphasis added).

[62] GH Stanton, 'The Ten Stages of Genocide' *Genocide Watch*: genocidewatch.org/genocide/tenstagesofgenocide.html.

[63] Bandura, 'Selective Moral Disengagement in the Exercise of Moral Agency' (n 59) 109.

automation, urbanisation and high mobility lead people to relate to each other in anonymous, impersonal ways'.[64] The risk that moral disengagement can occur unintentionally, as a result of moral carelessness rather than active wickedness, is something that seems important to bear in mind as we begin to apply the foregoing analysis in the HCLE context.

V. End-of-Life Narratives in Healthcare Law

It is worth outlining the main points that have been made so far. First, three main things have been noted from Nussbaum's consideration of dignity and the emotions in *Political Emotions*:

1. Respect for, or affirmation of dignity is a matter of recognition and inclusion in the community of moral equals; conversely, the denial or violation of dignity is a matter of exclusion.
2. 'Emotion-shaping' narratives perform an important role in the construction and maintenance of a 'decent society'; they foster emotional responses that are congruent with equal human dignity and 'keep at bay' emotional responses that are incompatible with equal dignity or that tend to threaten or undermine it.
3. Just as emotion-shaping narratives can foster dignity and resist inequality, they can also be deployed, either consciously or unconsciously, in exclusionary ways, when they provoke emotional responses that are liable to exclude certain individuals or groups from the community of moral equals.

Nussbaum herself does not apply these insights in the context of killing, but having considered killing narratives specifically, I now want to add the following claims of my own:

4. 'Killing narratives', whatever else they might also be, are 'emotion-shaping' processes; as such, they either affirm or deny equal human dignity, since their emotional content will be either congruent with dignity (inclusive, recognising) or inimical to it (exclusionary).
5. Dehumanising and abjectifying narratives are two specific (and distinct) types of exclusionary, dignity-incongruent narratives which sometimes accompany killings.

I want now to begin to apply the foregoing in the HCLE context. An interesting point of contrast is that in the examples discussed so far, it has seemed uncontroversial to assume that the killing processes involve a *violation* of the dignity of the victims. In HCLE discourse, by contrast, 'dignity' is not infrequently cited as a

---

[64] Ibid.

factor weighing *in favour* of permitting certain types of killing, such as euthanasia and assisted suicide.[65]

Here, I will make no claims about the objective moral status of particular end-of-life practices. My claim is rather that, if we are eager to know whether particular practices are (or would be) congruent with human dignity or not, we should be interested in examining the emotional content of the discourses around them. Do the discourses reflect and foster dignity-congruent emotions such as love, compassion, sympathy, empathy and recognition, or do they embody and promote emotions which tend to undermine dignity, such as fear, disgust, revulsion, and asymmetric pity? The literature on healthcare law and ethics is replete with narratives about the end of life whose emotional content could be analysed in this way,[66] but such a study is far beyond the scope of this chapter, which aims simply to introduce the idea that anyone who cares about dignity *ought* to be alert to the emotional content of killing narratives, including those in the healthcare context. In order to begin to illustrate how a dignity-analysis of end-of-life narratives in the healthcare context might unfold, I will simply offer some examples of narratives where there seems to be evidence of the 'wrong' sort of emotional content.

I begin with two narratives that Kristin Savell has identified as 'abjectifying'.[67] The first concerns 'Ms B',[68] a healthy, intelligent, professional woman in her forties who was suddenly rendered quadriplegic by a spinal haemorrhage. She was not terminally ill, but was dependent on artificial ventilation, and there was no realistic prospect that her condition would improve sufficiently to enable her to breathe independently in future. The healthcare professionals treating Ms B sought to persuade her to enter rehabilitation, but Ms B decided instead to exercise her right to refuse the life-sustaining medical treatment she was receiving (ventilation) in order to bring her life to an end. Because the team caring for Ms B had become emotionally attached to her, they found her decision difficult to accept. Doubts were raised regarding her capacity to make the decision, and the matter ended up before the English High Court. Savell reflects that, 'in constructing an intelligible account of her decision to die, Ms B invoked an *abject* body, vulnerable and open, a space of suffering and violation'.[69] Ms B's self-narrative emphasised her dependence, her isolation and the severity of her disability. Ultimately, in upholding her capacity to make the decision, the then Dame Elizabeth Butler-Sloss P agreed that for some patients like Ms B, 'life in that condition may be worse than death'.[70]

[65] See, for example, R Dworkin, *Life's Dominion: An Argument About Abortion, Euthanasia, and Individual Freedom* (New York, Oxford University Press, 1993) 239.
[66] Potentially, this includes all judicial consideration of, and legal/ethical academic commentary on, end-of-life practices such as the refusal of life-sustaining treatment, withholding and withdrawing treatment, the doctrine of double effect, assisted suicide and euthanasia.
[67] K Savell, 'A Jurisprudence of Ambivalence: Three Legal Fictions Concerning Death and Dying' (2001) 17 *Cultural Studies Review* 52: epress.lib.uts.edu.au/journals/index.php/csrj/article/view/1973/2138 on 7 January 2015.
[68] *Ms B v An NHS Hospital Trust* [2002] EWHC 429 (Fam).
[69] Savell (n 67) 60 (emphasis added).
[70] *Ms B v An NHS Hospital Trust* [2002] EWHC 429 (Fam), [94].

Mr Rossiter, also discussed by Savell, was another quadriplegic patient whose own personal narrative emphasised his level of indignity and suffering.[71] He cited his inability to move, talk, blow his nose, clear phlegm, or wipe tears; the constant danger of bedsores; and the fact that he had to be catheterised, have his stools cleaned away, and be changed frequently because of leaks and soiling. Savell interprets this narrative as depicting the 'grotesqueness of his physical condition' and Mr Rossiter's 'symbolic reduction to an "infantile 'non person' or 'open person' status"'.[72]

The example of Mr Rossiter vividly recalls Nussbaum's discussion of shame, and in particular, her observation that the 'purest' form of shame is 'a painful emotion directed at the self'.[73] One of the most interesting features of the narratives of Mr Rossiter and Ms B is that they are examples of *self*-abjectification; the kind of exclusion inherent in abjectification is, as these narratives demonstrate, an exclusion that one can perform in relation to oneself. Arguably, however, one cannot abjectify oneself in isolation; the exclusionary narrative a patient constructs in order to render her *own* existence or condition abject cannot be *limited* to herself. Once articulated and disseminated, it can also work abjectification on others whose condition is comparable to that of the author: I may intend only to record my own shame, but I may end up by humiliating others. I will return to this point in concluding.

Further examples of exclusionary end-of-life narratives can be found in the language of the judges in the House of Lords in the landmark case of *Airedale NHS Trust v Bland*.[74] Anthony Bland was the final victim of the Hillsborough stadium disaster on 15 April 1989, when 96 Liverpool fans were killed and 766 injured at a football match between Liverpool FC and Nottingham Forest FC, when a failure of police control led to overcrowding on one of the standing terraces. As the catastrophic events of that day unfolded, Bland was crushed in the crowds, sustaining broken ribs, punctured lungs and a lack of oxygen to the brain which left him with severe and irreversible brain damage. He was 18-years-old at the time of the disaster, and died in hospital in 1993, having spent the intervening four years in a persistent vegetative state.

In the speeches of the Law Lords, references to Bland's non-existent quality of life,[75] his lack of awareness of his environment[76] and his lack of any meaningful

---

[71] Mr Rossiter's case was heard in the Australian High Court as *Brightwater Care Group (Inc) v Rossiter* [2009] WASC 229, and is discussed in Savell (n 67).

[72] Savell (n 67) 61, quoting DD Waskul and P van der Riet, 'The Abject Embodiment of Cancer: Patients' Dignity, Selfhood and the Grotesque Body' (2002) 25 *Symbolic Interaction* 487, 499.

[73] Nussbaum, *Political Emotions: Why Love Matters for Justice* (n 10) 360. Although most people would presumably regard shame as an inappropriate emotional response to physical disability (emotions, including shame, can obviously be misplaced), what matters is that Mr Rossiter seems to have experienced it.

[74] *Airedale NHS Trust v Bland* [1993] AC 789.

[75] Ibid, 878–79 (Lord Browne-Wilkinson): 'If the quality of life of a person such as Anthony Bland is non-existent since he is unaware of anything that happens to him, has he a right to be sustained in that state of living death and are his family and medical attendants under a duty to maintain it?'.

[76] *Airedale NHS Trust v Bland* [1993] AC 789 passim.

interests[77] arguably combine to produce what Haslam has called automaton-like, or object-like dehumanisation. Tellingly, Lord Mustill opened his speech in the case as follows:

> My Lords, the *pitiful* state of Anthony Bland and the suffering of his devoted family must attract the sympathy of all. The devotion to duty of the medical staff, and the complete propriety of those who have faced up to the painful dilemma must equally attract the *respect* of all. This combination of *sympathy* and *respect* can but yield an urgent desire to take up the burden, to reach a conclusion on this deep moral issue of life and death, and to put that conclusion into effect as speedily and humanely as possible.[78]

Here, Anthony Bland is the recipient of asymmetric pity, whereas the symmetrical emotions of sympathy and respect are reserved for everyone else: the suffering relatives and the dutiful professionals. Later, Lord Mustill concludes that 'the continued treatment of Anthony Bland can no longer serve to maintain that combination of manifold characteristics which we call a personality'.[79] This echoes Lord Hoffmann's remarks in the Court of Appeal in the same case that 'the very concept of having a life has no meaning in relation to Anthony Bland. He is alive but has no life at all',[80] and that

> the stark reality is that Anthony Bland is not living a life at all. None of the things that one says about the way people live their lives—well or ill, with courage or fortitude, happily or sadly—have any meaning in relation to him.[81]

Statements like these reveal a view of Bland's existence as more 'object-like' than 'person-like' (indeed, the clinical term used to describe Bland's condition, 'vegetative', also has connotations of objecthood). Insofar as the judicial narratives portray Bland as existing at the boundary between personhood and objecthood, bearing features of both categories but conforming cleanly to neither, they are vividly abjectifying, and incompatible with respect for the patient's human dignity.

The rhetoric of the judges in the English Court of Appeal in the well-known case of *Re A*[82] is also illuminating, but more ambivalent; it contains both dignity-affirming and dignity-denying elements. The case concerned conjoined twins born in Manchester who would both certainly die if left in their conjoined state. Surgical separation would give the stronger twin, 'Jodie', a chance of survival, but would not guarantee it. The weaker twin, 'Mary', would inevitably die during the procedure. The Appeal Court judges make explicit and repeated references to the girls' 'dignity', and in particular, the language of 'monsters' and 'monstrosity' (used

---

[77] Ibid, 897 (Lord Mustill): 'The distressing truth which must not be shirked is that the proposed conduct is not in the best interests of Anthony Bland, for he has no best interests of any kind'.

[78] Ibid, 885, emphases added.

[79] Ibid, 899.

[80] Ibid, 829.

[81] Ibid, 830.

[82] *Re A (Children) (Conjoined Twins: Surgical Separation)* [2001] Fam 147.

in the past in relation to conjoined twin births) is firmly repudiated as 'totally unacceptable, indeed repugnant and offensive to the dignity of these children'.[83] In another notable passage Lord Justice Ward reflects on 'how we sympathise with [the parents'] predicament, with the *agony* of their decision—for now it has become ours'.[84] All of this seems to point towards the 'right sort' of emotional response, and to invite the audience to join the judges in including both girls within the community of equal human dignity.

As they reason their way through the legal issues, however, all three of the judges also deploy narratives in which the girls' bodies (and thus their existences) are marked out as abject. Ward LJ considers that 'the only gain I can see [for Mary] is that the operation would, if successful, give Mary [in death] the bodily integrity and dignity which is the natural order for all of us'.[85] Brooke LJ echoes this sentiment, saying that '[t]he doctrine of sanctity of life respects the integrity of the human body. The proposed operation would give these children's bodies the integrity which nature denied them'.[86] Walker LJ wonders whether 'the mere fact of restoring [Mary's] separate bodily integrity, even at the moment of death, can be seen as a good in itself and as something which ought to be achieved in the best interests of Mary as well as Jodie'.[87] He concludes that the operation is in Mary's best interests because 'for the twins to remain alive and conjoined in the way they are would be to deprive them of the bodily integrity and human dignity which is the right of each of them'.[88]

Underpinning all of this is a typically liberal view of subjecthood, exemplified in Walker LJ's statement that '[e]very human being's right to life carries with it, as an intrinsic part of it, rights of bodily integrity and autonomy—the right to have one's own body whole and intact'.[89] David Punter has noted that 'the law cannot permit … the exceptional body'.[90] In *Re A* it seems that the twins' conjoined state was regarded by the judges as being so abject, so unliveable and intolerable, that it was preferable for these girls to be dead (but separate) than alive and conjoined.

In some cases, dignity is denied not obliquely, but very explicitly. Take, for example, the appeal of Tony Nicklinson, which came before the UK Supreme Court in 2014.[91] The appeal concerned three applicants: Tony Nicklinson, Paul Lamb and a man known in the proceedings only as 'Martin'. All of the applicants were quadriplegic and all wished to be assisted in ending their lives. By the time the appeal

---

[83] Ibid, 182.
[84] Ibid, 173 (emphasis added).
[85] Ibid, 184.
[86] Ibid, 240.
[87] Ibid, 251.
[88] Ibid, 258.
[89] Ibid, 259.
[90] D Punter, *Gothic Pathologies: The Text, the Body and the Law* (Basingstoke, Palgrave Macmillan, 1998) 45.
[91] *R (Nicklinson and another) v Ministry of Justice* [2014] UKSC 38.

reached the Supreme Court, Mr Nicklinson was deceased: having been denied a judgment in his favour in the lower courts, he had opted to end his life by refusing food and starving to death, which was the only means lawfully available to him. Delivering the leading judgment in the Supreme Court, Lord Neuberger says of the applicants that 'each of [them] was suffering such a distressing and undignified life that he had long wished to end it'.[92] Mr Nicklinson is quoted as saying that his life was 'dull, miserable, demeaning, undignified and intolerable'.[93] Paul Lamb regards his life 'as consisting of a mixture of monotony, indignity and pain'.[94] The applicant known as 'Martin' considers his life to be 'undignified, distressing and intolerable', and he wishes it to end 'as soon as possible'.[95] All of this is reported in Lord Neuberger's judgment in a matter-of-fact way, without any countervailing declaration of the law's respect for the sanctity of the applicants' lives, or of its view of them as embodying an inherent human dignity. Sanctity and dignity are mentioned by Lord Neuberger and his colleagues,[96] but only in the abstract (and somewhat negatively), not in an attempt to affirm the inherent dignity of these particular applicants. Such explicit denial of dignity occurs wherever people claim that their own lives lack dignity, or where others describe their lives, or circumstances, as undignified.

A final observation before concluding this brief survey is that perceptions of the body and of embodiment are key to the emotion-shaping processes which affirm or deny dignity. Oliver points out that, in what she calls 'modern philosophical discourse', 'the body has figured as an abject entity, secondary or even irrelevant to the construction of a human subject that is posited as rational, autonomous, and largely disembodied'.[97] The 'more biological, more corporeal, more natural'[98] a being is, the further away it is from the ideal of liberal subjecthood, namely the 'stable, thinking being'.[99] The more 'insistent' the body is—in other words, the greater the extent to which the physical or corporeal interrupts or intrudes upon prized mental processes like rationality and autonomy—the more fearful, disgusting and abject the subject is perceived to be, and the less fully human. At the extreme end of the spectrum is a condition of 'pure "bodyhood"'[100] in which the human being seems to be no more than a physical object, positively *inviting* the denial of dignity inherent in object-like dehumanisation.

[92] Ibid, [2].
[93] Ibid, [3].
[94] Ibid, [8].
[95] Ibid, [9].
[96] See, for example, ibid, [90] (Lord Neuberger); [191] (Lord Mance); [199] (Lord Wilson); [208], [209] and [214] (Lord Sumption); [311] (Lady Hale); and [357] and [358] (Lord Kerr).
[97] Oliver (n 34) 94.
[98] Ibid, quoting E Grosz, *Volatile Bodies: Toward a Corporeal Feminism* (Bloomington, IN, Indiana University Press, 1994).
[99] Oliver (n 34) 94.
[100] Z Hanafi, *The Monster in the Machine: Magic, Medicine, and the Marvelous in the Time of the Scientific Revolution* (Durham, NC, Duke University Press, 2000) 96.

VI. Conclusion

As is the case with many other types of killing, killing in the healthcare context may have a narrative dimension. Acts (or proposed acts) whereby individuals' lives will be ended (whether by themselves or others, and whether by act or omission) are often accompanied and surrounded by narratives seeking to explain, justify, or legitimise them.

This chapter has observed that many killing narratives are exclusionary and hostile to dignity because they dehumanise and/or abjectify their subjects; the narratives of dehumanisation and abjectification that accompany atrocity killings like genocide and gay sexual homicide clearly do these things. But this need not necessarily be the case. Some killing narratives focus on the killer's state of mind, and say nothing about the humanity of the victim at all—criminal law narratives of self-defence, provocation and temporary insanity are examples. To discover whether a particular narrative is dignity-denying or not, we need to unpack its emotional content and discover whether that content is more likely to affirm equal human dignity, or to deny it. If we discover that dignity-congruent emotions such as compassion, empathy and love comprise the emotional heart of the narrative, this may point towards dignity-affirmation. If we find that the narrative is driven by asymmetric pity, shame, humiliation, revulsion, fear, disgust, or horror, this suggests that it is likely to deny, undermine or violate dignity.

Some important caveats must be acknowledged, however. First, a narrative which is apparently dignity-congruent may be dishonest. It may be paying lip service to compassion, empathy, respect and love, but concealing a genuine motivation in anti-dignity emotions like horror or disgust. Second, a narrative may be genuinely ambivalent; it may shape both dignity-promoting *and* dignity-violating emotions. In *Re A*, for example, although in many places the judges emphasise dignity and insist on respect for the separate personhood of each twin, in other places there is evidence of dignity-denying emotions such as pity and horror. As I have noted in another context, however, 'abjection ... is by definition an *ambivalent* response. It consists predominantly in fear and revulsion ... but with an accompanying sense of identification with, and sympathy for, the abject entity'.[101] Thus, 'the existence of seemingly-positive statements is not incompatible with an abjection-response'.[102] Third, as noted above, even if a narrative appears to be animated by the 'right' emotions towards the person immediately in contemplation, it may still have the potential to violate dignity by designating abject or unliveable zones for others.

---

[101] M Ford, 'Nothing and Not-Nothing: Law's Ambivalent Response to Transformation and Transgression at the Beginning of Life' in SW Smith and R Deazley (eds), *The Legal, Medical and Cultural Regulation of the Body: Transformation and Transgression* (Farnham, Ashgate, 2009) 21, 43 (emphasis in original).
[102] Ibid.

A general point can be made here about legislation to permit assisted suicide and/or euthanasia. Any legislation to permit these practices, unless it intends to make them equally available to all citizens, must set out a list of criteria describing the circumstances in which they would be permitted. Arguably, however, the identification of such criteria delineates an 'abject realm', a zone of 'unliveableness'. In practice, it might be seen as amounting to a formal state endorsement of a person's own assessment of his or her life as abject.

This effect is sharpened when such an 'abject zone' exists alongside a general policy of suicide prevention or reduction. The Health and Sport Committee of the Scottish Parliament noted, in its Stage 1 Report on the Assisted Suicide (Scotland) Bill in 2015, that:

> Where legislation to permit assisted suicide exists alongside a wider policy of suicide prevention, the eligibility criteria in the legislation serve to differentiate between circumstances in which suicide is to be regarded as a tragedy and prevented wherever possible, and circumstances in which suicide is to be regarded as a reasonable choice, to be facilitated and supported.[103]

The Report expressed concern that this may 'communicate an offensive message to certain members of our community (many of whom may be particularly vulnerable) that society would regard it as "reasonable", rather than tragic, if they wished to end their lives'.[104]

Giving evidence to the UK House of Lords Committee on one of Lord Joffe's Assisted Dying for the Terminally Ill Bills, one witness was disturbed by the idea of the law drawing lines 'between those who "qualify" to be assisted in killing themselves and those whom society would seek to prevent from committing suicide'.[105] Her concern seemed to be that such line-drawing would do existential harm to those in the same or similar circumstances who do *not* wish to die. As these individuals continue to live, they inhabit a liminal zone, living lives which are, in some sense, officially abject and 'beyond the pale'. The same danger arises in relation to *judicial* narratives about the end of life; for example, when the Court in the case of Ms B agreed that for her, 'life ... may be worse than death'.[106]

Finally, it is important to note that dignity is only *one* moral and legal standard; a practice which does not violate dignity may nevertheless violate another important standard, for example the principle of the sanctity of life which, like dignity, is a legal as well as a moral value.

Unpacking the emotional content of end-of-life debates in healthcare law can provide us with information about whether *particular* narratives are congruent with dignity or hostile to it; but this information alone cannot tell us whether

[103] Scottish Parliament Health and Sport Committee, *Stage 1 Report on Assisted Suicide (Scotland) Bill*, 6th Report, Session 4 (2015) para 279.
[104] Ibid, para 280.
[105] Select Committee on the Assisted Dying for the Terminally Ill Bill, *Volume II: Evidence* (HL 2004–05, 86-II) (London, The Stationery Office, 2005) Q1973 (Michele Wates).
[106] Dame Elizabeth Butler-Sloss P in *Ms B v An NHS Hospital Trust* [2002] EWHC 429 (Fam).

individual instances of ending life (let alone whole practices such as assisted suicide, euthanasia, treatment withdrawal and so on) involve the promotion or the
violation of human dignity. It may be that dignity-congruence or dignity-violation
can only be determined on a case by case basis, and that it may not be fruitful to
try to assess the dignity-congruence of practices in the abstract. Narratives about
whole practices do exist, of course, but their *emotional* content tends to consist in
references to, and anecdotes from, individual cases. Commenting on the second
reading of Lord Falconer's Assisted Dying (HL) Bill, Montgomery has acknowledged 'the grip that personal stories have on our lawmaking processes'.[107] Yet even
in individual cases, narrative will only be one source of information in establishing the normative status of the central act of ending life as dignity-congruent or
incongruent, and there may well be a plurality of narratives in a given case which
promote or deny dignity to a greater or lesser degree.

All of this must mean that, while we should be alert to the potential value of
narratives as a source of information about the dignity-status of various forms
of killing, we should not expect the information we glean from them to be deci-
sive. Moreover, even when the emotional content of the narratives surrounding
an act of killing appear clearly dignity-congruent, we ought also to be checking
the act against other moral values before deciding once and for all that the act is
(or would be) morally im/permissible. Narrative does not provide a complete picture of dignity, and dignity does not provide a complete picture of morality. Nevertheless, it would be worthwhile systematically to examine and analyse the content
of the emotion-shaping narratives that feature in the public discussion (including
judicial and scholarly discussion) of end-of-life practices such as assisted suicide,
euthanasia and the withholding and withdrawing of life-sustaining treatment,
given the potential of such narratives for signposting threats to dignity.

---

[107] J Montgomery, '"To Be or Not To Be?" Is that the Question?' Nuffield Council on Bioethics
website, posted 18 July 2014: nuffieldbioethics.org/blog/2014/question/.

6

Empathy for Victims in Criminal Justice: Revisiting Susan Bandes in Victimology

ANTONY PEMBERTON[*]

I. Introduction

Where in other areas of legal scholarship the notion of law and emotions might meet enduring resistance, this is certainly not true for Victimology. Indeed the understanding that emotions play a key role in the way victims of crime and abuse of power experience legal processes all but goes without saying. Assuaging the burden—the 'secondary victimisation'[1]—of the criminal justice process has from the outset been couched in emotional terms, while the positive value of participation is increasingly portrayed in such a way as well.[2] A victimologist therefore, with an interest in justice processes, is automatically involved in law and emotions scholarship, even without any explicit awareness of this fact.

This is not to say that the debates surrounding the role of emotions in law are unfamiliar terrain to scholars involved in victimological research; indeed it is a recurrent phenomenon. However, the perception of an emotional essence to victims' issues, combined with the relative novelty of considering the position of victims within criminal justice processes, means that the kernel and outcome of these debates are understood as concerning the appropriate place *for victims* in law rather than the appropriate place for *emotions*. Both the victims' (supposed) nature as emotional beings, as well as particular emotions associated with victimisation deemed particularly problematic—anger, outrage, hatred and their

---

[*] International Victimology Institute, Tilburg. Work on this chapter was supported by a Veni-grant (451-13-019) from the Dutch Science Foundation (NWO).

[1] See JE Williams, 'Secondary Victimisation: Confronting Public Attitudes About Rape' (1984) 9 *Victimology* 66.

[2] See A Pemberton and S Reynaers, 'The Controversial Nature of Victim Participation: The Case of the Victim Impact Statements' in E Erez, M Kilchling and JA Wemmers (eds), *Therapeutic Jurisprudence and Victim Participation in Criminal Justice: International Perspectives* (Durham, NC, Academic Press, 2011).

connection to revenge—often feature in these discussions.[3] The questions at issue are whether it is true, problematic and/or valuable that the victim's input in the process is emotionally charged,[4] and similarly whether it is true and/or problematic that the emotions victims experience are vengeful in nature.[5]

One of the upshots of this is that much of the normative discussion about victims' emotions in criminal justice focuses on the issue of revenge, which, although it is an important topic, drowns out consideration of the more subtle and complex ways in which victims' emotions can interact *with* or be expressed *in* justice processes and the extent to which legal processes can and should respond to these emotions. A classic text in the Law and Emotions canon that deals with a victimological subject does do so, and much of its line of thinking merits renewed attention. It is Susan Bandes' *Empathy, Narrative and Victim Impact Statements* (ENV) that appeared in the University of Chicago Law Review in 1996.[6]

In this paper Bandes offers an incisive analysis of two concepts—empathy and narrative—which are of lasting importance in understanding the complexities of the position of victims of crime in criminal justice.[7] As I will argue, this value only increases when divorced from the immediate topic of concern to Bandes, whose 'interest in victim impact statements was originally propelled by concern about— or, more accurately, outrage over—the result in Payne'.[8] This, of course, refers to the landmark US Supreme Court decision in *Payne v Tennessee*,[9] which allowed victim impact evidence at the sentencing phase in capital cases.

---

[3] See for instance, the contributions to the edited volumes of A Crawford and J Goodey, *Integrating a Victim Perspective Within Criminal Justice* (Aldershot, Ashgate, 2000); and A Bottoms and J Roberts, *Hearing the Victim. Adversarial Justice, Crime Victims and the State* (Cullompton, Devon, Willan Publishing, 2010).

[4] E Erez, M Kilchling and JA Wemmers (eds), *Therapeutic Jurisprudence and Victim Participation in Criminal Justice: International Perspectives* (Durham, NC, Academic Press, 2011).

[5] For instance, JJM Van Dijk, 'Free the Victim: A Critique of the Western Conception of Victimhood' (2009) 16 *International Review of Victimology* 1; L Sherman and H Strang, 'Empathy for the Devil' in S Karstedt, I Loader and H Strang (eds) *Emotions, Crime and Justice* (Oxford, Hart Publishing, 2011); BAM Van Stokkom, 'Victim Needs, Well-Being and Closure: Does Revenge Satisfy?' in E Erez, M Kilchling and JA Wemmers (eds), *Therapeutic Jurisprudence and Victim Participation in Criminal Justice: International Perspectives* (Durham NC, Academic Press, 2011); A Pemberton, 'Too Readily Dismissed? A Victimological Perspective on Penal Populism' in H Nelen and JC Claessen (eds), *Beyond the Death Penalty* (Antwerp, Intersentia, 2011).

[6] SA Bandes, 'Empathy, Narrative and Victim Impact Statements' (1996) 63 *University of Chicago Law Review* 361.

[7] See also, A Pemberton, 'Respecting Victims of Crime. Key Distinctions in a Theory of Victims' Rights' in I Vanfraechem, A Pemberton and FN Ndahinda (eds), *Justice for Victims. Perspectives on Rights, Transition and Reconciliation* (Oxford, Routledge, 2014); A Pemberton, PGM Aarten and E Mulder, 'Beyond Restoration, Retribution and Procedural Justice: The Big Two of Agency and Communion in Victims Perspectives on Justice' (manuscript under review, 2016); A Pemberton, PGM Aarten and E Mulder, 'Stories as Property. Narrative Ownership as a Key Construct in Victimology' (manuscript under review, 2018). The way I understand narrative and empathy and the latter's distinction from sympathy will be discussed below.

[8] See ENV 361. See also, A Sarat, 'Vengeance, Victims and the Identities of Law' (1997) 62 *Social & Legal Studies* 163.

[9] *Payne v Tennessee* 501 US 808 (1991). This was a mere four years after the Court had ruled the opposite in *Booth v Maryland* 482 US 496 (1987).

This is so for a number of reasons. At the most general level the relevance of re-examining Bandes' insights applies to a wider context, other jurisdictions and to a broader conception of victims' rights. In particular, the reasoning in *Payne* can stifle debate by setting up a straw man, that can and should be criticised, but has the unfortunate by-effect of skewing discussion towards issues that only arise in or are intimately connected with the particular context of the death penalty. Any trial that can lead to capital punishment should be viewed with concern, but it also casts a long shadow over the purpose of the proceedings, including the framing of the perspectives of participating actors, whether the judge, the jury or indeed the victim. Given the issues at stake in a capital case, the value of debating *Payne* is difficult to overstate for legal practice in the United States; however the portability of this specific context is limited, which in turn restricts the contribution to victimological theory elsewhere.

In this chapter I shall recapitulate and build on some of the main observations made by Bandes. As we shall see in the next section, Bandes first argues the impossibility of excluding emotion and narrative in (criminal) legal processes, unmasking the argument for such an exclusion as instead privileging certain emotions and narratives over others. Second, she points to the necessary connection between empathy and narrative, which I will extend to include a wider emotional pallet. Third, she argues for the importance of context in normatively assessing empathy and narratives. Agreeing that neither is necessarily benign, I will extend the understanding of context to include the distinction between the normative evaluation of empathy and narrative as underlying a certain *practice/institution*, from doing the same concerning particular *actions* within that practice/institution. Finally, Bandes notes the importance of understanding the way the legal context interacts with empathy and narrative. Criminal law imposes particular frames on victims' narratives, and the criminal legal context shapes the stories victims choose to tell about their experience. This is not only due to the formal processes of participation and the goals and ends criminal law foresees for victims' input, but also to the meaning victims ascribe to criminal processes and interacting with its actors.

I will draw upon these arguments in the section which follows. Drawing on Bandes' original title, the key issue here is first that fully *empathising with victims* will lead to an understanding of the *essentially narrative nature* of their experience. Sense and meaning making after victimisation involve narration, while the impact of relatively severe forms of victimisation can be understood in the challenges it poses towards victims' sense of continuity and coherence in their life story, throughout time and in conjecture with collective narratives in their social environment. Victimisation poses a threat to victims' sense of personal agency, and to connection with others, including the community as a whole, while victimisation narratives have the tendency to stretch forwards and backwards in time.

This will lead me to argue, secondly, that the criminal justice process is a *part of* rather than *a reaction to* the narrative of victimisation. The legal context has particular narrative qualities, not only due to its specific organisational characteristics, but also because it contributes to the victim's narrative both when it is and when it is not involved in the reaction to victimisation. Whether victims' narratives feature in criminal justice or not, criminal justice features in victims' narratives. Much of the underlying motivation of victim participation in criminal justice can therefore be helpfully reinterpreted as a means to connect the victim's narrative to the criminal justice process. We will develop the importance of inclusion of such *communion*-based motives in this desire and argue how this can give rise to new ways of conceiving of practice and purpose of victim input.[10]

Finally, I will show that understanding the competing narratives surrounding victim input in criminal justice can illuminate some of the negative experiences subsumed under the term *secondary victimisation*. Similarly, the imposition of these competing narratives upon the victim's perspective underlies practices that are victimological in name only. The victim impact statements (VIS) in the aftermath of *Payne* are one particular example of this phenomenon.

This will lead me to conclude that although I concur with Bandes' position in the discussion of *Payne v Tennessee*, including her adoption of empathy and narrative to make her case, they can also support a decidedly more positive evaluation of victim participation in criminal justice.

II. Revisiting Empathy, Narrative and Victim Impact Statements

A. The Impossibility of Excluding Emotion and Narrative in Legal Proceedings

In line with a large body of research, Bandes argues that neither emotion nor narrative can be excluded from legal proceedings.[11] She argues that 'There can be no debate about whether narrative belongs in the law. Such an argument would begin from the faulty assumption that we have a choice about whether to permit narratives into legal discourse'.[12]

Indeed, the argument against emotion and narrative in law turns out, on closer inspection, to be a manner of privileging certain narratives and certain emotions over others, under the pretext of speaking in 'an universal voice of reason'.[13] It is a

---

[10] See Pemberton, Aarten and Mulder, 'Beyond Restoration' and 'Stories as Property' (n 7). The particular meaning of 'communion' in this context and its juxtaposition with agency will be discussed in detail below.

[11] See also, P Ewick and SS Silbey, 'Subversive Stories and Hegemonic Tales' (1995) 29 *Law & Society Review* 197; J Bruner, *Making Stories: Law, Literature, Life* (Cambridge, MA, Harvard University Press, 2000).

[12] ENV 385.

[13] ENV 387.

particular instance of the *hegemonic character* of certain narratives.[14] This hegemony applies not only to the content of the story, but also concerning the kind of story that is appropriate, the question of who is entitled to tell stories, the settings in which stories are appropriate and the way stories are perceived. Hegemonic narratives pre-empt other narratives, in which their quality of appearing self-evident is an important factor. As Bandes notes, 'Often, one story (usually the dominant story) drowns out or pre-empts another (usually the alternative story). Because it is the dominant story, its character as narrative is invisible. The tale appears to tell itself'.[15]

This rhetorical strategy derives its force in part from the juxtaposition of two main modes of cognition: the *logico-paradigmatic* mode and the *narrative* mode.[16] The former attempts to fulfil the ideal of a formal, mathematical system of description and explanation, and deals in general causes and their establishment, while making use of procedures attempting to ensure verifiable reference and empirical truth. Narratives, on the other hand, explain events in terms of human or human-like intention and action, concerning the particular, the emotional and the idiosyncratic. Instead of abstraction from the particulars of a given situation, narrative seeks to make sense and give meaning to the experience contained in that situation, including the motives and intentions of the actor's behaviour. The seeming self-evidence of dominant narratives offers the possibility to retain the authority afforded to logico-paradigmatic-type arguments—rationality, efficiency, effectiveness[17]—within the rhetorical strategy, while positioning counter-narratives as mere 'stories'.

This strategy exploits the inherent *janus-face* that Francesca Polletta analyses in narratives.[18] She emphasises that the same stories may be seen as unique and special versus idiosyncratic and unrepresentative; universal and of interest to us all versus mundane and uninteresting; authentic versus deceptive and manipulative; and as an expression of potency versus an expression of powerlessness.[19] Bandes finds the reasoning of the US Supreme Court to be inconsistent in the way it allow emotions and narratives to play a role. Where emotions are endorsed they are portrayed as universal, authentic and special, where they are opposed they are portrayed as unrepresentative, distortions of reason and manipulations of justice. Her outrage flowed from several sources, including

---

[14] Ewick and Silbey (n 11); F Polletta, *It Was Like a Fever: Storytelling in Protest and Politics* (Chicago, IL, University of Chicago Press, 2006); F Polletta et al, 'The Sociology of Storytelling' (2011) 37 *Annual Review of Sociology* 109.

[15] ENV 386.

[16] J Bruner, *Actual Minds, Possible Worlds* (Cambridge, MA, Harvard University Press, 1986).

[17] As recently and rightly lampooned in David Graeber's profound critique of bureaucracy in his *The Utopia of Rules: On Technology, Stupidity and the Secret Joys of Bureaucracy* (New York, Melville House, 2015).

[18] See Pemberton Aarten and Mulder, 'Beyond Restoration' and 'Stories as Property' (n 7) and Polletta, *It Was Like a Fever* (n 14).

[19] See Polletta, *It Was Like a Fever* (n 14) 24–25.

indignation at the inconsistency of Chief Justice Rehnquist, who denounced compassion toward a civil rights plaintiff as an invalid ground for decision in *DeShaney v Winnebago County Department of Social Services*, yet invoked compassion toward crime victims in support of the Court's holding in *Payne*.[20]

B. Coincidence of Empathy and Narrative

Bandes considers empathy and narrative to be intimately connected. In her own words,

> the two strands should be more explicitly intertwined. Ordering events into a narrative is a key component of the ability to empathize with another's suffering: One [must] be able to run a narrative through one's mind about what happened to the sufferer to bring the individual to his or her current state, and what might be done to help. To empathize is to understand beginnings, middles and possible ends.[21]

A main issue that will be further elaborated below is that the coincidence of narrative and emotion can be generalised and enlarged in two ways. First, narrative is not only a key concept in the ability to empathise with another's *suffering*, but more generally to empathise with the *meaning* other persons grant to experience, situations and their lives in general.[22] The narrative mode of cognition is used in the situations where individuals try to make sense *of* and give meaning *to* the events and occurrences in their own lives.[23] Second, the unity of emotion and narrative runs deeper. Narrative relies on a dialectic relationship with expectations. The combination of expectations about the world with an event that is at odds with them functions as a main driver of the plot of a story, in which the characters attempt to cope with, resolve, integrate or overcome the unexpected event and its consequences.[24] Moreover, and relevant to the situation of victims of crime in particular, those deviations from the canonical that have moral consequences— relating to legitimacy, moral commitments and values—form the basis of stories.[25]

An event that stands out sufficiently from daily routine can also form the trigger for the type of appraisal that is characteristic of emotions.[26] This appraisal is inherently evaluative, in that it relates probable outcomes of the unexpected event to the individual's concerns.[27] In doing so it implicitly positions the event

---

[20] ENV 362.
[21] ENV 363.
[22] See J Bruner, *Acts of Meaning* (Cambridge, MA, Harvard University Press, 1990).
[23] Ibid. See also, D McAdams, *The Stories We Live By: Personal Myths and the Making of the Self* (New York, Guilford Press, 1993).
[24] See Bruner, *Actual Minds, Possible Worlds* (n 16); T Habermas and V Diel, 'The Emotional Impact of Loss Narratives: Event Severity and Narrative Perspectives' (2010) 10 *Emotion* 312.
[25] See Bruner, *Making Stories* (n 11) and Bruner, *Acts of Meaning* (n 22).
[26] See RS Lazarus, 'From Psychological Stress to the Emotions: A History of Changing Outlooks' (1993) 44 *Annual Review of Psychology* 1; K Oatley 'A Taxonomy of the Emotions of Literary Response and a Theory of Identification in Fictional Narrative' (1994) 23 *Poetics* 53.
[27] See Habermas and Diel (n 24).

in the individual's past and future selves, simultaneously redoubling the connection between emotion and narrative. Not only does this mean that narrative and emotion share the same nuclear episode, but it also underlies the characteristic of narrative as the main vessel for actively transmitting emotions, with narrative being crucial in the formation of collective emotions.[28] Understanding meaning therefore necessitates narrative, while transmitting meaning does so as well: narrative forms the bridge between both parties involved in an empathic relation.

C. The Importance of Context in the Normative Assessment of Empathy and Narrative

The main immediate conclusion made by Susan Bandes is that empathising with the victim's narrative in VIS in capital cases is morally undesirable. She expresses support for a positive presumption towards 'outsider' narratives, that is to say, narratives that dominant discourse chooses to neglect or suppress.[29] However, she argues that victims' narratives in VIS in capital cases are only superficially 'outsider' narratives; instead they reinforce what is already the dominant narrative of the trial, while endangering empathy for the even more 'outsider' narrative of the convicted offender. In the words of Bandes:

> Victim impact statements evoke not merely sympathy, pity, and compassion for the victim, but also a complex set of emotions directed toward the defendant, including hatred, fear, racial animus, vindictiveness, undifferentiated vengeance, and the desire to purge collective anger. These emotional reactions have a crucial common thread: they all deflect the jury from its duty to consider the individual defendant and his moral culpability.[30]

Given the stage of the trial in which VIS are submitted—following the guilty verdict of the offender—the offender's perspective is necessarily an 'outsider' narrative, not because his perspective is excluded, but because of the way the offender, his actions and often his other characteristics are viewed. The knowledge of the extent of his wrongdoing leads to psychological processes of increasing or maintaining a distance, of 'otherising' the offender, which places pressure on the extent to which empathic understanding is possible.[31] Again, as Bandes stated:

> More often, for the jury to empathetically connect with the defendant during the sentencing phase of a capital trial is an extremely difficult task. Not only has the defendant been convicted of a heinous crime—a fact that by itself sets him very much apart from the jury's experience—but he may be from a radically different socioeconomic milieu as well. Thus, the jury has difficulty making an empathetic connection.

---

[28] See B Rimé, 'Emotion Eicits the Social Sharing of Emotion: Theory and Empirical Review' (2009) 1 *Emotion Review* 60; K Oatley and PN Johnson-Laird, 'Basic Emotions in Social Relationships, Reasoning, and Psychological Illnesses' (2012) 3 *Emotion Review* 424.

[29] See Polletta, *It Was Like a Fever* (n 14).

[30] ENV 395.

[31] See JM Darley 'Social Organization for the Production of Evil' (1992) 3 *Psychological Inquiry* 199.

The more general point is to challenge the understanding that certain emotions are automatically benign, while similarly unsettling ideas that move too quickly from the observation of a silenced narrative to the conclusion that this narrative should be included. In both instances their value cannot be assessed outside the context. What narratives? Empathy for whom and why? Two issues merit preliminary attention in considering answers to these questions in the case of victims of crime. First, there is the variety in manners in which empathy is understood, including maintaining sufficient conceptual distinction from sympathy. Second, there is the level of abstraction upon which the concepts of empathy and narrative are deployed. I will discuss each of these issues in turn.

One very useful definition of empathy in the study of victimisation sees it as 'the attempt of one self-aware to understand the subjective experiences of another self'.[32] It involves the recognition of another world of experience, acknowledging another's reality and humanity and the awareness that the self is not exempt— at least in principle—from finding oneself in the same position.[33] However, as Bandes notes, in much of the literature empathy resembles 'something of a moving target'. In a similar vein Henderson explains that the word has several definitions, in particular: '1) feeling the emotion of another; 2) understanding the experience or situation of another, ... often by imagining oneself to be in the position of the other; [or] 3) action brought about by experiencing the distress of another'.[34]

Where empathy is focused on the victim's narrative, repeated confusion of empathy and sympathy further complicates matters.[35] Bandes notes that 'Ordering events into a narrative is a key component of the ability to empathize with another's *suffering*',[36] showing that she already understands victims' experiences in justice in a sympathetic manner. Sympathy is defined by Wispé as 'the heightened awareness of the suffering of another person as something to be alleviated'.[37] It is hard to envision sympathy without a measure of empathy: one can only reasonably be assumed to be moved by another's suffering if one can at least partially understand the other's plight. In turn, empathising with the experience of a victim will often, if not always, include increased awareness of what he or she has suffered, with the necessity of action to alleviate this suffering as a close corollary. However, this concurrence should not lead us to overlook the crucial distinction: empathy is concerned with understanding the point of view of the other, while

---

[32] See L Wispé 'The Distinction Between Sympathy and Empathy: To Call Forth a Concept, a Word is Needed' (1986) 50 *Journal of Personality and Social Psychology* 314, 318; Pemberton, 'Respecting Victims of Crime' (n 7).

[33] See MC Nussbaum, *Upheavals of Thought: The Intelligence of Emotions* (Cambridge, Cambridge University Press, 2001).

[34] ENV 373.

[35] Pemberton, 'Respecting Victims of Crime' (n 7).

[36] ENV 363 (emphasis supplied).

[37] Wispé (n 32) 318.

sympathy is concerned with increasing the wellbeing—from a negative point of departure—of the other, *irrespective* of the other's own view. Although sympathy is caused by the perception of another person's suffering, it is driven by the *distress felt by the observer*, upon viewing this suffering, rather than the perspective of the person suffering. Moreover, it predetermines the focus and direction of the victim's perspective. As Wispé notes, it is exactly the psychological process that involves the painful awareness of someone else's affliction as something that needs to be relieved. This precludes sympathising with someone's happiness, because why, except for malicious reasons would one want to terminate someone's happiness?[38]

I will return to some of the different potential upshots of this below, but for now it is sufficient to recognise that the focus of sympathy presupposes that victims' needs should be cast in a therapeutic guise, even when it relates to their position within criminal justice.

The importance of the level of abstraction in weighing the moral issues about victim involvement can be helpfully understood by a proposition put forward by John Rawls, whereby the moral argument concerning a *practice* might be of a different nature from the moral argument concerning *actions* under that practice.[39] For instance, according to Rawls punishment could be driven by retribution in individual cases (action), while the overall institution of punishment for crimes (practice) could be motivated by utilitarian calculi. Much of what Bandes finds disagreeable about VIS in capital cases involves empathising with victims within the action of sentencing. It becomes apparent however from her arguments that empathising with victims at the level of the *development of practice* is another matter. As she says: 'Quite to the contrary, though, victim impact statements may actually disempower, dehumanise, and silence victims. In short, victim impact statements offend human dignity—the victim's as well as the defendant's'.[40] In other words, involving empathy for the victim's position in arguments at the level of justifying *practice* can be deployed as an argument against VIS, even though and in fact *because* this practice involves the *action* of empathising with a victim's views.

As will be argued below, the general issue of empathising with victims' narratives cannot be settled on the particular practice of using VIS in capital cases. Rather, empathising with the victim's position in understanding and shaping practice can lead to the conclusion that other forms of victim input do not warrant the dismissal Bandes affords to VIS in her article.[41] To this end, it is necessary to understand the manner in which legal context interacts with victims' emotions and narratives. It is to this issue that we now turn.

---

[38] Ibid, 319.
[39] J Rawls, 'Two Concepts of Rules' (1955) 64 *Philosophical Review* 3.
[40] ENV 405.
[41] See also, Pemberton, 'Respecting Victims of Crime' (n 7).

D. The Particular Impact of Legal Context on
Emotions and Narratives

A final important issue raised by Bandes is the understanding that the legal arena is a particular context for emotions and narratives. In this connection she notes the distinction between the legal and therapeutic contexts. The therapist has considerable leeway in following the shape and form of the narrative of those who seek help, does not have to analyse their narratives in terms of veracity, and will view the narrative primarily in terms of its contribution to certain psychological outcomes. But the legal context can only allow narratives that follow a particular format, has to scrutinise them for their evidentiary value and cannot prioritise the emotional impact of the process, although it pays to refrain from being completely oblivious to 'therapeutic' impacts.[42]

Moreover, as Bandes amply demonstrates, the law has its own narrative with which participants will have to engage.[43] Certainly, this also applies to the therapeutic context, as the debates around False Memory Syndrome and the proposals of the positive psychology movement amply demonstrate.[44] Nevertheless, therapy's narrative context is considerably less explicit and dominant than that associated with the law. Legal narratives and the emotions that they prioritise can also vary from one context to the next. Reading Bandes' characterisation of the dominant narrative in capital cases in the American criminal law system from the vantage point of Dutch legal practice makes this point abundantly clear. Not only the practice of capital punishment, but also other structural features of the American criminal justice system—such as the draconian sentences, the widespread involvement of laypeople, the politicised nature of the process, including elected magistrates, the adversarial character of the process, the use of victim impact evidence after the guilty verdict—influence the dominant narrative of the criminal process at this point.[45] In any case it is hard to imagine making the same argument concerning Dutch criminal proceedings, with its inquisitorial process, and highly professionalised and appointed magistrates, whose years of legal training have instilled a deep dislike for anything related to vengeance and a natural tendency to

---

[42] In Pemberton and Reynaers (n 2), we referred to adequate understanding of therapeutic constructs in legal proceedings as *therapeutic coherence*.

[43] See Ewick and Silbey (n 11); and Bruner, *Making Stories* (n 11).

[44] For instance, Elizabeth Loftus' work on false memory syndrome, which concerns the way in which therapists succeeded in imposing a particular narrative of childhood trauma on the ambiguous memories of their clients: see E Loftus, 'The Reality of Repressed Memories' (1993) 48 *American Psychologist* 518. In the same way, the presidential address to the American Psychological Association of Martin Seligman in 1999, was a rallying cry against the negative slant in the framing of psychological experience in general, and of therapeutic narratives in particular: MEP Seligman (1999) 54 *American Psychologist* 552.

[45] See for instance, D Garland, The Culture of Control: Crime and Social Order in Contemporary Society (Oxford, Oxford University Press, 2001); and J Simon, Governing Through Crime: How the War on Crime Transformed American Democracy and Created a Culture of Fear (Oxford, Oxford University Press, 2007), both on the developments in the past decades in American criminal justice.

counteract populist pleas for ever increasing sentences.[46] The normative questions concerning emotion and narrative in the legal sphere therefore need to factor in the context in which they are deployed.

These specific features of the legal context interact with the narratives spoken and the emotions expressed, even beyond the extent of conformity with the dominant, hegemonic narratives. To a certain extent narratives are always socially constructed, while the experience of emotions cannot be fully grasped without reference to their social and cultural environment, but the legal context brings this social construction into sharp relief.[47] In this particular sense there is not a single victim narrative possible in a given situation, but a variety of narratives that are in part framed by the legal context in which they are elicited.

This is also part of the reason why drawing a direct analogy of the therapeutic setting to the legal process is mistaken. It overlooks the obvious fact that victims involved in the act of narrating are also aware of the place in which they tell their stories, as well as the function of the process in which they are offering their account, and will adjust their narrative accordingly.[48] This would already be true if the only difference was the public nature of the legal process, compared with the private and confidential nature of the therapist's consultation room, but it is further enhanced by the particular *meaning* of the justice process, including the extent to which the justice process and its actors form important representations of some of the most important norms and values that members of a community, including the victims, hold dear.[49] Where the criminal justice process does not act, in full or in part, this also conveys meaning; the importance of access to justice, or rather the lack of it, is particularly pronounced in the experience of victims of crime.[50] One upshot of this, as I will discuss below, is that it is not accurate to conceive of the criminal justice process as a reaction to a victimisation experience in the past; instead it is better understood as a part of the still unfolding narrative of the victimisation experience itself.

---

[46] See for instance, R Kool and M Moerings, 'The Victim Has the Floor' (2004) 12 *European Journal of Crime, Criminal Law and Criminal Justice* 46 on the reception of VIS in the Netherlands by the legal profession, which can be characterised as somewhere between lukewarm and overtly hostile.

[47] For the social construction of narratives see J Best, *Social Problems* (London, WW Norton & Company, 2008).

[48] I have been repeating this theme for a number of years now—see for instance, Pemberton and Reynaers (n 2); Pemberton, 'Respecting Victims of Crime' (n 7); A Pemberton and RM Letschert, 'Justice as the Art of Muddling Through: The Importance of Nyaya in the Aftermath of International Crimes' in C Brants and S Karstedt (eds), *Engagement, Legitimacy, Contestation: Transitional Justice and its Public Spheres* (Oxford, Hart Publishing, 2015).

[49] The norms transgressed by crime are those by which the 'political community defines itself as a law-governed polity': see RA Duff, *Punishment, Communication and Community* (Oxford, Oxford University Press, 2001).

[50] Ibid. See also, MS Laxminarayan, *The Heterogeneity of Crime Victims: Variations in Procedural and Outcome Preferences* (Nijmegen, Wolf Legal Publishers, 2012); MS Laxminarayan, J Henrichs and A Pemberton, 'Procedural and Interactional Justice: A Comparative Study of Victims in the Netherlands and New South Wales' (2012) 9 *European Journal of Criminology* 260; MS Laxminarayan and A Pemberton, 'The Interaction of Criminal Procedure and Outcome' (2014) 37 *International Journal of Law and Psychiatry* 564.

III. Empathy for the Victim's Narrative

A. Understanding the Narrative Nature of the Experience of Victimisation

Recently my colleagues and I argued the importance of narrative in the experience of victimisation.[51] We did this drawing on insights from personality psychology concerning cognition, identity and motivation. As noted above, the psychologist Jerome Bruner distinguished two main ways in which people attempt to understand the world around them: the *logico-paradigmatic* mode and the *narrative* mode. The former employs categorisation, abstraction, rationality and logical deduction, while its language does not admit contradiction and requires consistency. The latter, by contrast, deals in human or human-like intention and action and concerns the particular, the emotional and the idiosyncratic. Instead of viewing causality in abstracted and universal causes, it locates them in the actors' purposes in a storied manner and in a given situation: abstraction would make it harder rather than easier to understand the unfolding events. The driver of a story is most often the extraordinary or at least the unexpected. As literary theorist Kenneth Burke's analysis of the dramatic Pentad suggests, narratives deal with the situations where the actions driven by an agents' intentions do *not*—at least at first—succeed in reaching the intended goal.[52] Burke described the Pentad as an Agent who performs an Action to achieve a Goal in a recognisable Setting by the use of certain Means. A mismatch between two of these elements (Trouble), lies at the heart of narrative. Without this element of Trouble, a report rather than a narrative of events will do. Victimisation by crime and other forms of severe wrongdoing is a key example of this Trouble. As Burke himself summarised: 'If action, then drama; if drama, then conflict; if conflict, then victimage'. This is all the more so due to the essentially moral nature of the experience of victimisation. Theodore Sarbin's 'narratory principle', 'that human beings think, perceive, imagine, and make moral choices according to narrative structures' further summarises this connection.[53]

Narrative not only applies to particular instances in people's lives, but also to their lives as a whole. A main issue is the function of life narratives in the construction and maintenance of identity and personality. This perspective can be helpfully understood in personality psychologist Dan McAdams' theory of the threefold psychological self: the self as social actor, motivated agent and autobiographical

---

[51] See Pemberton, Aarten and Mulder, 'Beyond Restoration' and 'Stories as Property' (n 7); A Pemberton, *Victimology with a Hammer: The Challenge of Victimology*, inaugural lecture, Tilburg University (Tilburg, Prismaprint, 2015).

[52] K Burke, *A Grammar of Motives* (New York, Prentice Hall, 1945).

[53] TR Sarbin, 'The Narrative as a Root Metaphor for Psychology' in TR Sarbin (ed), *Narrative Psychology: The Storied Nature of Human Conduct* (New York, Praeger, 1986).

author.[54] The latter emerges in late adolescence and early adulthood, and refers to the self as storyteller, who ultimately aims to synthesise episodic information about the self into a coherent life story. The task of this autobiographical author is to maintain a sense of self-continuity. The self of today is the self of yesterday and the self of tomorrow. In addition it offers the means to maintain a sense of coherence with the wider cultural narrative of the group to which the individual belongs.[55] The connection between narrative identity and a person's culture is twofold: culture supplies the narrative scripts that individuals use to frame their own life story, while it is the means by which individuals embed their own experience within wider society. Within a life story certain 'nuclear episodes', autobiographical episodes of a particular and enduring relevance, play a key structuring role.[56] Negative life events, more so than positive ones, require narrative attention in one's life story; they demand an explanation, including the causes, the consequences and the meaning for the self and its relationship with others.[57] Severe forms of victimisation are clear examples of these nadir experiences. Beyond the negative impact on a victim's self-esteem and sense of self-control, they pose a particular narrative challenge, which can be summarised as a shattering of bedrock assumptions about continuity in their own lives and with the wider cultural narrative surrounding them.[58] As we have explained elsewhere:

> The narrative rupture in severe trauma not only concerns the continuity in one's life history, both backward—how to maintain a sense of continuity and connection with the past—and forward—including the sense of foreshortening or unpredictability about one's future—, it also endangers the implicit sense of connection and belonging with others.[59]

The shattering of assumptions in terms of victims' life stories can also be conceptualised in terms of the threat victimisation poses to both of what David Bakan has termed 'the fundamental modalities of human existence', namely *agency* and *communion*.[60] Where the former is apparent in the threat victimisation poses to

---

[54] McAdams, *The Stories We Live By* (n 23); DP McAdams, 'The Psychological Self as Actor, Agent and Author' (2013) 8 *Perspectives on Psychological Science* 272.

[55] E Erikson, *Identity and the Life Cycle* (New York, WW Norton & Company, 1959); DP McAdams and JL Pals, 'A New Big Five: Fundamental Principles for an Integrative Science of Personality' (2006) 61 *American Psychologist* 204; PL Hammack and A Pilecki, 'Narrative as a Root Metaphor from Political Psychology' (2012) 33 *Political Psychology* 75.

[56] See McAdams, *The Stories We Live By* (n 23).

[57] M Crossley, 'Narrative Psychology, Trauma and the Study of Self-Identity' (2000) 10 *Theory & Psychology* 527.

[58] R Janoff Bulman, Shattered Assumptions: Towards a New Psychology of Trauma (New York, Free Press, 1992).

[59] Pemberton, Aarten and Mulder, 'Beyond Restoration' and 'Stories as Property' (n 7).

[60] D Bakan, *The Duality of Human Existence: Isolation and Communion in Western Man* (Boston, MA, Beacon Press, 1966). More recently they have been re-christened as the 'Big Two' of human motivation: see AE Abele and B Wojciszke, 'Agency and Communion from the Perspective of Self Versus Others' (2007) 93 *Journal of Personality and Social Psychology* 751. This so-called Big Two of human motivation also doubles as the two main meta-themes in life narratives: see for instance, DP McAdams et al, 'Themes of Agency and Communion in Significant Autobiographical Scenes' (1996) 64 *Journal of Personality* 339.

a victim's sense of control, esteem and respect[61] the latter is often neglected.[62] However, the threat to communion is of at least equal importance. Any existing or symbolic relationship with the offender is damaged, but the impact on communion can also concern more symbolic matters of unity and togetherness, love and friendship. As Neil Vidmar explains, 'an offence is a threat to community consensus about the correctness—that is the moral nature—of a rule and hence the values that bind social groups together'.[63] The significance of this is that the trauma of victimisation cannot be fully understood through the metaphor of something that is broken or in need of repair. This medicalised model neglects the dynamic quality of victimisation in which the autobiographical narrative will have to absorb or adapt to the victimisation experience.[64] In this respect the victim's self has changed, irrespective of any enduring impact on the victim's psycho-social functioning.

The narrative connection between past, present and future is reflexive. New information about the past can lead to reinterpretation of the present, while the past is open to review in the light of experiences in the present. This reflexive nature is particularly true of victimisation narratives, as the experimental research by social psychologist Roy Baumeister and his colleagues demonstrates,[65] and has been described by Stephen Pinker in terms of the 'moralization gap'.[66] The 'moralization gap' refers to the differences in moral tone, impact, importance of context factors and time frame between the narratives of victims and of perpetrators. The latter tend to offer justifications for what happened, attribute the event to outside causes, minimise the impact on the victim and see the event as a moment in time. Victims, in contrast, emphasise the moral nature of the experience and its injustice, even to the extent of seeing intentions and malevolence where there is none; they may locate the cause in the person of the offender and his intentions, and will often highlight the impact of the offence, while stretching its time frame both forwards and backwards in time.

The first important upshot of this is that victim experience maintains a strong perceptual link between the past, present and future. Severing the link with the past entails a process involving a conscious decision of forgiveness, which as Trudy

---

[61] N Shnabel and A Nadler, 'A Needs-Based Model of Reconciliation: Satisfying the Differential Emotional Needs of Victim and Perpetrator as a Key to Promoting Reconciliation' (2008) 94 *Journal of Personality and Social Psychology* 116; I Simantov-Nachlieli, N Shnabel and A Nadler, 'Individuals' and Groups' Motivation to Restore Their Impaired Identity Dimensions Following Conflict: Evidence and Implications' (2013) 44 *Social Psychology* 129; M Wenzel et al, 'Retributive and Restorative Justice' (2008) 32 *Law and Human Behavior* 375.

[62] See Pemberton Aarten and Mulder, 'Beyond Restoration' and 'Stories as Property' (n 7).

[63] N Vidmar, 'Retribution and Revenge' in J Sanders and VL Hamilton (eds), *Handbook of Justice Research in Law* (New York, Plenum Press, 2000).

[64] See also, LC Hyden, 'Illness and Narrative' (1997) 19 *Sociology of Health & Illness* 48.

[65] RF Baumeister, *Evil: Inside Human Violence and Cruelty* (New York, Henry Holt & Company, 1997).

[66] S Pinker, *The Better Angels of Our Nature: The Decline of Violence in History and its Causes* (London, Allen Lane, 2011).

Govier has emphasised means that 'The past shall not be forgotten, but it will be the past'.[67] The second is that the victim's views on the sentence of the offender will be predictably biased and therefore should not be seen as an independent source of evidence to determine that sentence. The victim may have a unique and relevant perspective to offer on the harm suffered, but cannot lay claim to a similar perspective on the sentence the offender should undergo.[68]

B. Narratives of Victimisation and Criminal Justice

The extended time frame of victimisation narratives—which in the case of a collective trauma can literally span millennia[69]—also means that the aftermath of the victimisation experience, including the criminal justice reaction, is often better understood as *part* of the victim's narrative, rather than something that merely follows it. In this way, the victim's experience within the criminal justice process offers ample opportunity for reinterpretation of the victimisation event itself. This is particularly clear in the cases in which the end result of a case is an acquittal, particularly if the victim witnessed the commission of the crime. This has been well documented in intimate partner violence and rape cases.[70] Acquittal is particularly painful in these cases, as it calls into question whether what happened to the victim was actually a crime at all.[71] More generally, the outcome of the trial influences the experience due to what it signals to and about the victim. In this connection, Kenworthy Bilz argues that criminal punishment is essentially a referendum on the social standing and worth of the victim. A successful punishment indicates that the community values the victim. A failure to punish indicates something less—perhaps indifference towards the victim, perhaps even disdain.[72] The question posed by crime's transgression of the worth or even existence of these shared values is answered affirmatively in the former case, negatively in the latter. In narrative terms the tragedy of victimisation can transform into the plot

[67] T Govier, 'Public Forgiveness: A Modest Defense' in B Van Stokkom, N Doorn and P Van Tongeren (eds), *Public Forgiveness in Post-Conflict Contexts* (Antwerp, Intersentia, 2012) 26. I have noted elsewhere that 'forgiveness as a counterpoint to victimisation also relates to the way it changes the temporal perspective on an event. More precisely, it entails situating wrongdoing in the past', and that 'forgiveness means that wrongdoing will not steer our course in the present, nor does it have moral implications for the future. Full forgiveness implies that the victim of an act, "wipes the slate clean"': A Pemberton, 'Terrorism, Forgiveness, Restorative Justice' (2014) 4 *Onati Socio-Legal Series* 369. See also, L Allais, 'Wiping the Slate Clean: The Heart of Forgiveness' (2008) 36 *Philosophy & Public Affairs* 33. In this sense it serves as an end point to the narrative of victimisation. The only way in which the victimisation experience can resume to have purchase on the present, is by the wrongful deed being unforgiven anew.

[68] Pemberton, 'Respecting Victims of Crime' (n 7).

[69] V Volkan, *Bloodlines: From Ethnic Pride to Ethnic Terrorism* (New York, Farrar and Strauss, 1997).

[70] See for instance, PA Frazier and B Haney, 'Sexual Assault Cases in the Legal System: Police, Prosecutor and Victim Perspectives' (1996) 20 *Law and Human Behavior* 607.

[71] SF Colb, '"Whodunit" Versus "What Was Done": When to Admit Character Evidence in Criminal Trials' (2001) 79 *North Carolina Law Review* 939.

[72] JK Bilz, 'The Puzzle of Delegated Revenge' (2007) 87 *Boston University Law Review* 1059, 1108.

of 'overcoming the monster' in the former case, or the irony of the meaningless of the victim's circumstances in the latter.[73]

Having said this, interpreting the impact of the criminal justice process on the experience of victims solely as a function of retribution asserts a too narrow frame on a victim's justice experience. In this connection, we argue that the framework of agency and communion can illuminate this issue. Victimisation by crime threatens the victim's agency and sense of communion, which in turn produces a mirror image of motivations to rebuild them. This rebuilding of agency and communion is largely an exercise in sense- and meaning-making, and therefore a necessarily narrative endeavour. Narrating the experience serves to understand the events, for instance the offender's intentions, the victims' own reactions and subsequent experience.[74]

Retributive justice or a desire to commit acts of revenge can be part of this rebuilding of agency, but are not the only avenues to do so. Reasserting the victim's agency and status can also proceed without any involvement of the offender. Elements of restorative justice,[75] particularly concerning value restoration—that is to say, reaffirming the consensus about the moral nature of the rule transgressed by the crime[76]—can also be conceptualised as communion. In a more general sense, the damage to a victim's sense of communion triggers the motivation to reconnect, to re-establish a sense of unity and togetherness, in line with the repeated finding that the experience of social support and acknowledgement are among the main factors that help victims cope.[77]

An important issue is that in some cases behaviour may be guided by motives that are obviously agency or communion related, but that in others this distinction is often more subtle. In the same way behaviour may also be guided by a mix of agency and communion depending on the meaning a person gives to this behaviour. Given the fact that the same behaviour might result from very different motives, Horowitz and others argue that 'the goal-directed act itself may be unclear. Only when we can locate the behavior in the person's hierarchy of motives do we understand its meaning'.[78] Instead of attempting to locate behaviour in a hierarchy of motives, it is often assumed or asserted to be agency-driven. The rational actor of economics is a particularly clear and egregious example,[79]

---

[73] For an analysis of plotlines, see C Booker, *The Seven Basic Plots: Why We Tell Stories* (New York, Continuum, 2004). For the application to the situation of victims of crime, see Pemberton, Aarten and Mulder, 'Beyond Restoration' and 'Stories as Property' (n 7).

[74] See Bruner, *Acts of Meaning* (n 22).

[75] See generally, G Johnstone, *Restorative Justice: Ideas, Values, Debates* (Cullompton, Devon, Willan Publishing, 2002).

[76] See Wenzel et al (n 61).

[77] CR Brewin, B Andrews and JD Valentine, 'Meta-Analysis of Risk Factors for Posttraumatic Stress Disorder' (2000) 68 *Journal of Consulting and Clinical Psychology* 748.

[78] LM Horowitz et al, 'How Interpersonal Motives Clarify the Meaning of Interpersonal Behavior: A Revised Circumplex Model' (2006) 10 *Personality and Social Psychology Review* 67.

[79] K Polanyi, *The Great Transformation: The Political and Economic Origins of Our Time* (Boston, Beacon Press, 1948/2001).

but Bernard Rimé's discussion of the inability to understand the social sharing of emotions between adults as a means to connect with others rather than achieving some self-focused goal or other reveals that the 'fallacy of the solely agentic human', to coin a phrase, is a much more widespread phenomenon.[80]

Understanding the focus of victims on criminal justice as solely agency based frames both academic debate and official narratives concerning the purpose of their participation. The fact that most research indicates that victim input does not impact sentences[81] might have given sighs of relief to those who deemed such influence unwarranted anyway, but also repeatedly ignites debate about the point of victim participation: 'victim impact statements don't work, can't work', as one contribution concluded.[82] In similar vein, more recent research has reconceived victim participation as a means to achieve personal emotional benefit, with the expression of emotions leading to reduction of fear, anger, stress symptoms and even to closure or healing.[83] Indeed, the Dutch VIS programme explicitly mentions such emotional consequences—'a beginning of emotional repair'—as its primary victim-oriented goal.[84]

The issue here is not so much that the empirical evidence for these agency-oriented goals is very thin,[85] but instead that communion-based motivations are neglected. Nevertheless, there is already good reason to view victims' desire to participate in criminal justice processes as largely if not predominantly communion-driven, with the results from research into victims' experience in restorative justice programmes and VIS emphasising the importance of 'expressive or communicative motives'[86] and 'other-oriented motives', which are both communion-oriented in nature.[87] Indeed José Mulder's recent research on the experience of victims with criminal injuries compensation reveals that even with monetary outcomes, the main issue is the symbolic expression of belonging and acknowledgement that accompanies it, rather than monetary gain per se.[88]

---

[80] The way Rimé juxtaposes the wealth of research into communion concepts (for instance attachment) in children and young adolescents, with its dearth in similar research into adults is highly illuminating. It gives rise to the misunderstanding that adults emote solely to achieve catharsis from emotions, and/or to influence the people with whom they are communicating: see Rimé (n 28).

[81] See E Erez, 'Who's Afraid of the Big Bad Victim? Victim Impact Statements as Victim Empowerment and Enhancement of Justice' [1999] *Criminal Law Review* 545; JV Roberts 'Listening to the Crime Victim: Evaluating Victim Input at Sentencing and Parole' (2009) 38 *Crime and Justice: A Review of Research* 347.

[82] A Sanders et al, 'Victim Impact Statements: Don't Work, Can't Work' [2001] *Criminal Law Review* 447.

[83] KME Lens et al, 'Delivering a Victim Impact Statement: Emotionally Effective or Counterproductive?' (2015) 12 *European Journal of Criminology* 17.

[84] KME Lens, A Pemberton and S Bogaerts, 'Heterogeneity in Victim Participation: A New Perspective on Delivering a Victim Impact Statement' (2013) 10 *European Journal of Criminology* 479.

[85] Lens et al, 'Delivering a Victim Impact Statement' (n 83).

[86] Roberts (n 81); Lens et al, 'Delivering a Victim Impact Statement' (n 83); JV Roberts and E Erez 'Communication in Sentencing: Exploring the Expressive Function of Victim Impact Statements' (2004) 10 *International Review of Victimology* 223.

[87] D Bolivar, 'For Whom is Restorative Justice?' (2013) 1 *Restorative Justice* 190.

[88] JDWE Mulder, *Compensation: The Victims' Perspective* (Nijmegen, Wolf Publishing, 2013).

One communion-based element that is often conspicuously absent is understanding the potential difference in the meaning of seemingly identical outcomes, depending on participation. This has of course been repeatedly highlighted by research on procedural justice.[89] More to the point here, the work of Mario Gollwitzer and others shows that what is important in revenge and vengeance is not the degree of suffering of the offender, but instead the extent to which the message contained in the hard treatment and censure of the offender is connected to the harm previously visited on the victim.[90] There is a large chasm in meaning between 'the offender received a fair sentence for the crime' and 'the offender received a fair sentence for the crime he committed *against me*'.[91] Understanding the outcome of the process in the latter sense is contingent on the sense of connection felt by the victim towards the process. Excluding victim narratives from the process is a clear challenge to this sense of connection. Here the notion of narrative entitlement is important.[92] It concerns the narrative privilege normally afforded to people with first-hand knowledge of events.[93] This sense of entitlement is brought into sharp relief due to the narrative challenges posed by victimisation; maintaining a sense of coherence depends upon the construction of a 'successful' story.[94] Denying this narrative entitlement in a justice process disconnects victim experience from the process, while simultaneously sending a negative message concerning the value society affords the victim, thereby diminishing the victim's sense of agency.

C. Narrative and Emotional Issues in Framing Victim Participation

Elsewhere my colleagues and I have discussed some of the main points in this section at greater length, calling for *narrative ownership* as the main prism to understand victims' issues in justice processes.[95] We have argued that different social-psychological and sociological phenomena, as well as institutional processes, place predictable pressure on the victims' attempts to develop a coherent narrative of their experience. The same phenomena are also helpful in understanding the framing of victim participation, which can in turn have the much

---

[89] T Tyler, 'Procedural Justice, Legitimacy and the Effective Rule of Law' (2003) 30 *Crime and Justice: A Review of Research* 283.

[90] M Gollwitzer, 'Justice and Revenge' in ME Oswald, S Bieneck and J Hupfeld-Heinemann (eds), *Social Psychology of Punishment of Crime* (Hoboken, Wiley, 2009); M Gollwitzer, M Meder and M Schmitt, 'What Gives Victims Satisfaction When They Seek Revenge?' (2011) 41 *European Journal of Social Psychology* 364.

[91] Bilz (n 72).

[92] E Ochs and L Capps, 'Narrating the Self' (1996) 25 *Annual Review of Anthropology* 19.

[93] Ibid.

[94] See more extensively, Pemberton, Aarten and Mulder, 'Beyond Restoration' and 'Stories as Property' (n 7).

[95] Ibid.

maligned consequence of using victims for ends which are not in their interest: that is to say, victimological in name only.

The latter point is hardly new. In the 1980s Robert Elias argued that the way 'law and order' campaigns deploy victims' interests can be tantamount to political manipulation.[96] In the same way, Stuart Scheingold and others viewed with much concern the use of individual anecdotes of a small number of high-profile victims as a means to frame crime problems, and to suggest how the criminal justice system should respond in a far wider range of situations.[97] More generally, political campaigns involving victim policy can often use stereotypical depictions in the way they frame issues[98] This also applies to social movements, for instance victim support or proponents of restorative justice whose frame has considerably more empirical support.[99]

Beyond the lack of connection between the stereotypical narrative and the actual experience of large groups of individual victims, the frame can readily transform from a shorthand depiction of social reality to a normative demand, in which acknowledgement and recognition are dependent on the extent to which victims live up to the demands of the stereotype.[100] The notion of *following the plot* is a particular element of this.[101] Francesca Polletta's analysis of the relationship between the narrative structure of victims' accounts and the extent to which they are supported or believed demonstrates the limited leeway victims have in straying from the story affixed to their experience. An example is the use of the frame of the 'battered women' of the 1980s in the struggle to gain sufficient attention for the phenomenon of intimate partner violence. Here the main narrative adopted cast the victims in terms of a mental health problem—that of 'battered women syndrome'—which enabled victims to accrue benefits in terms of help and compensation in the criminal justice system, as well as reduction of any culpability for retaliatory violence towards their erstwhile tormentor, but also reduced the

---

[96] R Elias, *Victims Still. The Political Manipulation of Crime Victims* (London, Sage Publications Ltd, 1993).

[97] S Scheingold, T Olson and J Pershing, 'Sexual Violence, Victim Advocacy and Republican Criminology: Washington's Community Protection Act' (1994) 28 *Law & Society Review* 729.

[98] See Joel Best's excellent analysis in his book: J Best, *Random Violence: The Way We Talk About New Crimes and New Victims* (Berkeley, CA, University of California Press, 1999). I should add that this is not peculiar to victimisation issues or even to crime policy more generally, as the literature on the phenomenon of framing illustrates. The importance of painting a straightforward causal and moral picture is also observed elsewhere within social movements and political agenda setting: see RD Benford and DA Snow, 'Framing Process and Social Movements: An Overview and Assessment' (2000) 26 *Annual Review of Sociology* 611; R Entman 'Framing Bias: Media Distribution in the Distribution of Power' (2007) 571 *Journal of Communication* 163.

[99] See A Pemberton 'Victim Movements: From Diversified Need to Varying Criminal Justice Agendas' (2009) 22 *Acta Criminologica* 1.

[100] Pemberton, 'Respecting Victims of Crime' (n 7).

[101] Polletta, *It Was Like a Fever* (n 14); F Polletta, 'How To Tell a New Story About Battering' (2009) 15 *Violence Against Women* 1490; F Polletta et al, 'The Limits of Plot: Accounting For How Women Interpret Stories of Sexual Assault' (2013) 1 *American Journal of Cultural Sociology* 289.

extent to which they would be taken seriously or understood as reasonable. As Polletta explains:

> So the woman who has killed her abuser faces two equally unacceptable options. She can assert her agency, telling a story of her actions in which she appears and in control of herself. But then she might not be seen as victimised at all. Or, she can emphasize her victimisation. But then her actions may be seen as unreasonable. They are to be excused through an act of judicial solicitude rather than justified by her experience of abuse.[102]

In the latter case any benefits of being a victim come at the cost of being substantially disempowered, in the sense of being seen as weak and vulnerable, feeble and passive. Rather than the subject of empathic respect, the victim becomes the object of sympathy. In the former case she might not be seen as feeble or weak, but it is likely she will be blamed for her actions, and seen as an offender rather than as a victim. Polletta's analysis reveals how difficult it is to switch roles midstream: the victim is expected to stick to the narrative throughout the procedure on pains of suspension of belief and credibility. This applies not only to the victim's story, but also to the victim's display of emotions.[103]

This duality of sympathy and blame can also be understood through the lens of what has been called the 'justice motive'.[104] The basic tenet of this is that people have an innate need to believe that the world is just: good things happen to good people and bad things happen to bad people. The occurrence of an event that conflicts with this need (something bad happening to a good person, or vice versa) leads to justice-related distress, which in turn elicits cognitive, affective and/or behavioural reactions on the part of observers of this event. The justice motive can lead to helpful behavioural responses to injustice and misfortune, such as compensation, reparation and support, but also to negative reactions to those suffering from the consequences, like distancing, re-evaluation of the outcome, negative re-evaluation of appearance and character, and blaming. The narrative consequences of the negative reaction are clear.[105] Victim blaming for instance remakes the victim from the positive protagonist, to someone who, if not villainous himself or herself is at least sufficiently reckless to warrant moral censure. Positive re-evaluation of the outcome transforms the damaging experience into a difficult, but ultimately worthwhile, opportunity to learn and grow.

However, even in the more positive sympathetic reactions, the main driver of action—the desire of the observer to relieve the distress of the victim—can have negative narrative consequences. In particular, it recasts the victim into a supporting role, becoming the subject in the observer's endeavour to alleviate his or

---

[102] Polletta, *It Was Like a Fever* (n 14) 134.

[103] KME Lens et al, 'You Shouldn't Feel That Way!: Extending the Emotional Victim Effect Through the Mediating Role of Expectancy Violation' (2014) 20 *Psychology, Crime & Law* 326.

[104] See M Lerner, *The Belief in a Just World: A Fundamental Delusion* (New York, Plenum Press, 1980); C Hafer and L Begue, 'Experimental Research on Just-World Theory: Problems, Developments and Future Challenges' (2005) 131 *Psychological Bulletin* 128.

[105] Ibid.

her suffering.[106] In the unfolding of this tale the contribution of the victim to the story lies in the extent to which this suffering can be alleviated. Jan van Dijk coined the phrase 'secondary victim blaming' to describe the phenomenon of negative reactions to victims who opt for a more active position and/or do not care to be defined solely in terms of suffering.[107] Sympathy is contingent on the victim playing the role defined by the observer. As van Dijk himself observes, angry and active victims do not fit this mould.

This sympathetic stance also lays a claim on the expectations of how the narrative of justice can or should unfold. In particular, the widespread use of the term 'closure' is revealing in this respect.[108] The final verdict in the trial is often supposed to be an end point in the victim's narrative, who subsequently is enabled to 'move on' with his or her life. Although victims may indeed experience some benefit from this, the view that this could amount to 'closure' in this sense has neither empirical nor theoretical foundation. What makes this issue even more poignant is that the expectancy of closure becomes stronger the more severe the crime is, even though the crime's severity will make closure less likely to emerge.[109] Instead of closure and moving on, the reality of the outcome of the trial is better understood as making the best of an extremely bad situation. Not only is closure too much to expect, but this is also true for more than a modicum of justice.[110] The term 'closure' is better viewed as a projection of what third parties want than of a realistic prospect for victims. As Rianne Letschert and I have argued elsewhere:

> Part of the reason that our reaction to crime remains so heavily focused upon (punishing) the offender, rather than 'restoring' the victim, is that the former can be more readily conceived in terms amenable to the justice motive than the latter. Our distress at the murder is easily reconciled with the outrage at the murderer; not so much with sympathy for the victim's family. Our need for closure in respect to this distress might be quenched by the cathartic act of sentencing the murderer and his subsequent removal to prison; it is instead contradicted by viewing the enduring pain and the often life-long recovery process of the victim's family.[111]

---

[106] Pemberton, 'Respecting Victims of Crime' (n 7).

[107] Whereas 'primary' victim blaming is rooted in the victimisation itself, 'secondary' victim blaming concerns a negative reaction to the victim's reaction following victimisation: see van Dijk (n 5).

[108] Pemberton and Reynaers (n 2). See also, SA Bandes, 'Victims, "Closure", and the Sociology of Emotion' (2009) 72 *Law and Contemporary Problems* 1.

[109] In this connection Harvey Weinstein devoted his final editorial of the *International Journal of Transitional Justice* to the misuse of 'closure' in transitional justice processes following large-scale political conflict, including crimes against humanity and genocide: HM Weinstein, 'Editorial: The Myth of Closure: The Illusion of Reconciliation. Final Thoughts on Five Years as Co-Editor in Chief' (2011) 5 *International Journal of Transitional Justice* 1.

[110] As Rianne Letschert and I have noted, 'fully acknowledging the victimological reality of the aftermath of severe crime rapidly brings to the surface the difficulty of conceiving what might plausibly be viewed as justice. Hannah Arendt noted that the reality of the Holocaust "explodes the limits of the law", a highly accurate description. However, the limits of the law—but also other institutions of justice—are breached at less extreme levels of injustice as well. One of the key problems with the notion of restorative justice is precisely that where the need for restoration is the greatest, the impossibility of actually doing so is most keenly felt': Pemberton and Letschert (n 48).

[111] Pemberton and Letschert (n 48).

There are therefore two reasons why victims' narratives should be seen as the type of 'outsider' narratives that Bandes finds meriting inclusion in the legal process. One is that they offer a clear insight into the limits of justice in countering wrong-doing. Excluding the victims from view reinforces the need to believe that justice can always be done. The neat fit between sentencing the offender and the resolu-tion of third parties' distress at injustice can give rise to the misunderstanding that everything is essentially 'back to normal'. In an insightful analysis of the way media portrays crime, sociologist Jack Katz described this as the 'moral workout'.[112] The way newspaper readers process, and the way media ends up portraying severe cases of crime, entails focusing our emotional energy on confirming the rightness of our existing view of the world. The victims, even as heroes and angels, figure in a scripted role play that ends up confirming that our existing point of view was morally right. The anguish is neutralised, the crime or victimisation is objectified and society moves on. This however is not an avenue that is open to the victims themselves, for whom the moment that society does move on is often one of great distress.[113]

Beyond the general tension between society's need for closure and the victim's enduring narrative, many individual victims' stories can also be viewed as 'outsider' narratives due to their lack of conformity to that which is imposed on their experi-ence. As Bandes has rightly understood, left to itself the hegemonic narrative of criminal law is not likely to offer much leeway; where it allows victims input in the process it will seek to do so in a manner in keeping with this hegemonic narrative. That the narrative in VIS in capital cases is a particularly unappealing instance makes this poignantly clear. Other criminal legal contexts will be more critical of vengeance; indeed the angry, vengeful victim is most often the one whose contri-bution is viewed with concern.[114] The more general denominator is however that victims whose reality does not follow the plot laid out for them by the hegemonic narrative will suffer negative consequences.

IV. Conclusion

Susan Bandes' insights concerning victims within criminal justice processes, including her emphasis on the importance of empathy and narrative in doing so,

[112] See J Katz, 'What Makes Crime News?' (1987) 9 *Media, Culture & Society* 144: 'Crime is in today's newspaper, not because it contradicts the beliefs readers had yesterday, but because readers seek oppor-tunities to shape up moral attitudes they will have to use today. Like vitamins useful in a body only for a day, like physical exercise whose value comes from its recurrent practice, crime news is experienced as interesting by its readers because of its place in a daily moral routine'.
[113] M Peelo, 'Framing Homicide Narratives in Newspapers: Mediated Witness and the Construction of Virtual Victimhood' (2006) 2 *Crime, Media, Culture* 159.
[114] See van Dijk (n 5).

are fundamental in gaining a clearer understanding of the main issues in offering victim input in criminal justice. In a variation on her original ideas, I have sought to clarify that empathising with victims' experience means understanding its essentially narrative nature, and that any discussion of the appropriate place for victims' emotions in the practice of law needs to incorporate this fact. Victimisation poses a challenge to a victim's sense of continuity, forwards and backwards in time, but also in conjuncture with his or her surroundings. As people maintain this sense of continuity through life narratives, rebuilding the story of their lives in a way which accommodates or assimilates their experience is of vital importance. A key issue is that victimisation poses a threat to both agency and communion; the mirror image of this is to seek to rebuild both agency and communion in the way victims use narrative in an attempt to come to terms with their experience.

What I have argued is that we have been too keen to interpret the victim's involvement in criminal justice in terms of agency, and that rethinking his or her views on criminal justice from a communion-oriented standpoint offers important insights. Rather than, or in addition to getting back at the offender, connecting to other members of community and symbolic representations of shared group values are important concerns. Criminal justice, as a representation of our shared morality, is a particularly important vessel for such a sense of communion. Experiencing a connection with this process in this sense in itself contributes to recovering something that was lost or damaged by the experience of victimisation. It is the act of empathy itself that offers this connection, rather than empathising with the victim as a means for the victim to achieve some ulterior goal.

Narrating is similarly important in and of itself. Offering the victim the possibility to share his or her narrative in a legal context connects the victim's narrative both to the process and to the actors involved in it. This is so whether this is focused on the sentence of the offender or on a more therapeutic goal. Indeed, these types of goals appear to be a function of the hegemonic narrative of criminal justice itself, and of the attempts of third parties to assuage their distress at injustice, rather than an expression of the emotional needs of victims. Instead of framing victim participation in criminal justice in general, and VIS in particular, as a means to influence the sentence of the offender, it is better understood and conceived of as a way of re-establishing communion between the victim's actual and lived experience and the criminal justice process.

7

Re-Emotionalising Regulatory Responses to Child Sex Offenders

ANNE-MARIE MCALINDEN[*]

I. Introduction

Contemporary discourses on crime and justice have been marked by what scholars have termed 'the emotionalization' of crime and punishment.[1] Such tendencies have been especially notable in relation to public and official discourses concerning the presence of sex offenders, particularly those who offend against children, in the local community. This category of offender tends to generate a range of negative emotions amongst the general public ranging from fear, anxiety, hatred and feelings of disgust relating to 'child sex offenders' to anger and moral indignation. While the contemporary criminological literature cited above tends to imply a more linear and one-dimensional relationship between emotions, crime and 'justice' responses, the broader and generally older psychological literature highlights the rather more complex relationships between emotions, cognition and appraisal.[2] This chapter highlights that such complexities and what might be termed 'degrees of emotion' are also evidenced in public responses to sex offenders against children.

Existing work on 'moral panic'[3] has tended to focus on fear and anxiety as the predominant emotive components of public responses to the risk posed by sex

---

[*] Professor, School of Law, Queen's University Belfast.
[1] See especially, K Laster and P O'Malley, 'Sensitive New-Age Laws: The Reassertion of Emotionality in Law' (1996) 24 *International Journal of the Sociology of Law* 21; W De Haan and I Loader, 'On the Emotions of Crime, Punishment and Social Control' (2002) 6 *Theoretical Criminology* 243; S Karstedt, 'Emotions and Criminal Justice' (2002) 6 *Theoretical Criminology* 299.
[2] See eg, CA Smith and PC Ellsworth, 'Patterns of Cognitive Appraisal in Emotion' (1985) 48 *Journal of Personality and Social Psychology* 813; RS Lazarus and CA Smith, 'Knowledge and Appraisal in the Cognition-Emotion Relationship' (1988) 2 *Cognition and Emotion* 281; JS Lerner and D Keltner, 'Beyond Valence: Toward a Model of Emotion-Specific Influences on Judgement and Choice' (2000) 14 *Cognition and Emotion* 473.
[3] S Cohen, *Folk Devils and Moral Panics* (London, Paladin, 1972).

offenders.[4] This literature, which equates collective emotive public reactions to sex offenders with public 'panic' does not meaningfully engage with the complexity of a wider range of emotions. In this respect, reactions rooted in other emotions such as anger and moral outrage might be rather different, however, from those rooted in fear and anxiety.[5] In the main, while fear and anxiety relating to the presence of sex offenders in the local community are often to the forefront of immediate and expressive public reactions, these are often reinterpreted and replaced subsequently with anger and moral opprobrium at the failure of the authorities to deal adequately with the problem in punitive terms. As Karstedt has argued '[a]nger, disgust and contempt are the main forms of expressing moral indignation and of automated responses to crimes, perpetrators and criminal justice'.[6] In short, the public anxiously reacts to sex offender risk and also angrily reacts to perceived wrongdoing on the part of the authorities in failing to actively and effectively manage such risks.[7] As discussed in the second part of the chapter, reflecting on and taking account of this full range of public emotions in relation to sex offenders is a vital part of developing more forward-thinking and vanguard forms of public involvement and nuanced legal and policy responses to sex offender reintegration.

By way of example, high-profile cases such as the Sarah Payne case, discussed more fully below, act as a fulcrum for public fears and concerns about the risks posed to children by predatory strangers. The openly emotional response of the local community to the presence of sex offenders in their area has typically resulted in 'disintegrative shaming'[8] via vigilante attack and ostracism of known sex offenders.[9] This is usually followed or accompanied by public protests and campaigns and displays of anger and outrage at the failure of the authorities to 'name and shame' sex offenders—to publicly identify known sex offenders and their whereabouts. Indeed, more recently, the controversial adoption of 'Sarah's Law' across much of the United Kingdom is indicative of populist, retributivist policy-making[10] in response to public clamours for the authorities to 'name and shame'

---

[4] A McAlinden, *The Shaming of Sexual Offenders: Risk, Retribution and Reintegration* (Oxford, Hart Publishing, 2007).

[5] I am grateful to one of the anonymous reviewers for alerting me to this point. See eg, the work of Lerner and Keltner who found that fear and anger have opposite effects on perceptions of risk—whereas fearful people expressed pessimistic risk estimates and risk-averse choices, angry people expressed optimistic risk estimates and risk-seeking choices: JS Lerner and D Keltner, 'Fear, Anger, and Risk' (2001) 81 *Journal of Personality and Social Psychology* 146.

[6] S Karstedt, 'Handle with Care: Emotions, Crime and Criminal Justice' in S Karstedt, I Loader and H Strang (eds), *Emotions, Crime and Justice* (Oxford, Hart Publishing, 2011).

[7] I am grateful to one of the anonymous reviewers for alerting me to this broad distinction.

[8] J Braithwaite, *Crime, Shame and Reintegration* (Sydney, Cambridge University Press, 1989).

[9] A McAlinden, 'The Use of "Shame" with Sexual Offenders' (2005) 45 *British Journal of Criminology* 373; W Edwards and C Hensley, 'Contextualising Sex Offender Management Legislation and Policy: Evaluating the Problem of Latent Consequences in Community Notification Laws' (2001) 45 *International Journal of Offender Therapy and Comparative Criminology* 83.

[10] AE Bottoms, 'The Philosophy and Politics of Punishment and Sentencing' in C Clarkson and R Morgan (eds), *The Politics of Sentencing Reform* (Oxford, Oxford University Press, 1995).

sex offenders.[11] For the most part, however, the law and legal frameworks find it difficult to address and engage with the complex and often unruly range of emotional public responses principally because they make the task of the state and state agents (including the police and probation services) extremely difficult in seeking to secure the effective risk management and reintegration of sex offenders.

Emotions nonetheless can also be used in a more positive context and, when channelled effectively, may provide a legitimate means of addressing the myriad of problems associated with the community reintegration of sex offenders. Contrary to much of the existing literature, this analysis argues that emotions may have a constructive role to play in the legal and policy frameworks governing sex offender risk management. Schemes based on restorative justice and 'reintegrative shaming',[12] such as circles of support and accountability, have been used on an ad hoc basis across the United Kingdom and elsewhere as a pragmatic means of reintegrating sex offenders and addressing collective community concerns.[13] Such schemes accord emotions such as 'shame' and 'remorse' a central role within justice processes.[14] While acknowledging the concerns of critics, principally in terms of how unruly emotions might be managed in this context, this analysis contends that infusing this area of law and regulatory policy with a more tolerant, progressive and nuanced version of emotion may ultimately inform a more 'emotionally intelligent' or 'intuitive' system[15] of sex offender risk assessment and management. A regulatory framework which is more receptive to public concerns about sex offenders may in turn offer increased legitimacy for professionals and the public in dealing with contentious issues surrounding sex offender reintegration.

The structure of the chapter is as follows. The next section will examine the core themes arising from the theoretical literature on 'emotions and criminal justice' as a precursor to analysing the drivers of penal policy on sex offender risk management in more detail. The third section will analyse the core aspects of regulatory

---

[11] See eg, A Ashenden, 'Policing Perversion: The Contemporary Governance of Paedophilia' (2002) 6 *Cultural Values* 197; A Williams and B Thompson, 'Vigilance or Vigilantes: The Paulsgrove Riots and Policing Paedophiles in the Community: Part 1: The Long Slow Fuse' (2004) 77 *Police Journal* 99.

[12] Braithwaite (n 8).

[13] McAlinden, *The Shaming of Sexual Offenders* (n 4); RJ Wilson, JE Picheca and P Michelle, 'Evaluating the Effectiveness of Professionally-Facilitated Volunteerism in the Community-Based Management of High-Risk Sexual Offenders: Part One—Effects on Participants and Stakeholders' (2007) 46 *The Howard Journal* 289; C Wilson, A Bates and B Völlm, 'Circles of Support and Accountability: An Innovative Approach to Manage High-Risk Sex Offenders in the Community' (2010) 3 *The Open Criminology Journal* 48; A Bates, R Macrae, D Williams and C Webb, 'Ever-increasing Circles: A Descriptive study of Hampshire and Thames Valley Circles of Support and Accountability 2002–09' (2012) 18 *Journal of Sexual Aggression* 355.

[14] SM Retzinger and TJ Scheff 'Strategy for Community Conferences: Emotions and Social Bonds' in B Galaway and J Hudson (eds), *Restorative Justice: International Perspectives* (Monsey, NY, Criminal Justice Press, 1996); B Van Stokkom, 'Moral Emotions in Restorative Justice Conferences: Managing Shame, Designing Empathy' (2002) 6 *Theoretical Criminology* 339; N Harris, L Walgrave and J Braithwaite, 'Emotional Dynamics in Restorative Conferences' (2004) 8 *Theoretical Criminology* 191.

[15] See eg, Sherman in relation to criminal justice more generally: L Sherman, 'Reason for Emotion: Reinventing Justice with Theories, Innovations and Research—The American Society of Criminology 2002 Presidential Address' (2003) 41 *Criminology* 1.

frameworks on risk from which the public are usually excluded as 'irrational' threats to professional, expert-led risk management strategies.[16] At the same time, the process of law-making in this particular area of criminal justice cannot be said to be devoid of sentiment, as public concerns about the presence of high-risk sex offenders in the local community invariably come to infuse populist penal policies on risk.[17] The fourth part of the chapter will thus explore public responses to the reintegration of sex offenders in the aftermath of high-profile cases which are often marked by anger, fear and abhorrence concerning sex offenders and attendant mistrust of the authorities. These emotive responses, which are typically based on highly polarised moral sentiments about victims and perpetrators of sexual offending concerning children, ultimately become embedded in reactionary, risk-averse policies on sex offending. The fifth part of the chapter will examine the role of restorative justice as a pragmatic means of addressing public emotion concerning contentious sex offender issues, as well as the victim's affective needs in seeking closure and offender engagement, and the offender's needs in terms of resettlement. Finally, the chapter will draw out the broader implications for law and policy-making in taking account of emotions within criminal justice and in moving from elitist to participatory modes of legal decision-making.[18]

II. The Emotionalisation of Crime and Punishment

Social theorists such as Durkheim[19] and Elias[20] have long recognised that criminal justice or penal policies are deeply rooted within the emotional culture of societies. During the last half of the twentieth century, the 're-assertion of emotionality in law'[21] and the permeation of legal and policy discourses with 'emotions and the non-rational'[22] has proliferated many neo-liberal societies,[23] changing the criminal justice landscape. Several writers have since acknowledged the affective dimensions of criminology and the complex interplay between emotions, crime, punishment and social control.[24] Garland, for instance, has pinpointed the

---

[16] H Kemshall and J Wood, 'Beyond Public Protection: An Examination of Community Protection and Public Health Approaches to High-Risk Offenders' (2007) 7 *Criminology and Criminal Justice* 203, 207, 209–10.

[17] Bottoms (n 10).

[18] G Johnstone, 'Penal Policy Making: Elitist, Populist or Participatory?' (2000) 2 *Punishment & Society* 161.

[19] E Durkheim, *Moral Education* (New York, Dover Publications, 2002, first published in 1961).

[20] N Elias, *The Civilising Process* (Oxford, Blackwell, 1994, first published in 1939).

[21] Laster and O'Malley (n 1) 22.

[22] Ibid.

[23] This type of 'political economy' is characterised by incapacitation as the dominant penal ideology, high rates of imprisonment and social exclusion of deviants, and typified by the US and England and Wales: see M Cavadino and J Dignan, 'Penal Policy and Political Economy' (2006) 6 *Criminology and Criminal Justice* 435.

[24] See eg, De Haan and Loader (n 1); Karstedt, 'Emotions and Criminal Justice' (n 1).

'emotional tone' within contemporary neo-liberal discourse and public policy on crime in Anglo-American jurisdictions.[25] Sparks and others have also explored the role of fear of crime within contemporary penality and the relationship between media discourses and the demand for more punitive justice responses or 'something to be done'.[26] These concerns are typified by what Bottoms has famously termed 'populist punitiveness'[27] and the enactment of a burgeoning amount of punitive penal sanctions—such as mass imprisonment and sex offender notification—'that consciously give voice and legislative effect to the emotive demands of citizens'.[28] Indeed, as Karstedt notes, the 'return of emotions' to criminal justice has occurred in two main arenas: 'the emotionalization of public discourse about crime and criminal justice, and the implementation of sanctions in the criminal justice system that are explicitly based on—or designed to arouse—emotions'.[29] This analysis will explore both of these dimensions in relation to public discourses concerning sex offenders against children.

Historically, emotions were integral to the informal resolution of disputes where parties settled their feuds in public, absent a formal role of the state, and which were often subject therefore to 'the excesses of private vengeance'.[30] As discussed throughout this chapter, despite the advent of a formal, modern criminal justice system, we have not lost sight of the display of public emotion and the desire for vengeance in relation to certain categories of crime or victim. As an illustration of this point, Laster and O'Malley highlight, inter alia, broader contemporary developments within criminal law in rape and sexual assault cases. 'Special measures' for vulnerable witnesses,[31] and restrictions on sexual history evidence, common to many jurisdictions, were enacted out of 'deference to the emotional well being of victims and witnesses'.[32] Yet, as other commentators have also contended, such concerns have the potential to erode some of the basic ideological protections of the adversarial process, including the right to be confronted by one's accuser and other truth-finding mechanisms, thereby undermining the potential for fair and judicious outcomes for defendants.[33] Moreover, as discussed further below, these

---

[25] D Garland, *The Culture of Control: Crime and Social Order in Contemporary Society* (Oxford, Oxford University Press, 2001) 10–11.

[26] R Sparks, *Television and the Drama of Crime: Moral Tales and the Place of Crime in Public Life* (Buckingham, Open University Press, 1992). See also W Hollway and T Jefferson, 'The Role of Anxiety in Fear of Crime' in T Hope and R Sparks (eds), *Crime, Risk and Insecurity: Law and Order in Political Discourse and Everyday Life* (London, Routledge, 2000).

[27] Bottoms (n 10).

[28] De Haan and Loader (n 1) 247.

[29] Karstedt, 'Emotions and Criminal Justice' (n 1) 301.

[30] Laster and O'Malley (n 1) 24.

[31] Special measures include screening the witness from the accused, evidence given in private, or by live link, and video-recorded evidence-in-chief: Criminal Evidence (NI) Order 1999, or in the context of England and Wales: Part II; Youth Justice and Criminal Evidence Act 1999, Part II, Ch 1.

[32] Laster and O'Malley (n 1) 26.

[33] See eg, L Hoyano, 'Striking a Balance Between the Rights of Defendants and Vulnerable Witnesses' [2001] *Criminal Law Review* 948; J McEwan, 'Vulnerable Defendants and the Fairness of Trials' [2013] *Criminal Law Review* 100.

emotional and spiritual concerns of law have tended to 'compete and co-exist' with more technocratic, rational and normative approaches.[34] Indeed, more broadly, criminologists have also noted the increasingly 'volatile' and 'contradictory' nature of postmodern penal policies,[35] due in large part to the infusion of public emotion and sentiment into otherwise actuarial, managerial and professional-based strategies.

Penal policy-making within neo-liberal societies such as the United States and the United Kingdom[36] in particular are characterised by what Bouris refers to as 'the politics of victimhood'.[37] A number of interrelated factors have contributed to the emotionalisation of crime and punishment within such societies which can be distilled to the centrality of victims within contemporary discourses on criminal justice. As De Haan and Loader argue, 'the victim of crime has become the symbol *par excellence* of the late modern condition, and protecting victims' rights the predominant ideological justification of criminal justice'.[38] More generally, victims of crime have gone from being 'the forgotten actor'[39] of criminal justice policy to being the bedrock of political discourses on 'law and order'.[40] Victim-centric discourses have underpinned the contemporary regulatory regime with the co-optation of the crime victim providing 'an all-purpose justification for measures of penal repression'.[41] As McEvoy and McConnachie argue, victims' rights or needs 'become intrinsically linked to the punishment of perpetrators' and 'punishing the wicked [becomes] the most satisfying method of honouring the righteous victim'.[42] Much of this rhetoric, however, which is often used to spearhead a punitive reform agenda, is symbolic only with a veneer of victim-centricity.[43] Indeed, this symbolic instrumentalisation of victims 'in the service of severity'[44] is perhaps most acute in relation to victims of sexual offences. Punitive policy-making discourses engage victims and offenders in a

---

[34] Laster and O'Malley (n 1) 22.

[35] D Garland, 'The Commonplace and the Catastrophic: Interpretations of Crime in Late Modernity' (1999) 3 *Theoretical Criminology* 353; P O'Malley, 'Volatile Punishments: Contemporary Penality and the Neo-Liberal Government' (1999) 3 *Theoretical Criminology* 175; A Crawford, 'Joined-Up but Fragmented: Contradiction, Ambiguity and Ambivalence at the Heart of New Labour's "The Third Way"' in R Matthews and J Pitts (eds), *Crime, Disorder and Community Safety: A New Agenda* (London, Routledge, 2001).

[36] See above, n 23.

[37] E Bouris, *Complex Political Victimhood* (Bloomfield, CT, Kumarian Press, 2007).

[38] De Haan and Loader (n 1) 245.

[39] L Zedner, 'Victims' in M Maguire, R Morgan and R Reiner (eds), *The Oxford Handbook of Criminology*, 3rd edn (Oxford, Oxford University Press, 2002) 419; R Mawby and S Walklate, *Critical Victimology: International Perspectives* (London, Sage Publications Ltd, 1994).

[40] R Elias, *Victims Still: The Political Manipulation of Crime Victims* (London, Sage Publications Ltd, 1993); MD Dubber, *Victims in the War on Crime: The Use and Abuse of Victims' Rights* (New York, New York University Press, 2006).

[41] Garland, *The Culture of Control* (n 25) 143.

[42] K McEvoy and K McConnachie, 'Victimology in Transitional Justice: Victimhood, Innocence and Hierarchy' (2012) 9 *European Journal of Criminology* 527, 530.

[43] See eg, R Elias (n 40); Dubber (n 40).

[44] A Ashworth, 'Victims' Rights, Defendants' Rights and Criminal Procedure' in A Crawford and J Goodey (eds), *Integrating a Victim Perspective Within Criminal Justice* (Aldershot, Ashgate, 2000).

'zero-sum game'[45] where the emphasis on championing victims' interests simultaneously fuels negative images of offenders and emotive attitudes towards them. The claims for recognition of the suffering of victims made on their behalf by an angry and vengeful public have resulted in an array of 'emotive and ostentatious' forms of punishment[46] against sex offenders, particularly those who pose a risk to children.

Legislative campaigns to enact more punitive measures against sex offenders are often named after specific child victims in high-profile cases.[47] Measures such as 'Megan's Law' or 'Jessica's Law' in the United States, 'Sarah's Law' in the United Kingdom or 'Natalie's Law' in Germany call for community notification and other restrictive measures on the movement of sex offenders. These 'memorial laws'[48] are used rhetorically to 'lever up punitiveness'[49] and help contribute to the 'emotionalisation' of discourses on crime and justice. Such cases often become 'signal crimes' in providing a focal point for broader and often irrational, or at least misplaced, concerns about the risks posed by sex offenders in the community.[50] Concerns about 'justice' for particular child victims are often amplified in the media to underline the need for protection of an undifferentiated and hypothetical class of *all* potential child victims as 'vulnerable citizens'.[51] As a result, sex offenders against children are singled out as meriting 'extralegal' punishment because of the ubiquitous risk they are seen as presenting.[52] This 'differential justice'[53] has manifested itself in a policy of 'radical prevention'[54] with sexual offenders by means of preventive detention and restrictions placed on dangerous offenders in the community. As discussed further below, the state's prioritisation of the dangers posed by potential sex offenders over other forms of deviant behaviour is driven in large part by media fuelled popular discourses concerning risk. Through a 'politics of vindictiveness',[55] resulting law and order policies give public expression to feelings of moral and collective outrage, appearing to meet the 'deep-seated psychological

---

[45] P O'Malley, 'The Uncertain Promise of Risk' (2004) 37 *Australian & New Zealand Journal of Criminology* 323; see also Garland, *The Culture of Control* (n 25).

[46] J Pratt, 'Emotive and Ostentatious Punishment: Its Decline and Resurgence in Modern Society' (2000) 2 *Punishment & Society* 417.

[47] A McAlinden, 'The Governance of Sexual Offending Across Europe: Penal Policies, Political Economies and the Institutionalisation of Risk' (2012) 14 *Punishment & Society* 166.

[48] C Valier, *Memorial Laws: Victims, Law and Justice* (London, Cavendish, 2005).

[49] Zedner, 'Victims' (n 39) 447.

[50] M Innes, 'Signal Crimes and Signal Disorders: Notes on Deviance as Communicative Action' (2004) 55 *British Journal of Sociology* 335.

[51] P Ramsay, 'Overcriminalization as Vulnerable Citizenship' (2010) 13 *New Criminal Law Review* 262.

[52] Pratt (n 46).

[53] B Weaver and F McNeill, 'Public Protection in Scotland: A Way Forward?' in A Williams and M Nash (eds), *Handbook of Public Protection* (Abingdon, Willan Publishing, 2010) 274.

[54] B Hebenton and T Seddon, 'From Dangerousness to Precaution: Managing Sexual and Violent Offenders in an Insecure and Uncertain Age' (2009) 49 *British Journal of Criminology* 343, 344.

[55] J Young, 'Merton with Energy, Katz and Structure: The Sociology of Vindictiveness and the Criminology of Transgression' (2003) 7 *Theoretical Criminology* 389.

and affective needs'[56] of the public for punishment and vengeance. The next two sections will seek to examine some of these core themes further, and to draw out the interchange and tensions between emotions and official and public responses to sexual crime.

III. Law Without Emotion? Regulatory Frameworks on Sex Offender Risk Assessment and Management

Contemporary criminal justice policies, particularly those pertaining to dangerous or 'risky' offenders, have also been characterised by what Feeley and Simon have termed 'actuarial justice'.[57] Actuarial justice is shaped by concerns with efficient processing and the classification and management of offenders according to assessed levels of future risk. In this vein, there has been an increasing emphasis on notions of 'risk', 'regulation' and 'governance' for a minority of criminals for whom exceptional forms of punishment and control are thought necessary.[58] According to this 'new penology'[59] regulation rather than punishment becomes the core orientation of criminal justice. This new way of thinking about penal policy 'shifts focus away from the traditional concerns of the criminal law and criminology', which have focused on 'retributive judgment' for individual offenders, and redirects it towards 'the language of probability and risk'.[60] As a result, a range of 'new techniques' has developed which focus on managing the dangerous and deploying targeted interventions with selected 'at risk' groups such as violent or sexual offenders.[61] As noted above, sex offenders in particular are singled out for special consideration because of the emotive nature of the crime, particularly where children and the vulnerable are concerned. Recent regulatory initiatives for sex offenders range from preventative detention and restrictions placed on their

---

[56] A Freiberg, 'Affective Versus Effective Justice: Instrumentalism and Emotionalism in Criminal Justice' (2001) 3 *Punishment and Society* 265.

[57] M Feeley and J Simon, 'Actuarial Justice: The Emerging New Criminal Law' in D Nelken (ed), *The Futures of Criminology* (London, Sage Publications Ltd, 1994).

[58] L Zedner, 'Fixing the Future? The Pre-emptive Turn in Criminal Justice' in B McSherry, A Norrie and S Bronitt (eds), *Regulating Deviance: The Redirection of Criminalisation and the Futures of Criminal Law* (Oxford, Hart Publishing, 2009).

[59] M Feeley and J Simon, 'The New Penology: Notes on the Emerging Strategy of Corrections and its Implications' (1992) 30 *Criminology* 449.

[60] Ibid, 449–50.

[61] Ibid, 450. See also J Simon, 'Managing the Monstrous: Sex Offenders and the New Penology' (1998) 4 *Psychology, Public Policy, and Law* 452; H Kemshall and M Maguire, 'Public Protection, Partnership and Risk Penalty: The Multi-agency Risk Management of Sexual and Violent Offenders' (2001) 3 *Punishment & Society* 237.

whereabouts and activities on release from custody, such as notification and vetting, to the development of multi-agency panels to assess and manage risk.[62]

The development of multi-agency public protection arrangements (MAPPA) across the United Kingdom exemplifies this regulatory shift. In these the core criminal justice agencies (police, probation, prisons) work together with a host of other agencies (such as housing, health, education and social services) to assess, classify and manage violent and sexual offenders according to their levels of risk.[63] The underlying goal is to target those who pose the greatest risk to the public by allocating and managing resources effectively.[64] While offenders at the lowest level of risk (category 1) are managed by a single agency, those at the highest level of risk (category 3) are managed on a multi-agency basis.[65] Within this framework, as Kemshall and Wood highlight, the task of public protection and risk management 'has been the preserve of professionals and vested with a few key agencies such as police and probation'.[66] In England and Wales and Northern Ireland, selected members of the public have also been recruited as 'lay advisers' to contribute to the strategic risk management of offenders. For the most part, however, elitist and professional discourses on risk[67] have actively striven 'to avoid, modulate or neutralize excited "popular" demands'.[68] This has meant that public and popular sentiments concerning sex offenders are officially excluded from decision-making processes and are instead characterised as 'irrational' and a potential threat to expert-led risk-management strategies.[69] As noted above and discussed further below, the public reaction to the placement of sex offenders in the local community has often ranged from fear and anxiety to anger and resentment, with the tendency at best to ostracise sex offenders and at worst to physically attack suspected offenders or their known residence.[70] Such vengeful reactions tend to make the work of statutory and voluntary agencies extremely difficult because they undermine effective risk management.

---

[62] N Rose, 'Government and Control' (2000) 40 *British Journal of Criminology* 321; A McAlinden, 'Vetting Sexual Offenders: State Over-extension, the Punishment Deficit and the Failure to Manage Risk' (2010) 19 *Social & Legal Studies* 25.

[63] See eg, in the context of England and Wales, ss 67–68 of the Criminal Justice and Courts Services Act 2000 as amended by s 325 of the Criminal Justice Act 2003.

[64] R Lieb, 'Joined-up Worrying: The Multi-Agency Public Protection Panels' in A Matravers (ed), *Sex Offenders in the Community: Managing and Reducing the Risks* (Cullompton, Devon, Willan Publishing, Cambridge Criminal Justice Series, 2003).

[65] H Kemshall, 'Risk Assessment and Management of Known Sexual and Violent Offenders: A Review of Current Issues' (2001) London, Home Office, Police Research Series Paper No 140; Kemshall and Maguire (n 61).

[66] Kemshall and Wood (n 16) 203.

[67] RV Ericson and KD Haggerty, *Policing the Risk Society* (Oxford, Clarendon Press, 1997).

[68] De Haan and Loader (n 1) 247.

[69] Kemshall and Wood (n 16) 209–10.

[70] See eg, R Winton, 'Monrovia Neighborhood Protests Drive Sex Offender Out of Home', *LA Times*, 29 August 2000; 'Pipe Bomb at Offenders' Hostel in North Belfast', BBC News NI Online, 18 October 2011.

However, as Sparks argues, drawing on the work of Garland,[71] risk is a 'mixed discourse', encompassing 'moral, emotive and political as well as calculative' dimensions.[72] Indeed, at the same time, as part of the broader contemporary trend of emotionalising crime and punishment, the development of normative regulatory frameworks on sexual offending is underpinned by public sentiment. Public concerns around sex offending against children have become embedded within pre-emptive approaches to sex offender risk management. In this respect, risk-based policy is also grounded in a 'wider politics of fear and insecurity'[73] concerning sex offenders. Professional, scientific and objective risk assessments, as the hallmarks of 'actuarial justice',[74] are often subjected to emotive, sweeping and typically misplaced assumptions about future risk. The desire to pre-emptively govern risky behaviours or categories rather than simply risky individuals[75] has led to the development of a range of broadly exclusionary and precautionary regulatory policies on sex offending which often conflate anxiety and risk.[76] Misguided public fears about the ubiquitous risk posed by sex offenders—in particular that posed by 'predatory paedophiles' or 'stranger danger'—have fed into and infused regulatory penal policies on risk. By way of example, measures such as notification or vetting are based on the erroneous assumption that simply having knowledge of the whereabouts of a few known individuals will keep communities and children safe.[77] Indeed, as discussed further in the final section, the challenge becomes how to meaningfully and constructively engage the public in policy discourses within the current 'politics and culture of fear',[78] the climate of moral opprobrium and the vehement societal reaction which exists concerning sex offending against children.

In the United States, the advent of what have become known as 'shame penalties'[79] with certain classes of offenders, including sex offenders, exemplify the use of the courts and the criminal justice system as 'a public space of emotions'.[80] Historically, punishment was a public spectacle where shaming and

---

[71] D Garland, *Punishment and Modern Society: A Study in Social Theory* (Oxford, Clarendon Press, 1990).

[72] R Sparks, 'Degrees of Estrangement: The Cultural Theory of Risk and Comparative Penology' (2001) 5 *Theoretical Criminology* 159, 169.

[73] T Seddon, 'Dangerous Liaisons: Personality Disorder and the Politics of Risk' (2008) 10 *Punishment & Society* 301, 312.

[74] Feeley and Simon, 'Actuarial Justice' (n 57).

[75] P O'Malley, *Risk, Uncertainty and Government* (London, The Glasshouse Press, 2004) 318–19.

[76] Hebenton and Seddon (n 54) 354.

[77] McAlinden, 'Vetting Sexual Offenders' (n 62).

[78] F Furedi, *Politics of Fear: Beyond Left and Right*, 2nd edn (London, Continuum International Publishing Group Limited, 2006); F Furedi, *Culture of Fear Revisited*, 2nd rev edn (London, Continuum International Publishing Group Limited, 2006).

[79] TM Massaro, 'Shame Culture and American Criminal Law' (1991) 89 *Michigan Law Review* 1880; DR Karp, 'The Judicial and the Judicious Use of Shame Penalties' (1998) 44 *Crime & Delinquency* 277.

[80] Karstedt, 'Emotions and Criminal Justice' (n 1) 302.

public humiliation were used in order to exact punishment for an offence.[81] In the contemporary context, some scholars have argued that the requirement for sex offenders to register their names and addresses and notification of this information to the community is synonymous with putting someone in a public stock, to a brand on the forehead, or to *A Scarlet Letter*.[82] While the United Kingdom has a much narrower version of public disclosure under 'Sarah's Law', under 'Megan's Law' in the United States sex offenders may be required to self-identify as a convicted sex offender by, for example, wearing a scarlet letter 'S' on the front of their clothing or handing out handbills or flyers to their neighbours which contain a picture, physical description and details of their offences.[83]

More particularly, in response to the limitations of prison and parole, a minority of American judges have begun to use shaming sanctions as part of the conditions of probation. These generally take two forms—signs and apologies.[84] In relation to the former, in one case the Oregon Court of Appeals placed a convicted child molester on probation for five years subject to a condition, among others, that he place a sign on both sides of his car and on the door of his residence in three-inch lettering which read: 'Dangerous Sex Offender—No Children Allowed.'[85] In relation to the latter, in other cases the courts have required sex offenders to place advertisements in the local newspaper publicising their offences or urging others to sex treatment.[86] As Karstedt argues, '[w]hat is striking about these sentences, is not only the explicit use of emotion, but the way it is done, the great emphasis placed on their publicness'.[87] These types of shame penalties have found favour among judges and the public because they appear to satisfy the retributive impulse in at least two ways: the symbolic moral and public condemnation of the offence, combined with the practical imposition of some form of suffering in the threat of stigma and social exclusion.[88] Not surprisingly several commentators have questioned whether this is appropriate terrain for judges,[89] not least because of

[81] M Foucault, *Discipline and Punish: The Birth of the Prison* (London, Penguin, 1977) 3–72. Punishments such as hanging, drawing and quartering, the stocks and the pillory, flogging and branding were carried out publicly and in ceremonial fashion, designed to inflict physical suffering in tandem with social disgrace.
[82] See eg, AL Van Dujn, 'The Scarlet Letter Branding' (1999) 47 *Drake Law Review* 635; M Earl-Hubbard, 'The Child Sex Offender Registration Laws: The Punishment, Liberty, Deprivation and Unintended Results Associated with the Scarlet Letter Laws of the 1990s' (1996) 90 *North Western Law Review* 788. Hawthorne's fictional account of seventeenth-century Boston tells the story of Hester Prynne, an adulteress forced to wear a scarlet letter 'A' embroidered on the front of her dress to show her crime, embodying Puritan society's use of punishment by humiliation and shame: N Hawthorne, *The Scarlet Letter* (London, Penguin Books Ltd, 1994, first published in 1850).
[83] A Bedarf, 'Examining Sex Offender Community Notification Laws' (1995) 83 *California Law Review* 885.
[84] Massaro (n 79); Karp (n 79).
[85] *State v Bateman*, 95 Or Ct App 456, 771 P 2d 314 (1989).
[86] Massaro (n 79) 1880.
[87] Karstedt, 'Emotions and Criminal Justice' (n 1) 302.
[88] Karp (n 79) 277–78.
[89] McAlinden, 'The Use of "Shame" with Sexual Offenders' (n 9).

the 'thin line between shame, humiliation and stigmatization'.[90] Public forms of shaming, however, and in particular the use of 'disintegrative shaming' are also evident in community responses to the reintegration of sex offenders.

IV. Emotive Public Responses to the Reintegration of Sexual Offenders

That sexual offending concerning children has become an intensely politicised and controversial area of policy-making within the last two decades is in large part due to the media construction and representation of such crimes.[91] However, legal and policy discourses surrounding 'actuarial justice'[92] and 'the new penology',[93] referred to above, which are heavily premised on scientific assessment and rational judgements about risk, cannot easily accommodate emotive public reactions to and understandings about sex offender risk. In this respect, there are a number of interrelated themes within contemporary media discourses which underlie the emotionalisation of public responses to this class of offender. First, there is the conflation of levels and types of risk. Sex offending against children has become synonymous with sexual offending as a whole. The word 'paedophile' in particular and the perceived threat posed by the 'predatory stranger' are deemed symptomatic of the wider omnipresent risks posed by sex offenders in the community, who are all deemed to pose the same degree of very high risk.[94] Second, following on from the previous point, risk is firmly located in the public sphere as a 'site of crime'.[95] As a result, cases which highlight the vulnerability of children in quasi-intrafamilial environments traditionally assumed secure, such as churches, care homes and schools, have a particular poignancy, often provoking public anger and eliciting outcry.[96] Indeed, the public appear to take comfort from the 'othering' of sex offending,[97] and become reluctant to visualise the risk in domestic terms[98] for fear of undermining the sanctity of the family and home as a place of safety and protection.[99] Third, there are particular stereotypical and sentimental views

---

[90] Karstedt, 'Emotions and Criminal Justice' (n 1) 302.
[91] C Greer, 'News Media, Victims and Crime' in P Davies, P Francis and C Greer (eds), *Victims, Crime and Society* (London, Sage Publications Ltd, 2007).
[92] Feeley and Simon, 'Actuarial Justice' (n 57).
[93] Feeley and Simon, 'The New Penology' (n 59).
[94] McAlinden, *The Shaming of Sexual Offenders* (n 4) 10–11.
[95] E Saraga, 'Dangerous Places: The Family as a Site of Crime' in J Muncie and E McLaughlin (eds), *The Problem of Crime*, 2nd edn (London, Sage Publications Ltd, 2001).
[96] McAlinden, *The Shaming of Sexual Offenders* (n 4) 19–20.
[97] D Spencer, 'Sex Offender as Homo Sacer' (2009) 11 *Punishment & Society* 219.
[98] C Greer, *Sex Crime and the Media: Sex Offending and the Press in a Divided Society* (Cullompton, Devon, Willan Publishing, 2003).
[99] Saraga (n 95).

about victims and, as a result, oppositional views about offenders, as epitomised in the sustained coverage of recent high-profile cases.[100] As discussed below, these viewpoints are typically juxtaposed around highly moralised, hierarchical notions relating to the good/innocence of the child victim and the evil/subhuman status of the offender.[101]

Sensationalist media reporting of sexual offences has a number of undesirable effects on the popular imagination. As Greer argues, media depictions of sex offending, particularly that concerning children, give the public important cues about how they should perceive the nature and extent of sexual crime, and how they should think, feel and respond to it.[102] In the main, the media are also influential in prompting or sustaining vengeful community attitudes in relation to sex offenders, often fuelling the cry for a more punitive criminal justice response.[103] The 'vicious policy cycle' which ensues represents an emotive and irrational response to sexual crime.[104] Punitive political rhetoric fuels public fear and anger concerning the presence of sex offenders in the community, which in turn produces a greater demand for more action and a more punitive society.[105] At the same time, resulting policies are also based on capturing known risk, located in the public sphere and belie the fact that the greatest risk to women and children lies not with predatory strangers but with those closest to them.[106] Resulting legislative frameworks, therefore, are premised on capturing the elevated levels of fear, anxiety and anger which exist concerning the risks posed by sex offenders against children. Indeed, such policies tend to inflate embedded levels of societal suspicion, mistrust and intolerance concerning potential sex offenders,[107] and create indiscriminate strategies which 'cast the net of suspicion on all'.[108]

By way of illustration of these themes, two of the most recent heart-rending and high-profile cases of child abduction and murder by known sex offenders relate to those of eight-year-old Sarah Payne and ten-year-old Soham schoolgirls, Holly Wells and Jessica Chapman. Sarah Payne was murdered in Sussex in July 2000 by known sex offender Roy Whiting while playing in a field near her grandparents' home. Holly and Jessica were murdered in 2002 by school caretaker Ian Huntley,

---

[100] A McAlinden, 'Deconstructing Victim and Offender Identities in Discourses on Child Sexual Abuse: Hierarchies, Blame and the Good/Evil Dialectic' (2014) 54 *British Journal of Criminology* 180.

[101] Ibid.

[102] Greer, *Sex Crime and the Media* (n 98).

[103] McAlinden, *The Shaming of Sexual Offenders* (n 4) 21. See also M Berry, G Philo, G Tiripelli, S Docherty and C Macpherson, 'Media Coverage and Public Understanding of Sentencing Policy in Relation to Crimes Against Children' (2012) 12 *Criminology and Criminal Justice* 567.

[104] McAlinden, *The Shaming of Sexual Offenders* (n 4) 27.

[105] P McCold, 'Restorative Justice and the Role of Community' in B Galaway and J Hudson (eds), *Restorative Justice: International Perspectives* (Monsey, NY, Criminal Justice Press, 1996).

[106] M Cowburn and L Dominelli, 'Masking Hegemonic Masculinity: Reconstructing the Paedophile as the Dangerous Stranger' (2001) 31 *British Journal of Social Work* 399.

[107] F Furedi and J Bristow, *Licensed to Hug: How Child Protection Policies are Poisoning the Relationship Between the Generations* (London, Civitas, 2008).

[108] R Ericson, *Crime in an Insecure World* (Cambridge, Polity Press, 2007) 259.

who had been previously known to the police for a range of allegations of sexual offences against women and young girls. In both cases, the victims represented the archetypal victim—young, innocent, passive and blameless—and conversely, the offenders epitomised the stereotypical offender who appears at the top of the offending hierarchy—the older, male, predatory 'paedophile'.[109] These particularly noteworthy cases were the subject of sustained media coverage, providing a focal point for public fears and concerns relating to the risks posed by sex offenders in the community. The highly moralised public discourse which results often hinges upon the juxtaposition of victims and offenders as 'angels' and 'monsters',[110] creating in the process a collective revulsion about sex offenders and in particular 'a universal loathing for the child abuser'.[111] Moreover, these particular cases are also illustrative of 'populist punitiveness'[112] and 'the impassioned demands of citizens for order',[113] as both were instrumental in changing the legislative and policy frameworks concerning sex offender risk management.

The Sarah Payne case led to the then *News of the World* newspaper's 'Name and Shame' Campaign which called for the authorities to publicly identify all known sex offenders. The campaign centred on the 'outing' of suspected and known paedophiles by printing their photographs and names and addresses, along with brief details of their offending history. Accompanying this was a demand for a 'Sarah's Law' which would provide for a child sex offender disclosure scheme. The campaign also coincided with public protests at the presence of sex offenders in the local community and vigilante activity on the Paulsgrove estate in Portsmouth, where a number of homes of suspected sex offenders were attacked causing two alleged sex offenders to commit suicide and one convicted sex offender to flee the area.[114] While there was initial reluctance on the part of the government to enact a broad form of community notification,[115] following the similarly styled 'Megan's Law' in the United States and a number of successful pilots,[116] 'Sarah's Law' ultimately came to fruition across the United Kingdom.[117] The measure

---

[109] McAlinden, 'Deconstructing Victim and Offender Identities' (n 100).

[110] C Wardle, 'Monsters and Angels: Visual Press Coverage of Child Murders in the USA and the UK, 1930–2000' (2007) 8 *Journalism* 263.

[111] F Furedi, *Moral Crusades in An Age of Mistrust: The Jimmy Savile Scandal* (Basingstoke, Palgrave Macmillan, 2013) 45.

[112] Bottoms (n 10).

[113] De Haan and Loader (n 1) 243.

[114] A Ashenden (n 11); Williams and Thompson (n 11).

[115] A Rutherford, 'Holding the Line on Sex Offender Notification' (2000) 150 *New Law Journal* 1359; T Thomas, 'Sex Offender Community Notification: Experiences from America' (2003) 42 *Howard Journal of Criminal Justice* 217.

[116] H Kemshall, J Wood and S Westwood et al, *Child Sex Offender Review* (CSOR) *Public Disclosure Pilots: A Process Evaluation*, 2nd edn (London, Home Office, 2010); V Chan, A Homes, L Murray, S Treanor and Ipsos Mori Scotland, *Evaluation of the Sex Offender Community Disclosure Pilot* (Scottish Government Social Research, 2010), available at: www.scotland.gov.uk/socialresearch.

[117] In the context of England and Wales see s 327A of the Criminal Justice Act 2003 (inserted by s 140 of the Criminal Justice and Immigration Act 2008) which places a duty on each MAPPA to consider disclosure to particular members of the public of an offender's convictions for child sexual offences where there is a risk of serious harm to a particular child or children.

provides for a limited form of community notification whereby parents or carers can request a criminal record check of those with unsupervised access to their children. The Bichard Inquiry[118] was set up in the aftermath of the Soham murders to investigate information-sharing systems and vetting practices in two police constabularies in England and Wales. The Inquiry ultimately led to a new and expansive legislative framework on pre-employment vetting and barring in the Safeguarding Vulnerable Groups Act 2006, designed to pre-emptively capture the potential risk posed to children and the vulnerable by would-be sex offenders.[119] The populist, cyclical nature of penal policy-making which draws on and gives expression to public sentiment concerning sex offenders has also been reflected in legislative debates in the United States. Lynch, for example, notes the emotional drive of American criminal justice policy-making which targets sex offenders and which is exemplified by 'emotional expressions of disgust' and 'fear of contagion' and 'pollution' by sex offenders, so reinforcing the victim–offender divide and the 'othering' of sex offenders.

This emotionally charged response of society to the placement of sex offenders in the local community may have a number of undesirable effects on the effective risk management and reintegration of sex offenders. As noted above in relation to the immediate aftermath of the Sarah Payne case, this can at worst result in vigilante attacks on suspected paedophiles or their residences. At best, it may serve to displace or increase the risk of reoffending by causing the offender to go underground in order to escape notice.[120] What has been termed 'disintegrative shaming'[121] relates to the process whereby sex offenders are labelled and stigmatised and singled out as different from the rest of the community. This 'public shaming' of sex offenders, exemplified by official measures such as community notification or public protests at the presence of sex offenders in their local community, has the net result of impeding and undermining rather than securing offender rehabilitation and public protection.[122] As Hebenton and Thomas have argued, this is fundamentally at odds with the criminal justice system's calculated knowledge of risk assessment and security where, in effect, the desire to manage the risk posed by sex offenders effectively ends up producing the opposite result.[123]

[118] M Bichard, *The Bichard Inquiry Report* (London, Home Office, 2004).
[119] McAlinden, 'Vetting Sexual Offenders' (n 62). The legislation has subsequently been scaled back under the Protection of Freedoms Act 2012, Part 5.
[120] McAlinden, 'The Use of "Shame" with Sexual Offenders' (n 9).
[121] Braithwaite (n 8).
[122] McAlinden, *The Shaming of Sexual Offenders* (n 4).
[123] B Hebenton and T Thomas, 'Sexual Offenders in the Community: Reflections on Problems of Law, Community and Risk Management in the USA and England and Wales' (1996) 24 *International Journal of the Sociology of Law* 427, 440–41.

V. Addressing Emotion in Discourses on Sexual Crime: The Role of Restorative Justice

It may be, however, that 'negative emotions'[124] concerning sexual offenders—'moral disgust, revulsion and feelings of vengeance',[125] together with anger, hatred and fear—can be used more effectively. In a number of jurisdictions, communities have adopted innovative 'reintegrative shaming'[126] practices with sexual offenders with the broad aims of reducing the incidence of child sexual abuse, preventing future offending and reintegrating the offender back into the community. These measures aim to engage local communities in the management and reintegration of sex offenders and to directly address wider concerns about the presence of released sex offenders in the local community. To begin with, it is proposed to briefly outline the core elements of restorative justice and reintegrative shaming which have provided a constructive means of addressing the pragmatic and affective needs of communities, victims and offenders impacted by sexual crime. The discussion will then move to a critical examination of circles of support and accountability as the primary example of reintegrative measures with sex offenders involving local communities in the processes of reintegration and risk management. Finally, the subsection will address the concerns of critics regarding restorative justice, particularly those relating to the 're-assertion of emotionality in law'.[127]

Restorative justice is in one sense an umbrella term that encompasses a range of practices and processes that seek to respond to crime in a more constructive way than through the use of conventional justice processes. Although its precise definition and scope remain subject to contention, the term is generally applied to non-adversarial processes between victims and offenders where the emphasis is on repairing harm to people and relationships through 'mediated encounters' rather than simply seeking to address the violation of legal norms via retributive punishment.[128] In relation to sexual offending specifically, advocates of restorative justice point to the failure of retributive or adversarial responses and the greater potential of restoration in meeting the affective needs of victims, offenders and communities in more cases.[129] Tony Marshall's much-cited definition is

---

[124] DM Kahan, 'The Progressive Appropriation of Disgust' in SA Bandes (ed), *The Passions of Law* (New York, New York University Press, 1999); RA Posner, 'Law and the Emotions' (2000) The Law School, University of Chicago, John M Olin Law and Economics Working Paper No 103.

[125] Karstedt, 'Emotions and Criminal Justice' (n 1) 303.

[126] Braithwaite (n 8).

[127] Laster and O'Malley (n 1) 22.

[128] DW Van Ness and KH Strong, *Restoring Justice* (Cincinnati, OH, Anderson Publishing Co, 1997); H Zehr, 'Doing Justice, Healing and Trauma: The Role of Restorative Justice in Peacebuilding' (2008) 1 *South African Journal of Peacebuilding* 1.

[129] J Braithwaite and K Daly, 'Masculinities, Violence and Communitarian Control' in T Newburn and E Stanko (eds), *Just Boys Doing Business? Men, Masculinity and Crime* (London, Routledge, 1994); McAlinden, *The Shaming of Sexual Offenders* (n 4).

instructive: '[A] process by which all the parties with a stake in a particular offence come together to resolve collectively how to deal with the aftermath of the offence and its implications for the future.'[130] This definition usefully captures the agreed core values and principles of restorative justice, and in particular the potential to address public emotion and the interests of local communities by: (1) empowerment of and respect for all the parties affected by the offence—typically the victim and the offender, but also their families and the wider community; (2) inclusive and non-coercive participation and decision-making—which seeks to strike an appropriate balance between the multiple interests at stake on a consensual and voluntary basis; and (3) a forward-looking or problem-solving orientation—which focuses, inter alia, on offender accountability and acknowledgement of wrongdoing and reintegrating offenders back into the community.[131]

A core element of restorative justice is Braithwaite's notion of 'reintegrative shaming'.[132] Braithwaite defines 'shaming' as the 'social processes of expressing disapproval which have the intention or effect of invoking remorse in the person being shamed and/or condemnation by others'.[133] The crux of the theory is that it is the ways in which society, the community and the family sanction deviance, rather than the state, which affects the extent to which offenders engage in future criminal behaviour. 'Shaming', therefore, is more important to crime control than retribution or punishment. Braithwaite argues that communitarian societies (those with a high degree of interdependence and strong cultural commitments to group loyalties) are better able than other societies (where there is a lower level of interdependence and greater concern with individualism) to informally sanction deviance and reintegrate lawbreakers by shaming the offence, rather than permanently stigmatising the offender through harsh formal penal measures.[134] There are two facets to reintegrative shaming: (1) the overt disapproval of the delinquent act (shaming) by socially significant others; and (2) the ongoing inclusion of the offender within an interdependent relationship (reintegration).[135] Thus, shaming is reintegrative when it reinforces an offender's membership in civil society. As discussed further below, these principles are reflected in the work of circles of support and accountability.

Indeed, unlike conventional criminal justice measures which, for the most part, seek to minimise or downplay emotion, emotions are seen as being core to the relational dynamics and outcomes of restorative or reintegrative processes. Restorative scholars contend that a major benefit of restorative justice in comparison to

---

[130] T Marshall, *Restorative Justice: An Overview: A Report by the Home Office Research Development and Statistics Directorate* (London, HMSO, 1999) 5.
[131] A Crawford and J Goodey (eds), *Integrating a Victim Perspective Within Criminal Justice* (Aldershot, Ashgate, 2000).
[132] Braithwaite (n 8).
[133] Ibid, 100.
[134] Ibid, 84–85.
[135] SX Zhang, 'Measuring Shame in an Ethnic Context' (1995) 35 *British Journal of Criminology* 248, 251.

conventional criminal justice is that it addresses the emotional dimension of crime and its aftermath.[136] As outlined above, the key emphasis is on repairing harm to people and relationships through 'mediated encounters' rather than simply seeking to address the violation of legal norms.[137] Within this broader context, some scholars highlight the critical role that emotions such as shame and guilt play in the reintegrative shaming process.[138] For some, shame is identified as 'the master emotion'[139] or 'the core emotional sequence'[140] within restorative processes, and within family group conferencing in particular. For other writers, however, given the restorative goal of repairing harm, a focus on the role of disapproval and the emotion of shame in justice processes is potentially misplaced. For these writers, the management and resolution of moral emotions such as empathy, remorse and guilt are much more potent and constructive elements than 'shame' in achieving reparative outcomes.[141] Whichever viewpoint one adopts, taken more broadly, in the emotional and relational dynamics of restorative conferencing, emotions such as empathy, remorse and guilt will become merged with feelings of shame, and it is ultimately the outworking and resolution of these moral emotions that is critical for successful restorative interventions.[142] Indeed, within the restorative process, 'shame management'[143]—allowing participants to tell their story, and the ritual of apology and forgiveness—offers a means of managing the emotions of shame for both the victim and the offender and in assisting in their psychological recovery.[144] Allowing victims a chance to tell their story and communicate the harm they have suffered to the offender, is the path to reducing victim shame[145] and displacing feelings of anger, indignation and resentment.[146] Similarly, encouraging

[136] H Strang, 'Justice for Victims of Young Offenders: The Centrality of Emotional Harm and Restoration' in A Morris and G Maxwell (eds), *Restorative Justice for Juveniles: Conferencing, Mediation and Circles* (Oxford, Hart Publishing, 2001); Sherman (n 15).

[137] Van Ness and Strong (n 128); Zehr, 'Doing Justice, Healing and Trauma' (n 128).

[138] J Braithwaite and V Braithwaite, 'Part I. Shame, Shame Management and Regulation' in E Ahmed, N Harris, J Braithwaite and V Braithwaite (eds), *Shame Management Through Reintegration* (Cambridge, Cambridge University Press, 2001); Harris et al (n 14).

[139] Retzinger and Scheff (n 14).

[140] DB Moore, 'Shame, Forgiveness and Juvenile Justice' (1993) 12 *Criminal Justice Ethics* 3; Harris et al (n 14).

[141] See eg, Karstedt, 'Emotions and Criminal Justice' (n 1); G Maxwell and A Morris, 'The Role of Shame, Guilt and Remorse in Restorative Justice Processes for Young People' in EGM Weitekamp and HJ Kerner (eds), *Restorative Justice: Theoretical Foundations* (Cullompton, Devon, Willan Publishing, 2002); Van Stokkom (n 14).

[142] See eg, MP Koss, 'Blame, Shame, and Community: Justice Responses to Violence Against Women' (2000) 55 *American Psychologist* 1332.

[143] E Ahmed, N Harris, J Braithwaite and V Braithwaite (eds), *Shame Management Through Reintegration* (Cambridge, Cambridge University Press, 2001).

[144] Moore (n 140).

[145] H Zehr, 'Journey to Belonging' in EGM Weitekamp and HJ Kerner (eds), *Restorative Justice: Theoretical Foundations* (Cullompton, Devon, Willan Publishing, 2002).

[146] N Harris, 'Evaluating the Practice of Restorative Justice: The Case of Family Group Conferencing' in L Walgrave (ed), *Repositioning Restorative Justice* (Cullompton, Devon, Willan Publishing, 2003) 127–28.

offenders to take responsibility for their actions and to express genuine empathy and remorse and an apology to their victims also helps the offender to resolve their shame leading to empathy and remorse in the offender.[147]

Measures which have embodied the hallmarks of restorative justice and reintegrative shame culture with considerable success are circles of support and accountability.[148] This model, which operates with high-risk sex offenders on release from prison, originated in Canada over two decades ago,[149] and has since been extended to other countries including the United Kingdom.[150] The model is based on the twin notions of safety and support—it addresses local community concerns surrounding public safety and the risk of reoffending and also the offender's support needs in terms of reintegration. The circle is focused on the development of an informal network built around the offender, as the core member, involving the wider community in partnership with state and voluntary agencies. The trained circle members enter into a signed agreement or 'covenant' which specifies each member's area of assistance. The scheme provides intensive support, guidance and supervision for the offender, mediating between the police, media and the general community to minimise risk and assist with the practical aspects of reintegration such as finding suitable accommodation and employment. The offender agrees to relate to the circle of support, pursue treatment and to act responsibly in the community. The offender has daily contact with someone from the circle each day in the high-risk phase just after release which gradually diminishes.[151] The aim is to control wrongdoing within a communitarian society and informally sanction deviance by reintegration into cohesive networks, rather than by formal restraint. The community is involved in expressing disapproval of the sex offending behaviour, but also in providing protection and redress for victims, and in supporting the offender in their efforts to desist and reintegrate. Within England and Wales, the model operates on a systemic, rather than organic, basis and may feed into MAPPA, the multi-agency framework for sex offender risk assessment and management outlined above. The growing number of evaluations of the schemes has demonstrated success on a number of levels, not least

[147] H Strang, *Repair or Revenge: Victims and Restorative Justice* (Oxford, Clarendon Press, 2002); Zehr, 'Journey to Belonging' (n 145).

[148] At the macro level, Truth and Reconciliation Commissions, which draw heavily on restorative principles, seek to resolve issues of anger, forgiveness and remorse within the context of broader conflict resolution processes: see generally, C Villa Vincenzo, 'A Different Kind of Justice: The South African Truth and Reconciliation Commission' (1999) 1 *Contemporary Justice Review* 403.

[149] C Cesaroni, 'Releasing Sex Offenders into the Community Through "Circles of Support"—A Means of Reintegrating the "Worst of the Worst"' (2001) 34 *Journal of Offender Rehabilitation* 85; MG Petrunik, 'Managing Unacceptable Risk: Sex Offenders, Community Response, and Social Policy in the United States and Canada' (2002) 46 *International Journal of Offender Therapy and Comparative Criminology* 483, 503–05.

[150] Following implementation in the Netherlands, the *Circles4EU* project, funded by the European Commission, has developed pilots in Bulgaria, Latvia and Catalonia, with further pilots planned in France, Hungary and Northern Ireland. See: www.circles4.eu/default.asp?page_id=133.

[151] McAlinden, *The Shaming of Sexual Offenders* (n 4) 168–73.

in protecting communities and reducing recidivism rates.[152] More particularly for present purposes, however, is the fact that they have also provided a pragmatic and constructive means of engaging communities as 'stakeholders' in the release and reintegration of high-risk sex offenders where, despite tentative beginnings, communities have been willing to play a constructive and supportive role in the process.[153]

Finally, it would be remiss not to address the concerns of critics of restorative justice, particularly those relating to the emotional dimensions of restorative justice processes. Opponents have highlighted the dangers inherent in a communitarian approach to justice more generally, chiefly related to the need to guarantee legitimacy,[154] accountability[155] and adequate safeguards.[156] It is not proposed to rehearse all of these in detail but rather, in tandem with current purposes, to highlight those pertaining to public engagement in justice processes. Chief among the concerns of critics, and also stemming from the 'emotional dynamics' which lie at the heart of the face-to-face nature of restorative justice processes, is the imbalance of power between the victim and the offender which, if not managed appropriately, may produce secondary victimisation.[157] Restorative justice processes, however, routinely work towards removing this power imbalance by focusing on the empowerment of victims or others directly affected by the crime in a positive and supportive context.[158] Moreover, within the context of circles of

---

[152] Wilson, Bates and Völlm, 'Circles of Support and Accountability' (n 13); S Hanvey, T Philpot, and C Wilson, *A Community-Based Approach to the Reduction of Sexual Offending: Circles of Support and Accountability* (London, Jessica Kingsley Publishers, 2011) 150–65. In one study there was a 70% reduction in the expected rate of recidivism in comparison to the control group: RJ Wilson, JE Pichea and M Prinzo, 'Evaluating the Effectiveness of Professionally-Facilitated Volunteerism in the Community-Based Management of High-Risk Sex Offenders: Part Two—A Comparison of Recidivism Rates' (2007) 46 *The Howard Journal* 327. More recently, evaluations of over 60 circle projects in England and Wales have demonstrated a significant improvement in the emotional wellbeing of the core member and a reduction in social isolation: Bates et al, 'Ever-increasing Circles' (n 13).

[153] A Bates, R Saunders and C Wilson, 'Doing Something About It; A Follow-up Study of Sex Offenders Participating in Thames Valley Circles of Support and Accountability' (2007) 5 *British Journal of Community Justice* 19; Wilson, Bates and Völlm, 'Circles of Support and Accountability' (n 13).

[154] R Paternoster, R Backman, R Brame and L Sherman, 'Do Fair Procedures Matter? The Effect of Procedural Justice on Spousal Assault' (1997) 31 *Law & Society Review* 163.

[155] D Roche, *Accountability in Restorative Justice* (Oxford, Oxford University Press, Clarendon Studies in Criminology, 2003).

[156] M Wright, 'The Court as Last Resort' (2002) 42 *British Journal of Criminology* 654. For a detailed discussion of the critiques of restorative justice and how they can be overcome in relation to violent and sexual crime see eg, B Hudson, 'Restorative Justice: The Challenge of Sexual and Racial Violence' (1998) 25 *Journal of Law and Society* 237; K Daly, 'Sexual Assault and Restorative Justice' in H Strang and J Braithwaite (eds), *Restorative Justice and Family Violence* (Melbourne, Cambridge University Press, 2002); A Morris, 'Critiquing the Critics: A Brief Response to Critics of Restorative Justice' (2002) 42 *British Journal of Criminology* 596; McAlinden, *The Shaming of Sexual Offenders* (n 4) 197–205.

[157] See eg, such criticisms in the context of domestic violence: KJ Cook, 'Doing Difference and Accountability in Restorative Justice Conferences' (2006) 10 *Theoretical Criminology* 107; S Jülich, 'Views of Justice Among Survivors of Historical Child Sexual Abuse: Implications for Restorative Justice in New Zealand' (2006) 10 *Theoretical Criminology* 125.

[158] See eg, Morris (n 156); A Morris and L Gelsthorpe, 'Re-visioning Men's Violence Against Female Partners' (2000) 39 *The Howard Journal* 412, 420.

support and accountability, it is usually members of the local community, rather than direct victims, who are involved in the restorative or reintegrative process with the offender.

In addition, critics of reintegrative shaming theory argue that a number of difficulties including the lack of social and norm cohesion in contemporary society, the difficulties in promoting social inclusion, and the contestable nature of the terms 'community' and 'partnership', mean that such schemes will not easily be implemented in Western societies.[159] In countering these claims, however, advocates contend that popular responses to sex offending demonstrate that: (1) there is clear consensus concerning the wrongness of sexual relationships between adults and children;[160] (2) the provision of public education about the nature of sexual crime and responses to it, would help dispel the commonly held myths and misconceptions, shift public opinion and promote social inclusion;[161] and finally, (3) the involvement of professional agencies in community-based schemes helps to keep the community in check while also ensuring state and organisational accountability.[162]

Within this broader context, the chief concern with restorative justice at the collective level, however, relates to its association with community or popular justice and the risk of 'vigilance turning into vigilante action'.[163] As outlined above, popular responses to sexual offending in the form of 'name and shame' campaigns and public protests at the presence of sex offenders in the local community can be repressive, retributive and vengeful.[164] Such values, however, are fundamentally at odds with the defining values of restorative justice and cannot, therefore, be part of it.[165] On the other hand, the schemes which have developed thus far demonstrate that the community is capable of responding to contentious issues surrounding the reintegration of sex offenders in a responsible and constructive manner. Moreover, operating measures such as circles of support within the rubric of the criminal justice system in conjunction with statutory and voluntary agencies helps ensure the provision of adequate safeguards and standards. It could mean, for example, that an offender's rights would be protected against a vengeful community, that a victim's rights would be protected against a community view which did not take the harm seriously, and that either party would have rights guaranteed against persuasion of the group by a stronger advocate.[166] Furthermore, if properly operated and applied, restorative justice schemes might also provide a process

---

[159] McAlinden, *The Shaming of Sexual Offenders* (n 4) 205–13.

[160] I Hacking, *The Social Construction of What?* (Cambridge, MA, Harvard University Press, 1999).

[161] D Grubin, 'Sex Offending Against Children: Understanding the Risk' (1998) London, Home Office, Police Research Series Paper 99.

[162] A Crawford, *The Local Governance of Crime: Appeals to Community and Partnership* (Oxford, Clarendon Press, 1999).

[163] S Ashenden, *Governing Child Sexual Abuse: Negotiating the Boundaries of Public and Private, Law and Science* (London, Routledge, 2004) 203.

[164] Morris (n 156) 609.

[165] Morris and Gelsthorpe (n 158).

[166] Hudson, 'Restorative Justice' (n 156) 256.

of education and engagement for vigilante groups, as well as an opportunity for
the wider community to approach the problems of managing sexual offenders in
the community in a more considered, less emotive way. Indeed, as discussed further in the final section, promoting these pragmatic benefits might help persuade
the public and policymakers that restorative schemes provide a realistic means of
engaging the community in the processes of sex offender management and reintegration and in particular of managing heightened levels of emotion concerning
sex offenders against children.

VI. Taking Account of Emotion in Sex Offender Risk Management: From Elitist to Participatory Modes of Decision-Making

Thus far the chapter has examined the contemporary emotionalisation of public and official discourses about sexual offenders and has explored restorative
schemes as a means of harnessing public sentiment about sex offenders, and of
engaging the public in emotive and contentious debates concerning sex offenders.
This concluding section will seek to pull together the benefits and residual challenges of taking account of emotion in the face of sex offender risk management
and reintegration, and in moving from elitist to participatory modes of decision-
making.[167] Infusing this area of law and regulatory policy with a more tolerant,
progressive and nuanced version of human emotion may ultimately inform a
more rational yet emotionally intelligent system of sex offender risk assessment
and management. Within this broader context, I would argue that there are at
least three principal advantages of re-emotionalising public and official discourses
on sex offender risk management and reintegration. These benefits relate to the
partnership approach between the community and statutory and voluntary sec-
tors; the emotional wellbeing and 'healing' of victims, particularly those related
to intra-familial abuse; and finally, a retreat from the 'othering' of sex offenders
with positive knock-on effects for a reduction in recidivism and more effective
reintegration.

First, a more rational and considered response would recognise the community as a critical dimension to the effective reintegration of offenders, rather
than a 'problem' which must be managed. Restorative approaches such as circles
of support have demonstrated that communities can take a more proactive and
effective role in securing offender reintegration and, moreover, have gained the
trust of the relevant agencies to work in this way. Circles of support have facilitated the reformulation of traditional state and community roles and an effective
partnership approach between the statutory, voluntary and community sector in

---

[167] Johnstone (n 18).

responding to contentious sexual offender issues. As noted above, a key benefit of a 'partnership approach to justice'[168] is that the involvement of professional agencies in community-based schemes helps to keep a potentially volatile community reaction in check while also ensuring state and organisational accountability.[169] In particular, involving the community in the process of offender resettlement on a more widespread basis would give them some ownership of the problem and a relevant stake with formal justice agencies in securing offender reintegration. In effect, consistent with Ericson and Haggerty's (1997) model of 'knowledge-risk-security', being part of the information or knowledge loop would also reduce their feelings of being at risk and increase their feelings of security.[170] Moreover, giving the local community a stake in sex offender reintegration and assuring them that their concerns are being addressed in a meaningful way would help to alleviate current tensions and feelings of anger, in particular surrounding the placement of sex offenders in the local community. This may be particularly the case in a society transitioning from decades of political conflict, such as Northern Ireland, where there are enhanced concerns relating to the legitimacy of the authorities and official decision-making.[171] In turn, a regulatory framework which is more receptive to public concerns about sex offenders may have increased legitimacy for professionals and the public in dealing with controversial issues surrounding sex offender reintegration.

Second, the fuller implementation of restorative measures may serve to alleviate many of the problems to date in effectively managing sex offenders in the community. In the main, 'the democratization and/or humanization of justice'[172] may help to diffuse hostile community reactions towards convicted sex offenders. As De Haan and Loader have contended more generally, more rational debates about sex offending involves fully acknowledging its emotional dimensions in order to have forms of social control that are more 'reasonable' and 'just'.[173] A move away from the 'otherness' of sex offending towards a recognition that sex offenders are 'of us' rather than 'other than us' may facilitate more rational and considered responses to sexual crime both on the part of policymakers and a concerned public.[174] As outlined above, circles of support and accountability have been used effectively to mediate between the media and the wider community in relation to concerns over the reintegration of high-risk sex offenders. Communities, for example, can offer support and encouragement towards offenders in the process of reintegration and change, while protecting them from wider community vengeance.[175]

---

[168] McAlinden, *The Shaming of Sexual Offenders* (n 4) 191–94.
[169] Crawford, *The Local Governance of Crime* (n 162).
[170] Ericson and Haggerty (n 67).
[171] A McAlinden, 'Public and Official Responses to Sexual and Violent Crime' in A McAlinden and C Dwyer (eds), *Criminal Justice in Transition: The Northern Ireland Context* (Oxford, Hart Publishing, 2015).
[172] De Haan and Loader (n 1) 248.
[173] Ibid, 250.
[174] McAlinden, 'Deconstructing Victim and Offender Identities' (n 100).
[175] McAlinden, *The Shaming of Sexual Offenders* (n 4) 192.

Moreover, recognising 'the humaneness of the perpetrator'[176] may also lead to more rational and effective criminal justice policies by making policymakers and society more fully aware of a wider range of potential risks to children including those which lie closest to home.

Third, giving victims the option to become involved in restorative processes may also help the emotional healing and wellbeing of victims. Restorative schemes can create favourable conditions for restoration, support victims and their needs and create a safe environment where inappropriate behaviour can be challenged.[177] As noted above, critics of restorative justice processes point principally towards the reinforcement of power imbalances in abusive relationships and the encouragement of repeat victimisation.[178] Child sexual abuse in particular is part of the broader category of gendered and sexualised violence which causes significant trauma for victims.[179] There is an important therapeutic dimension to restorative justice which is absent from formal criminal justice processes.[180] Giving victims the chance to tell their story, however, where they can 'put [their] claims in [their] own terms' and not 'have to accommodate to the dominant modes of legal/political discourse',[181] may have important cathartic benefits for victims. The experience of seeing that the offender is affected by genuine feelings of remorse and shame should also have a restorative effect for the victim.[182] Furthermore, reducing the emotive and punitive reactions on the part of the public to allegations of sexual abuse may ultimately help more victims to come forward at an earlier stage in the abusive process, thereby breaking cycles of abuse.[183] This may be particularly the case for victims of intra-familial abuse and their families who may wish to continue contact with the abuser and who simply want the abuse to stop rather than see the offender vilified or punished.[184]

In sum, criminology and criminal justice must deal with the instrumental as well as the sentimental aspects of penal policy.[185] Indeed, as Freiberg has contended, 'crime prevention strategies are more likely to be successful if they recognize and

---

[176] BCJ van Roermund, 'Rubbing Off and Rubbing On: The Grammar of Reconciliation' in EA Christodoulidis and S Veitch (eds), *Lethe's Law* (Oxford, Hart Publishing, 2001).

[177] McCold (n 105) 92–96.

[178] See eg, A Cossins, 'Restorative Justice and Child Sex Offences: The Theory and the Practice' (2008) 48 *British Journal of Criminology* 359.

[179] J Herman, *Trauma and Recovery* (New York, Basic Books, 1997).

[180] J Doak, 'The Therapeutic Dimension of Transitional Justice: Emotional Repair and Victim Satisfaction in International Trials and Truth Commissions' (2011) 11 *International Criminal Law Review* 263.

[181] BA Hudson, 'Beyond White Man's Justice: Race, Gender, and Justice in Late Modernity' (2006) 10 *Theoretical Criminology* 29, 34.

[182] L Walgrave and A Aersten, 'Reintegrative Shaming and Restorative Justice: Interchangeable, Complementary or Different?' (1996) 4 *European Journal on Criminal Policy and Research* 67, 77.

[183] McAlinden, 'The Use of "Shame" with Sexual Offenders' (n 9) 384.

[184] McAlinden, *The Shaming of Sexual Offenders* (n 4) 204–05.

[185] D Garland, 'The Culture of High Crime Societies: Some Preconditions of "Law and Order" Policies' (2000) 40 *British Journal of Criminology* 347.

deal with the role of emotions, symbols, irrationalism, expressionism ... in the criminal justice system'.[186] In this respect, restorative schemes offer a practical agenda for meeting the affective as well as effective needs of victims, offenders and communities affected by sexual crime.[187] They offer a better balance between pro-active responses to the risks posed by sex offenders in the community and reactive, knee-jerk responses after specific cases occur.[188] As such, the future focus and the wider appreciation of harm underpinning restorative policies have the potential to 'make obsolete the negative, punishment-orientated policies'[189] which character-ise contemporary public and official discourses in relation to sex offenders.

It is fully acknowledged, however, that the advocacy of such schemes does not rest easily within the current climate of public panic and fear which exists con-cerning sex offending against children. As Sutton has argued, the primary chal-lenge facing future crime prevention strategies is to 'develop philosophies and programmes which could compete with law and order at both the symbolic and practical levels'.[190] Indeed, the principal challenge for any future shift in criminal justice policy-making becomes how to overcome the contemporary public and political 'mood' relating to 'populist punitiveness'[191] and meaningfully and con-structively engage the public in policy discourses concerning sex offending. The starting point has to be informing the public about the realities of sex offend-ing, including the statistics demonstrating the success of restorative schemes with high-risk sex offenders, particularly in terms of reducing rates of reoffending. The dissemination of such information may help persuade the public that this is ulti-mately a more rational, constructive and effective way of managing the risks they feel such offenders pose.

---

[186] Freiberg (n 56) 266.

[187] L Presser and E Gunnison, 'Strange Bedfellows: Is Sex Offender Notification a Form of Com-munity Justice?' (1999) 45 *Crime & Delinquency* 299.

[188] H Goldstein, *Problem-Orientated Policing* (London, McGraw-Hill, 1990) 45–47.

[189] EGM Weitekamp, H-J, Kerner and U Meier, 'Community and Problem-Oriented Policing in the Context of Restorative Justice' in EGM Weitekamp and HJ Kerner (eds), *Restorative Justice in Context: International Practice and Directions* (Cullompton, Devon, Willan Publishing, 2003) 321.

[190] A Sutton, 'Crime Prevention: The Policy Dilemmas—A Personal Account' in P O'Malley and A Sutton (eds), *Crime Prevention in Australia* (Sydney, The Federation Press, 1997) 17.

[191] Bottoms (n 10).

8

Emotions and the Assessment of Credibility

JANE HERLIHY* AND STUART TURNER†

I. Introduction

The first theme of this collection suggests that emotions are, in some cases, pre-existing, or intrinsic to the cases being heard. In some analyses of legal tradition, the law takes on the role of decision-making *in spite of* such emotions, laying them aside, as far as is possible. As psychologist and psychiatrist, the authors of this chapter argue that it is neither possible nor desirable to put aside the emotional elements of claimants' accounts or of decision-makers' responses. In order to achieve justice, or international protection in the case of refugee decisions, the more important task is to understand the role of emotion, and to take it into account in a full and nuanced understanding of the claim.

This chapter, written by two non-lawyers (a psychologist and a psychiatrist) sets out to examine the role of emotion in relation to the difficult decision-making area of credibility assessment using two case examples—torture survivors seeking asylum in another country (involving Refugee Convention and human rights law) and victims of sexual assault including rape (involving criminal law). Torture survivors present themselves with an account of their experience but often with no physical scars and usually with no documentation of their experiences; yet they have to convince a decision-maker that they are at risk of persecution to gain refugee status. In the same way, the prosecution of rape often has to rely on subjective evidence concerning consent; survivors have to be able to persuade a judge or jury that their account of this experience is truthful, and in particular, since rape is often an act of someone known to the victim,[1] that they had not consented.

---

* Centre for the Study of Emotion and Law.
† Trauma Clinic, London.
[1] See for example, Ministry of Justice Home Office and the Office for National Statistics, *An Overview of Sexual Offending in England and Wales* (2013).

It will be argued that reliance on judicial 'common sense'[2] in these situations is often flawed and may lead to incorrect decisions.

In both examples there is a trauma history (hence a state of disturbed emotion, which may or may not amount to a psychiatric disorder), and in neither is there usually sufficient objective corroboration to determine the legal claim. Torture is typically denied by states that perpetrate it, and survivors do not present with medical or prison records from their country of origin. Similarly in the criminal prosecution of rape, while there may be forensic evidence of sexual activity, the issue of consent often comes down to the credibility of the alleged victim as opposed to that of the alleged perpetrator, a process that has been described as a 'credibility contest'.[3] Refugee law judges in their decision-making are advised to draw on 'common sense and experience',[4] suggesting that their experience in similar cases is seen to be sufficient to guide their understanding of individual and social behaviour in contexts of mortal danger in different cultural settings across the world. Although there may be a great deal of experience in specialist tribunals and courts, this reliance on 'common sense' ignores the potential contribution of specialist scientific knowledge in this process. In some cases, medico-legal reports may be submitted, but in the UK, these are in practice only commissioned by the legal representative of the client,[5] subject to available funds, and indeed subject to the availability of legal representation.[6] Similarly, in domestic courts, trials of sexual assault often involve a jury, and there is a similar principle that jury members carry 'common sense' and that extra 'expert' information can only be brought into the court if it is shown to be beyond the knowledge of the average person.[7]

In both of these areas of law, therefore, the notion of 'common sense' has been invoked as a guide for judges and juries to help them make decisions about people's claims. Psychological science offers a growing body of knowledge on human behaviour relevant to the lives and behaviours of people making these claims before the law, but it is unclear how much of this actually informs many of the decisions being made. In this chapter, after considering some of the relevant legal issues and potential pitfalls, the focus will be on the application of psychological science to these important matters, and to its potential contribution as a means of challenging common myths and assumptions, thus improving the quality of justice.

---

[2] Independent Asylum Commission, *Fit for Purpose Yet? The Independent Asylum Commission's Interim Findings* (2008) 34.

[3] L Ellison, 'The Use and Abuse of Psychiatric Evidence in Rape Trials' (2009) 13 *The International Journal of Evidence & Proof* 28.

[4] Independent Asylum Commission (n 2).

[5] A Good, 'Expert Evidence in Asylum and Human Rights Appeals: An Expert's View' (2004) 16 *International Journal of Refugee Law* 358.

[6] Such reports can contribute not only a clinical assessment of any emotional difficulties or psychological disorder in the individual, but also can introduce scientific literature to explain why such problems might prevent the person from presenting a coherent account of events.

[7] See Ellison (n 3), for a discussion of the 'helpfulness' criterion for the inclusion of expert witness testimony in criminal courts.

II. The Law

A. Refugees

When an individual flees their home country and enters a country that is a party to the Refugee Convention, they can ask for protection, or 'asylum'. The receiving state must then decide if the person fits the legal criteria for refugee status, in which case they must be afforded protection and rights.

The definition of refugee status was developed by a group of states that came together after the Second World War and drafted the Convention for the Protection of Refugees.[8] It was approved in Geneva in 1951 (hence it is commonly called the 'Geneva Convention' on refugees), and it came into force in 1954. In 2015, there were 145 signatories to the Geneva Convention.[9] A refugee, as defined in Article 1(2) of the Geneva Convention, is a person who

> owing to well-founded fear of being persecuted for reasons of race, religion, nationality, membership of a particular social group or political opinion, is outside the country of his nationality and is unable or, owing to such fear, is unwilling to avail himself of the protection of that country.

This definition has been broadened in respect of Africa, where the term 'refugee' has been extended in Article 1 of the OAU Convention to apply also

> to every person who, owing to external aggression, occupation, foreign domination or events seriously disturbing public order in either part or the whole of his country of origin or nationality, is compelled to leave his place of habitual residence in order to seek refuge in another place outside his country of origin or nationality.

Similarly, the 1984 Cartagena Declaration extended the definition of refugees in the Americas to

> persons who have fled their country because their lives, safety, or freedom have been threatened by generalized violence, foreign aggression, internal conflicts, massive violations of human rights or other circumstances which have seriously disturbed public order.[10]

The United Nations High Commissioner for Refugees (UNHCR), who has a key role with regard to the implementation of these obligations, emphasises that the process is one of *recognition*—a person 'does not become a refugee because of recognition, but is recognised because he is a refugee'.[11]

---

[8] United Nations, *Convention Relating to the Status of Refugees,* adopted 28 July 1951, entered into force 22 April 1954 (1951).

[9] United Nations High Commissioner for Refugees (UNHCR), 'States Parties to the 1951 Convention relating to the Status of Refugees and the 1967 Protocol': www.unhcr.org/3b73b0d63.html.

[10] See J Herlihy, C Ferstman and S Turner, 'Legal Issues in Work with Asylum Seekers' in JP Wilson and B Drozdek (eds), *Broken Spirits: The Treatment of Traumatized Asylum Seekers, Refugees, and War and Torture Victims* (New York, Brunner-Routledge, 2004).

[11] UNHCR, *Handbook on Procedures and Criteria for Determining Refugee Status under the 1951 Convention and the 1967 Protocol relating to the Status of Refugees* (Geneva) para 28.

All refugees are entitled to the protection of the principle of *non-refoulement*, which is defined in Article 33(1) of the 1951 Convention as follows:

> No Contracting State shall expel or return ('refouler') a refugee in any manner what-soever to the frontiers of territories where his life or freedom would be threatened on account of his race, religion, nationality, membership of a particular social group or political opinion.

This principle applies not only to refugees, but also to asylum seekers whose status has not yet been determined, and those seeking entry at a border.[12] *Non-refoulement* is also prohibited by the Convention against Torture, the European Convention on Human Rights, the American Convention on Human Rights, and the African Charter on Human and Peoples' Rights.[13]

The European Union Directive 2004/83/EC additionally provides for 'subsidiary protection', which is protection for individuals who do not qualify as refugees, but in respect of whom substantial grounds have been shown for believing that they would, if returned to their country of origin, face a real risk of suffering serious harm. Furthermore, Member States of the Council of Europe must consider the case law on Article 3 of the European Convention on Human Rights, which prevents the extradition of a person to another State where there are substantial grounds for believing that he would be in danger of being subjected to torture.[14] There are differences in the relief granted to those who qualify under the subsidiary protection or Article 3 but not the Refugee Convention; these vary across the different states of Europe.[15] There are also procedural differences in the ways that the different decision-making processes are implemented. In the UK, for example, the Refugee Convention, subsidiary protection and Article 3 are considered concurrently; in other jurisdictions, such as the Republic of Ireland, protection rights under the refugee Convention must be exhausted before the European Convention on Human Rights is considered.[16]

Refugee receiving states which are signatories to the 1951 Convention relating to the Status of Refugees, while bound to offer protection to persons fitting the definition of a refugee, are free to assess claimants by their own procedures. The UNHCR has issued a number of non-binding documents to guide the task. Thus, paragraph 195 of the UNHCR *Handbook* states that

> The relevant facts of the individual case will have to be furnished in the first place by the applicant himself. It will then be up to the person charged with determining his status

[12] UNHCR, *Conclusions of the Executive Committee No 6* (XXVIII 1977).

[13] See text above, nn 8–11.

[14] *Soering v UK* App no 14038/88 (ECHR, 7 July 1989) [91].

[15] See European Council on Refugees and Exiles (2009) Complementary Protection in Europe: www.refworld.org/pdfid/4a72c9a72.pdf; and the new Qualification Directive 2011/95/EU, designed to improve and make more uniform the decision-making and provisions for both refugees and those qualifying for subsidiary protection: eur-lex.europa.eu/legal-content/EN/TXT/PDF/?uri=CELEX:320 11L0095&from=EN.

[16] European Communities (Eligibility for Protection) Regulations SI No 518 of 2006 (article 4 in particular).

(the examiner) to assess the validity of any evidence and the credibility of the applicant's statements.[17]

Such statements usually involve a history of persecution, which goes towards establishing their 'well-founded fear' of return for one of the five Convention reasons.

Decision-making in most receiving countries has two or more stages, allowing for an initial decision and the possibility of an appeal process. In the UK, the initial decision is taken by a state-employed official, who interviews the claimant,[18] reviews any paperwork and either allows the claim or writes a 'Reasons for Refusal' letter, addressed to the claimant and signed 'on behalf of the Secretary of State'. The claimant may then appeal to an independent tribunal, consisting of a single judge, usually with an oral hearing.

B. Sexual Assault

As an example of the procedures involved in reporting and prosecuting sexual assault, we shall look at the law as it applies in the UK.[19] The prosecution of sexual assault (like reports of torture or other persecution) also necessitates the description of an event often in which only the people concerned were present. In order to initiate a process of prosecution, the survivor of a sexual assault must report the incident to the police. If this is immediately after the assault, an internal and external medical examination will usually be conducted in order to collect forensic evidence, and an initial statement is taken.[20] In the UK this is co-ordinated by a Specially Trained Officer (STO), who is trained in sexual offence investigative techniques.[21] The full statement of the incident is taken in a subsequent interview, either conducted or attended by the same STO. This interview is video recorded and is intended for use in any eventual court proceedings. In the course of the police investigation, the survivor should be kept up to date with progress, including being informed within 24 hours of any arrest. The survivor may be required to help with photo or video or (less often) live identification procedures. The decision as to whether or not to charge the suspect involves both an examination of the evidence and an assessment of public interest. The survivor may be called for a pre-trial witness interview. The decision to proceed to trial remains under review, for example as new evidence becomes available. The trial may then be conducted in a magistrates' court, heard by either a District Judge or three non-legally

---

[17] UNHCR, *Handbook* (n 11).

[18] This changes according to the asylum procedure in practice—some models favour one interviewer and decision-maker throughout, others separate these functions.

[19] The material in this section is taken largely from the Rights of Women publication, *From Report to Court: A Handbook for Adult Survivors of Sexual Violence*: rightsofwomen.org.uk/get-information/criminal-law/report-court-handbook-adult-survivors-sexual-violence. The advice in the handbook is based on the Sexual Offences Act 2003, which deals with offences that have taken place in England and Wales. Similar (but different) legislation deals with Northern Ireland and Scotland.

[20] Ibid.

[21] Ibid, 39.

qualified (lay) magistrates, or in the Crown Court, where the legal decisions (such as the admissibility of evidence) are made by the judge, while decisions about facts are made by a jury made up of 12 people selected at random from the public.

III. Credibility Assessment in the Legal Setting

In the academic literature authors have distinguished between the *credibility* of the person, which is matter of their honesty, and genuineness, and the *reliability* of their account, which refers to a judgement about the accuracy with which they are describing a given event.[22] Thus, the evidence of a credible witness may not be reliable.[23] In this chapter, we shall continue to use the term 'credibility' as this is widely applied, but we recognise that strictly speaking it is usually (and should be) the *reliability* of the narrative that is under consideration, rather than the credibility of the person.

A. Credibility Assessment in Refugee and Sexual Cases

In the context of refugee status determination, both state and judicial decision-makers have an unusually difficult task. There is often little or no specific corroborating evidence of any sort to add to the history given in support of the claim. The decision-maker may draw on country evidence, that is, reports gathered about current situations in general in the alleged country of origin. Other than this the judgement typically relies on an assessment of the credibility of the claimant and their account. This has to be performed within a highly politicised and media-dominated context of discussions about immigration, human rights and—rightly or wrongly—terrorism and crime.

Similarly in sexual assault cases, although there may be forensic evidence of sexual contact, in relation to adults this is often insufficient, as it usually does not address the central matter of consent.[24] For this reason, the narrative and the

---

[22] A Memon, 'Credibility of Asylum Claims: Consistency and Accuracy of Autobiographical Memory Reports Following Trauma' (2012) 26 *Applied Cognitive Psychology* 677.

[23] S Porter and L ten Brinke, 'Dangerous Decisions: A Theoretical Framework for Understanding How Judges Assess Credibility in the Courtroom' (2009) 14 *Legal and Criminological Psychology* 119, 120. In the refugee context there is also another dimension sometimes cited; notwithstanding clauses in the refugee Convention which exclude those convicted of certain criminal offences, judgements on the credibility of the asylum claimant can also take the decision-maker into unfortunate moral judgements about the 'worthiness' or general moral acceptability of claimants. See G Noll, 'Salvation by the Grace of State? Explaining Credibility Assessment in the Asylum Procedure' in G Noll (ed), *Proof, Evidentiary Assessment and Credibility in Asylum Procedures* (Leiden, Martinus Nijhoff Publishers, 2005). This draws interesting parallels between asylum claims and confession in the Roman Catholic Church.

[24] For a summary of the assessment of consent, see Rights of Women, *From Report to Court: A Handbook for Adult Survivors of Sexual Violence* (Rights of Women, 2014). See also J Temkin and B Krahé, *Sexual Assault and the Justice Gap: A Question of Attitude* (Oxford, Hart Publishing, 2008) 27.

credibility of the survivor take on a central role. Throughout the whole procedure there are a number of stages where credibility is crucial to the continuation of the process of obtaining justice. For example, the police may decide not to make any further investigation if they decide at the initial report that there is insufficient evidence.[25] Alternatively, individuals may themselves withdraw allegations for a variety of different reasons.[26] An important study by Hardy showed how this includes complainants' beliefs that they will not be believed.[27] This involved interviewing 22 people who had reported sexual assault within the previous 18 months and asking them to rate their memory for the event in terms of fragmentation and coherence. A questionnaire was used to assess how much the person had dissociated[28] at the time of the assault, and finally, the researcher asked the victim how likely it was that he or she would proceed with the case. There were significant positive correlations between peri-traumatic dissociation and self-reported memory fragmentation, between fragmented memory and self-reported account incoherence, and between account incoherence and likelihood of proceeding, leading to the conclusion that people who dissociated at the time of the assault were more likely to report fragmented memories. Moreover, the study concluded that 'people who provided the police with a more incoherent account of their sexual assault perceived themselves to be less likely to proceed with their legal case'.[29]

Even where the complaint is pursued, the decision of the prosecution to proceed to trial will also rely heavily on the perceived credibility of the allegation. The judge and/or jury will also have to decide whether to accept the narrative offered by the complainant or the defendant. Survivors of rape, after cross-examination in the courts, often describe a sense in which they feel that they have been on trial rather than the perpetrator, sometimes with tragic consequences.[30] Early observational studies of the prosecution of rape highlighted a focus on omissions and discrepancies in the victim/witness's statements and the way in which the centrality of the issue of consent leads to a focus on his or her credibility. Bohmer and Blumberg state that 'it is because of the difficulty of legally determining the issue of consent that cross-examination will be so much more harrowing for a rape

---

[25] L Kelly, J Lovett and L Regan, *A Gap or a Chasm? Attrition in Reported Rape Cases* (London Metropolitan University, Child and Woman Abuse Studies Unit, 2005).

[26] Temkin and Krahé (n 24) ch 1. See also C Saunders, 'The Truth, the Half-Truth, and Nothing Like the Truth' (2012) 52 *British Journal of Criminology* 1152 for an interesting attempt to understand the differing positions of academics and front line criminal justice professionals on the rates of false allegations of rape.

[27] A Hardy, K Young and EA Holmes, 'Does Trauma Memory Play a Role in the Experience of Reporting Sexual Assault During Police Interviews? An Exploratory Study' (2009) 17 *Memory* 783.

[28] Dissociation has been described as a 'disruption in the usually integrated functions of consciousness, memory, identity, or perception of the environment'—American Psychiatric Association, *Diagnostic and Statistical Manual of Mental Disorders DSM-IV-TR* (Washington DC, American Psychiatric Association, 1994). The mildest form of dissociation is daydreaming, but at the other extreme can involve feelings of 'depersonalisation' (feeling unreal, perhaps a sense of observing oneself from the outside, or from above) or 'derealisation', where the physical world seems unreal.

[29] Hardy, Young, and Holmes (n 27) 786.

[30] www.theguardian.com/society/2013/apr/13/rape-sexual-assault-frances-andrade-court.

victim than for a prosecuting witness in another type of criminal case'.[31] In order
to test this view, Brereton applied a comparative framework to court cases between
1989 and 1991 heard in the Melbourne County Court addressing allegations of
physical assault and of rape, investigating the cross-examination in each.[32] In a
comparison of transcripts he found no differences in the tactics of the defence
counsel, such as attacks on the character and credibility of the complainants, questions about drinking and 'mental stability', finding inconsistencies, questioning
expected behaviour, including prompt reporting of the crime. However, he did
find that rape complainants were, on average, questioned for twice as long as complainants in trials for assault[33] and in the examples cited, he demonstrated the
intimate nature of the questioning, thus allowing him to conclude that the process
was likely to be more traumatic for rape complainants. While these studies are now
quite old, and reforms have been introduced to the procedures they examined, a
more recent observational study in the UK has made similar findings.[34] Six trials
were observed, and the researcher's notes were analysed using critical discourse
analysis. The themes that emerged from the data were routine delays, the notion
of 'rational' behaviour, extreme interpretations of 'beyond reasonable doubt' and
'burden of proof', and winning the case as priority. The interpretation of reasonable doubt as 'any doubt' led to a focus on the victim, who, as a result, suffered
harsher manipulation tactics and more critical evaluations of their evidence.[35]

Bohmer and Blumberg also argued that the way in which such victims were
examined by the prosecution and defence served to stir up fears, insecurities,
embarrassment and irrational guilty feelings.[36] We shall show that this is not just
a matter of unpleasantness for these complainants, but can have an effect on how
they are perceived, potentially unfairly affecting the assessment of their credibility.

B. Pitfalls in 'Common Sense' Credibility Assessment

As we have seen, common sense, or 'the knowledge of the average person',[37] is
often a misleading guide to judging the validity of an individual's testimony. In
particular, scientific studies establish that common sense ideas about memory
are not always accurate or in accordance with the findings of empirical research.
For instance a study conducted in Norway[38] asked participants a number of

---

[31] C Bohmer and A Blumberg, 'Twice Traumatized: The Rape Victim and the Court' (1975) 58 *Judicature* 391, 395.
[32] D Brereton, 'How Different Are Rape Trials' (1997) 37 *British Journal of Criminology* 242.
[33] Rape cases had an average of 25 pages of evidence-in-chief and 55 pages of cross-examination; for
assault cases, this was 12 pages of evidence-in-chief and 27 pages of cross-examination.
[34] O Smith and T Skinner, 'Observing Court Responses to Victims of Rape and Sexual Assault'
(2012) 7 *Feminist Criminology* 298.
[35] Ibid, 311.
[36] Bohmer and Blumberg (n 31) 394.
[37] See text above, n 7.
[38] S Magnussen et al, 'What People Believe About Memory' (2006) 14 *Memory* 595.

fixed-response questions about aspects of memory, for which there are reasonably clear answers in the research literature. The authors concluded that, where people can draw on their own experience of memory phenomena, such as their age at their earliest memory, and where the research literature has confirmed folk psychology, they are accurate in their understanding of memory. However, a significant number of the respondents endorsed notions contrary to research, for example, that memory has a limited 'storage capacity' or that children have better or equally good memory abilities as compared with adults.

Further studies have used the same questions with judges in the US[39] and Norway,[40] concluding that both had limited knowledge of eyewitness memory factors, and that they often harboured beliefs and opinions that were at odds with current scientific knowledge.[41] Even psychologists and psychiatrists serving as expert witnesses have been found in some cases to harbour scientifically unproven ideas of human memory on issues such as the memory of small children, repression of adult traumatic memories, and recovered traumatic childhood memories.[42] Howe also illustrates this point with case examples of historic sexual abuse, where he shows how memory expertise drawing on the scientific literature would have avoided lengthy and costly prosecutions which then were dismissed at court once the memories claimed were assessed in the light of the scientific literature.[43] All of this underlines the importance of keeping up to date with the science.

These studies show that there is a consistent gap between a careful examination of scientific findings and the 'common sense' associated with decision-making in court. There is a need to educate and to continue to educate judges, juries and expert witnesses to ensure that fair and just determinations can be made, where necessary based on scientific understanding of memory.

Turning to the particular treatment of allegations of rape, Temkin and Krahé[44] have argued that in all of the decision-making process, from initial reporting to the police, through to courtroom conviction or acquittal and sentencing, those making the decisions (police, lawyers, judge or jury) are unduly influenced by their attitudes to rape and sexual assault. They suggest that, rather than turning to research evidence on how people behave during and after sexual violence, decision-makers are informed by widely held (but inaccurate) stereotypes of the typical rape—that it is most likely to be by a stranger, using threat or force, and

---

[39] RA Wise and MA Safer, 'What US Judges Know and Believe About Eyewitness Testimony' (2004) 18 *Applied Cognitive Psychology* 427 (detailing a study of 160 judges).

[40] S Magnussen et al, 'What Judges Know About Eyewitness Testimony: A Comparison of Norwegian and US Judges' (2008) 14 *Psychology, Crime & Law* 177 (detailing a study of 157 judges).

[41] Ibid, 185.

[42] A Melinder and S Magnussen, 'Psychologists and Psychiatrists Serving as Expert Witnesses in Court: What Do They Know About Eyewitness Memory?' (2015) 21 *Psychology, Crime & Law* 53.

[43] ML Howe, 'Memory Lessons from the Courtroom: Reflections On Being a Memory Expert on the Witness Stand' (2012) 21 *Memory* 576.

[44] Temkin and Krahé (n 24).

with active resistance on the part of the victim.[45] They also present data from studies of law students, barristers and community participants showing that decisions
made by people who score highly on measures of adherence to such 'rape myths'
are more likely to make judgements about what they believe happened in line with
those myths, rather than being driven by the evidence.[46]

Temkin[47] goes on to review how research evidence that counters the stereotypes
of rape might be introduced into credibility assessment in rape trials. In the past
this has not been very successful,[48] and Temkin ties this in to the actual experience in court of a trial that can last many days, the hearing of all the evidence, the
opportunity to construct a guiding narrative,[49] and the coming to preliminary
conclusions.[50] She concludes that 'myth busting is an essential activity that needs
to be undertaken within society at large, particularly in schools, as well as in the
context of education of the police, barristers, and judges'.[51]

Turning to the case of refugees, the present authors have taken a different
approach to examining the underlying knowledge base of judicial decisions in this
context. As we have seen, the law allows those who have been turned down for
refugee status to appeal to an immigration judge.[52] In order to clarify some of
the assumptions that immigration judges rely on in their decision-making in this
context, we[53] conducted a qualitative study of a series of UK determinations. UK
immigration judges are required to produce a written determination, outlining
the claim before them, the law on which they rely and the decisions that go to
make up the final decision whether to allow or dismiss the appeal. A copy of this
written determination is made available to the appellant.[54]

---

[45] Schema-driven processing is the way in which we draw on generic descriptions (including stereotypes) to make decisions, rather than taking the (more effortful) approach of examining the available
data—see ST Fiske and SE Taylor, *Social Cognition* (New York, McGraw-Hill 1991).

[46] Temkin and Krahé (n 24) Study 3.

[47] J Temkin, '"And Always Keep A-Hold of Nurse, For Fear of Finding Something Worse": Challenging Rape Myths in the Courtroom' (2010) 13 *New Criminal Law Review* 710.

[48] L Ellison and VE Munro, 'Turning Mirrors Into Windows?' (2009) 49 *British Journal of Criminology* 363.

[49] N Pennington and R Hastie, 'The Story Model for Juror Decision Making' in R Hastie (ed), *Inside
the Juror: The Psychology of Juror Decision Making* (Cambridge, Cambridge University Press, 1993).

[50] Research suggests that jurors form views about the verdict early on in the trial—see for example,
VP Hans, 'US Jury Reform: The Active Jury and the Adversarial Ideal' (2002) 85 *Saint Louis University
Public Law Review* 85.

[51] Temkin and Krahé (n 24) 734. This is a difficult area of study since it is prone to suggestions of
ideological bias. However, the present authors argue that this is all the more reason for renewed efforts
to bring hard evidence from scientific study into the investigative and judicial arenas for the prosecution of rape. We recognise that this will mean that experts in court will have to be able to demonstrate
that they are familiar with, and understand, current scientific advances.

[52] See text above, n 18.

[53] J Herlihy, K Gleeson and S Turner, 'What Assumptions About Human Behaviour Underlie Asylum Judgments?' (2010) 22 *International Journal of Refugee Law* 351.

[54] Using an initial sample of determinations, a coding structure was developed, which defined
assumptions about people's behaviour, intentions, motivations, knowledge, and what people do when
they are telling the truth. These definitions were then used to build a data set of 117 assumptions,
which were then subjected to an inductive and data-driven thematic analysis: Herlihy, Gleeson and
Turner (n 53) 355 ff.

Three major themes became apparent from this study. First, assumptions were made about how a truthful claimant *would have behaved in situations of fear or traumatic experience.* Thus, adverse interpretations were made on the basis of how the judge assumed that people should behave; for example, a husband who sent his wife to this country ahead of anyone in his own family, including his sister, who had been raped, was seen to be non-credible. Similarly, in assessing situations outside their personal experience, immigration judges also drew upon their sense of plausibility; thus in one case the judge considered it 'implausible that a family in fear, on seeing a man throw something over the fence and into their garden ... would go to investigate it'.[55]

Second, assumptions were made about how people *behave through the asylum-seeking process.* This included basing credibility judgements on whether the appellant applied for asylum immediately upon arrival, as well as the less obvious assumptions that claimants will know and use appropriate language and behaviour in the court. For example, of a man alleging persecution on the grounds of his sexuality, from a country where homosexuality is illegal, the judge wrote that, '[t]he appellant denies having slept with the sponsor, which the sponsor [a UK citizen] says has occurred'.[56] In another case, the judge apparently drew adverse conclusions from the fact that '[n]one of the three witnesses testified about any of the hardships faced by the appellant and her family'.[57] Both of these examples assume that the appellant and family or friends understand and have accepted both their role in the court and what they are expected to speak about. This theme also raises questions about cross-cultural communication in the court, and how well the 'rules of conversation'[58] of the different cultures (of court and appellant) are understood by all parties.

The third theme identified was to do with assumptions about the *nature of a truthful account.* Internal inconsistency in details across repeated questioning, late disclosure of material facts and lay assumptions about memory were all being relied upon to indicate a fabrication of a claim for protection. One judge wrote that:

> Given that rape is such a serious thing to happen to any woman, I would have expected a raped person to know when they were raped. This is not the type of event which I would expect a person to forget about or confuse.[59]

---

[55] Ibid, 358.

[56] Ibid, 360.

[57] Ibid.

[58] The Cooperative Principle of conversation, as first described by P Grice, 'Logic and Conversation' in P Cole and J Morgan (eds), *Syntax and Semantics, 3: Speech Acts* (Cambridge, Academic Press, 1975), states that in conversation we generally adhere to certain principles, or 'maxims' that ensure effective and collaborative communication. One example of this is the 'maxim of relevance' where one tries to be relevant, and say things that are pertinent to the discussion. This means that when Alice says 'where's Bill?' and Carol says 'he has a cold' the assumption is that he is not present because of his cold, since it is assumed that Carol is being relevant. The 'maxim of quantity'—where one tries to be as informative as one possibly can, and gives as much information as is needed, and no more—exemplifies the cross-cultural aspect of the assumptions, as seen in the enquiry 'how are you?' answered with differing quantities of information by conversationalists from different cultures.

[59] Herlihy, Gleeson and Turner (n 53) 361.

In another case, a judgement that an account was true was based on an assumption about the consistency of memory on the grounds that '[He] was able to with-
stand a cross examination ... that lasted for over one hour without any serious
discrepancies coming to light'.[60]

The important issue raised by this study lies not in the individual examples,
but in the assumptions on which they are based. We do not argue that it was necessarily inappropriate to draw these conclusions from the evidence in particular
cases. We do argue, however, that these matters concerning human behaviour, or
intention, or response to situations are all areas of psychological enquiry, some of
which have an extensive knowledge base. It is essential that this should be available
to decision-makers to inform their judgements and to prevent them mistakenly
relying on one of the unfounded assumptions or myths that still abound.

The contention raised by this study, therefore, is in line with previous studies
on knowledge of eye-witness testimony and on studies of the reliance on myths in
rape trials;[61] namely that, in such a crucial area, decisions based on assumptions
about people's behaviour, intentions and motivation should draw on the latest and
best available scientific knowledge.

IV. Psychological Science and the Claimant

In this part of the chapter we shall see how the current psychological literature can
inform our understanding of how people remember and relate past experiences.

A. Introduction to Memory

One of the most commonly used indicators of credibility in these cases is the consistency of an account over multiple telling.[62] This is a long-standing assumption,
and one entirely understandable from a lay perspective. Someone who is telling
the truth will be able to 'keep their story straight'; if it keeps changing then this
is because there are no 'underlying facts'.[63] However, the relevant literature now
shows overwhelmingly that these assumptions are based on a misunderstanding of

---

[60] Ibid, 362.
[61] See Temkin and Krahé (n 24).
[62] PA Granhag, LA Stromwall and M Hartwig, 'Granting Asylum or Not? Migration Board Personnel's Beliefs About Deception' (2005) 31 *Journal of Ethnic and Migration Studies* 29; J Jordan, 'Worlds
Apart? Women, Rape and the Police Reporting Process' (2001) 41 *British Journal of Criminology* 679;
Kelly, Lovett and Regan (n 25).
[63] There is an even more sophisticated version of this assumption; someone who knows that they
falsely gave an account of being tortured will be able to repeat the core of their story but will fall down
on the detail, giving different versions on repeat questioning.

how memory works. There are different ways of looking at memory, for example memory for facts (semantic memory); memory for experiences (episodic memory); memory for dangerous events (fear memory); and memory for how to do things (procedural memory).[64] Autobiographical memory is generally described as the combination of semantic knowledge and episodic memory, giving us a description of events experienced in our lives, and this is the type of memory that is required when reporting persecution in the asylum process or sexual assault for prosecution. Accordingly, this is the area on which we focus here.

Autobiographical memory serves a number of functions.[65] First, the recalling and telling of episodes from the past helps us to develop, maintain and nurture social bonds. Second, our personal past is our guide to our behaviour in the present: it gives us examples of key events that helped to develop our moral and emotional responses, and it helps us explain to ourselves and others the decisions we make about life directions. Accordingly, our stories of the past will be updated and developed in the light of new understandings about ourselves and the world. Consequently, our autobiographical memories guide our definition and expression of our own identities and sense of self, and the changing self, maintaining our sense of 'biographical identity'.[66] In the context of experiences that challenge the self, memories can be modified and refined in order to protect, or rebuild this sense of self.

In general, scientific study now demonstrates that autobiographical memory is an exercise of *reconstruction*, not *reproduction*, as was once thought. As we have pointed out in our previous research:

> Contrary to common lay opinion, research over the last 50 years has provided compelling evidence to suggest that autobiographical remembering is not an exact replaying of an event. This type of memory is a reconstruction of events based on several elements and subject to distortion as well as failure (forgetting or false remembering).[67]

Thus, we see a chasm of misunderstanding. The legal systems we have examined demand, or expect consistent, detailed, coherent memories in order to establish legal evidence. However as we have seen, human autobiographical memory has developed to be socially interactive, flexible and open to being updated and refined.[68]

---

[64] See Hungarian Helsinki Committee, *Credibility Assessment in Asylum Procedures—A Multidisciplinary Training Manual, 2013, Volume 1*: www.refworld.org/docid/5253bd9a4.html for a fuller explanation of the different types of memory.

[65] For a fuller review of autobiographical memory and the asylum process, see J Herlihy, L Jobson and S Turner, 'Just Tell Us What Happened to You: Autobiographical Memory and Seeking Asylum' (2012) 26 *Applied Cognitive Psychology* 661.

[66] Ibid, 663.

[67] Ibid, 662.

[68] To illustrate a potential example of this, a young man interviewed twice about a police interrogation said on the first occasion 'we were slapped around', but on a later occasion 'we were badly beaten': J Herlihy, P Scragg and S Turner, 'Discrepancies in Autobiographical Memories: Implications for the Assessment of Asylum Seekers: Repeated Interviews Study' (2002) 324 *British Medical Journal* 324, 327.

When it comes to more dramatic and potentially distressing events, studies of returning veterans[69] and refugees show that people often change their answers to a checklist of events. These are not questions about trivial experiences. In the military studies, for example, there are events such as encountering mines or booby traps, or being shot at. This phenomenon is not yet fully understood—it may be related to changes in the symptoms of post-traumatic stress,[70] depression,[71] or the form of the questions (more or less specific).[72] Unravelling this is likely to be of particular relevance to interviewers in legal procedures.

One very robust finding in the literature shows that, when events are distressing, there is a focusing of attention on the 'central' details of the event.[73] In one classic experiment,[74] participants watched one of two video recordings of a simulated armed bank robbery, at the end of which the robbers ran away past a young boy with a rugby shirt with a number on the back. The recordings were identical for each group, except that in one version, at the end one of the robbers turned and shot the boy in the face, while in the other the robbers merely ran away. The researchers found that the participants who watched the video with the shooting were less likely to be able to recall the number on the boy's shirt, compared with those who had watched the 'non-traumatic' video. This effect has been replicated, and a distinction is now made when talking about disturbing or distressing memories, between the 'central' details of a story—that is, what is important to the gist of the narrative or the emotional content of the account—and 'peripheral' details, such as the number on a boy's rugby shirt (before he is shot), or indeed the date of a beating while in detention, or the exact number and dress of people involved in a gang rape. More recent research has shown that memory for both central and peripheral details declines over time, with normal forgetting, but memory for central details declines more slowly.[75]

[69] S Southwick et al, 'Consistency of Memory for Combat-Related Traumatic Events in Veterans of Operation Desert Storm' (1997) 154 *American Journal of Psychiatry* 173; DW King et al, 'Posttraumatic Stress Disorder and Retrospectively Reported Stressor Exposure: A Longitudinal Prediction Model' (2000) 109 *Journal of Abnormal Psychology* 624; IM Engelhard, MA van den Hout and RJ McNally, 'Memory Consistency for Traumatic Events in Dutch Soldiers Deployed to Iraq' (2008) 16 *Memory* 3.
[70] King et al (n 69).
[71] PK Schraedley, RJ Turner and IH Gotlib, 'Stability of Retrospective Reports in Depression: Traumatic Events, Past Depressive Episodes, and Parental Psychopathology' (2002) 43 *Journal of Health and Social Behavior* 307.
[72] K Krinsley et al, 'Consistency of Retrospective Reporting About Exposure to Traumatic Events' (2003) 16 *Journal of Traumatic Stress* 399.
[73] S-A Christianson, 'Remembering Emotional Events: Potential Mechanisms' in S-A Christianson (ed), *The Handbook of Emotion and Memory: Research and Theory* (copy of chapter; book in DSW, Lawrence Erlbaum Associates Inc, 1992).
[74] E Loftus and T Burns, 'Mental Shock Can Produce Retrograde Amnesia' (1982) 10 *Memory & Cognition* 241.
[75] T Lanciano and A Curci, 'Memory for Emotional Events: The Accuracy of Central and Peripheral Detail' (2011) 7 *Europe's Journal of Psychology* 323.

Finally, Granhag and others tested the notion of 'keeping the story straight', in a context resembling legal interviewing.[76] They asked pairs of participants either to make up (as if for an alibi), or to recall having lunch together (the lunch was provided to half of the participants). All of the participants were then individually interrogated twice, using a structured interview. When their accounts were analysed, contrary to the common assumptions about credibility assessment in legal procedures, both liars' and truth-tellers' accounts were equally inconsistent over time, in terms of number of repeated themes, omissions and contradictions.[77]

B. Emotion and Memory

All of these factors can be aggravated in situations of high emotion. Thus, when Brereton compared the cross-examination of complainants in rape and assault trials, he saw no significant differences in the approach of the cross-examiners, but did end by noting that

> [i]t is also probable that being a complainant in a rape trial is frequently a more traumatic experience than being a complainant in an assault trial, because of the intimate nature of the matters which are canvassed in rape trials, the length of time which the complainant must spend in the witness box [on average twice as long as the assault complainants], and the degree of trauma associated with the offence itself.[78]

This raises not just the issue of the care which needs to be taken of these witnesses, but also the important question of exactly how the emotional impact of both the offence and the court experience might affect the quality of the evidence being considered. As an example, consider a man who has been repeatedly sexually assaulted, while imprisoned in a state that is known to use torture. He has managed to get to a safe country and has indicated that he wants to claim asylum. However, he says only that he was detained and beaten, but is vague and his story keeps changing. He feels very ashamed that he was raped, and has an overwhelming urge not to think or talk about this experience. Consequently he is refused asylum by the state, on the basis that he is not credible. His lawyer helps him to prepare an appeal and he appears at the tribunal and discloses the sexual assault. He appears very distressed on cross-examination, and as a result he is barely

---

[76] PA Granhag, LA Stromwall and A-C Jonsson, 'Partners in Crime: How Liars in Collusion Betray Themselves' (2003) 33 *Journal of Applied Social Psychology* 848.

[77] Interestingly, in frank contradiction to the assumption that liars are more likely to 'embellish a story', it was found that it was the truth-tellers who added significantly more new themes to their initial statements. These findings support the authors' *repeat versus reconstruct* hypothesis, which suggests that liars will try to repeat what they stated during previous interrogations, whereas truth-tellers will try to reconstruct what they actually experienced.

[78] Brereton (n 32) 259.

coherent. The judge rejects his claim on the basis of inconsistency and incoherence, also suspecting that the appellant's advisers may have coached him before the hearing. In this case, a genuine claimant has been disadvantaged specifically by his emotional responses to these experiences—the initial assault and the subsequent interrogation.

C. Traumatic Memory

After a particularly shocking experience, it is common to develop an emotional memory of specific aspects of the event.[79] This is a sensory 'snapshot' of the traumatic moment—perhaps just the sound of screams, the image of a face, the smell of smoke, or a feeling of pain; it is without narrative structure, and, crucially, does not have a sense of being in the past, but is 're-experienced', as if it were happening in the present. These memories are not available for updating, in contrast to our normal memories, which we might change in the light of new information, or a new listener.[80] They are not voluntary, as normal memories, but triggered, by external or internal cues, such as the sight of someone in uniform, a pain, or a feeling of guilt. They probably serve an important evolutionary function. This is part of an extremely rapid danger alerting system, as a result of which we can attend very rapidly to other events in which the same sensory pattern (signature) is evident and can start to take steps to respond—even before the information reaches our conscious mind.[81]

So after an emotionally charged adverse experience, we may have a combination of normal autobiographical memories, subject to voluntary recall and all the distortions of normal memory identified above, and in addition, these sensory traumatic memories. The autobiographical memories have a beginning, middle and end, a sense of being in the past, and may be updated should new information become available. The sensory traumatic memories, however, do not have a beginning, middle and end, are not date-stamped and are not subject to updating in the same way. Indeed there is good evidence that these traumatic memories are never totally forgotten, although over time they will be less likely to be accessed.[82]

---

[79] C Brewin, T Dalgleish and S Joseph, 'A Dual Representation Theory of Posttraumatic Stress Disorder' (1996) 103 *Psychological Review* 671; C Brewin, 'A Cognitive Neuroscience Account of Posttraumatic Stress Disorder and its Treatment' (2001) 39 *Behaviour Research and Therapy* 373; C Brewin et al, 'Intrusive Images in Psychological Disorders: Characteristics, Neural Mechanisms and Treatment Implications' (2010) 117 *Psychological Review* 210.

[80] Indeed this is one of the tasks of psychological therapy: to make such memories available in such a way that updating information can be incorporated, in order that the memory can be integrated into the rest of the person's identity and life story. For example, in a car accident one might have a very strong thought that 'I'm going to die'. In PTSD the memory of this moment can cause ongoing fear and distress, if not 'updated' with the knowledge 'I did not die'.

[81] C Brewin et al, 'Intrusive Images in Psychological Disorders: Characteristics, Neural Mechanisms and Treatment Implications' (2010) 117 *Psychological Review* 210.

[82] Ibid.

D. Post-Traumatic Stress Disorder (PTSD) and Depression

Most people recover from traumatic experiences, given time and the right kinds of family and social support.[83] However, for some people, a pattern develops of persistent, intrusive, distressing re-experiencing of the event, strong efforts to avoid the triggers of the memories, emotional numbing, distorted beliefs and a variety of other symptoms, such as sleep disturbance, irritability, anger, loss of concentration and a tendency to be easily startled and excessively aware of potential threat. These comprise the core symptoms of Post-Traumatic Stress Disorder (PTSD).[84] However, even without reaching the threshold of a diagnosis, these symptoms can seriously impede the process of making a claim for protection. PTSD avoidance symptoms in particular may include conscious avoidance, such as an effort not to speak or think or have feelings about the traumatic event. However, they can also include avoidance which is not under the conscious control of the individual, such as emotional numbing, or dissociation—'cutting out'—under even moderate stress.

Perhaps not surprisingly, in the face of managing such extreme emotion, many people with PTSD also show the symptoms of depression; indeed it has been said to be 'the norm rather than the exception'.[85] What is useful here is to consider not just the categoric diagnosis, but the symptoms, which include persistent low mood, loss of pleasure or interest in activities previously enjoyed, sleep problems, fatigue or loss of energy, diminished ability to think or concentrate or indecisiveness, feelings of worthlessness or excessive guilt, and recurrent thoughts of death or of harming or killing oneself,[86] all of which might impair an individual's ability to present a coherent and credible account in a legal process. The diminished ability to think or concentrate in depression can be sufficiently marked to resemble the effects of traumatic brain injury or dementia.

Again, it is not necessarily the diagnosis of depression which holds the key to understanding the possible difficulties for an asylum seeker or survivor of rape with the legal processes she or he has to traverse. However, it is important to examine the individual symptoms that may be present and the effects of these. For example, asylum seekers are often asked factual questions about their country in order to establish their provenance, and feelings of worthlessness might lower a person's confidence in their memory and knowledge, leaving them appearing unsure—and hence not credible. Similarly, poor concentration, or simply not having slept for more than a few hours together for many months, can make a

---

[83] B Andrews, CR Brewin and S Rose, 'Gender, Social Support, and PTSD in Victims of Violent Crime' (2003) 16 *Journal of Traumatic Stress* 421.

[84] American Psychiatric Association, *Diagnostic and Statistical Manual of Mental Disorders*, 5th edn (American Psychiatric Association, 2013).

[85] ML O'Donnell, M Creamer and P Pattison, 'Posttraumatic Stress Disorder and Depression Following Trauma: Understanding Comorbidity' (2004) 161 *American Journal of Psychiatry* 1390, 1390.

[86] American Psychiatric Association (n 84).

person poorly equipped for lengthy, detailed interviews about their present and past circumstances.

As noted above, the full complement of these symptoms of PTSD and depression will not happen to everyone who experiences a potentially traumatic event. There is evidence, however, that some types of event are more likely to precipitate these more extreme emotional responses for longer than just the immediate aftermath of the event. A community survey in Detroit from 1998 (when much of the focus on PTSD was on veterans, particularly from Vietnam) showed that assaultive violence and rape were most likely to give rise to PTSD.[87] More recent studies also find that rape and sexual assault are the events most likely to be associated with PTSD, for both men and women.[88]

E. Inconsistencies and PTSD

Emotional responses to major traumatic events, including PTSD, unfortunately stand to increase the risk of inconsistent recall. This is particularly important since, if discrepancies are used to infer lack of credibility, it raises the potential for a systematic bias in the decision-making process to the detriment of those who are genuinely traumatised.

Two studies, which specifically focused on the consistency of refugees' memory, had complementary findings. In the first, UK programme refugees—meaning they had been given blanket permission to stay in the UK, thus not having to engage with individual asylum claims—were interviewed about one traumatic and one non-traumatic experience on two occasions.[89] These interviews were unrelated to any legal process, and there was no obvious motivation for any deception. Approximately 30 per cent of the details they gave about these events changed between interviews.[90] They were also asked to rate whether the details were central to the narrative or emotional gist of what happened, or if they were peripheral to the experience.[91] Statistical analysis then showed that the highest rates of discrepancies between the interviews were for peripheral details of traumatic events, such as questions on the exact date that a traumatic event happened—exactly the kinds of details that are required of a 'credible' asylum claimant. The other finding from this study was that, for people with higher levels of PTSD symptoms, a longer time between interviews was associated with a higher rate of discrepancies.

[87] N Breslau et al, 'Trauma and Posttraumatic Stress Disorder in the Community: The 1996 Detroit Area Survey of Trauma' (1998) 55 *Archives of General Psychiatry* 626.

[88] M Creamer, P Burgess and AC McFarlane, 'Post-traumatic Stress Disorder: Findings from the Australian National Survey of Mental Health and Well-Being' (2001) 31 *Psychological Medicine* 1237; D Lee and K Young, 'Post-traumatic Stress Disorder: Diagnostic Issues and Epidemiology in Adult Survivors of Traumatic Events' (2001) 13 *International Review of Psychiatry* 150.

[89] Herlihy, Scragg and Turner (n 68).

[90] Ibid, 326.

[91] Ibid, 325.

Another study of 376 Bosnian refugees used a checklist approach seen in studies of veterans and, again, found that many of the answers changed over a three-year period.[92] The events investigated were not trivial; they included experiences such as being 'present while bombs or other weapons exploded' and seeing or hearing 'beatings, injuries, or killings of family'.

F. Shame and the Disclosure of Sexual Violence

Following experiences of sexual violence torture, different patterns of psychological responses have been observed, and again these are of great relevance in the present context. In the study of 376 Bosnian refugees already described,[93] there was one particularly noteworthy finding to do with the reporting of sexual abuse and rape. One question asked was whether the participant had heard or seen rape or sexual abuse of someone (by a non-family member). At the first interview, 115 participants responded positively to this question, but no one did so at the follow-up interview three years later. It seems unlikely that these were events that had been merely forgotten. Further, in spite of this high rate of reporting of witnessing *others* being raped in the initial assessment, and in spite of studies showing the extensive prevalence of wartime rape in Bosnia,[94] none at all reported at either interview having been raped *themselves*. These findings suggest that there are other factors influencing people's ability to recall or to report sexual violence, some of which we explore below.

A study of survivors of torture at a London treatment centre showed that generally the intrusive symptoms of PTSD are common—sudden distressing memories, nightmares and flashbacks.[95] However, this study also showed that in survivors of sexual violence, the avoidance symptoms of PTSD are more prevalent. This effect has been replicated and linked to dissociation and shame. Thus, in a study of 27 asylum seekers in the UK,[96] Bögner et al found that compared with participants with a history of non-sexual torture, those with a history of sexual torture scored higher on measures of PTSD-avoidance symptoms, PTSD symptoms overall, dissociation, shame and difficulty in disclosing their histories at their immigration interview. Across both groups, there was a positive association between their

[92] RF Mollica, KR Caridad and MP Massagli, 'Longitudinal Study of Posttraumatic Stress Disorder, Depression, and Changes in Traumatic Memories Over Time in Bosnian Refugees' (2007) 195 *The Journal of Nervous and Mental Disease* 572.

[93] Ibid.

[94] A Richters, 'Sexual Violence in Wartime' in PJ Bracken and C Petty (eds), *Rethinking the Trauma of War* (London, Free Association Books Ltd, 1998); D Kozaric-Kovacic et al, 'Rape, Torture and Traumatization of Bosnian and Croatian women: Psychological Sequelae' (1995) 65 *American Journal of Orthopsychiatry* 428.

[95] C van Velsen, C Gorst-Unsworth and S Turner, 'Survivors of Torture and Organized Violence: Demography and Diagnosis' (1996) 9 *Journal of Traumatic Stress* 181.

[96] D Bögner, J Herlihy and C Brewin, 'Impact of Sexual Violence on Disclosure During Home Office Interviews' (2007) 191 *British Journal of Psychiatry* 75.

difficulty in disclosing sexual violence and higher levels of total PTSD symptoms, PTSD avoidance symptoms, shame, depression and dissociation.[97] The importance of this study is that people who fail to disclose sexual violence at the very first possible opportunity are under suspicion, and are very often judged to be fabricating evidence.[98] This is also seen in allegations of rape and sexual assault in the domestic context. Bögner's study[99] thus provides further support to the hypothesis that people who have been sexually assaulted are systematically at a disadvantage when it comes to claiming protection and justice.

Shame has therefore emerged as a potentially important factor affecting disclosure after sexual assault.[100] This emotion produces an intense urge to hide; not a rational decision, but a visceral sense of being defective and unworthy.[101] It is also capable of causing and maintaining the symptoms of PTSD.[102] Interviewers, lawyers, judges and all those trying to make sense of people who have survived shame-inducing experiences need to be aware of this possible response that can severely interfere with normal conversations or other interactions.

These issues are most studied in women, but probably apply equally to men. Sorsoli and others identified personal barriers for men to the disclosure of sexual violence, most commonly 'shame and concerns about emotional safety' and 'intentional avoidance'.[103]

G. Depression, PTSD and Overgeneral Memory

When asked to give a memory of a personal event, specific in time and place, most people are able to do this (for example, dancing at John's party last week). People with depression[104] or PTSD,[105] however, are more likely to give memories which are either 'extended' (last longer than one day—for example 'when we were on holiday') or 'categoric' (similar events experienced several times—for example 'when I used to go Salsa dancing'). There is a high prevalence of PTSD and

[97] Ibid, 78.
[98] H Muggeridge and C Maman, 'Unsustainable: The Quality of Initial Decision-Making in Women's Asylum Claims' (*Asylum Aid*, 2011).
[99] Bögner, Herlihy and Brewin (n 96).
[100] Ibid.
[101] DA Lee, 'Compassion-Focused Cognitive Therapy for Shame-Based Trauma Memories and Flashbacks in Post-Traumatic Stress Disorder' in N Grey (ed), *A Casebook of Cognitive Therapy for Traumatic Stress Reactions* (Abingdon, Routledge, 2009).
[102] D Lee, P Scragg and S Turner, 'The Role of Shame and Guilt in Traumatic Events: A Clinical Model of Shame-Based and Guilt-Based PTSD' (2001) 74 *British Journal of Medical Psychology* 451.
[103] L Sorsoli, M Kia-Keating and FK Grossman, '"I keep that Hush-Hush": Male Survivors of Sexual Abuse and the Challenges of Disclosure' (2008) 55 *Journal of Counseling Psychology* 333, 341–42.
[104] MG Williams et al, 'Autobiographical Memory Specificity and Emotional Disorder' (2007) 133 *Psychological Bulletin* 122.
[105] R McNally et al, 'Autobiographical Memory Disturbance in Combat-Related Posttraumatic Stress Disorder' (1995) 33 *Behaviour Research and Therapy* 619.

depression amongst survivors of rape and sexual violence,[106] so if this phenomenon is not properly understood in the court, it is possible that an account from someone unable to retrieve specific memories is judged as being 'vague' and thus not credible.

This is also important in asylum decisions, because there is an assumption that detail is indicative of a true account. For instance, as one judge said in our study of assumptions in UK determinations, 'There was a texture and richness to the details of her evidence that indicates that this was true'.[107]

A recent study has also shown higher levels of overgeneral memory in people seeking asylum with PTSD and depression, suggesting that it is possible to be telling the truth, but not to be able to provide 'texture and richness' (of detail).[108]

There are also suggestions that there is a cultural element to 'overgeneral' memory. Most of the studies in the literature have been conducted with Western-culture participants. Hofstede categorised countries as having individual or independent cultures (typical of Australia, New Zealand, Western Europe or North America), or collective or interdependent cultures (typical of regions such as Asia, Middle East, Africa and South America), and this has given rise to research on social and cognitive differences between people from those two groups.[109] Reviewing studies of the development of memory, and in particular the specificity of memories, Jobson writes: 'Cultures emphasizing interdependence do not value specificity of autobiographical memories because the aim of the relatedness self is to achieve interdependence, and the retrieving of specific autobiographical memory has the potential to undermine this objective'.[110] In an empirical study, Jobson asked people from a range of backgrounds to describe, in writing, an everyday memory and a trauma memory.[111] Each memory was rated as 'specific' if it gave details such as date, time, people or location, and suggested a specific episode, or 'general' if the event described occurred regularly or repeatedly, was difficult to date and could not be so linked. Rather than rely on the categorisation of country of origin, Jobson used a more individual measure of culture.[112] Significantly more of the

---

[106] HS Resnick et al, 'Prevalence of Civilian Trauma and Posttraumatic Stress Disorder in a Representative National Sample of Women' (1993) 61 *Journal of Consulting and Clinical Psychology* 984; Creamer, Burgess and McFarlane (n 88).

[107] Herlihy, Gleeson and Turner (n 53). This example did not appear in our published paper of this study, but was one of the data items analysed.

[108] B Graham, J Herlihy and C Brewin, 'Overgeneral Memory in Asylum Seekers and Refugees' (2014) 45 *Journal of Behavior Therapy and Experimental Psychiatry* 375.

[109] G Hofstede, 'Cultural Dimensions': www.clearlycultural.com/geert-hofstede-cultural-dimensions/; G Hofstede and GJ Hofstede, *Cultures and Organizations: Software of the Mind* (New York, McGraw-Hill, 2005).

[110] L Jobson, 'Cultural Differences in Specificity of Autobiographical Memories: Implications for Asylum Decisions' (2009) 16 *Psychiatry, Psychology and Law* 453, 454.

[111] Ibid.

[112] 'The 'Twenty Statements Test' (MH Kuhn and TS McPartland, 'An Empirical Investigation of Self-Attitudes' (1954) 19 *American Sociological Review* 68) asks people to write statements beginning 'I am', and has been used to measure cultural differences in people's sense of self—for example, more

participants whose culture was rated as 'independent' gave specific accounts, compared with those rated 'interdependent'.

Given that the 'interdependent' cultures in this study are mostly commonly associated with the refugee-producing areas of the world, and the 'independent' cultures are those where the rules are mostly defined for access to refugee protection, Jobson warns that: 'Culture impacts on specificity and needs to be considered when deeming an autobiographical memory as credible or not in legal settings, such as in asylum decision-making processes'.[113]

Overgeneral memory—perhaps even too derogatory a term in this context—is likely to be present for asylum seekers, both because of their cultural background and because of PTSD.[114] Relying heavily on dates and other specific details to establish the credibility of people seeking protection is therefore not in line with the psychological literature.[115]

H. Recognising Emotional Distress

There is a further complexity, and it concerns the degree to which emotional difficulties are recognised in individual cases. For someone seeking asylum, early contact with professionals rarely includes anyone with clinical training. For someone reporting rape, this has been improved by the training of Specially Trained Officers (STOs) and the development of multidisciplinary centres such as the Havens in London, but these are not universal. The straightforward answer for a lawyer is to commission a psychologist or psychiatrist to prepare a report, but how is he or she to know when this is necessary?

Psychiatrists and psychologists are specifically trained to recognise, assess, diagnose and work with disorders of emotion, but most actors in the asylum process do not have this background. When UK immigration lawyers have clients whom they suspect may be having psychological difficulties, they may ask for a medico-legal assessment by a qualified mental health expert. A recent study by Wilson-Shaw and others explored how immigration lawyers make this decision.[116] In-depth interviews with a sample of immigration lawyers found that, as well as considering the legal decision about the utility of an expert report for the case, they relied on the presentation of the claimant, identifying elevated levels of sadness,

relational (I am a daughter, I am a friend) versus more individual (I am a teacher, I am interested in sport). See also Q Wang, MD Leichtman and SH White, 'Childhood Memory and Self-Description in Young Chinese Adults: The Impact of Growing Up an Only Child' (1998) 69 *Cognition* 73.

[113] Jobson (n 110) 457.

[114] B Graham, 'Overgeneral Memory in Asylum Seekers and Refugees: The Influences of PTSD and Cultural Background' (DClinPsych, University College London, 2012).

[115] See also HE Cameron, 'Refugee Status Determinations and the Limits of Memory' (2010) 22 *International Journal of Refugee Law* 469.

[116] L Wilson-Shaw, N Pistrang and J Herlihy, 'Non-Clinicians' Judgments About Asylum Seekers' Mental Health: How do Legal Representatives of Asylum Seekers Decide When to Request Medico-Legal Reports?' (2012) 3 *European Journal of Psychotraumatology*: dx.doi.org/10.3402/ejpt.v3i0.18406.

upset, aggression or withdrawal as possible indicators of a problem. Depression was not usually considered important to the case, and would rarely trigger a referral for clinical assessment, even though, as we have seen, depression can have profound implications for the way in which an individual is able to recall and present their experiences.[117] The conclusion was that: 'Representatives and decision makers may rely on lay understandings of distress that do not necessarily fit with all possible presentations of psychological disorder ... presentations of PTSD which are less well-understood by lay decision makers may pass unrecognised'.[118] This issue was further explored using an experiment by Rogers and others in which an actor recounted the same asylum story employing four different sets of behavioural presentations.[119] First, he showed the typical signs of having PTSD; second, he exhibited cues indicating he was lying; third, he presented both cues of PTSD and lying; and finally, a neutral account. All of the behavioural expressions were derived from the literature on PTSD and on deception,[120] and were validated by expert clinicians. Students instructed in asylum decision-making then rated each presentation as to its credibility. The presentation deemed most credible was the PTSD-alone account. However, the least credible presentation was the one combining PTSD and deception elements, raising difficult questions for the assessment of victims of trafficking, who have often been coerced to lie about their circumstances. Further questions asked participants to explain their decision-making process, in order to better understand their reasoning. The answers pointed to an effect called 'emotional congruence' which has also been seen in studies of rape trials. This is where the emotion fits with the assessor's expectation of a response to any given event. For example, in one study, the perceived credibility of a (simulated) rape victim's statement increased when the victim showed despair.[121] In the Rogers actor study,[122] one participant said, 'he seemed understandably traumatised by events'.[123]

PTSD for one person may be a question of extreme fear, but in another it may be maintained by strong feelings of shame.[124] Similarly, some people with PTSD symptoms appear visibly anxious or fearful, whereas others may be withdrawn, even 'numb'. Such flattened affect, or seeming lack of emotion, can also be a feature of depression. The findings of these studies both suggest that fear-based PTSD is reasonably well recognised and seen to be understandable

---

[117] MG Williams et al, 'Autobiographical Memory Specificity and Emotional Disorder' (2007) 133 *Psychological Bulletin* 122.

[118] Wilson-Shaw, Pistrang and Herlihy (n 116) 7.

[119] H Rogers, S Fox and J Herlihy, 'The Importance of Looking Credible: The Impact of the Behavioural Sequelae of Post-Traumatic Stress Disorder on the Credibility of Asylum-Seekers' (2014) 21 *Psychology, Crime & Law* 139.

[120] For example, see A Vrij, *Detecting Lies and Deceit: Pitfalls and Opportunities*, 2nd edn (Chichester, John Wiley, 2008).

[121] G Kaufmann et al, 'The Importance of Being Earnest: Displayed Emotions and Witness Credibility' (2003) 17 *Applied Cognitive Psychology* 21.

[122] Rogers, Fox and Herlihy (n 119).

[123] Ibid, 9.

[124] Lee, Scragg and Turner (n 102).

(that is to say, emotionally congruent with the observer's expectations) in the context of an account of persecution, but that other less common presentations of distress, with less clear emotional expression, may be less well recognised. It is therefore important that these studies be replicated with actual decision-makers.

V. Psychological Science and the Decision-Maker

So far we have been focusing mainly on the emotion of the claimant, who is usually the only witness to events. However, those tasked with making the decision, whether jury member, judge, tribunal member or state-employed decision-maker, are also part of the process. Each of these brings their own knowledge of and assumptions about the world.

Graycar, referring to the personal and cultural backgrounds of judges, suggests that

> we need to pay careful attention to what judges know about the world, how they know the things they do, and how the things they know translate into their activities as judges … Judicial notice may resemble a window that judges try to look through but that has reflective glass in it: so it is really a mirror. When judges look at it they see what they think is 'human nature', 'human experience' and 'ordinary or reasonable people'. What they are really seeing is the society they know. (And they do not see that they are looking in a mirror.)[125]

Jarvis, similarly, concludes from a survey of UK immigration judges[126] that:

> Some respondents realize that they are looking into a mirror and, recognizing the effect of who and what they are upon their ability to fairly assess credibility, try to look through the glass in order to carry out the exercise, whilst acknowledging that sometimes they forget that the mirror is there. Others have not yet seen the mirror; or if they have, are not admitting to its existence.[127]

It is impossible to have no cultural background, or not to be alive at a certain historical moment, but the decision-maker's task is to recognise these limitations, and to be aware of the differences that might apply to the person about whom they must make judgements.

A. Emotion and Judging

It is not only the cultural and social background of the decision-maker that is important. Another significant factor in some areas of law is the distressing nature

---

[125] R Graycar, 'The Gender of Judgments: An Introduction' in M Thornton (ed), *Public and Private Feminist Legal Debates* (Oxford, Oxford University Press, 1991).
[126] Jarvis questioned 27 judges, and conducted 10 follow-up interviews.
[127] C Jarvis, 'The Judge as Juror Re-visited' (2003) *Winter Immigration Law Digest* 7, 10.

of the material presented. In her study of emotions in judging Maroney argues that 'traditional legal theory either presumes that judges have no operative emotions … or mandates that any such emotions be actively suppressed'.[128] Asylum claims can entail accounts of some of the most atrocious acts that humans perpetrate upon each other, usually in the name of state or political ideology. Similar issues may arise in the criminal prosecution of rape.

The effects on lawyers and other decision-makers of working regularly with such material are not well known, but there are some indications that they are felt. A study of claims heard by the Refugee Review Board of Canada[129] described highly emotionally charged hearings, with board members being sarcastic with claimants, expressing anger, dismissing or trivialising horrific events, and laughing amongst themselves. Similarly, a recent academic legal study of the UK Asylum and Immigration Tribunal reports 'strategies of detachment' and 'denial' as ways of coping with the 'emotional impact' of asylum work.[130]

A useful construct here is the concept of Vicarious Traumatisation (VT), an umbrella term often used to describe the psychological effects—well documented in therapists working with psychological trauma[131]—of exposure to other people's traumatic experiences. It can involve symptoms that mirror the symptoms of PTSD, such as having nightmares about a claimant's trauma, or forgetting particularly stressful parts of the account; or it can mean a more pervasive change of beliefs and attitudes, seeing the world as a more dangerous, untrustworthy place.

In one study of judges, researchers interviewed 105 Family Court judges, and found indications of VT in 63 per cent.[132] Another study compared criminal lawyers with academic lawyers; the criminal lawyers reported higher levels of subjective distress, VT, depression, stress and cognitive changes relating to safety and intimacy compared with their non-criminal colleagues.[133] In immigration lawyers, a recent qualitative study drew on a model of 'emotional burden' and highlighted the ways in which lawyers were attempting to balance the conflicting roles of 'empathic advocate' and 'objective fact-finder'.[134] However, no quantitative

---

[128] TA Maroney, 'Law and Emotion: A Proposed Taxonomy of an Emerging Field' (2006) 30 *Law and Human Behavior* 119, 132.

[129] C Rousseau et al, 'The Complexity of Determining Refugeehood: A Multidisciplinary Analysis of the Decision-making Process of the Canadian Immigration and Refugee Board' (2002) 15 *Journal of Refugee Studies* 43.

[130] H Baillot, S Cowan and VE Munro, 'Second-Hand Emotion? Exploring the Contagion and Impact of Trauma and Distress in the Asylum Law Context' (2013) 40 *Journal of Law and Society* 509.

[131] L McCann and LA Pearlman, 'Vicarious Traumatization: A Framework for Understanding Psychological Effects of Working with Victims' (1990) 3 *Journal of Traumatic Stress* 131; CR Figley (ed), *Compassion Fatigue: Coping with Secondary Traumatic Stress Disorder In Those Who Treat the Traumatized* (New York, Brunner/Mazel, 1995); KW Saakvitne and LA Pearlman, *Transforming the Pain: A Workbook on Vicarious Traumatization* (New York, WW Norton & Company, 1996).

[132] P Jaffe et al, 'Vicarious Trauma in Judges: The Personal Challenge of Dispensing Justice' (2003) 54 *Juvenile and Family Court Journal* 1.

[133] LP Vrklevski and J Franklin, 'Vicarious Trauma: The Impact on Solicitors of Exposure to Traumatic Material' (2008) 14 *Traumatology* 106.

[134] C Westaby, '"Feeling Like a Sponge": The Emotional Labour Produced by Solicitors in their Interactions With Clients Seeking Asylum' (2010) 17 *International Journal of the Legal Profession* 153.

assessment of VT in immigration lawyers has been attempted. Similarly, we know of no study of VT in decision-makers in rape trials.

What has been observed are decision-makers' attempts—not necessarily deliberately—to avoid distress, which can involve 'trivialization of horror, cynicism, and lack of empathy'.[135] Similar effects have been observed in the context of the recent war crimes tribunal in Cambodia—another locus of extremely distressing material—where the repeated interjections of President Nil Nonn in the first trial of Khmer Rouge leaders, instructing witnesses to 'control their emotion' have been widely cited as indications of his own struggle with the levels of emotion brought into the court.[136] Such responses to horrific material are described in one study as 'psychological self-protection'.[137] It is easy to see how they might have significant effects on the decisions made about people seeking asylum, although this has yet to be shown empirically. Nor have potential links between VT and decision-making been explored in this crucial area.

B. Tolerating Uncertainty

Legal professionals are taught to discover facts in order to uncover the truth and to make definite decisions.[138] Nowhere is this clearer than in refugee or humanitarian protection decisions, where the risks involved can be either a wrongful return of an individual who may then face further torture (or even death), or a decision to allow individual immigrants to remain in the host country against a tide of social, governmental and media pressure.[139] In this context, Thomas describes the unique nature of asylum decision-making:

> Asylum adjudication, as Sedley LJ once explained, does not involve a conventional lawyer's exercise of applying a litmus test to ascertained facts but 'a global appraisal of an individual's past and prospective situation in a particular cultural, social, political and legal milieu, judged by a test which, though it has legal and linguistic limits, has a broad humanitarian purpose' ...[140] The task of prognosticating the risk of persecution or illtreatment must usually be undertaken on the basis of incomplete, uncertain and limited evidence. Also, underlying the decision exercise are unusually high error costs which arise from the acute and pervasive tension between maintaining immigration control and protecting individual rights: asylum adjudication raises the constant problem of

---

[135] Rousseau et al (n 129) 49.

[136] See JD Ciorciari and A Heindel, 'Trauma in the Courtroom' in B Schaak, D Reicherter and C Youk (eds), *Cambodia's Hidden Scars: Trauma Psychology in the Wake of the Khmer Rouge* (Documentation Center of Cambodia, 2011).

[137] Rousseau et al (n 129) 60.

[138] Michael Kagan (personal communication); see also the discussion in M-B Dembour and E Haslam, 'Silencing Hearings? Victim-Witnesses at War Crimes Trials' (2004) 15 *European Journal of International Law* 151 especially notes 24 and 163 on what constitute facts in criminal law trials.

[139] See for example: www.freemovement.org.uk/2012/07/19/judge-hung-out-to-dry/ for a discussion of two recent newspaper articles criticising UK immigration judges for their rulings.

[140] *R v Immigration Appeal Tribunal and Secretary of State for the Home Department, ex parte Shah* [1997] Imm AR 145, 153 (HC) cited in the text.

either refusing protection to the genuine claimant or affording protection to the non-genuine claimant.[141]

In most cases the final outcome—especially where the individual is returned to their country of origin—is unknown. In terms of judging whether someone is lying in order to make a claim, such a lack of feedback precludes being able to learn from experience. In terms of the 'emotional burden' of the work, however, it means that decision-makers have to learn to tolerate the uncertainty of never knowing whether or not their decision was correct, and whether or not it had disastrous consequences for the individual concerned. Indeed, the very notion of a standard of proof suggests a tolerance of uncertainty; however, this does not guarantee that, in the culture and thinking of lawyers and judges, it is easy to accept and live with the uncertainty inherent in making decisions to return people to what they claim will involve torture and possibly death.[142]

In the area of psychological therapy, Mason[143] wrote about 'tolerating uncertainty', proposing a model of certainty/uncertainty crossed with safety/unsafety, giving a range of possible positions: (1) unsafe certainty (Mason's example is of a father whose describes his son as 'out of control' and brings him to therapy to be 'fixed'); (2) unsafe uncertainty (the person who is lost and can see no way forward); (3) safe certainty (the 'expert position',[144] important in surgeons); and (4) safe uncertainty—where curiosity and change become possible. According to Mason, the fourth of these positions is to be preferred for the therapist, but what position can the immigration judge inhabit in order to do his or her job? The task of judges is to make a final decision, and their training and tradition say they must be certain—but certainty is often simply impossible in this area of decision-making.

Adding the inherent uncertainty of these decisions to the knowledge of potential torture and death of the refused claimant puts a heavy burden on any decision-maker. An error does not simply mean that a person has an unwarranted penalty, it can mean the difference between life and death. Maroney shows how requiring calm and equanimity in such a role is to add to the burden, citing the—hopefully extreme—example of a judge who was removed from office in Florida, following his being 'callous, rude, condescending, and abusive':

> By constantly 'striving to demonstrate calm in difficult situations', [his psychiatrist] testified, the judge eventually 'placed himself' in a state of 'emotional over-control'. His drive to control his emotions became so strong that he was unable to 'incorporate emotions

---

[141] R Thomas, 'Consistency in Asylum Adjudication: Country Guidance and the Asylum Process in the United Kingdom' (2008) 20 *International Journal of Refugee Law* 489, 491.

[142] Michael Kagan (personal communication).

[143] B Mason, 'Towards Positions of Safe Uncertainty' (1993) 4 *Human Systems: The Journal of Systemic Consultation and Management* 189.

[144] H Anderson and H Goolishian, 'The Client is the Expert: A Not-Knowing Approach to Therapy' in S McNamee and K Gergen (eds), *Social Construction and the Therapeutic Process* (London, Sage Publications Ltd, 1992).

into his life without worrying he would display inappropriate anger'—which, inevitably and ironically, he did.[145]

Requiring 'safe certainty' for judges in this impossible area of decision-making is to impose a burden which can be bad for judges[146] and bad for the people about whom the decisions must be made.[147] It may also raise the stakes in terms of judges' confidence, that is, requiring them to exude and if possible feel confidence, which 'has its own downsides, perhaps because it discourages self-examination and learning'.[148]

The importance of this issue does not lie in attacking or criticising those who are taking on one of our most difficult humanitarian tasks. Rather, Maroney proposes a model of 'emotional regulation', drawing on psychological research and parallels from the training of doctors (who also have to make important decisions, with incomplete data, in the face of gruesome realities).[149] Such a model could be integrated into training programmes, without prejudice or judgement about those participating.

The other frequent factor in asylum decision-making is the knowledge that at least some of the people before the decision-maker may be using systems of humanitarian protection deceitfully. Without going into the structural and political reasons why this might be happening, the fact remains that some people do exaggerate accounts, use stories given to them by agents and hide or change details in order to protect themselves or others. Continually having to consider whether or not one is being lied to would test the most liberal of assessors, and may lead some judges to become 'hardened'.[150]

Maroney's proposed programme of 'emotional regulation' may well provide a useful approach for actors in areas of law with high levels of uncertainty. In addressing consistency and methodology, Jarvis advocates 'education and training delivered to judges with open minds'[151]—and this would be the way forward to address the emotional burden of making decisions that rely so heavily on the credibility of the people involved. For example, a promising programme of training on 'Psychological Factors Affecting Decision-Makers' has been rolled out to UK asylum caseworkers, followed up by regular 'reflection groups'. A systematic evaluation of this programme would be useful to indicate ways forward. Given what Maroney refers to as the 'persistent cultural script of judicial dispassion',[152] decision-makers, emotion researchers and practitioners need to agree on the size and shape of the problem (to include the limitations of taking a simple common sense approach and the emotional burden of the consequence of making a bad decision) to ensure that any such interventions are maximally effective.

---

[145] TA Maroney, 'Emotional Regulation and Judicial Behavior' (2011) 99 *California Law Review* 1481.

[146] Ibid.

[147] Ibid; Rousseau et al (n 129); Baillot, Cowan and Munro (n 130).

[148] Maroney, 'Emotional Regulation and Judicial Behavior' (n 145) 1549, fn 389.

[149] Ibid.

[150] Baillot, Cowan and Munro (n 130).

[151] Jarvis (n 127) 16.

[152] TA Maroney, 'The Persistent Cultural Script of Judicial Dispassion' (2011) 99 *California Law Review* 629.

VI. Conclusions and Recommendations

In this chapter, we have briefly reviewed the topic of credibility and the pitfalls in taking a naive approach to its determination. We have looked at two areas of law where credibility takes centre stage, due to there generally being little or no corroboration from witnesses, documentation, or other evidence. The reliance on credibility assessment in deciding international protection claims and sexual violence allegations raises the risk of subjectivity and inconsistency both within and between decision-makers. One solution is to turn to the science of psychology for information on how people might present a claim—whether for international protection or for justice following an assault. We have considered the potential contribution of modern psychological science, ranging from concepts of memory to the effect of emotion on the nature and accuracy of recall. In refugee law there is already a model for the use of external expertise in decision-making. Decision-makers are required to be familiar with information about the alleged country of origin of a claimant in order to test their account of persecution.[153] If they were similarly required to be familiar with the current science on memory, the disclosure of distressing personal experiences and responses to fear, they would not be relying on subjective assumptions about these matters, just as they should not in their assessment of country situations.

We have also considered the impact of this work on decision-makers and the quality of their decisions. We have not considered in this chapter other potentially important, but difficult, areas such as the value of offering support for witnesses, mainly because we lack a sufficient body of science. However, the main messages we wish to communicate are that common sense is not always the best guide for valid decisions and that psychological science has both a current body of knowledge and the potential for further research in relation to the assumptions commonly used by decision-makers. In keeping with the premises of this collection we argue that it is only by working across disciplinary boundaries to understand the role of emotion in legal decision-making that the best possible decisions can be made, even in the most difficult task of credibility assessment. This will involve not simply the training of experts, decision-makers, judges and juries concerning existing knowledge, but also the defining of a shared agenda for future research, thus gradually improving the quality of justice.

---

[153] The 2015 policy instructions to state decision-makers in the UK state that 'Caseworkers must be familiar with the current CIG [County Information and Guidance] reports (or COIS [Country of Origin Information Service] reports) before an interview to ensure that the claimant is given an opportunity to explain any inconsistencies between their account and the COI [Country of Origin Information]'. (Home Office, 'Asylum Policy Instruction: Assessing credibility and refugee status' (2015): www.gov. uk/government/uploads/system/uploads/attachment_data/file/397778/ASSESSING_CREDIBILITY_ AND_REFUGEE_STATUS_V9_0.pdf.

9

Emotional Transitions in Social Movements: The Case of Immigrant Rights Activism in Arizona

KATHRYN ABRAMS[*]

I. Introduction

How does emotion structure legal disputes? Much of the literature on law and emotions assumes this is a question that we ask in an institutional setting— a courtroom or judge's chambers, a legislature, or a lawyer's office. But, as legal theorists have argued,[1] most disputes have a vital trajectory that occurs before participants formally engage legal institutions; emotion infuses and structures these settings as well. In this chapter I will explore the role of emotion in one such context: the social movement that aims to influence the law. Social movement organisations crystallise and mobilise claims for change on behalf of collectivities who have suffered some injury or injustice. Some aim simply to provide solidarity or raise consciousness; many others seek formal recognition or remedy for their claims, often by engaging legal institutions. Emotional expression, management and display are critical to the way that social movement organisations do their work: as they motivate and organise their members, and as they approach legal actors and the public. Studying how emotion functions and changes in the context of social movements, however, does more than illuminate the process of making the *law*; it also sheds new light on *emotions*. Because emotions in the social movement setting have a collective dimension—that is, they are shaped by scripts and assumptions that are shared by members of the group as a whole—analysing them can supplement understandings of emotion in the law and emotions literature that are often individual in character.

In this chapter I will explore the emotional trajectory of a vital movement for social justice: the US movement for immigrant rights. This movement seeks to

[*] Herma Hill Kay Distinguished Professor of Law, UC-Berkeley School of Law.
[1] See eg, W Felstiner, R Abel and A Sarat, 'The Emergence and Transformation of Disputes: Naming, Blaming, Claiming' (1980) 15 *Law & Society Review* 631.

reform the American immigration system and, more specifically, to seek legal status or relief from deportation, for more than 11 million immigrants who are present in the United States without authorisation.[2] Led increasingly by undocumented activists themselves, this movement has mobilised immigrants and addressed the public in ways that involve strong affective appeals: that is, emotion has been prominent on the face of movement narratives and actions. More strikingly, the emotional appeal of the movement has changed over time, encompassing a wider range of affective performances, and foregrounding more critical and contentious emotions. This change is a challenging move for a group which lacks legal status and is still contending for recognition in the political domain. In this chapter I offer an explanation of this controversial shift.

This explanation revolves around the concept of an 'emotional habitus', introduced by Deborah Gould in a recent study of AIDS activism in the United States.[3] Gould describes an emotional habitus as a set of taken-for-granted assumptions among members of a group that help them to translate their affects, or experienced bodily intensities, into distinct, articulable emotions, and tell them what kinds of emotions are appropriate to feel, express, or display.[4] Although the emotional habitus of a group is often constant over time, it may also change, when members negotiate salient changes in their self-conceptions or encounter political developments which cause them to reinterpret the political environment in which they operate. I argue that both kinds of factors have produced a change in the emotional habitus of undocumented activists, leading them to view expressions of frustration, indignation, anguish and outrage as legitimate and potentially productive forms of political engagement.

In section II, I describe the emotional dimension of recent immigrant rights mobilisations, highlighting in particular a broadening and pluralising of the emotional repertoire of undocumented activists.[5] A movement that began in a register of

---

[2] There were 11.3 million undocumented immigrants in the United States as of 2014. Pew Research Center, '5 Facts About Illegal Immigration in the US', 19 November 2015: www.pewresearch.org/fact-tank/2015/11/19/5-facts-about-illegal-immigration-in-the-u-s/.

[3] D Gould, *Moving Politics: Emotion and ACT UP's Fight Against AIDS* (Chicago, IL, University of Chicago Press, 2009).

[4] Ibid, 32–39.

[5] In this examination, I draw on a qualitative empirical study of the immigrant rights movement in Arizona, particularly that portion of it populated and led by undocumented immigrants. Arizona is considered to be 'ground zero' in the state policy of 'enforcement by attrition', an effort to compel undocumented immigrants to leave or 'self-deport' by passing successive waves of anti-immigrant legislation, affecting the ability of undocumented immigrants to live, work and receive various kinds of benefits (including access to higher education) in the states in question. The difficulties faced by immigrants in Arizona have made the emergence of a robust movement of undocumented activists there an important object of study. This research, which consisted of semi-structured interviews with more than 80 activists, and observation and informal interviews with six social movement organisations, was conducted between 2012 and 2015, with follow-up in 2016. Interviews or ethnographic information from this study will be described under the rubric of 'Arizona Immigrant Rights Project'. (All interview transcripts and field note references are on file with the author.) I supplement this research with analysis of secondary source, media coverage and participant narratives from undocumented activism at the

aspiration and hope, engaging legislative institutions in a posture of petition and trust, added first a discourse infused with critique, frustration and indignation, and ultimately a mode of defiant protest, marked by expressions of anguish and outrage and demands for political accountability. While all three modes of affective expression remain prominent in the movement, the broadening of its affective range and its growing recourse to more defiant emotional postures remain controversial choices, particularly for a movement of non-citizens. In section III, I investigate the reasons for these shifts. I introduce Gould's concept of 'emotional habitus', and identify a set of factors that appear to have produced changes in the emotional habitus of undocumented activists. In section IV, I conclude by suggesting some important implications that this may have for our understanding of the nature of law and its relationship to emotion.

II. Undocumented Activism: A Broadening Emotional Repertoire

The past decade has been a tumultuous period in immigration politics. Immigrant rights activists, led increasingly by undocumented immigrants,[6] have struggled against anti-immigrant legislation at the state level, and mobilised for immigration reform legislation and executive relief from deportation at the federal level. The period from 2006 to 2010 marked the ascent of 'attrition by enforcement': a state strategy that intensified enforcement against undocumented immigrants and denied them a host of benefits, from bail to in-state tuition and state-funded college scholarships, to induce them to return to their countries of origin.[7] The high water mark of this effort was Arizona's SB 1070, which made undocumented presence or labour into crimes, and authorised police, in the course of any legal stop, to ask for identification from anyone they suspected of being in the country without authorisation.[8] During this same period pro-immigrant forces waged an

---

national level. I am grateful to all of those I have spoken with or observed in action, for their generosity in sharing their stories with me, and for the courage of their example.

[6] The term 'undocumented immigrants' refers to immigrants who are present in the United States without authorisation: they have neither a legal status (such as citizenship or permanent legal residency, conferred by the Immigration and Naturalization Act or related legislation) nor legal presence (ie, permission to be present in the United States without formal legal status, such as a form of deferred action implemented as a matter of executive discretion). Immigrants may be undocumented because they have crossed the border without apprehension, or because they have come to the United States on some form of visa, and remained after the visa has expired, so 'falling out' of legal status.

[7] For a discussion of the strategy of 'attrition by enforcement' by its legal architect (who also advised the Arizona legislature), see K Kobach, 'Reinforcing the Rule of Law: What States Can and Should Do to Reduce Illegal Immigration' (2008) 22 *Georgetown Immigration Law Journal* 459.

[8] National Conference of State Legislatures, 'Analysis of Arizona's Immigrant Enforcement Laws': www.ncsl.org/research/immigration/analysis-of-arizonas-immigration-law.aspx (revised 28 July 2011).

unsuccessful effort to pass the DREAM Act, a federal law which would have created a path to citizenship for undocumented immigrants brought to the United States as children. This law failed, most conspicuously in 2010, when it was defeated by five votes in the Senate; yet undocumented activists pressed President Obama successfully to grant Deferred Action for Childhood Arrivals (DACA), an executive mandate that suspended deportation and granted work permits to many undocumented youth, for a renewable period of two years. Following a 2012 election in which undocumented activists mobilised the Latino vote, movement activists worked for Senate passage of a comprehensive immigration reform Bill, which would have included a path to citizenship for most of the nation's 11 million undocumented immigrants.[9] When that Bill was thwarted in the House of Representatives, activists set their sights again on President Obama, pressing for deferred action for undocumented adults.[10] In November 2014, Obama announced a programme of Deferred Action for Parents of Americans, which would have provided renewable relief from deportation and work permits to the undocumented parents of American citizens and legal permanent residents.[11] This relief, however, was enjoined by the federal courts as an invalid exercise of executive power, and will be addressed by the US Supreme Court in the 2015–16 term.[12]

Throughout this period, undocumented activists, both youth and adults, mobilised against state restrictions and in favour of federal reforms. In the personal narratives through which undocumented immigrants introduced themselves to the public, and in the movement actions, which ranged from voter canvassing and legislative lobbying to hunger strikes and civil disobedience, emotions were prominent on the face of activists' appeals. Yet the tenor of these emotions, and the stances they conveyed towards the government, changed strikingly over this decade. Early narratives, protests and other forms of self-presentation by activists were delivered in a carefully modulated affective tone, which emphasised the determination and aspiration that immigrants shared with citizens. This hopeful stance was buttressed by trust or confidence in the federal institutions responsible for immigration policy. This early emotional stance did not disappear from view; indeed, it emerged strongly among activists in the campaign for comprehensive immigration reform in 2013–14.[13] Yet as the decade progressed, and activists faced

---

[9] Seung Min Kim, Senate Passes Immigration Reform Bill, politico.com, 27 June 2013: www.politico.com/story/2013/06/immigration-bill-2013-senate-passes-093530.

[10] *DREAMers Switch to Civil Disobedience to Help Cause*, UPI.com, (26 August 2013, 3:09 pm): www.upi.com/Top_News/US/2013/08/26/Dreamers-switch-to-civil-disobedience-to-help-cause/ UPI-95551377544151/ (describing shift in strategy suggested by direct action protests at the Immigration and Customs Enforcement (ICE) building and immigration facility).

[11] Remarks by the President in Address to the Nation on Immigration: www.whitehouse.gov/ the-press-office/2014/11/20/remarks-president-address-nation-immigration.

[12] *United States v Texas*, 86 F Supp 3d 591, 677 (SD Tex 2015), aff'd F 3d (No 15-40238, 5th Cir, 9 November 2015, cert granted (19 January 2016).

[13] See eg, Statement of Maria Gabriela ('Gaby') Pacheco before the Senate Judiciary Committee, 22 April 2013; Statement of Jose Antonio Vargas before the Senate Judiciary Committee, 13 February 2013.

federal inaction and state escalation, new affective strands emerged in their public actions. Particularly in settings where government action was hostile, or where pro-immigrant changes were postponed or thwarted, activists' discourse grew more critical and their affective stance more aggrieved. They began to voice emotions which went beyond broadly shared states of aspiration. Emotions such as frustration, indignation, or grief, which activists increasingly manifested in public contexts, were used to highlight hardships they had endured specifically as undocumented immigrants. When Congress failed to enact comprehensive reform in 2014, and activists shifted to a demand for deferred action to address record-level deportations, stark expressions of the pain of family separation and outraged condemnation of federal enforcement came to the fore.

A. Managed, 'Universalising' Emotions

Young people were the first undocumented immigrants to organise, at both state and federal level. Some were enlisted by national immigrant rights organisations to share their stories with Congress, in support of the DREAM Act. Others organised themselves, as state strategies of 'attrition by enforcement', created barriers to their higher education.

In their public presentations, both in Congress and elsewhere, youth offered narratives of their lives in the United States, putting a human face to a controversial issue and highlighting the qualities that made them desirable as prospective Americans. As sociologist Walter Nicholls has pointed out, these stories highlighted academic achievement, cultural assimilation and innocence in connection with the family's decision to migrate without authorisation.[14] These elements can be found in a narrative offered to Congress by DREAMer Ola Kaso:

> I was five years old, but I remember it like it was yesterday. Apprehensively, I teetered into the perplexing classroom. Students spoke in a language completely foreign to me. The teacher, too, spoke and pointed in a certain direction. What did she want me to do? Where did she want me to go? I stood there frozen still and silent like a statue ... I've come a long way since that day 13 years ago. I've become proficient in the English language and I've excelled in my studies. Since the third grade, I've been placed in advanced programs ... I have taken every advanced placement course my high school has offered and I've earned a 4.4 GPA doing so. I earned a 30 on ACT with English being my highest score. In high school I was a varsity athlete ... I juggle all my schoolwork, after-school activities and community service projects while also having a job. I have completely immersed myself within the American culture of which I so strongly desire to become a citizen. I am currently enrolled in the University of Michigan ... I ultimately aspire to become a surgical oncologist ... I wish to remain in this country to make a difference ... to help American citizens.

---

[14] W Nicholls, *The DREAMers: How the Undocumented Youth Movement Transformed the Immigrant Rights Debate* (Stanford, CA, Stanford University Press, 2013) 47–73.

... Despite all my hard work and contributions, I face removal from the only country I've ever considered home ... I am a DREAM Act student. I was brought to this country when I was five years old. I grew up here. I am an American at heart. There are thousands of other dreamers just like me ... All we are asking for is a chance to contribute to the country that we love. Please support the DREAM Act.[15]

While embodying the paradigmatic substantive elements of the early DREAMer statements, this narrative is also typical in its emotional tone. The affective presentation of this DREAMer is carefully controlled. She recounts a series of challenging obstacles—from entering a classroom whose language she could not understand, to facing removal after years of committed work—yet her response to these obstacles remains matter-of-fact. The primary emotions she projects are hope and determination ('I juggle all my schoolwork, after-school activities and community service projects while also having a job ... all we are asking is to have a chance to contribute to the country that we love.') The tenacious, aspiring emotional tone that marks early DREAMer testimony might be described as universalising, in that it highlights the affective similarities between immigrants and citizens that lie beneath factual differences in their circumstances. Both apply themselves with determination and hope; both aspire to better for themselves and their families. It also creates validating parallels between undocumented immigrants and the upwardly mobile, successfully integrated immigrants of generations past.[16] These stories inevitably relate frustrations; exposing the public to the challenges faced by undocumented youth is part of the purpose of these statements. Yet the affective tone of these narratives, which remains even, hopeful and determined, frames such challenges less as injustices imposed by the immigration system on undocumented migrants, than as obstacles to be surmounted through the formidable perseverance of talented, motivated youth. Emotions of frustration, indignation, or resentment—particularised emotions of undocumented immigrants which might set them apart from their documented audiences—are kept carefully off-stage.

Adult activists responding to 'attrition by enforcement' also projected universalising emotions, which were both confluent with and distinct from those expressed by DREAMers. When SB 1070 was passed in Arizona, for example, undocumented immigrants, Latinos and their allies mobilised in resistance.[17] These protests sought to represent the experiences and emotions of undocumented immigrants, by reframing them not as violent criminals, but as human

---

[15] Ola Kaso, 'DREAM Act Student Delivers Testimony (before Senate)': www.youtube.com/watch?v=1Pa029Yi1eA (uploaded 28 June 2011). The fact that a narrative in this form was offered in 2011 illustrates the fact that earlier emotional stances in this movement do not disappear; they are simply joined by new forms of affective communication which may (or may not) predominate.

[16] See eg, W Nicholls, 'Making Undocumented Immigrants into a Legitimate Political Subject: Theoretical Observations from the United States and France' (2013) 30 *Theory, Culture & Society* 82, 97 (describing DREAMer conformity to a 'nationalising' norm: being 'law-abiding and hardworking residents in search of a better life').

[17] See eg, Jordan Flaherty, 'In Arizona A Human Rights Summer' *YES! Magazine* (30 July 2010): www.yesmagazine.org/people-power/in-arizona-a-human-rights-summer.

beings and hard workers. Undocumented immigrants took part in these protests but were rarely explicit about their status. T-shirts that asked 'do I look
undocumented to you?' or signs that identified the bearer as a 'hard worker not a
criminal'[18] were displayed both by those who had some form of legal status and
those who did not. This practice underscored the ambiguities of a regime that
invited racial profiling, but also provided cover to those whose self-identification
could trigger their detention or deportation. The self-presentation of protesters,
including undocumented immigrants, was also infused with emotion, but the
emotions manifested had a very specific range: protesters manifested steadfast-
ness and dignity, pride in hard work or in being part of a history of immigration
to the United States.

The valence of these emotions was slightly different from those projected by
DREAMers: dignity registered more strongly than ambition, pride was connected
less with distinction or accomplishment than with responsible labour, commitment to family, and perseverance. Yet there were also important continuities,
including hope for a better life and determination to achieve it. These latter emotions carried a universalising message: though the circumstances of these immigrants might be different from those of legislators, or privileged members of the
public, their hope and perseverance would be likely to seem familiar to those who
observed them, and similar as well to 'successful' immigrants from previous historical waves. What remained largely backstage in these early protests was the par-
ticularity of the undocumented experience: the fear, shame, or outrage sparked
by being the targets of this new regime. Documented Latinos leaders sometimes
voiced emotions of embarrassment or outrage, describing with indignation the
vulnerability of all Latinos to SB 1070's law enforcement stops.[19] But the feelings
of fear, precariousness and uncertainty triggered in undocumented immigrants by
this law were expressed primarily within their own communities.

B. Self-Disclosure and the Particularised Emotions
of Undocumented Experience

In the period between 2010 and 2012, the emotional range of undocumented
activism began to shift. The hope and determination that infused early DREAM
narratives did not disappear from view; but activists also began to communicate
a broader array of emotions. As national debate intensified, first over the prospect of comprehensive immigration reform, and then over the 2010 DREAM Act,

---

[18] This apparel and signage has been prevalent in rallies and marches I have observed as part of the
Arizona Immigrant Rights Project; it is also conspicuous in the many photographs taken of movement
activities.

[19] Interview with former state Senator Alfredo Gutierrez, Arizona Immigrant Rights Project
(legislation creating attrition by enforcement generated sense of vulnerability and anger among
documented Latinos).

DREAMers began to assert their independence from national pro-immigrant non-profits,[20] and press for reform in their own voices and settings. Most conspicuously, undocumented youth began to speak publicly about their status, which they described as 'coming out' as 'undocumented and unafraid'.[21] Beginning with 'National Coming Out of the Shadows Day' orchestrated by Chicago's Immigrant Youth Justice League (IYJL) on 10 March 2010,[22] and continued in March of each subsequent year, undocumented activists across the United States revealed their identities in public rallies or protests and advocated for change. This practice, patterned explicitly on lesbian, gay, bisexual, and transgender (LGBT) coming out,[23] sought to humanise a group that had been sharply stigmatised, by associating it with specific individuals. But it also sought to refuse the shame and anxiety that had been imposed by that stigma. A public refusal of stigma, in which activists declared themselves to be not only 'unafraid' but 'unashamed' and 'unapologetic', signalled a subtle but palpable shift in emotional communication. DREAMers spoke of their experience in ways that blended hope with indignation, impatience, even defiance. This narrative, from 'Coming Out Week' in Georgia in 2011, provides an example:

> I am undocumented and unafraid. I will no longer wait for someone to save me while I am being denied access to an education. I will no longer sit by and watch politicians demonize us to build up their campaigns. I will no longer be apologetic for speaking my native language and for embracing my culture. I am a proud Georgian and a proud Mexicana.[24]

In this statement, we see several elements of a new emotional stance. The feeling of trust towards the nation and its political processes that undergirded congressional narratives has been replaced by wariness and even indignation. Determination is inflected by impatience ('I will no longer') rather than by simple perseverance. Pride is present but emerges from new sources: a willingness to help oneself ('I will no longer wait for someone to save me') and to claim one's culture even as one embraces an identity as a member of an American state. Notably, the narrative highlights not only emotions that undocumented immigrants share with lawmakers or the documented public, but emotions arising specifically from struggles associated with their status.

---

[20] Walter Nicholls documents this transition in Nicholls, *The DREAMers* (n 14) 74–98.

[21] For descriptions and analyses of this move, see Nicholls, *The DREAMers* (n 14) 118–42; C Beltran, '"Undocumented, Unafraid, and Unapologetic": DREAM Activists, Immigrant Politics, and the Queering of Democracy' in D Allen and J Light (eds), *From Voice to Influence: Understanding Citizenship in a Digital Age* (Chicago, IL, University of Chicago Press, 2015).

[22] Immigrant Youth Justice League, National Coming Out of the Shadows Day! Chicago Undocumented Youth Kick Off National 'Coming Out of the Shadows' Actions on 10 March 2010, 17 February 2010: www.iyjl.org/national-coming-out-of-the-shadows-day/.

[23] For a thoughtful discussion of this parallel, see RC Villazor, 'The Undocumented Closet' (2013) 92 *North Carolina Law Review* 101.

[24] Georgina Perez, 'Georgia DREAMers' (5 April 2011): www.youtube.com/watch?v=mTeh1m0qiEU.

The 'undocumented and unafraid' also expressed new emotions through acts of civil disobedience, sitting-in at legislative offices or blocking public streets.[25] These riskier political acts[26] conveyed the growing urgency and sense of grievance experienced by undocumented activists, as well as their frustration with the more limited emotional range employed by earlier youth activists. Arizona DREAMer Daniel Rodriguez explained this broader emotional range, commenting on the decision of the first undocumented activists to engage in civil disobedience, at the Tucson office of Senator John McCain:

> A lot of people have said these were acts of desperation: I wouldn't call them acts of desperation, I would call them acts of anger. People are angry that nothing has been done, people are angry that these deportations are happening, people are angry that one day your friend or husband is no longer there next to you, that your family that raised you is no longer there. So I wouldn't say it's an act of desperation, I'd say that it's the next step from everything that we've already done, but it's also an act of anger that people are not dealing with this issue yet … When we have been working for this issue for so long and we know that we have done it the 'right' way, and not … ruffled anyone's feathers, and not done anything that's given us a bad image, six years, seven years, eight years, nine years, and we still don't see any change … The[se activists] went down there because … they just can't deal with, having another year when we don't have change … they just think, I need to put myself out there, I need to be the catalyst for this change, in order for me to motivate other students.[27]

In this statement Rodriguez straightforwardly acknowledges anger, an emotion not publicly claimed by undocumented activists in earlier phases of activism,[28] and explains the reasons for its emergence. Moreover, Rodriguez's explanation foregrounds features of undocumented experience that are unfamiliar to most members of the public: having your friend or partner or family member suddenly taken and deported. It also describes the federal government—once approached with trust by undocumented immigrants—as the source of continuing injustices

---

[25] Ted Hesson, '9 DREAMer Actions that Advanced Immigration Reform, abc.com', 10 August 2013: abcnews.go.com/ABC_Univision/dreamer-protests-advanced-immigration-reform/story?id= 19915997# (describing, inter alia, sit-ins at the office of Senator John McCain, at President Obama's Re-election Campaign Headquarters in Denver, and in the middle of a public street in Georgia).

[26] Even this symbolic form of confrontation was an incalculable risk for undocumented youth, as arrest could readily result in their deportation. In fact, some of those involved with the movement believed that undocumented activists arrested for civil disobedience would be immediately deported. See Arizona Immigrant Rights Project, interview with Luis A ('Oh, my god [I thought], they're going to get deported. And they [didn't]. They're here; they're happy right now. And some of them are undocumented; some of them have work permits. But it was the unknown…').

[27] Daniel Rodriguez, speaking about the DREAM 5 '5 DREAMers who staged the first sit-in by undocumented activists at the AZ office of Senator John McCain), 18 May 2010: www.youtube.com/watch?v=fviT-u7DMSQ.

[28] Anger is a potentially risky emotion for undocumented immigrants, particularly when they face hostile or unresponsive audiences. Not only might displays of anger reinforce the stigma of criminality or aggression which has been imposed on undocumented immigrants in places like Arizona, but for some audiences, anger may also raise the question whether those without status could have expectations of the state whose disappointment could be a legitimate source of anger.

against undocumented communities. This kind of self-presentation aims to elicit the support of the public, not by suggesting that undocumented immigrants are similar to themselves, but by mobilizing citizens' sense of injustice about the difficulties immigrants have confronted.

This period saw a similar broadening of emotional repertoire in state-based activism against 'attrition by enforcement'. In protests against Maricopa County (Arizona) Sheriff Joe Arpaio, whose racial profiling, workplace raids and bluntly anti-immigrant stance made him the scourge of immigrant communities, undocumented adults, as well as youth, increasingly came out as 'undocumented and unafraid'. Some engaged in the acts of civil disobedience which, in early protests against SB 1070, had been performed primarily by citizens. These protests were marked by a confrontational tone, and a candid evocation of the pain that Arpaio had visited on undocumented communities. Because many of these participants did not come to activism through DREAM Act politics, their path to the frank expression of grievance was different from that for those DREAMers described above. Here it emerged as a form of defiance of an official who aimed to terrorise undocumented communities, a means of demonstrating—as protesters asserted—that 'we will not comply'.[29]

In 2012, for example, during the *Melendres* trial,[30] four undocumented activists called a 'people's press conference' and came out as undocumented and unafraid. They then sat down in the middle of a busy intersection outside the federal courthouse to await arrest. The emotions of this protest were palpable in the statement of one activist, who said:

> My name is Leticia Ramirez. I've been in the community for 18 years. I am a mother of three kids. And I'm here to tell Arpaio that he's been chasing our community, he's been chasing our people, and I'm here to tell him that I'm making his job easy ... I'm not going to stand for what he's been doing to my community, and come and get me.[31]

Ramirez's statement conveys the corrosive fatigue produced by years of fear and intimidation, and its transformation into anger and defiance ('I'm not going to stand for what he's been doing to my community ... come and get me'). Her act

---

[29] Unzueta Carrasco and Hinda Seif affirm this point: 'Participating in civil disobedience, like fighting individual deportations, is not just about changing immigration law and immigration policies, it is about owning the risk of deportation with the knowledge that we can challenge deportability. Perhaps this is the most powerful challenge to the power of the nation-state to control its populations through fear and the threat of criminalization and expulsion'—U Carrasco and H Seif, 'Disrupting the Dream: Undocumented Youths Reframe Citizenship and Deportability Through Anti-Deportation Activism' (2014) 12 *Latino Studies* 279.

[30] *Melendres v Arpaio*, No PHX-CV-07-02513-GMS (D Az, 24 May 2013) (findings of fact and conclusions of law). In this case Melendres alleged that the Maricopa County Sheriff's office was liable for racial profiling of Latinos in violation of the Fourth and Fourteenth Amendments of the US Constitution. It resulted in a detailed consent decree and the appointment of an independent monitor to supervise training and policing in the Maricopa County Sheriff's Office.

[31] A Goodman, '"No Papers, No Fear": As Arpaio Fights Arizona Suit, 4 Undocumented Immigrants Reveal Their Status' *Democracy Now* (26 July 2012): www.democracynow.org/2012/7/26/no_papers_no_fear_as_arpaio.

of civil disobedience marks her rejection not only of Arpaio's regime, but of the posture—terrorised and silent—that it prescribes for her. Though she does not elaborate on what she has experienced, the magnitude of the risk she is willing to take, in courting arrest as an undocumented mother of small children, signals the extent of her suffering and her refusal to submit to stigmatisation and surveillance.

C. Pain and the Emotions of Accountability

Beginning as early as mid-2013, those who were focused on fighting for legal status and those who were focused on resisting oppressive immigration enforcement converged on a shared effort to fight deportations and demand an executive programme of deferred action for adults as well as youth.[32] This convergence followed a concerted yet unsuccessful push for comprehensive immigration reform, in which many undocumented activists felt their new-found political voices eclipsed by the machinations of legislators and the reassertion of control by national pro-immigrant non-profits.[33] The campaign for executive relief, frequently referred to as 'Not1MoreDeportation',[34] brought new forms of emotion management, expression and display to the fore.

This campaign comprised two kinds of efforts: social-media-based struggles against individual deportations, and larger public events at which those with loved ones or friends in detention or deportation proceedings engaged in civil disobedience designed to highlight and thwart mechanisms of immigration enforcement.[35] Both kinds of action shared a common substantive theme: the sundering of family ties through record-level detention and deportations was a not only betrayal by the Obama Administration but a violation of the humanity of those targeted. This message was communicated through a distinctive emotional repertoire; the shift in activists' critique—from claims of injustice to claims of immorality—was underscored by yet another shift in emotional register, from anger and frustration, to outrage and demands for governmental accountability.[36] Moreover, the pain of family separation was communicated

---

[32] See eg, 'An Open Letter to the Immigrant Rights Movement: Our Families Can't Wait', 15 January 2014 (circulated by email and social media); Aura Bogado, 'A Group of Immigration Activists Disrupt ICE Colorlines.com, Wednesday 16 October 2013: colorlines.com/archives/2013/10/shutting_down_ice.html.

[33] K Abrams, Arizona Immigrant Rights Project, interviews with Reyna M, Erika A, Yadira G and Ileana S.

[34] See generally: www.notonemoredeportation.com/.

[35] See eg, Y Alaniz, 'From LA to DC, Young Activists Take Up Civil Disobedience for Immigrant Rights', February 2014: www.socialism.com/drupal-6.8/articles/la-dc-young-activists-take-civil-disobedience-immigrant-rights.

[36] By contrasting 'anger' and 'outrage' I mean primarily to emphasise a transition from a sense of grievance arising from the violation of socially-situated norms of fairness (it is unfair for Obama to claim public support for DREAMers and then fail to act to secure their higher education and/or deport their parents) to a sense of grievance arising from the violation of universal moral norms (it is violation of the basic humanity of immigrants to separate their families through detention and deportation).

by anguished, first-person narratives in which those suffering the detention or deportation of a family member abandoned practices of emotional self-restraint, in favour of searing, intimate expressions of the losses that were being imposed by federal immigration enforcement.

A key example of this affective approach was a video created by Arizona DREAMer Erika Andiola, in January 2013, to fight her mother's deportation.[37] When Andiola's mother and brother were taken from their home by ICE agents, Andiola recorded a statement in which she recounted the circumstances of their detention and pleaded for help in fighting her mother's imminent deportation. In the video, Andiola is distraught and weeping visibly as she says:

> Hello, my name is Erika … my mother and my brother were just taken by Immigration. They just came to my house, they knocked on my door. My brother was outside with the neighbor. They just came to ask for my mom. They said they were not going to do anything to her. My mom came outside and they took her, for no reason. And then they asked me if my brother was related to me. I said yes, he's my brother. They just took him, they just took him—they didn't want to tell me why. They just said that they needed to go because they were here illegally, and that they shouldn't be here. This needs to stop. We need to do something, we need to stop. We need to stop separating families. This is real, this is so real. This is not just happening to me, this is happening to families everywhere. We cannot let this happen anymore. I need everybody to stop pretending like nothing is wrong, to stop pretending like we're just living normal lives, because we're not. This could happen to any of us at any time.[38]

While Andiola's video draws on a love between family members that may be broadly shared, there is nothing universal about the pain it so starkly conveys. Andiola's anguish arises from a kind of inhumanity that is unfamiliar to many in her audience; it is directly related to her family's undocumented status. She abandons, and even critiques, the posture of normalcy and cheerful aspiration that has been part of DREAMers hopeful stance, adding 'I need everyone to stop pretending like we're just living normal lives because we're not. This could happen to any of us at any time'. Also notably, Andiola films herself at the moment of

---

This distinction between anger and outrage tracks one salient dimension of the distinction drawn by Dirk Lindebaum and Deanna Geddes between 'personal anger' and 'moral anger': see D Lindebaum and D Geddes, 'The Place and Role of (Moral) Anger in Organizational Behavior Studies' (2015) *Journal of Organizational Behavior* (published online in Wiley Online Library wileyonlinelibrary.com) doi: 10.1002/job.2065. Another distinguishing feature of moral anger (outrage) that is germane here is that moral anger (outrage) produces a strong action tendency aimed at correcting the violation and preventing it in the future, even at significant personal cost to the actor, whereas personal anger may not. We see this tendency in the Not1More campaign's call for accountability on the part of President Obama, which take forms that may expose activists to significant personal risk.

[37] Some DREAMers who led the shift toward a focus on deportation were galvanised by their own experience with the detention or deportation of family members. See Open Letter (n 32). See also Arizona Immigrant Rights Project, interviews with Reyna M, Erika A, Yadira G, Julio Z.

[38] The video can be found at www.huffingtonpost.com/2013/01/11/erika-andiola-undocumented-immigrant_n_2456792.html.

greatest impact, before she has had the opportunity to assimilate her fear, anger and grief; in so doing she makes absolutely clear the emotional pain of family separation. While this timing reflected practical necessity—it was essential to spread the word quickly order to fight her mother's deportation—it also allowed her to capture, in the most visceral way possible, the pain produced by immigration enforcement.[39] Andiola's video captured not simply vulnerability but immediate loss: it materialised for viewers the raw pain inflicted on hundreds of families each day through immigration enforcement practices.[40]

Public demonstrations during this period also foregrounded this kind of visceral suffering. In April 2014, undocumented activists from Phoenix organised a 60-mile march into the Arizona desert, culminating in a public vigil at the immigration detention centre at Eloy.[41] At the end of the vigil, an organiser asked participants who had children in detention at Eloy to speak to them via a public address system, noting that protesters could often be heard inside the facility. The expressions of love and anguish that followed were difficult to witness—in both their intimacy and their pain—as they echoed off the concrete canyons of the facility.[42] Although the self-disclosure required by this part of the action was an exhausting experience for the parents involved, participants treated it as a demanding but necessary expedient, to impress upon an apparently indifferent world the suffering that had been imposed upon them by federal immigration enforcement.

The emotions of anguish that characterised this period of activism were intertwined with emotions intended to elicit accountability: outrage at the inhumanity of the Administration's enforcement policies, and determination to hold the Administration accountable for this treatment.[43] These latter emotions emerged

[39] The feelings of shock, empathy and outrage sparked by Andiola's appeal led viewers to call ICE and contact their elected representatives; following this, the scheduled deportation was stopped at the last minute: J Hing, Release of DREAMer Erika Andiola's Family Highlights Youth Movement's Power', 11 January 2013: www.colorlines.com/articles/release-dreamer-erika-andiolas-family-highlights-youth-movements-power.

[40] The Not1MoreDeportation campaign has generated dozens of videos that aim to secure the release of those held in immigration detention or facing deportation; most express palpable emotional pain, as a way of communicating the costs of family separation: see eg, Petition for the release of Norma Edith Bernal Gutierrez, in April 2014: www.youtube.com/watch?v=Ep9eeQTJqqc&feature=youtu.be.

[41] 'Immigrant Activists March from Phoenix to Immigrant Detention Center' *Latino Daily News* (Thursday 3 April 2014): www.hispanicallyspeakingnews.com/latino-daily-news/details/immigration-activists-to-march-from-phoenix-to-immigrant-detention-center/29545/.

[42] I witnessed these speeches on Saturday 5 April, 2014. Arizona Immigrant Rights Project, notes from 3 April 2014 trip.

[43] Outrage has sometimes been theorised by social movement scholars as the emotion that is most important in mobilising prospective activists: see eg, J Jasper, 'The Emotions of Protest: Affective and Reactive Emotions In and Around Social Movements' (1998) 13 *Sociological Forum* 397, 413–14. See also generally W Gamson, *Talking Politics* (Cambridge, Cambridge University Press, 1992). However, undocumented activists have only recently begun to voice outrage in public contexts. In the early stages of the movement, undocumented immigrants were able to mobilise around emotions such as hope, pride and determination. However, as political frustrations have continued, and as they have gained a

forcefully in actions that sought to intervene in the machinery of immigration enforcement. By tying themselves to deportation buses, or chaining themselves together across the entrances to deportation facilities, protesters highlighted the Obama Administration's record-level deportations,[44] and pressed the President to adopt executive relief from deportation on the model of DACA. The outrage and desire for accountability that infused many 'Not1More' actions are powerfully captured by a video from an April 2014 action to shut down an ICE facility in Boston. The speaker is himself a citizen, a rarity in such actions; but the standpoint from which he speaks—as the son of an undocumented woman who has been criminalised and whose family endures the constant risk of separation—is the standpoint from which most undocumented protest arises in this campaign. The distinctive mix of emotions that characterised this phase of activism is displayed in his impassioned remarks:

> [M]y mother crossed the border to this country some thirty years ago. She existed 27 years as an undocumented person, and I should say, as this government would like to label her body as an illegal human being, something that is incomprehensible, something that is inhumane. That was the woman that birthed me, that was the woman that raised me to be the person that I am today, to stand with here demanding justice, to stand here and say to this country: YOU are the one that is inhumane, YOU are the one that is breaking rules, YOU are the one that is breaking laws. YOU are breaking laws of humanity, YOU are breaking laws of dignity, YOU are breaking laws of respect.[45]

The speaker's outrage at the fear and the dehumanisation to which immigrant families have been subjected is joined with a fierce and focused claim for accountability, when he adds:

> I direct [this] message directly to the President of the United States of America, Barack Obama. That is for you, as the son of an immigrant, as the son of someone else who comes from a different land, you should know better than any that we deserve rights, that we deserve dignity, and you should be recognizing our families, you should be recognizing our communities. This message is for you, Mr President.[46]

---

sense of authorisation through their organising and some political successes, most notably President Obama's grant of Deferred Action for Childhood Arrivals (DACA) to DREAMers, undocumented activists have been more inclined to organise around indignation and outrage. See Arizona Immigrant Rights Project, interviews with Yadira G, Erika A, Reyna M.

[44] There remains some statistical controversy about whether Obama or George W Bush has deported more immigrants: L Jacobson, 'Has Barack Obama Deported More People Than Any Other President?' *Politifact* (10 August 2012): www.politifact.com/truth-o-meter/statements/2012/aug/10/american-principles-action/has-barack-obama-deported-more-people-any-other-pr/ (finding that at the end of his first term, Obama had not deported more people than Bush did in two terms, but that his monthly deportation numbers were higher). However, it is widely claimed by undocumented activists that Obama has deported record numbers of undocumented immigrants.

[45] 'The Most Passionate Speech You May Ever Have Heard' (17 April 2014): www.youtube.com/watch?v=lSStVYqxcno.

[46] Ibid.

III. Understanding Emotional Transitions in Undocumented Activism

These shifts in the emotional repertoire of undocumented activists, which foreground anger, indignation and outrage, have been dramatic and potentially consequential. The tactics through which activists enacted these emotions placed them at risk of arrest, detention and deportation. More directly, the display of contentious emotions and critical stances towards the state were daring for those who lacked legal status, and, in some cases, legal presence. They risked alienating key segments of their audience:[47] administration officials who believed they had supported undocumented immigrants under exceptionally adverse circumstances,[48] or citizens who questioned the entitlement of those without status publicly to critique US policy. Columnist Ruben Navarette, for example, derided undocumented leaders for 'thinking of themselves as full-fledged Americans who can get away with the kind of in-your-face-agitation that has been prevalent since the 1960s'. He concluded, 'their arrogance and radicalism alienates supporters and puts them in jeopardy'.[49] The evident challenges involved in these transitions raise important questions. What changes in assumptions have made activists once wary of 'ruffling feathers' willing to take these kinds of risks? More broadly, what events or processes change the view that members of a social movement take of particular emotions?

A literature analysing emotion in social movements[50] has begun to approach these kinds of questions. Early works treated emotion as a source of the irrationality of social movements: the passions that turned a crowd into a mob.[51] More recent scholarship on emotion has sought to counter a rationalist turn in social movement analysis, by describing the ways that many social movement phenomena—from emergence, recruitment and mobilisation, to florescence and

---

[47] For a superb analysis of the challenges involved in a more confrontational stance, interpreted through the lens of 'civility', see L Volpp, 'Civility and the Undocumented Alien' in A Sarat (ed), *Civility, Legality, and Justice in America* (Cambridge, Cambridge University Press, 2014) 69.

[48] President Obama, for example, has publicly expressed frustration with more confrontational DREAMer protests, claiming that he is an ally and activists should be protesting against Republicans. See eg, Latino Rebels.com, 3 November 2014: www.latinorebels.com/2014/11/03/obama-to-dreamer-you-need-to-go-protest-the-republicans-video/.

[49] R Navarette, 'A DREAMers Nightmare' *San Jose Mercury News* (15 January 2013): www.mercurynews.com/ci_22379873/ruben-navarrette-dreamers-nightmare.

[50] For examples of such works, see H Flam and D King (eds), *Emotions and Social Movements* (London, Routledge, 2005); J Goodwin, J Jasper and F Polletta (eds), *Passionate Politics: Emotions and Social Movements* (Chicago, IL, University of Chicago Press, 2001).

[51] H Blumer, 'Collective Behavior' [1939] in AMcC Lee (ed), *Principles of Sociology* (New York, Barnes and Noble, 1969). This view of the role of emotion in social movements dates back to G Le Bon, *The Crowd* (New York, Viking, 1960 (1895)), and includes works that analyse the susceptibility of particular kinds of people to the emotions of the crowd: see eg, O Klapp, *The Collective Search for Identity* (New York, Holt, Rinehart and Winston, 1969); E Hoffer, *The True Believer* (New York, Harper and Row 1951).

decline—can be explained or illuminated by the functioning of emotion.[52] Some of this scholarship has followed the invitation of sociologist Arlie Hochschild, who has worked in familial and organisational contexts, to consider processes of 'emotion management'[53]—that is, how movement actors consciously or less consciously control or direct their own emotions so as to elicit emotions in others or achieve the larger goals of the movement.[54] Rarer are works that have followed Hochschild's invitation to investigate 'feeling rules': shared assumptions, both explicit and implicit, that help group members to understand what they are feeling and what emotions should be experienced and expressed in particular contexts.[55]

Deborah Gould, however, has brought a related enquiry to the domain of social movements, using the concept of 'emotional habitus':

> Operating beneath conscious awareness, the emotional habitus of a social group provides members with an emotional disposition, with a sense of what and how to feel ... with ways of figuring out and understanding what they are feeling. An emotional habitus contains an emotional pedagogy ... [that confers] on some feelings and modes of expression an axiomatic, natural quality, and mak[es] other feeling states ... unfeelable and inexpressible.[56]

A social movement group's emotional habitus bears not simply on feelings but on political action, 'because feelings play an important role in generating and foreclosing political horizons, sense of what is to be done and how to do it'.[57] Gould is interested in how emotional habitus shapes political action and, importantly, how *shifts* in emotional habitus fuel new political expressions and strategies. Gould argues that during the late 1980s, the emotional habitus of the LGBT groups fighting the AIDS epidemic underwent a dramatic transition. Gays and lesbians, who had met the government's wilful neglect of the epidemic with stoicism and a steadfast commitment to caring for their sick, began to mobilise in

---

[52] J Goodwin, J Jasper and F Polletta, 'Why Emotions Matter' in J Goodwin, J Jasper and F Polletta (eds), *Passionate Politics: Emotions and Social Movements* (Chicago, IL, University of Chicago Press, 2001). See also sources cited at n 51.

[53] A Hochschild, *The Managed Heart* (Berkeley, CA, University of California Press, 1983) 7.

[54] J Goodwin and S Pfaff, 'Emotion Work in High-Risk Social Movements: Managing Fear in the US and East German Civil Rights Movements' in J Goodwin, J Jasper and F Polletta (eds), *Passionate Politics: Emotions and Social Movements* (Chicago, IL, University of Chicago Press, 2001); N Whittier, 'Emotional Strategies: The Collective Reconstruction and Display of Oppositional Emotions in the Movement Against Child Sexual Abuse' in J Goodwin, J Jasper and F Polletta (eds), *Passionate Politics: Emotions and Social Movements* (Chicago, IL, University of Chicago Press, 2001).

[55] Hochschild (n 53) 56–75.

[56] Gould (n 3) 34. Gould takes from Bourdieu the notion of 'habitus' as 'socially constituted, commonsensical, taken-for-granted understandings ... in any social grouping that, operating beneath conscious awareness, on the level of bodily understanding, provide members with a disposition or orientation to action, a "sense of the game" and how best to play it': ibid, 33. But as she notes, she does not simply transpose this understanding into the emotional realm; she acknowledges certain differences in her view of the way an emotional habitus functions. For example, while Bourdieu tends to emphasise the stabilisation and reproduction of habitus, Gould acknowledges this tendency while also emphasising, as I describe above, its potential for change: ibid, 38–39.

[57] Ibid, 32.

angry, militant street protests. The catalyst for this shift, Gould argues, was not a development within the epidemic itself, but the Supreme Court's opinion in *Bowers v Hardwick*,[58] upholding Georgia's anti-sodomy statute against a constitutional challenge. The opinion, which denied gays and lesbians the right of privacy, and exiled them from the Constitution with the blunt language of homophobia, created a 'moral shock'[59] which caused them to reappraise themselves and their relation to the state.

Gay and lesbian activists, Gould argues, had struggled with a deep ambivalence, their pride in their identities confronting yet never fully conquering the shame instilled by a homophobic society. Particularly in an epidemic traceable to sexual behaviour, this ambivalence fuelled a 'politics of respectability' in which responsible care of the sick demonstrated the ability of the LGBT community to behave as 'good gays'. *Hardwick* showed the futility of this path; not only had this strategy failed, but the community was so thoroughly marginalised that it had nothing left to lose through a change in political strategy. At the same time the decision helped to resolve gay and lesbian ambivalence in direction of pride and indignation; confronting them with frank, official homophobia, *Hardwick* 'encouraged lesbians and gay men to channel blame and shame about AIDS away from themselves and toward the homophobic institutions of society'.[60] Finally, *Hardwick* allowed a new interpretation of governmental inaction in the early phases of the AIDS crisis; it suggested that state and society viewed gay men as expendable—indeed as 'better off dead'.[61] These insights helped 'crystalize into anger'[62] the many, sometimes inchoate effects produced by the devastation of the epidemic. In so doing, they created a new political horizon. Spurred by leaders to 'turn anger, fear, grief into action',[63] gays and lesbians responded with the angry, disruptive direct action of ACT UP.[64]

I argue that a similar shift in emotional habitus has occurred in the immigrant rights movement, or, more specifically, in that portion of it led and populated by undocumented activists. The dynamics of that shift are both similar to and different from the transition described by Gould in AIDS activism. In both cases, a deep ambivalence about identity prompted an initial affective stance which reflected, at least in part, a 'politics of respectability'.[65] In both cases the transition enabled the

---

[58] *Bowers v Hardwick*, 478 US 186 (1986).
[59] Gould (n 3) 134–36. See also J Jasper and J Poulsen, 'Recruiting Strangers and Friends: Moral Shocks and Social Networks in Animal Rights and Anti-Nuclear Protests' (1995) 42 *Social Problems* 493.
[60] Gould (n 3) 136.
[61] Ibid, 137.
[62] Ibid, 142.
[63] Ibid, 130.
[64] ACT UP (AIDS Coalition to Unleash Power) is an organisation founded at the height of the AIDS epidemic in 1987, to advocate for people with AIDS, and transform medical research, treatment and legislative policies through the use of confrontational direct action tactics (including die-ins and agency shut-downs). See generally D Crimp, *AIDS Demo Graphics* (Seattle, WA, Bay Press, 1990).
[65] The term has its origins in an early twentieth-century ideology of the US black middle class, through which elites policed the behaviour and appearance of working-class or poor blacks, on the

emergence of activism marked by indignation, outrage and confrontational tactics. But the nature of the transition and the precipitating factors in the two cases were different. Undocumented activists did not experience a single 'moral shock' equivalent to *Bowers v Hardwick*; it was a more gradual transition with several moments of reappraisal. And the sense of membership that undocumented activists ultimately saw as betrayed by government action had different sources: it was not the presumptive entitlement of otherwise privileged citizens to which Gould points; it was a growing sense of de facto citizenship forged by years of concerted and creative political engagement. The resulting consciousness—which combined a sense of de facto membership with a recognition of extreme precarity—was less a resolution of ambivalence than a willingness to reveal it through political action. In what follows, I build on this argument. Although I support it with evidence, from my own research and from others' sources, I offer it less as a conclusion than a set of hypotheses: further investigation and analysis will be required to elaborate and confirm them. But the provisional insight they provide into how and why the implicit emotional assumptions of a social movement can change may enhance our understanding of the collective, socially-structured emotions that influence the law.

The emotional habitus reflected in early DREAMer narratives, as with early AIDS activism, arose in part from ambivalence about identity. As scholars such as Abrego, Menjivar, and Gonzales have argued,[66] the self-conception of undocumented immigrants is shaped in the first instance by 'illegality', the pervasive stigma that emerges from legal, political and media-based understandings of what it means to be undocumented. Abrego and Menjivar have described as 'legal violence' the effects of immigration laws on youth, adults and families who lack permanent legal status.[67] Immigration laws and their enforcement forge a deep association between undocumented status and criminality, and separate

---

theory that such efforts at self-improvement would 'uplift the race': see F Harris, 'The Rise of Respectability Politics' *Dissent* (Winter 2014): www.dissentmagazine.org/article/the-rise-of-respectability-politics. In the context of immigration politics, the 'politics of respectability' consists of personal or organisational efforts to structure the self-presentation and claims-making of undocumented immigrants around norms of 'deservingness' (such as those captured in the early DREAMer narrative), without questioning the way that 'deservingness' has been defined by mainstream (liberal, democratic) institutions: G Negron-Gonzales, L Abrego and K Coll (eds), 'Complicating the Politics of Deservingness: A Critical Look at Latina/o Undocumented Youth' (2012) 9 *Association of Mexican American Educators Journal*: amaejournal.utsa.edu/index.php/amae/issue/view/27.

[66] C Menjivar and L Abrego, 'Legal Violence: Immigration Law and the Lives of Central American Immigrants' (2012) 117 *American Journal of Sociology* 1380; L Abrego, 'The Legal Consciousness of Undocumented Latinos: Fear and Stigma as Barriers to Claims-Making by First- and 1.5-Generation Immigrants' (2011) 45 *Law & Society Review* 337; R Gonzales, 'Learning to be Illegal: Undocumented Youth and Shifting Legal Contexts in the Transition to Adulthood' (2011) 76 *American Sociological Review* 602.

[67] Menjivar and Abrego (n 66). Menjivar and Abrego's data, which draws on interviews with Central American immigrants, includes not only those who are undocumented but those who are in various forms of Temporary Protected Status. In my discussion I consider the implications of their thesis specifically for those who are undocumented.

undocumented status from notions of rights or recourse. Many undocumented immigrants internalise the highly stigmatised identities created by law, which adds to ongoing fears of enforcement, a sense of shame, isolation and powerlessness to improve their circumstances. Menjivar and Abrego relate the wrenching story of a Guatamalan immigrant apprehended in a workplace raid, who, despite the explanations of his lawyer, stated repeatedly that 'I'm illegal. I have no rights. I'm nobody in this country. Just do what you want with me'.[68] Though youth may be spared this sense of complete abjection through their socialisation within American educational institutions, they may also suffer feelings of hopelessness, immobility, or self-derogation. Gonzales argues that young immigrants emerge from the protective educational environment created by *Plyler v Doe*[69] into a world in which their post-secondary educational opportunities are sharply curtailed and their employment prospects are not decisively different from those of their parents. He characterises the despair, immobilisation and gradual adaptation to a socially marginal life in the on the edges of the low-wage job market as 'learning to be illegal'.[70] As one undocumented youth described it: 'I don't want to finish school ... I know that after this, I will have nothing. I feel that my life will be over. I want to stay back a year, so at least I can continue to go to school'.[71]

This socialisation to the stigma of illegality made mobilising undocumented immigrants an ambivalent undertaking. Undocumented communities desperately needed legal change, but had neither the legal status nor the kind of self-conception from which political claims might readily spring. One answer emerged in the DREAM Act strategy: to rest claims to legalisation on the distinctive strengths of a segment of the undocumented population.[72] The paradigmatic emotions reflected in early DREAMer narratives respond in many ways to the deficits in self-conception produced by 'illegality'.[73] While their emphasis on academic

[68] Ibid, 1404 (citing Julia Preston, 'Immigration Quandary: A Mother Torn from Her Baby' *New York Times* (17 November 2007).

[69] *Plyler v Doe*, 457 US 202 (1982) held that state school districts are required by the Equal Protection clause of the Fourteenth Amendment to the Constitution to provide a K-12 public education to undocumented youth brought to the United States as children.

[70] Abrego (n 66).

[71] Menjivar and Abrego (n 66) 1410.

[72] As Nicholls argues, this strategy emerged at the national level from pro-immigrant non-profits led by citizens. See Nicholls, *The DREAMers* (n 14) 41–73. Yet a similar strategy emerged from among undocumented youth themselves, in states where out-of-state tuition requirements threatened to place college beyond the reach of undocumented students. When Arizona's Proposition 300 (2006) imposed out-of-state tuition on undocumented students and eliminated state scholarships, Arizona State University brought together more than 100 undocumented scholarship recipients to explain the changes and explore possible private scholarship options. Students quickly glimpsed the experience they shared, and the mutual support they might provide as they struggled to continue their education. Organizing first around the search for scholarships, they soon learned about the federal DREAM Act, and began coalesce with DREAMers nationwide to support it. Arizona Immigrant Rights Project, Interviews with Dulce M, YG, Julio Z.

[73] Nicholls has emphasised the way that DREAMer narratives counter the stigma of illegality in the minds of legislators—Nicholls, *The DREAMers* (n 14) 41–73. My argument is different: namely, that these narratives, and the emotional stances they embody, also served to combat stigma in the consciousness of DREAMers themselves.

success or mastery of English appeals to potential audiences, it also fosters and amplifies pride that DREAMers feel in their accomplishments. Making the claim, playing the role and experiencing the response it elicits—from members of Congress or the public—enables DREAMers to feel a greater sense of desert. Serving as the symbol of immigrant ingenuity and accomplishment helps to *ameliorate* the feelings of stigma with which they have been struggling. Considered another way, however, activists' embrace of this emotional stance *reflects* the sense of stigma that 'illegality' creates. The submerging of frustration or despair in a consistent narrative of pride, hope and trust reflects a deferent posture towards prospective audiences: a careful avoidance, as DREAMer Daniel Rodriguez put it, of anything that would 'ruffle ... anyone's feathers' or 'give ... us a bad image'.[74] This cautious emotional self-management exemplifies a 'politics of respectability', an effort to advance by being—affectively as well as academically—the 'good immigrant'. The change in emotional habitus that allows a loosening of this constraint arises both from a continuing amelioration of the ambivalence experienced by undocumented activists about their identities, and from a reassessment of what their political circumstances require. It creates a new 'political horizon', in which the expression of confrontational emotions and the undertaking of disruptive political actions seem plausible and even advantageous.

The failure of the DREAM Act in 2010 caused a major reappraisal of many elements of strategy, including the affective. DREAMers who had projected a compliant, hopeful image for close to a decade had little to show for their efforts; they began to wonder whether they had pursued the right path. To be well mannered when one is being neglected or exploited for political benefit, to have faith when that faith is not vindicated, seems less like strategy and more like passivity or blind deference.[75] DREAMers reached conclusions like that voiced by Daniel Rodriguez: when years of one approach produce no results, another approach is required.[76] Registering the frustration or anger that arose from the government's inaction seemed like the 'next step' in the trajectory of activism; it also seemed likely to catalyse activists whose energies were flagging with the lack of governmental response.[77]

The failure of the DREAM Act also allowed DREAMers to register the personal costs of the emotional stance they had cultivated for so long. Though the pride they had voiced in their accomplishments was undoubtedly genuine, DREAMers had laboured to submerge many other emotions as they framed their self-presentation: pride in ethnic or racial identities that was muted by emphasis on assimilation; frustration over the present restriction of their options; uncertainty

[74] Rodriguez (n 27).
[75] The debate over the 'politics of respectability' (see above, n 65), also extends to this more tactical question.
[76] Rodriguez (n 27).
[77] Rodriguez makes both these arguments in explaining DREAMers' anger and their choice of civil disobedience: see above, n 27.

about the meaning of their parents' ongoing sacrifice. Facing a period in which no new legislation would be imminently on the horizon, they felt an impetus to 'be more open with how complex our lives really are'.[78] They sought and created new venues—'improvisational' vehicles, in Gould's term—in which they could express the many facets of their identities and the range of emotions they evoked. One such vehicle was the online site 'DREAMers Adrift',[79] an 'artivists' collective, which encouraged DREAMers to explore the meaning of their status through video, spoken word and graphic arts. In registers ranging from anger and sadness to humour and irony, contributors reflected on the frustration, tedium, solidarity and even awkwardness of their undocumented lives. Although contributors seemed at first to eschew more traditional political discourse for more personal or artistic explorations, the impetus to make these more complex depictions part of public discourse was fuelled by a second development, the process of coming out as 'undocumented and unafraid'.[80]

The act of self-revelation, as LGBT activists had discovered years earlier, managed fear by taking control over the circumstances by which one's status was revealed.[81] It fought stigma by claiming undocumented status as an identity that could be a source of pride and affirmation—even without the displays of achievement or assimilation that were thought to be necessary in DREAMers stories. The 'Coming Out of the Shadows' actions, ignited in the struggle for the 2010 DREAM Act and proliferating in the years that followed, produced these effects. The rallying cries of this effort, 'undocumented and unafraid' or 'undocumented, unafraid, and unapologetic' functioned as what William Reddy has called 'emotives': descriptions of one's feeling state that have normative, and performative effects.[82] As Deborah Gould explains, when LGBT activists said 'we are angry',

---

[78] Carrasco and Seif (n 29) 288.

[79] See www.facebook.com/DreamersAdrift/.

[80] Ultimately the 'artivists' of Dreamers Adrift found that their more emotionally varied self-presentations could be mobilised for explicitly political purposes. For example, a video by the co-founders of the site used an ironic, rap-inspired message to President Obama, to challenge the Administration's failure to deliver a programme of deferred action.

> This video's for you, you know who you are. Yeah, we saw your speech. Yeah I guess you did have some valid points. We get it, you're [inaudible] our broken immigration system. We get it, we know that you support DREAM Act students. But what we don't get, what doesn't make sense to us, is why you refuse to use your executive powers to *end our pain*. There are DREAMers right now who are about to get deported. And what are *you* doing to help them? Mean what you say. Say what you mean. Simply saying you support the DREAM Act is not getting us anywhere. Oh, and by the way, we are not your political pawns, so don't use us for ad space on your campaign trail. Obama, don't deport my mama; Obama don't deport my mama.

See Dreamers Adrift, www.facebook.com/DreamersAdrift (May 16, 2011).

[81] One activist from the IYJL described a similar effect of engaging in civil disobedience while undocumented. She observed: '[T]here is no greater way to break your fear than to get arrested. The one thing you're most afraid of, but on your own terms'—Carrasco and Seif (n 29) 296.

[82] W Reddy, 'Emotional Liberty: Politics and History in the Anthropology of Emotions' (1999) 14 *Cultural Anthropology* 256, 266–71. Reddy describes 'emotives' as '[e]motional utterances of the type "I feel afraid" or "I am angry"—which I will call first-person, present-tense emotion claims—[that]

they were not simply describing their own feelings, they were saying that it was understandable and legitimate to be angry, and that other participants should feel angry too.[83] Similarly, in challenging DREAMers nationwide to come out as 'undocumented and unapologetic', the IYJL invited them to see undocumented status as something for which no one should have to apologise—whether or not they had mastered English or been the valedictorian of their high school class. And by declaring themselves 'undocumented and unafraid', activists came to feel less fearful, regardless of whether they had felt that way at the moment of revealing their status. These effects arose in part from observing how the declaration worked in others: as one Arizona DREAMer observed, 'as people started telling their stories and started coming out [you] started noticing that it wasn't really something to be afraid of; that it was something that you could live with and that you were okay with'.[84] But the performative effects also arose from seeing the impact of the phrase on the public:

> Even if people were still afraid, even if they were dying inside ... [y]ou had to put on that face, where it was—you know what; I'm not afraid ... When you sa[id] so, certainly people believe[d] you ... so even if it started as ... an empowerment phrase, it became true.[85]

Coming out was itself an exercise in the emotions of defiance; those who were undocumented were *supposed to feel* afraid, ashamed, apologetic. This practice thus enabled activists to feel more comfortable voicing the varied emotions and moods that flowed from undocumented experience.

But undocumented activism did not simply ease fear and stigma; it also fostered feelings of greater authorisation in relation to the state. These effects began as early as DREAM Act activism; the ability of DREAMers to join a human face and a set of tangible details to the abstraction of being 'undocumented' enabled them to testify in the halls of Congress, forming relationships and gaining first-hand understanding of the political process. But two events in 2012 strengthened this sense of authorisation and appreciation of the accountability of the state. One, not surprisingly, was the announcement of Deferred Action for Childhood Arrivals (DACA) in June 2012. The grant of even temporary legal presence made many DREAMers feel a greater sense of membership, and an empowerment to work on behalf of those who did not have such protection.[86] But more specifically, DREAMers felt that their activism had held the Obama Administration accountable: escalating direct action protests at Obama re-election campaign headquarters in spring

---

have 1) a descriptive appearance; 2) a relational intent; and 3) a self-exploring or self-altering effect': ibid, 268.

[83] Gould (n 3) 37–39 (describing emotives and citing Reddy), and 142–43 (describing the naming of anger and outrage in AIDS activism).
[84] Arizona Immigrant Rights Project, interview with Carla C.
[85] Ibid.
[86] Arizona Immigrant Rights Project, interviews with Yadira G, Dulce M.

2012 had made it clear that some relief from deportation would be necessary if Obama hoped to win the support of Latino voters.[87] But political confidence and appreciation of governmental accountability stemmed from a second source as well: the civic engagement work performed by undocumented activists in the 2012 election. Rallied by the announcement of DACA, thousands of undocumented teenagers and some undocumented adults worked to register and turn out Latino voters. Activists without status shared a role that had traditionally been performed by citizens, gaining exposure to dynamics of political participation and of electoral accountability. A canvasser from Phoenix, for example, emphasised a key lesson drawn from his efforts: voters have the right to tell their representatives, '[w]e need you to fix this, or else, if you don't fix this, we will hold you accountable and the same way that we bring you in, we have the right to take you out of office'.[88] These concrete and varied experiences gave undocumented activists a sense of investment in the political system that was similar to that experienced by politically-engaged citizens. As one Arizona DREAMer declared:

> Don't you dare tell me that I don't have a voice ... I have family members; I have friends; I have community leaders, community members who care about me, and they're going to be voting for something that I care about. I do have a voice in that sense, because even though I might not have the right to vote, I have made the choice to empower those who can.[89]

This emergent sense of membership produced a huge surge of effort behind the campaign for comprehensive immigration reform (CIR) in 2013. But when CIR began to stall, and ultimately to fail, the same sense of authorisation and of state accountability allowed activists to voice new emotions. What produced the final shift towards the expression of pain and outrage was the recognition that though the legislation had failed, the enhanced enforcement—which had begun as a 'down-payment' on bipartisan immigration reform—would continue. Activists felt a keen sense of betrayal by an administration claiming to support them, but was willing to inflict unprecedented pain on their communities. They also felt the enormous vulnerability of undocumented adults—the parents of DREAM activists—now that prospects of legalisation had evaporated. In some ways, voicing the raw pain of family separation seemed intuitive: these were powerful bonds that would continue to be threatened by detention and deportation. Moreover, the strong emotions connected to these bonds had been submerged in youth-focused campaigns for the DREAM Act and DACA, and had only recently emerged in

---

[87] See Matt Bareto, Thomas Schaller and Gary Segura, 'DACA's Three Year Anniversary' *Huffington Post* (15 June 2015): www.huffingtonpost.com/latino-decisions/dacas-three-year-annivers_b_7585586. html (DACA re-energised support from Latino voters which was flagging after Obama's decision to move slowly on immigration reform in his first term).

[88] Arizona Immigrant Rights Project, interview with Sergio R.

[89] Arizona Immigrant Rights Project, interview (1) with Reyna M.

the campaign for CIR.[90] These intuitions were fortified, however, by high-profile examples such as the video by Erika Andiola discussed above.[91] Andiola's visible anguish functioned as kind of emotive, making it acceptable, even imperative, to give public voice to private pain when one's relatives are taken. Andiola's video also made clear that ongoing susceptibility to the pain of separation is part of what being a DREAMer is. Her statement that 'we have to stop pretending that we're just living normal lives, because we're not. This could happen to any of us at any time' was the final blow to self-depictions that submerged fear, pain and vulnerability. Seeing a DREAMer who felt the confidence to speak to legislators, and to be arrested at their offices, voice this kind of anguish and desperation demonstrated that the contradictory persona of the DREAMer embodies all of these affective dimensions. The shift in the emotional habitus of undocumented immigrants did not so much resolve as recast their ambivalence; though their growing sense of authorisation mitigated their stigma, it did not mitigate their susceptibility to family separation. Their broader emotional vocabulary enabled them to express this combustible combination of growing agency and persisting vulnerability.

IV. Conclusion

A full theorisation of the emotional transitions of undocumented activists must await further investigation and the continuing maturation of this young movement. But this preliminary analysis suggests what law and emotions scholars can learn from exploring the evolving feeling rules of social movements. First, this analysis extends our view of 'law' and the processes through which it is produced. 'Law' is more than the work product of legal decision-makers, or the immediate processes of adjudication, legislation and rule-making through which such products are produced. Law also comprehends longer-term processes of public deliberation and mobilisation, through which those who experience the law's effects and have stakes in its revision engage with actors empowered to make formal legal change. When we propose to study 'law and the emotions', those longer-term, social and political processes must be the objects of our attention as well.

Second, this analysis suggests that to ask, as this volume does, how 'law responds to pre-existing emotions' is to pose an important yet incomplete question. The emotions to which law responds are not naturally-occurring phenomena. They

---

[90] A focus on parents had emerged during the campaign for CIR: the '11 million dreams' and 'our parents are the original dreamers' discourse mobilised by United We DREAM emphasised adults in the push for a path to legalisation. See 'Celebrating Parents, The Original DREAMers' Blog: *Define American* (14 March 2013): www.defineamerican.com/blog/post/celebrating-parents-the-original-dreamers. Yet, like the campaign for CIR as a whole, this focus on adults was voiced in a register of hope and aspiration, rather than pain and accusation.

[91] Above, n 38.

are products of complex social formation, shaped both by the experience of living under the law, and engaging with lawmakers over the law. This ongoing interaction explains the movement, in the emotions of undocumented activists, from hopeful aspiration to aggrieved indignation to outraged anguish. Understanding the law's response to emotions means more than understanding a pattern of one-directional influence: rather, it means tracing and examining a long, reverberating interplay between human beings and legal institutions.

10

Mediation and Emotions: Perception and Regulation

CHARLIE IRVINE* AND LAUREL FARRINGTON†

Information ... has no meaning until its significance is evaluated by a person.[1]

Feeling—emotionality—is the sixth sense, the sixth critical human filter through which we make sense of the universe.[2]

I. Introduction

Mediation and more formal legal processes have much in common: their subject matter is disputes; their participants are disputants; and an independent third party plays a key part in their resolution. Yet there are significant differences. In adjudicative processes that third party is the decision-maker; her perception of the facts and evaluation of what is just are definitive. The parties' perceptions of facts and justice are secondary, and can quite reasonably be biased and self-serving. In mediation the parties are the decision-makers. Their perceptions of the facts and evaluations of justice carry the day.

We argue that it is the necessity of this context (rather than personal inclination) that drives mediators to focus on the emotional realm. As this chapter sets out, there are clear links between emotion and perception. If parties are emotionally aroused by anger, fear or a sense of injustice it will influence their perceptions and thus their judgements about what is true or false, right or wrong.[3] Formal

---

* Senior Teaching Fellow, University of Strathclyde.
† Mediator and doctoral student, University of Strathclyde.

[1] RS Lazarus, *Fifty Years of the Research and Theory of RS Lazarus: An Analysis of Historical and Perennial Issues* (London, Lawrence Erlbaum Associates, 2014) xx.

[2] E Ryan, 'The Discourse Beneath: Emotional Epistemology in Legal Deliberation and Negotiation' (2005) 10 *Harvard Negotiation Law Review* 231, 232.

[3] See, for example, JS Keltner and D Keltner, 'Fear, Anger, and Risk' (2001) 81 *Journal of Personality and Social Psychology* 146; F Gino and ME Schweitzer, 'Blinded by Anger or Feeling the Love: How Emotions Influence Advice Taking' (2008) 93 *Journal of Applied Psychology* 1165.

adjudication sidesteps this phenomenon by delegating decision-making power to the third party, although some question the capacity of judges to immunise themselves against 'catching' the emotions of others.[4] Mediation imposes a different discipline: the job is not done until first and second party decision-makers agree. If emotions affect their perceptions, mediators have little choice but to work with those emotions until the parties' perceptions of facts and justice overlap sufficiently for them to reach consensus.[5]

Some years ago one of the authors of this chapter conducted a workplace mediation between two senior colleagues, a man and a woman with long-standing enmity. The woman set out a litany of slights, offences and outrageous behaviour by the man, who had 'risen through the ranks' of the organisation. In her eyes he was aggressive, loud and thoughtless. He responded by cataloguing her many failings (in his eyes) as a senior manager. She retorted that another senior colleague supported her view. The man seemed temporarily silenced; then shook his head and stood up, leaving the room. He was clearly close to tears.

The woman was astonished. She said 'That's not Bob.[6] I've known him eighteen years and I've never seen him like that'. Although the man was considerably embarrassed by the episode it transformed the atmosphere of the mediation. There followed a period of mutual problem-solving for which both parties took responsibility. Ultimately they wrote an agreement about how they would work together in future. This episode illustrates both the significance of emotions and their 'recursive' quality: while the environment may trigger the emotion, 'emotions can and often do change the environment'.[7]

Mediation provides a useful lens through which to consider the place of emotion in disputes. Its multidisciplinary roots embrace law, psychology, economics, international relations and, more recently, neuroscience.[8] Mediators themselves have shown ambivalence about emotions, with practice lurching between intrusive fascination[9] and denial. Indeed, one prominent pioneer even questioned the usefulness of emotional information.[10] Commercial mediators have tended to stress pragmatic solutions and efficiency. As the chapter by Clare Huntington

---

[4] TA Maroney, 'Angry Judges' (2012) 65 *Vanderbilt Law Review* 1207.

[5] The mediator has been characterised as 'the self-limiting intervenor'—C Irvine, 'Mediation's Values: An Examination of the Values Behind Five Mediation Texts' (unpublished Masters dissertation, Birkbeck College, University of London, 2006): papers.ssrn.com/sol3/papers.cfm?abstract_id=1686195, 27.

[6] Not his real name.

[7] JJ Gross, 'Emotion Regulation' in M Lewis, JM Haviland-Jones and L Feldman Barrett (eds), *Handbook of Emotions*, 3rd edn (New York, Guilford Press, 2008) 499.

[8] Cloke identifies 40 disciplinary sources—see K Cloke, 'Let a Thousand Flowers Bloom: A Holistic, Pluralistic and Eclectic Approach to Mediation' (Winter, 2007) *ACResolution* 26.

[9] Menkel-Meadow describes 'a peculiarly intrusive focus on feelings'—C Menkel-Meadow, 'The Many Ways of Mediation: The Transformation of Traditions, Ideologies, Paradigms, and Practices' (1995) *Negotiation Journal* 217, 223. This appears to be a fairly accurate description.

[10] J Haynes and G Haynes, *Mediating Divorce: Casebook of Strategies for Successful Family Mediation* (San Francisco, CA, Jossey-Bass, 1989).

shows,[11] other domains, such as family law, favour mediation precisely because of its capacity to deal with emotional concerns.

This chapter starts with an overview of the approach to emotion within the mediation 'canon'[12] before considering two domains that hold promise: empathy and emotion regulation. Our perspective is shaped by findings from neuroscience and psychology suggesting that the distinction between emotion and rationality is a false dichotomy.[13] In this view emotions play a key role in perception (how we receive data from the outside world) and judgement (how we evaluate those data). Both are central to the legal system, playing critical roles in establishing truth and justice. The chapter has three sections:

— The developing understanding of emotion in mediation.
— The nature of empathy and its significance in mediation practice.
— The way in which emotional self-regulation is harnessed and supported by mediators.[14]

We conclude that mediation offers the justice system a setting in which emotions are integrated into decision-making. For mediators, emotions are not just an unfortunate by-product of disputes but a key factor in their resolution, providing both information and motivation. We describe in some detail the operation of empathy and emotion regulation in mediation; this should prove useful both for mediators and others such as lawyers, judges and arbitrators who become enmeshed in other people's conflict.

II. Mediation and Emotion

Law has long been wary of emotion. 'Blind justice' portrays the ideal judge as unaffected by human influence. Maroney recognises 'the traditional view of emotion— a view strongly reflected in legal theory—as a savage force that unseats rationality, distorts judgment, manifests in impulsive aggression, and imperils social bonds'.[15] This view chimes with older notions of the passions' rightful place as slave to reason,[16] and serves to position law as the heir of Enlightenment ideas opposing rationality to emotion and superstition. As MacIntyre claims, 'the lawyers, not the philosophers, are the clergy of liberalism'.[17]

---

[11] See Huntington, ch 2.

[12] Irvine, 'Mediation's Values' (n 5).

[13] A Damasio, *Descartes' Error*, revd edn (London, Vintage Books, 1994).

[14] JJ Gross, 'The Emerging Field of Emotion Regulation: An Integrative Review' (1998) 2 *Review of General Psychology* 271.

[15] Maroney, 'Angry Judges' (n 4) 1209. Maroney also revisits these themes in the current collection: see ch 12.

[16] R Solomon, 'The Philosophy of Emotions' in M Lewis, JM Haviland-Jones and L Feldman Barrett (eds), *Handbook of Emotions*, 3rd edn (New York, Guilford Press, 2008).

[17] A MacIntyre, *Whose Justice? Which Rationality?* (London, Duckworth, 1988) 344.

Mediation and its close relation, negotiation, have been influenced by this history. Many mediators are lawyers; after all, lawyers and the courts are gatekeepers to and consumers of their work. This position 'in the shadow of the law'[18] may explain why mediators have adopted significant elements of the law's approach: ideas like 'neutrality', 'without prejudice' and the goal of a legally binding outcome.[19] It may also account for their ambivalence about emotion: as Mayer says, 'folk wisdom suggests that a negotiator (1) should avoid getting emotional and (2) is a passive recipient of the whims of emotion'.[20] Meanwhile, Riskin states that: 'Negotiators—especially those trained in law—commonly address this problem by trying to exclude emotions from negotiation and to focus solely on so-called objective, rational factors, such as money'.[21] Moore suggests mediators 'neutralize' anger;[22] Strasser and Randolph assert that 'to remain in conflict with another defies rational scrutiny';[23] Roberts claims mediators transform interactions by 'embodying the principles of objectivity and reasonableness'.[24] In a similar vein, Haynes sought to limit the reach of mediation on this ground: 'Conflict over issues is resolvable in mediation: conflict over behaviour is resolvable in therapy'.[25]

Reviewing mediation's approach to emotion, we acknowledge different models of practice. Some, such as Bush and Folger's 'Transformative Mediation'[26] and Winslade and Monk's 'Narrative Mediation'[27] are explained in a single volume. The 'mainstream model'[28] is more diffuse, drawing inspiration from several sources, as we shall see below.

---

[18] R Mnookin and L Kornhauser, 'Bargaining in the Shadow of the Law: The Case of Divorce' (1979) 88 *Yale Law Journal* 950.

[19] See JM Sabatino, 'ADR as "Litigation Lite": Procedural and Evidentiary Norms Embedded within Alternative Dispute Resolution' (1998) 47 *Emory Law Journal* 1289.

[20] B Mayer, *The Dynamics of Conflict Resolution: A Practitioner's Guide* (San Francisco, CA, Jossey-Bass, 2000) 43; see also D Shapiro, 'Negotiating Emotions' (2002) 20 *Conflict Resolution Quarterly* 67; TZ Reeves, 'Practicing with the Heart as Metaphor' (Spring, 2010) *ACResolution*; and Irvine, 'Mediation's Values' (n 5).

[21] L Riskin, 'Further Beyond Reason: Emotions, the Core Concerns, and Mindfulness in Negotiation' (2010) 10 *Nevada Law Journal* 290, 294.

[22] CW Moore, *The Mediation Process: Practical Strategies for Resolving Conflict*, 2nd edn (San Francisco, CA, Jossey-Bass, 1996), cited in R Friedman, J M Brett, C Anderson, M Olekalns, N Goates and CC Lisco, 'The Positive and Negative Effects of Anger on Dispute Resolution: Evidence From Electronically Mediated Disputes' (2004) 89 *Journal of Applied Psychology* 369, 369.

[23] F Strasser and P Randolph, *Mediation: A Psychological Insight into Conflict Resolution* (London, Continuum, 2004) 23.

[24] M Roberts, *A–Z of Mediation* (Basingstoke, Palgrave MacMillan, 2014) 66.

[25] Haynes and Haynes (n 10) 2.

[26] RAB Bush and JP Folger, *The Promise of Mediation: The Transformative Approach to Conflict* (San Francisco, CA, Jossey-Bass, 1994); RAB Bush and JP Folger, *The Promise of Mediation: The Transformative Approach to Conflict*, 2nd edn (San Francisco, CA, Jossey-Bass, 2005).

[27] J Winslade and G Monk, *Narrative Mediation: A New Approach to Conflict Resolution* (San Francisco, CA, Jossey-Bass, 2001).

[28] Irvine, 'Mediation's Values' (n 5) 17.

A. The Mainstream Model

Also known as the facilitative or problem-solving approach, this model is pervasive in the Western world. Most mediation training uses it, although practitioners have adapted it to a range of contexts.[29] One canonical document is *The Mediator's Handbook*, first published in 1982.[30] Evoking Quaker principles of consensual decision-making, its seven-step structure[31] is surely one of the field's most influential ideas. The *Handbook* abounds with references to individual emotions,[32] reflecting our observation above that, when clients are decision-makers, mediators must take them as they are: 'The mediator provides a structure for parties to increase honest communication, air emotions, and solve problems. In effect mediation gives angry people a chance to bring out the best in themselves'.[33] Unsurprisingly, among the characteristics and skills of a good mediator the *Handbook* lists 'comfortable with high emotion, arguments, interruptions, tears'.[34] Its 'conflict core' includes emotions such as annoyance and disagreement.[35] Regarding goals, the *Handbook* reflects a common mediator aspiration to go beyond mere settlement. Its hope is for conflict to be 'transformed',[36] and among the characteristics of conflict transformation is 'easing their emotional state'.[37] Three pages are devoted to emotionally difficult situations, including 'extreme anger', 'anguish, crying' and 'the silent one'.[38]

It seems, then, that this founding document of mainstream mediation is at ease with emotion, treading a 'via media' between intrusion and suppression: 'Accept but don't press for emotions'.[39] High or negative emotion is viewed as a manifestation of conflict; resolve the conflict and the emotion will reduce. Mediators should condition themselves neither to overreact to, nor to ignore, emotional displays.

---

[29] The 'facilitative/evaluative' debate, while significant, does not propose a new model; rather it is descriptive of variations within mainstream practice—see LL Riskin, 'Understanding Mediators' Orientations, Strategies, and Techniques: A Grid for the Perplexed' (1996) 1 *Harvard Negotiation Law Review* 7; LL Riskin, 'Decision Making in Mediation: The New Old Grid and the New New Grid System' (2003) 79 *Notre Dame Law Review* 1.

[30] JE Beer with E Stief, *The Mediator's Handbook*, 3rd edn (Gabriola Island, BC, New Society Publishers, 1997).

[31] (1) Opening statement; (2) Uninterrupted time; (3) The exchange; (4) Setting the Agenda; (5) Building the Agreement; (6) and (7) Writing the Agreement and Closing: ibid, 4–5.

[32] For example, 'angry and hopeless' (ibid, 3); 'stubborn, angry' and 'friendly' (ibid, 4); 'upset' (ibid, 5); 'uneasy' (ibid, 8); 'anxiety' (ibid, 10); 'annoyance' (ibid, 11); 'anxiety, anger, hostility, depression, and even vengeance' (ibid, 12); and 'resentment, hatred, frustration, jealousy, fear, outrage, grief' (ibid, 39).

[33] Ibid, 9.

[34] Ibid, 23.

[35] Ibid, 11.

[36] A hope shared by the Transformative Mediation model—see section II.B below.

[37] Beer and Stief (n 30) 15.

[38] Ibid, 84–86.

[39] Ibid, 39.

Another keystone of mainstream mediation is a negotiation text: Fisher, Ury and Patton's *Getting to Yes*.[40] Its core idea, 'principled negotiation', has been widely adopted by mediators. However, its first principle may have created an impression of discomfort with emotions. The injunction to 'separate the people from the problem'[41] bears a surface resemblance to legal negotiators' conventional wisdom, described above, to exclude emotion and focus on facts.[42] Its intention, however, is the opposite: 'separate the relationship from the substance; deal directly with the people problem'.[43] Emotion is a key concern: 'In a negotiation, particularly a bitter personal dispute, feelings may be more important than talk'.[44] Subsequent guidance resembles emotion regulation:[45] 'First recognise and understand emotions, theirs and yours'; 'Make emotions explicit and acknowledge them as legitimate'.[46]

Despite the success of *Getting to Yes*, its authors have been accused of naivete and idealism.[47] Possibly as a result they have developed and expanded their ideas. Ury's *Getting Past No* includes advice resonant with emotion regulation: 'You obviously can't eliminate your feelings, nor do you need to do so. You need only to disconnect the automatic link between emotion and action'.[48] Strategies for disarming one's negotiation counterparts[49] include acknowledging their emotions and helping them save face. In 2005 Fisher and Shapiro's *Beyond Reason* dealt explicitly with emotions.[50] This book offers practical tools enabling negotiators to work with their own and their counterparts' emotions via five 'core concerns': appreciation, affiliation, autonomy, status and roles. Praised as a 'structured, portable methodology'[51] it teaches negotiators to attend to these five concerns so as to understand and influence emotion.

---

[40] R Fisher, W Ury and B Patton, *Getting to Yes: Negotiating Agreements Without Giving In* (London, Random House Business Books, 1991).

[41] Ibid, 17.

[42] See text above, nn 15–17.

[43] Fisher, Ury and Patton (n 40) 21.

[44] Ibid, 30.

[45] See below, section IV.

[46] Fisher, Ury and Patton (n 40) 30, 31. The injunction to 'allow the other side to let off steam' (ibid, 32) seems dated, however, and the notion of 'venting' has been criticised; see KG Allred, 'Anger and Retaliation in Conflict: The Role of Attribution' in M Deutsch and P Coleman (eds), *The Handbook of Conflict Resolution: Theory and Practice* (San Francisco, CA, Jossey-Bass, 2000) 249.

[47] See, for example, J White (with response by R Fisher) 'The Pros and Cons of "Getting to Yes"' (1984) 34 *Journal of Legal Education* 115; JC Freund, *Smart Negotiating: How to Make Good Deals in the Real World* (New York, Simon & Schuster, 1992); JL Graham, L Lawrence and WH Requejo, *Inventive Negotiation: Getting Beyond Yes* (New York, Palgrave Macmillan, 2014).

[48] W Ury, *Getting Past No: Negotiating with Difficult People* (London, Century Business, 1991) 29.

[49] The term 'counterpart' is commonly used in the negotiation literature to convey the idea that negotiation is best understood as a co-operative venture where the result depends on the other party's consent. Later we use the term 'disputants' to refer to those whose negotiations are sufficiently unsuccessful to require the intervention of a third party such as a mediator, arbitrator or judge.

[50] R Fisher and D Shapiro, *Beyond Reason: Using Emotions As You Negotiate* (New York, Viking Press, 2005).

[51] E Ryan, 'Building the Emotionally Learned Negotiator' (2006) *Negotiation Journal* 209, 218.

Another 'mainstream' text, Mayer's *The Dynamics of Conflict Resolution*, both acknowledges and integrates emotion.[52] His 'three dimensional' model of conflict sees resolution proceeding along cognitive, emotional and behavioural dimensions.[53] If people feel less strongly about the dispute, emotional resolution is achieved. Emotions are volatile and mercurial, however, and it can feel like 'one step forward, one step back'. Examples of 'emotional resolution' include:

— Feeling they are accepted as individuals and their personalities and values are not under attack.
— Feeling they can maintain dignity or 'face'.
— Having their core needs respected and addressed.
— Having enough time to gain perspective and experience healing.
— Having others accept their feelings as valid and values as legitimate.
— Feeling genuinely and non-judgementally heard.[54]

Mayer mentions apology and forgiveness,[55] and suggests true resolution of conflict must occur on all three dimensions: behavioural, emotional and cognitive.[56]

B. Transformative Mediation

In 1994 two critics of mainstream mediation practice, Bush and Folger, launched what they claimed was a radical alternative in *The Promise of Mediation*.[57] Substantially rewritten in 2005[58] this book is a stinging rebuke to the traditional approach, which they accused of 'squandering' mediation's potential in order to 'shore up institutional processes that operate to control, contain and settle conflict'.[59] Instead, they propose a different model, that of 'transformative mediation'. This rejects the notion of achieving resolution by solving problems and settling disputes. The promise of mediation is fulfilled instead by focusing on the parties' relationship, with mediators supporting 'empowerment' and 'recognition'. Thus, 'parties can recapture their sense of competence and connection, reverse the negative conflict cycle, re-establish a constructive (or at least neutral) interaction, and move forward on a positive footing'.[60]

---

[52] Mayer (n 20).
[53] Ibid, 98.
[54] Ibid, 103, 104.
[55] Ibid, 104.
[56] Ibid, 99, 108. Mayer considers cognitive resolution the hardest to achieve.
[57] Bush and Folger, *The Promise of Mediation* (1994) (n 26). The idea of conflict transformation is not original to these authors—see, for example, Beer and Stief (n 30); JP Lederach, *Preparing for Peace: Conflict Transformation Across Cultures* (Syracuse, NY, Syracuse University Press, 1995).
[58] Bush and Folger, *The Promise of Mediation* (2005) (n 26), further re-stated in JP Folger, RAB Bush and D Della Noce (eds), *Transformative Mediation: A Sourcebook* (New York, Institute for the Study of Conflict Transformation, 2010).
[59] Bush and Folger, *The Promise of Mediation* (2005) (n 26) 1.
[60] Ibid, 53.

The overarching theory of transformative mediation[61] holds that conflict renders people weak and self-absorbed. The by-products of weakness include 'confusion, doubt, uncertainty, and indecisiveness',[62] while self-absorption makes them 'suspicious, hostile, closed'.[63] The authors rarely explicitly mention emotions although they acknowledge that fear, blame and anger contribute to conflict escalation.[64] Transformative mediation aims to deal with this weakness and self-absorption by restoring human agency and social connectedness.[65] This is manifest in the twin notions of 'empowerment shift ... from weakness to greater strength' and 'recognition shift ... from self-absorption to greater understanding of the other'.[66] To these phenomena Bush and Folger attribute many of mediation's benefits such as restored relationships and improved 'sense of competence and connection'.[67] 'Weak and self-absorbed' parties are thus transformed to become 'strong and responsive'.[68] Words like 'positive' and 'constructive' pepper the text.[69] Any emotional dimension to these benefits is not spelled out. 'Empathy' is defined as 'the capacity to understand the situations and perspectives of others',[70] entirely omitting affective components.[71] One might conclude that transformative mediation shares Enlightenment prejudices favouring rationality over emotion.

However, the authors later went on to legitimise the expression of emotion and voice criticism of those who don't follow suit: 'To ignore, sidestep, or stifle expressions of emotion is ... to squander the opportunities for empowerment and recognition that these expressions present'.[72] This sentence illustrates the 'single track' nature of transformative mediation. Emotions are useful insofar as they support the model's intellectual architecture.

Transformative mediation is used by the US Postal Service, claiming some credit for improving that organisation's famously combative employment culture.[73] However, it has been criticised for its authors' early claim that the model could

---

[61] C Irvine, 'Transformative Mediation: A Critique' (unpublished Masters assignment: papers.ssrn.com/sol3/papers.cfm?abstract_id=1691847).

[62] Bush and Folger, *The Promise of Mediation* (2005) (n 26) 49.

[63] Ibid, 49.

[64] Ibid, 51 citing JZ Rubin, DG Pruitt and SH Kim, *Social Conflict: Escalation, Stalemate, and Settlement*, 2nd edn (New York, McGraw-Hill, 1994).

[65] Citing the communitarian philosophy of A Etzioni, *The New Golden Rule: Community and Morality in a Democratic Society* (London, Profile Books, 1996) and the social psychology of Rubin, Pruitt and Kim (n 64).

[66] Bush and Folger, *The Promise of Mediation* (2005) (n 26) 75.

[67] Ibid, 52, 53.

[68] Ibid, 55. For a critique of empowerment see S Cobb, 'Empowerment and Mediation: A Narrative Perspective' (1993) 9 *Negotiation Journal* 245.

[69] See, for example, Bush and Folger, *The Promise of Mediation* (2005) (n 26) 53, 54, 56.

[70] Cobb (n 68) 250.

[71] See section III below.

[72] JP Folger and RAB Bush, 'Transformative Mediation and Third-Party Intervention: Ten Hallmarks of a Transformative Approach to Practice' (1996) 13 *Mediation Quarterly* 263, 271; and see LB Bingham, 'Transformative Mediation at the United States Postal Service' (2012) 5 *Negotiation and Conflict Management Research* 354, 360 (mediators inhibited or supported recognition depending on their tolerance for strong emotions).

[73] Bingham (n 72).

not be combined with others,[74] and also because of its rejection of settlement,[75] the shortcomings in its underlying theory of moral development[76] and for being 'grandiose, intransigent, and exclusivist'.[77]

C. Narrative Mediation

Another approach is seen in *Narrative Mediation*, by Winslade and Monk. Stories are central: 'the narrative metaphor draws attention to the ways in which we use stories to make sense of our lives and relationships'.[78] Although not the first to apply a narrative lens to mediation,[79] the book elevates it into a coherent model. Steeped in social constructionist philosophy, its authors view stories as creating rather than reporting reality.[80] Stories of disputes both describe and contribute to conflict, typically preventing consideration of alternative explanations. The mediator's job is to create space for alternative storylines. While, as with transformative mediation, the main thrust of the activity seems cognitive,[81] emotions are recognised insofar as they inform people's narratives. One of the book's case studies mentions 'hurt'; 'injustice, betrayal'; and 'guilt and self-blame'.[82] The mediator's goal is to 'deconstruct'[83] such stories and work with parties to construct an 'alternative' or 'preferred' narrative.[84]

The emphasis on building a trusting relationship draws heavily on the model's therapeutic roots[85] reflecting Rogerian ideas of 'unconditional positive regard'.[86] The authors cite Gergen's claim that we are 'born into relatedness',[87] an approach

[74] J Lande, 'How Will Lawyering and Mediation Practices Transform Each Other?' (1997) 24 *Florida State University Law Review* 839, 856.

[75] M Williams, 'Can't I Get No Satisfaction? Thoughts on the Promise of Mediation' (1997) 15 *Mediation Quarterly* 143.

[76] J Seul, 'How Transformative is Transformative Mediation? A Constructive Developmental Assessment' (1999) 15 *Ohio State Journal on Dispute Resolution* 135; L Gaynier, 'Transformative Mediation: In Search of a Theory of Practice' (2005) 22 *Conflict Resolution Quarterly* 397.

[77] R Condlin, 'The Curious Case of Transformative Dispute Resolution: An Unfortunate Marriage of Intransigence, Exclusivity, and Hype' (2014) 14 *Cardozo Journal of Dispute Resolution* 621.

[78] Winslade and Monk (n 27) 3.

[79] See Cobb (n 68).

[80] V Burr, *An Introduction to Social Constructionism* (London, Routledge, 1995).

[81] A similar phenomenon has been noted in relation to negotiation scholarship—see, for example, IS Fulmer and B Barry, 'The Smart Negotiator: Cognitive Ability and Emotional Intelligence in Negotiation' (2004) 15 *International Journal of Conflict Management* 245.

[82] Winslade and Monk (n 27) 6, 13, 18.

[83] Ibid, 72.

[84] Ibid, 82.

[85] The authors acknowledge in particular M White and D Epston, *Narrative Means to Therapeutic Ends* (New York, WW Norton & Company, 1991).

[86] Carl Rogers, pioneer of client-centred therapy, regarded 'unconditional positive regard' as one of the key conditions for therapists to promote growth—C Rogers, *On Becoming a Person* (Boston, MA, Houghton Mifflin, 1961).

[87] Winslade and Monk (n 27) 40 citing KJ Gergen, *The Saturated Self: Dilemmas of Identity in Contemporary Life* (New York, Basic Books, 1991) 243.

aligning with social baseline theory, which holds that social connection, not isolation, is the human norm.[88] They reject, however, suggestions that emotions are
inherent or 'essential', viewing them along with other aspects of experience as constructed in discourse: 'It does not make sense to say that people have thoughts
or feelings on the inside that precede their expression. It makes more sense to
speak about how discourses and linguistic formulations make up our subjective
experience'.[89] There is therefore much to play for in mediation, where individuals
can construct and reconstruct their emotional world.

Notwithstanding scant reference to emotions, narrative mediation offers much
to the emotional domain. Its recognition that culture influences how we construct reality raises the possibility of dialogue about the emotional expressions
legitimised within particular cultures. Its relational practices create conditions for
building empathy between mediator and parties.[90] And instead of locating conflict
within individuals it lifts the mediator's gaze to the wider system: 'The person is
not the problem; the problem is the problem'.[91]

D. Further Developments

Mediation has not been immune from wider and more recent developments in
psychology and neuroscience. While in 2000 it could be said that 'lack of detailed
attention to emotions and relationships is the biggest gap in our understanding
of conflict',[92] the influence of neuroscience, cognitive psychology and perhaps the
maturing of the field have yielded contributions from a range of writers. Below,
we provide an overview of some of the more interesting and relevant connections.

In 2001 Jones and Bodtker argued for the centrality of emotion in conflict, challenging the 'false duality of rationality vs emotionality'.[93] They urged mediators
not to see emotion as a 'side effect' but rather as a 'framer ... a social construction through which the disputant defines the conflict reality'.[94] Their prescription

---

[88] '[S]ocial relatedness and its psychological correlates constitute the normal, baseline ecology of the
functional human brain'—JA Coan and EL Maresh, 'Social Baseline Theory and the Social Regulation
of Emotion' in JJ Gross (ed), *Handbook of Emotion Regulation*, 2nd edn (New York, Guilford Press,
2014).

[89] Ibid, 39.

[90] See section III.A below.

[91] Winslade and Monk (n 27) 131 citing M White, 'The Externalizing of the Problem and the
Re-authoring of Lives and Relationships' in M White, *Selected Papers* (Adelaide, Dulwich Centre
Publications, 1989).

[92] S Retzinger and T Scheff, 'Emotion, Alienation, and Narratives: Resolving Intractable Conflict'
(2000) 18 *Mediation Quarterly* 71, 71; although see LS Schreier, 'Emotional Intelligence and Mediation
Training' (2002) 20 *Conflict Resolution Quarterly* 99, 100 (claiming by 2002 that there was a surge of
interest in emotions in mediation).

[93] TS Jones and A Bodtker, 'Mediation With Heart in Mind: Addressing Emotion in Mediation
Practice' (2001) 19 *Negotiation Journal* 217, 224.

[94] Ibid, 223.

for emotionally-confident mediators includes advice on dealing with 'emotional flooding ... being swamped by emotion to the extent that one cannot function or think effectively'[95] and 'emotional contagion', the tendency to 'catch' others' emotions.[96] They suggest that cognitive reappraisal[97] holds promise when emotions are triggered by conflict, but caution that this requires skill on the part of the mediator. Their emotion-eliciting and reappraising questions are similar to the 'externalising conversation' techniques of narrative mediation:[98] the approach could be characterised as 'externalising emotions'.[99] In effect the mediator invites someone experiencing an emotion to step a little distance away from it; observe, describe and reflect on it; then decide how to respond.[100]

In 2006 Jones presented a model explaining how individuals experience emotions. A triggering event is followed by appraisal (interpretation of the triggering event) leading to an emotion (appropriate to that interpretation). The emotion produces somatic reactions (physiological changes preparing us for the action we need to take) which in turn lead to action tendencies (the disposition to behave in keeping with all of the foregoing).[101] Sometimes known as the 'path to action'[102] this model reflects research by 'appraisal theorists' such as Lazarus.[103] Damasio states: 'Emotion and feeling, along with the covert physiological machinery underlying them, assist us with the daunting task of predicting an uncertain future and planning our actions accordingly'.[104] Emotion and thinking are intimately linked, and each requires the other for accurate perception. Damasio also links mind and body; emotions work by comparing new perceptual data to a 'background feeling', the 'image of the body landscape when it is not shaken by emotion'.[105]

The implications for law and mediation are clear: if accurate perception is important we must attend to the emotional domain. Jones challenges mediators to become emotionally literate because working with conflict inevitably means working with emotions. First, mediators should learn to decode emotions;[106]

---

[95] Ibid, 228–32.

[96] Ibid, 232–33. For a further discussion of emotion contagion as a component of empathy see section III.E below.

[97] For an explanation of cognitive reappraisal see section IV.A below (n 186).

[98] Winslade and Monk (n 27) 79.

[99] A technique associated with drama therapy—ie, 'externalising the internal' in P McFarlane, *Drama Therapy: Developing Emotional Stability* (London, David Fulton Publishers, 2005) 92.

[100] Similar to self-empathy—see section III.E below.

[101] TS Jones, 'Emotion in Mediation: Implications, Applications, Opportunities, and Challenges' in MS Herrman (ed), *The Blackwell Handbook of Mediation: Bridging Theory, Research, and Practice* (Oxford, Blackwell Publishing, 2006) 277, 278–79.

[102] K Patterson, J Grenny, R McMillan and A Switzler, *Crucial Conversations: Tools for Talking When Stakes are High* (New York, McGraw-Hill, 2002) 99.

[103] Lazarus, *Fifty Years of the Research and Theory of RS Lazarus* (n 1).

[104] Damasio (n 13) xxiii.

[105] Ibid, 151. See also C Irvine, 'Building Emotional Intelligence: A Grid for Practitioners' in M LeBaron, C MacLeod and AF Acland (eds), *The Choreography of Resolution: Conflict, Movement, and Neuroscience* (Chicago, IL, American Bar Association, 2013) 107.

[106] Jones provides detailed guidance for the identity-based emotions of anger, shame and contempt: Jones (n 101) 287–93.

second, they should use elicitive questioning to help parties identify their emotional experience; and finally they should help parties reappraise their emotions.[107] Barker also calls for emotional literacy, suggesting that mediators should 'stay with the heat' because emotions 'often hold the key to unlocking conflict at a profound level'.[108]

Schreier's 2002 survey of 36 mediation training organisations[109] confirmed her hypothesis that insufficient attention was given to teaching mediators to deal skilfully with emotions.[110] Attitudes appeared to be changing with trainers calling for mediators to develop skills in both handling emotions and in emotional self-regulation. One spoke of the 'old way (repressing emotion in the room) and the new way (allowing it in)'.[111]

Bowling and Hoffman's influential 2003 collection *Bringing Peace into the Room* proposed a systemic conception of the mediator's role.[112] Questioning the conventional view of mediators as neutral, they suggest they are 'being influenced by the process as much as influencing it'.[113] Thus, 'the feelings the mediator experiences may be vital material that the mediator can use—albeit judiciously—in helping the parties reach a resolution'.[114] The authors champion reflective practice because mediation requires head and heart. Similarly, Johnson and others challenge mediators to develop emotional intelligence, focused on four areas: 'Self-Awareness', 'Self-Management', 'Social Awareness' and 'Social Skills'.[115] And Gehris warns against ignoring emotion, suggesting mediators learn to recognise emotions via facial expressions,[116] speech, body language and discussion.[117] Techniques include acknowledgement, active listening, expressing empathy and drawing on the mediator's own emotional response.[118]

---

[107] Ibid.

[108] E Barker, 'Tips for Dealing with Emotion in Mediation' (2003): www.mediate.com/articles/ebarker2.cfm.

[109] This involved 34 organisations from the United States and one each from Canada and the Netherlands.

[110] Schreier (n 92).

[111] Ibid, 109.

[112] D Bowling and DA Hoffman (eds), *Bringing Peace into the Room: How the Personal Qualities of the Mediator Impact the Process of Conflict Resolution* (San Francisco, CA, Jossey-Bass, 2003).

[113] D Bowling and DA Hoffman, 'Bringing Peace into the Room: The Personal Qualities of the Mediator and their Impact on the Mediation' in D Bowling and DA Hoffman (eds), *Bringing Peace into the Room* (n 112) 13, 23.

[114] Ibid, 24.

[115] ME Johnson, S Levine and LR Richard, 'Emotionally Intelligent Mediation: Four Key Competencies' in D Bowling and DA Hoffman (eds), *Bringing Peace into the Room: How the Personal Qualities of the Mediator Impact the Process of Conflict Resolution* (San Francisco, CA, Jossey-Bass, 2003) 151, 153.

[116] Drawing on Paul Ekman's approach—see P Ekman, *Emotions Revealed: Understanding Faces and Feelings* (London, Phoenix, 2003).

[117] MS Gehris, 'Good Mediators Don't Ignore Emotion' (2005) 46 *New Hampshire Bar Journal* 28.

[118] Ibid, 32, 33.

Negotiation research has also highlighted the importance of emotions. Potworowski and Kopelman distinguished between 'Emotional Intelligence' (a trait) and their proposed model of 'Negotiation Expertise in Emotion Management' (NEEM) (which can be learned).[119] The capacity for NEEM requires '*sensitivity, ability,* and *inclination*'[120] so that the negotiator learns to distinguish the other party's helpful, unhelpful and irrelevant emotions. Gaspar and Schweitzer noticed the importance of emotion in deception and developed a model taking account of 'incidental' and 'integral' emotions en route to the 'anticipated emotion' that the deception is designed to achieve.[121] Decision-making by negotiators is affected by both incidental emotions (such as feeling annoyed because of a difficult journey or grateful because a stranger held open a lift door) and integral emotions (such as being stressed by a deadline or irked by the counterpart's demeanour). Intriguingly they cite Ruedy et al's research on the 'cheater's high', a recently detected phenomenon where 'undetected dishonesty can induce feelings of elation'.[122]

Picard and Siltanen noticed the significance of both positive and negative emotions to learning in their 'insight model' of mediation.[123] They are critical of Fisher and Shapiro's[124] proposal that negative emotions be blocked or suppressed during negotiation: 'to block negative emotions is to inhibit significant moments in the learning that are hoped for in any model of mediation'.[125]

In 2006 Maiese urged mediators to rethink 'the reason–emotion dichotomy'.[126] She contended that emotions are central to the emergence and escalation of conflict and that cognitive reappraisal holds significant promise for resolution. She proposed that mediators supplement standard techniques of 'active or empathic listening, appreciative inquiry, and dialogue' with 'ritual, art and joking',[127] though she conceded that such emotional appraisal techniques might be too 'touchy-feely' for some.[128]

---

[119] G Potworowski and S Kopelman, 'Strategic Display and Response to Emotions: Developing Evidence-based Negotiation Expertise in Emotion Management (NEEM)' (2008) 1 *Negotiation and Conflict Management Research* 333.

[120] Ibid, 336.

[121] JP Gaspar and ME Schweitzer, 'The Emotion Deception Model: A Review of Deception in Negotiation and the Role of Emotion in Deception' (2013) 6 *Negotiation and Conflict Management Research* 160.

[122] Ibid, 171 citing N Ruedy, C Moore, F Gino and M Schweitzer, 'The Cheater's High: The Unexpected Affective Benefits of Unethical Behaviour' (2013) 105 *Journal of Personality and Social Psychology* 531.

[123] C Picard and J Siltanen, 'Exploring the Significance of Emotion for Mediation Practice' (2013) 31 *Conflict Resolution Quarterly* 31.

[124] Fisher and Shapiro (n 50).

[125] Picard and Siltanen (n 123) 46.

[126] M Maiese, 'Engaging the Emotions in Conflict Resolution' (2006) 24 *Conflict Resolution Quarterly* 187, 188.

[127] Ibid, 189.

[128] Ibid, 194.

This work prefigured a project conceived by LeBaron exploring the potential of dance for conflict resolution, resulting in an international conference in 2011 and, in 2013, an edited collection re-emphasising the mind—body connection in conflict work.[129] One of the present authors attended the conference and the bodywork alerted him to the tradition in which he had been trained, caricatured as 'mediating from the neck up', meaning to ignore the physical, and thereby emotional realm.[130] He proposed a grid capturing two dimensions of conflict: intensity and volume (Figure 1).[131] 'Intensity' describes the force of an emotion for the person experiencing it; 'volume' to the force with which it is transmitted. The latter dimension is related to 'strategic display': instrumental reasons for displaying a particular emotion at a particular volume.[132]

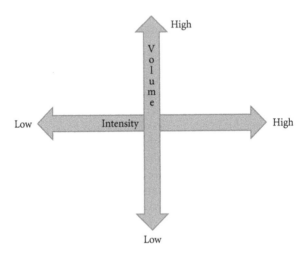

Figure 1: The Emotional Grid

Recently, we updated the grid with a third dimension: valence, the positivity or negativity with which an emotion is experienced (Figure 2). Research suggests that a central driver of behaviour is the attempt to reduce negative emotion and increase positive.[133]

<hr />

[129] M LeBaron, C MacLeod and AF Acland (eds), *The Choreography of Resolution: Conflict, Movement, and Neuroscience* (Chicago, IL, American Bar Association, 2013).

[130] Irvine, 'Building Emotional Intelligence' (n 105) 108. See also E Beausoleil and M LeBaron, 'What Moves Us: Dance and Neuroscience Implications for Conflict Approaches' (2013) 31 *Conflict Resolution Quarterly* 133.

[131] Irvine, 'Building Emotional Intelligence' (n 105) 114.

[132] Potworowski and Kopelman (n 119).

[133] BL Frederickson and MA Cohn, 'Positive Emotions' in M Lewis, JM Haviland-Jones and L Feldman Barrett (eds), *Handbook of Emotions*, 3rd edn (New York, Guilford Press, 2008) 777.

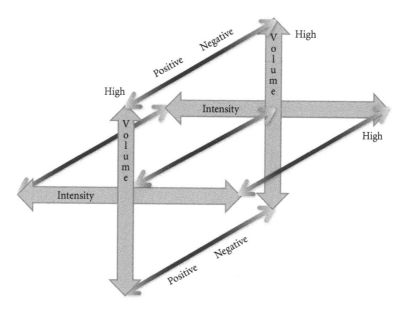

Figure 2: The Emotional Grid, 3D Version

The grid conceptualises mediators' work by drawing attention to the split between the emotionally private and public realms. Mediators know the intensity and valence of their own emotions; they can choose (to an extent) how much they display and how much is kept private. Disputants also choose (effortfully or automatically) how much emotion to display (the 'volume'). So mediators must make judgements about what and how much disputants are making public. There is a sense of co-authoring, reflecting the view that emotions are socially constructed[134] and that mediators may usefully have a hand in that construction.

The upshot of these developments is to put emotions firmly at the theoretical core of mediation. As a 2011 student text asserts: 'Both mediators and lawyers can contribute greatly to the process of settlement by dealing with emotional forces'.[135] We now consider the mechanisms by which mediators may do so, examining the role of empathy before considering how mediators and mediation may contribute to the regulation of emotion.

---

[134] See Winslade and Monk (n 27). See also DW Augsburger, *Conflict Mediation Across Cultures: Pathways and Patterns* (Louisville, KY, Westminster/John Knox Press, 1992).

[135] D Golann and J Folberg, *Mediation: The Roles of Advocate and Neutral*, 2nd edn (New York, Aspen Publishers, 2011) 177.

III. The Significance of Empathy

A. Introduction

Empathy is a key ingredient in mediation, both in its use by the mediator and the manner in which the process offers disputants opportunities to give and receive it. We outline empathy as a concept, including background, definition and components, suggesting that empathy is a synergy of emotion and reason. We then explain how the mediator works with emotion and emotion regulation to facilitate empathic understandings and agreement.

B. The Nature of Empathy

In the words of Simon Baron-Cohen: 'Empathy is the ability to identify what someone is thinking or feeling and to respond to their thoughts and feelings with an appropriate emotion'.[136] When we empathise, we imagine what it feels like to be in that person's mental state. Importantly, we are motivated to respond to another's distress with empathic concern.[137]

Empathy has been described as a process, attitude, behaviour, event, trait, skill and capacity.[138] Coined as *Einfuhlung* by nineteenth-century German philosophers of aesthetics, it originally described the attempt to understand art from a dual perspective by mirroring and projecting self in the work.[139] It is generally measured as dispositional (trait) yet can also be described as situational (context-dependent). In other words, empathy can be measured as a feature of personality which is more or less stable across time,[140] or it can be conceptualised as an individual response to a specific other or situation, which may vary depending, for example on the degree of shared values and preferences.[141] Empathy is usually measured through physiological tests, brain scans and self-reporting questionnaires. Scores vary across the population: those with traits associated with personality disorder and some with autistic spectrum difficulties (ASD) show lower levels and such people have been described as having low or 'zero degrees of empathy' or even an

---

[136] S Baron-Cohen, *Zero Degrees of Empathy: A New Theory of Human Cruelty* (London, Allen Lane, 2011) 12.

[137] See below, section III.E.

[138] V Lucas, 'The Art and Science of Empathy' (2014) 21 *European Journal of Palliative Care* 69.

[139] R Vischer, 'On the Optical Sense of Form: A Contribution to Aesthetics' cited in D Howe, *Empathy: What it is and Why it Matters* (London, Palgrave Macmillan 2013).

[140] MH Davis, *Empathy: A Social Psychological Approach* (Boulder, CO, Westview Press 1994).

[141] L Cameron, *Metaphor and Reconciliation: The Discourse Dynamics of Empathy in Post-Conflict Situations* (London, Taylor & Francis, 2010). Cameron's viewpoint is that the decision whether or not to engage in empathy is often situation-specific and involves choice.

'empathy disorder'.[142] Additionally, empathy fluctuates within individuals in the short term and across the lifespan. It is influenced by early experience, gender, education, occupation and wealth. People empathise more with those familiar and similar and where there is shared experience.[143] They are less empathic when tired, stressed, unwell, suppressing emotion or highly aroused as in conflict situations.[144] These latter two circumstances are highly relevant in mediation.

C. The Origins of Empathy: Evolution and Attachment

Empathy is a requirement for co-operation and is as important to survival as the practical skills involved in the acquisition of food and shelter.[145] We seem hardwired to give and receive empathy, and social connections can be considered a basic human need.[146] In the same way, loneliness may be as detrimental to physical health as smoking.[147]

Dependence on others for our sense of identity and self-worth may explain why shared understandings are so valued and, conversely, why it is felt so distressing when these are fractured by conflict.[148] Relis found that disputants engaged in mediation for medical negligence valued communication, having a voice and the opportunity to express themselves and receive acknowledgment of harm. These non-legal, human concerns contrasted with lawyers' preoccupation with financial settlement.[149]

The need for connection is mirrored by the urge to achieve it: as Beausoleil and LeBaron put it, 'we are neurologically wired for mutual understanding and feeling'.[150] Bowlby's Attachment Theory posits that an attentive, empathic caregiver creates a physically and emotionally secure environment, helping to regulate a child's emotions and, crucially, reduce stress. The child can then develop into an emotionally secure adult, able to regulate her emotions, and become an emotionally attuned parent in turn.[151] Secure adult attachment bonds, based on empathy, are mutually supportive as well as emotionally regulating, as in successful couple

---

[142] Baron-Cohen (n 136) 111.

[143] SD Preston and FBM de Waal, 'Empathy: Its Ultimate and Proximate Bases' (2002) 25 *Behavioural and Brain Sciences* 1.

[144] This may explain Bush and Folger's insight at section II.B above, that conflict brings about weakness and self-absorption.

[145] C Darwin, *The Descent of Man and Selection in Relation to Sex* (London, John Murray, 1871) 80.

[146] This view aligns with 'social baseline theory'; see section II.C and n 88.

[147] J Holt-Lunstad, TB Smith and JB Layton, 'Social relationships and mortality risk: a meta-analytic review' 27 July 2010, *PLoS Med*: journals.plos.org/plosmedicine/article?id=10.1371/journal.pmed.1000316, 7.

[148] See Ury (n 48); and Jones (n 101).

[149] T Relis, *Perceptions in Litigation Mediation: Lawyers, Defendants, Plaintiffs, and Gendered Parties* (Cambridge, Cambridge University Press, 2011); and see also Riskin, 'Further Beyond Reason' (n 21).

[150] Beausoleil and LeBaron (n 130) 144.

[151] EJM Bowlby, *Attachment and Loss: Attachment*, vol 1 (London, Hogarth Press, 1969).

relationships. Indeed, Baron-Cohen has described the capacity for empathy as 'the internal pot of gold'.[152]

However, those whose caregivers were unresponsive, erratic or under-responsive, or behaved inappropriately, often lack empathy and have difficulty managing emotion.[153] Learned expectations of how others will meet one's needs tend to determine the choice of emotion regulation strategies. While powerful predictors of behaviour, these strategies can be challenged and altered by experience: emotional events and encounters including situations encouraging self/other–reflection such as therapy[154] and perhaps also mediation.

D. Empathy and Neuroscience

We begin with the child–parent bond. Empathic attunement involves the release of powerful bonding hormones in both parent and child. Situations of fear and distress activate the attachment system and the child seeks out his caregiver. Exploratory behaviour ceases until a sense of security is restored. Then the attachment system is deactivated and, as the child's emotions become regulated, the exploratory system is reactivated. Cognitive activity is again possible and the child resumes play and learning.[155] Importantly, in this two-way process the caregiver experiences automatic activation of the caregiving system and an overriding need to respond. This is both a physical and psychological phenomenon; separation is painful to both, and children can even die as a result of being emotionally abandoned.[156] This need for attachment figures (and the need to respond as caregiver) continues into adulthood and is particularly apparent at times of perceived stress and threat, as it is in situations of conflict. Similar physiological responses are activated by loss through divorce or bereavement.[157]

Both giving and receiving empathy appear to increase its potential. Volunteering and certain kinds of meditation[158] seem to improve the capacity for empathy. Feeling understood by another through receiving empathy can assist emotion regulation: such relationships can change and improve growth, development and the formation of neural connections in the brain. From infancy onwards as the partly-formed brain develops through experience and learning the child is enabled to

---

[152] Baron-Cohen (n 136) 105.

[153] Bowlby, *Attachment*, vol 1 (n 151).

[154] LA Travis, NJ Bliwise, JL Binder and HL Horne-Moyer, 'Changes in Clients' Attachments Styles Over the Course of Time-limited Dynamic Psychotherapy' (2001) 38 *Psychotherapy* 149.

[155] Bowlby, *Attachment*, vol 1 (n 151).

[156] J Rifkin, *The Empathic Civilisation* (Cambridge, Polity, 2010).

[157] EJM Bowlby, *Attachment and Loss: Separation, Anxiety and Anger*, vol 2 (London, Hogarth Press, 1973); and EJM Bowlby, *Attachment and Loss: Loss, Sadness and Depression*, vol 3 (London, Hogarth Press, 1980).

[158] CA Hutcherson, EM Seppala and JJ Gross, 'Loving-kindness Meditation Increases Social Connection' (2008) 8 *Emotion* 720.

manage and make sense of self and world. This plasticity of the brain continues throughout life.[159]

Something similar can occur in adult therapeutic and other helping relationships; in the words of Cozolino: 'By activating processes involved in attachment and bonding, as well as moderating stress in therapy, empathic attunement may create an optimal biochemical environment for enhancing neural plasticity'.[160] Again, as Howe puts it:

> Empathic relationships help clients to tolerate and regulate arousal and affect. Emotional regulation is key to successful therapy. Under conditions of increased safety and lowered stress, brains and their neural circuits can grow ... When brains are able to process information without distortion, cognitive flexibility rises, reflections improve, behavioural options increase and responses become more creative.[161]

While mediation is not therapy, there is sufficient overlap in their forms and functions to suggest that these observations apply here too. This is supported by Relis' research into litigants' perceptions, which indicated that disputants judged the effectiveness and acceptability of mediators according to their 'human attributes, including warmth, caring and protectiveness'.[162] They were valued for being 'fair, fatherly, very understanding and respectful', with some clients quoted as saying that the mediator was 'calming and trustworthy' and 'not going to let anything *happen* or let anyone say anything'.[163]

E. The Components of Empathy

Empathy can be divided into two main categories: 'affective' and 'cognitive' empathy. Affective empathy, also called 'emotional', 'mirrored' or 'primitive' empathy refers to automatic components involving reflex responses rather than reflection and cognition.[164] An example is 'emotion contagion'[165] where, through loss or absence of self–other boundary, one catches others' emotions. This can result in 'personal distress', in the sense of an emotional, aversive response to another's real or imagined upset in a self-preoccupied manner.[166] An example would be a hysterical reaction to the sight of another's blood loss at the scene of an accident.

---

[159] RJ Davidson and BS McEwan, 'Social Influences on neuroplasticity: stress and interventions to promote wellbeing' (2012) 15 *Nature Neuroscience* 689.

[160] L Cozolino, *The Neuroscience of Psychotherapy: Healing the Social Brain* (London, WW Norton & Company, 2002) cited in Howe (n 139) 145.

[161] Ibid.

[162] Relis (n 149) 12.

[163] Ibid, 203.

[164] Baron-Cohen (n 136).

[165] See above, n 96.

[166] This appears to be the sense in which Jones and Bodtker use the term (see n 93).

Affective empathy is enhanced by the closeness and quality of the relationship between giver and receiver, leading to 'the blurring of self and other'.[167]

'Sympathy', from the Greek, 'feeling with', has been used synonymously with affective empathy.[168] However, it is now more commonly described as spontaneous concern for another's distress as opposed to an understanding of the experience causing the upset.[169] Further, it overlaps with 'empathic concern':[170] a spontaneous desire that motivates towards helping another in need. Unlike personal distress it is often the springboard for altruistic behaviour; in our hypothetical accident this person responds by calling an ambulance and comforting the injured.

Whereas affective empathy is reactive and immediate, cognitive empathy requires reflection, effort and control and clear self–other differentiation. It requires the capacity for 'self-awareness' and 'self-empathy': an ability to recognise, observe and evaluate personal thoughts and feelings non-judgementally and, importantly for mediation, to identify personal triggers and self–other boundaries.[171] It includes the key capacity for 'emotion regulation', which as we shall see denotes a range of strategies for appropriately managing, containing and expressing emotion.[172] Another cognitive empathy component is perspective taking, which, crucially, enables thinking about what the world might look like from another's stance. Perspective taking is an effortful, imaginative and comparative process of shifting back and forth between self-perspective (thinking about one's own past experiences, inclination and responses) and other-perspective (using knowledge about the person's characteristics and context). It also draws on general information to inform the particular situation.[173]

There is much debate about what should and should not be included in a definition of empathy. In our view, it requires an integration and congruence of head, heart and good intention. This 'head–heart' or 'gut–brain' continuum is clear in empathic communication, which is automatic yet potentially enhanced by conscious learning. People can be taught to improve the listening skills and 'rapport' which are essential for relating to others.[174] Cognitive empathy is reflected in

[167] L Beckes, J Coan and K Hasselmo, 'Familiarity Promotes the Blurring of Self and Other in the Neural Representation of Threat' (2013) 8 *Social Cognitive & Affective Neuroscience* 670.

[168] J Duffy, 'Empathy, Neutrality and Emotional Intelligence: A Balancing Act for the Emotional Einstein' (2010) 10 *Queensland University of Technology Law & Justice Journal* 44.

[169] L Wispé, 'The Distinction Between Sympathy and Empathy: To Call Forth a Concept a Word is Needed' (1986) 50 *Journal of Personality and Social Psychology* 314.

[170] CD Batson, J Fultz and PA Schoenrade, 'Distress and Empathy: Two Qualitatively Distinct Vicarious Emotions with Different Motivational Consequences' (1987) 55 *Journal of Personality* 19.

[171] GG Gallup and SM Platek, 'Cognitive Empathy Presupposes Self-Awareness: Evidence from Phylogeny, Ontogeny, Neuropsychology and Mental Illness' (2002) 25 *Behavioral and Brain Sciences* 36.

[172] See below, section IV.

[173] A Gerace, A Day, S Casey and P Mohr, 'An Exploratory Investigation of the Process of Perspective Taking in Interpersonal Situations' (2013) 4 *Journal of Relationships Research* 6.

[174] And significant in negotiation success: see K Kilm, NLA Cundiff and SB Choi, 'The Influence of Emotional Intelligence on Negotiation Outcomes and the Mediating Effect of Rapport: A Structural Equation Modeling Approach' (2014) 30 *Negotiation Journal* 49.

the ability to verbalise, check and question the accuracy of one's understanding of another's experience and to use non-verbal communication in a considered, deliberate and targeted way.

In the health sector empathy as a blend of reason and emotion has been termed 'intelligent kindness'.[175] It is offered for people with Autistic Spectrum Disorder[176] and may also help people with personality-disordered traits.[177] It is implicit in diversity training and anti-bullying initiatives. These skills can be also be practised by mediators and supported and developed within disputants as we discuss later.

F. Motivation and the Effort of Empathy

Whereas affective empathy is automatic, the components of cognitive empathy are demanding and often subject to failure. Preston argues that, while we may attempt to imagine another's experience based on our own, we can only be sure of accuracy if the other gives feedback.[178] We often make mistakes: there is a tendency to stereotype individuals who are different from ourselves and, conversely, the risk of false assumption that someone perceived as similar to ourselves will respond as perhaps we think we might. As Coplan says, 'To stay focused on the target individual and move us beyond our own experiences, perspective taking requires mental flexibility and relies on regulatory mechanisms to modulate our level of affective arousal and suppress our own perspectives'.[179]

G. Empathy in Mediation and the Role of Emotion Regulation

While mediation is often seen as part of the justice system, it can also be viewed as a psychological intervention that enables disputants to give and receive empathy. We now argue that this is linked to emotion regulation provided by both process and mediator. Emotion and cognition are inseparable and down-regulation of negative emotion increases the ability for perspective taking. Disputants then become motivated and enabled to develop empathy. The resultant connections and mutual understandings will then help lead to sustainable agreements.

---

[175] J Ballatt and P Campling, *Intelligent Kindness: Reforming the Culture of Healthcare* (London, RCPsych Publications, 2011).

[176] Baron-Cohen (n 136) 104.

[177] E Hepper, C Hart and C Sedikides, 'Moving Narcissus: Can Narcissists Be Empathic?' (2014) 40 *Personality and Social Psychology Bulletin* 1079.

[178] SD Preston, 'A Perception Action Model for Empathy' in TFD Farrow and PWR Woodruff (eds), *Empathy in Mental Illness* (Cambridge, Cambridge University Press 2007) 428.

[179] A Coplan, 'Will the Real Empathy Please Stand Up? A Case for Narrow Conceptualisation' (2011) 49 Spindel Supplement *Southern Journal of Philosophy* 40, 58.

IV. Emotion Regulation

A. Emotion Regulation in Theory

The recent and 'slippery' concept of 'emotion regulation'[180] recognises that individuals need to manage, adapt and express emotions in an appropriate and acceptable way, by 'shaping which emotions one has, when one has them, and how one experiences or expresses these emotions'.[181] Emotion regulation can be intrinsic, as when the individual regulates his own emotion, or extrinsic, as in seeking to influence another's emotional state: for example, a parent calming a tearful child. Frequently it is both, as where the emotional landscape of the parent is altered by the change in the child.[182]

Gross also describes emotion regulation's 'impact on emotion dynamics'.[183] This affects various aspects of emotion, including both how an emotion is experienced in mind and body and how it is communicated. There are differences in the time taken for emotion to surface and in development, duration, intensity and expression. Different processes may be engaged to alter 'the emotional trajectory'.[184] These can be automatic or controlled or both: 'a continuum of emotion regulation possibilities that range from explicit, conscious, effortful, and controlled regulation to implicit, unconscious, effortless and automatic regulation'.[185]

In this connection, Gross proposes five 'families' of emotion regulation processes, categorised according to the point at which the emotion is generated. Early processes anticipate emotions; then come real-time reactions to current emotions; these are followed by responses after emotion is experienced. Briefly, the groups work as follows, with examples from a workplace setting:

— *Situation selection*: anticipatory avoidance of situations likely to arouse negative emotions and seeking out others which might bring relief (for instance by delaying meeting a difficult colleague or by offloading to workmates around the water cooler).
— *Situation modification*: changing an aspect of the situation itself (for instance having to attend and bringing along a friendly workmate for moral support).

---

[180] Gross, 'Emotion Regulation' (n 7) 499.
[181] JJ Gross, 'Conceptual and Empirical Foundations' in JJ Gross (ed), *Handbook of Emotion Regulation*, 2nd edn (New York, Guilford Press, 2014) 6.
[182] Gross, 'Emotion Regulation' (n 7) 500.
[183] Gross, 'Conceptual and Empirical Foundations' (n 181) 7.
[184] Ibid.
[185] Ibid.

— *Attentional deployment*: thinking about something else (for instance by lingering over agenda items to avoid controversial ones; or by considering something pleasant like a good dinner and bottle of wine waiting at home).

— *Cognitive change*: altering one's thinking about one's own thoughts and feelings or about a situation through reappraisal, distancing or use of humour in order to change its emotional significance. These strategies can be employed to help down-regulate negative emotion ('the meeting is only half an hour'; 'she's more nervous than I am').[186]

— *Response modulation*: engaging in behavioural techniques such as relaxation and breathing exercises or, more negatively, the use of drugs and alcohol. It also includes emotional suppression. Examples include smiling although feeling angry and upset, and back home, pouring a glass of wine.

Observations about the value of emotion regulation for judges[187] seem doubly apposite for mediators and their clients. To return to our introduction, if it is important for a sole judicial decision-maker to notice, manage, learn from and regulate her emotions, how much more so for mediators working with non-judicial decision-makers in conflict? While to those with legal training this may seem unachievable,[188] mediation abounds with examples of settlement or, better, transformation. That suggests that achieving emotion regulation is an essential part of the mediation process, albeit that mediators may not always conceptualise their role in these terms. In the pages which follow we shall investigate how this may be achieved.

B. Emotion Regulation in Mediation Practice

We now describe a standard mediation process through the lens of the above research on empathy and emotion regulation.[189]

---

[186] Cognitive reappraisal describes a phenomenon whereby an individual alters an emotion, not by suppression, but by thinking differently about the original stimulus. For example, if I see a threatening shape in the street on a dark night I may experience fear. If I discover it is in fact the shadow of a tree I no longer need feel that emotion. Rather than suppressing my fear the reappraisal allows me to feel an emotion appropriate to the new situation. Research on cognitive reappraisal has confirmed its help in regulating emotion, while suppression can increase blood pressure. However, evidence is accumulating that no strategy is always effective. Much depends on context with the idea emerging of a flexible repertoire of emotion regulation strategies: see AS Troy, AJ Shallcross and IB Mauss, 'A Person-by-Situation Approach to Emotion Regulation: Cognitive Reappraisal Can Either Help or Hurt, Depending on the Context' (2013) 24 *Association for Psychological Science* 2505.

[187] TA Maroney, 'Emotion Regulation and Judicial Behavior' (2011) 99 *California Law Review* 1485, 1517–21.

[188] For a summary of the deficits in legal education see J Lande and JR Sternlight, 'The Potential Contribution of ADR to an Integrated Curriculum: Preparing Law Students for Real World Lawyering' (2010) 25 *Ohio State Journal on Dispute Resolution* 247.

[189] We should acknowledge that here we have idealised and simplified the mediation process in the interests of clarity. Later we discuss mediations that are unusually challenging—see section IV.C below.

i. Pre-Mediation

Mediators commonly start by meeting disputants individually.[190] Each party may have constructed and become locked into an emotional narrative and mythology, oft-rehearsed and 'tightly woven'[191] through repetition. This may be the first opportunity for disputants to have their story heard. They are likely to be experiencing negative emotions such as anger, rage, fear, sadness and disappointment. In this meeting they should experience empathy: a self-aware mediator will listen non-judgementally with an attitude of acceptance and respect.[192] In this way, rapport and trust are achieved and a sense of emotional safety created. The pre-mediation meeting provides a forum for disclosure and reappraisal, which promotes the process of perspective taking as described above.[193] This is achieved through the mediator's use of open and exploratory questions.

When a disputant offers an observation accompanied by an evaluation, the mediator can invite reflection on alternative explanations. Raising questions in a factual yet empathic manner, from a position of curiosity rather than challenge, can sow seeds of uncertainty that may lead a person to review their opening position. Explaining the mediation process alerts parties to the fact that they may discover previously unknown information. This in itself can be viewed as 'anticipatory reappraisal'.[194] Appropriate questions may also assist the rehearsal of strategy: for example the mediator may ask, 'If the other party says this ..., how do you think you will react?' The answer may prompt discussion on the choice of emotion regulation strategy and, crucially, include reassurances that the mediator will manage the process so as to prevent harm.

By the end of this meeting, a skilful mediator will have established rapport through empathic attunement and communication; and will be perceived by the disputant as trustworthy and capable of steering him or her safely through difficult emotional waters. Akin to early life attachment described above,[195] the disputant can start to experience curiosity rather than fear, and may come to realise that the other party too has a 'story', that 'right and wrong' may not be the issue, that

---

[190] Although less common in commercial and court-annexed mediation, this practice is typical in the fields of family, employment and community mediation. See C Irvine, 'Intake Interviews in Family Mediation: Some Thoughts from Scotland' (April 2003) *Mediation in Practice*: papers.ssrn.com/sol3/papers.cfm?abstract_id=1823327,12.

[191] See section II.C above, and Winslade and Monk (n 27).

[192] Described as 'The Mediator's "Presence"'—Bowling and Hoffman, *Bringing Peace into the Room* (n 112) 21.

[193] See Jones and Bodtker (n 93) and the discussion of perspective taking at section III.E above.

[194] Maroney, 'Emotion Regulation and Judicial Behavior' (n 187) 1517–21 explains how doctors prepare to cope with emotionally challenging situations, such as informing relatives of a patient's death, by telling themselves that they are professionals doing a job. She calls this 'anticipatory reappraisal' because it usually occurs in advance of the encounter and reduces the prospect of experiencing distressing emotions. In the same way parties can be prepared for mediation by viewing it as a necessary step on the path to resolution.

[195] See above at section III.D.

the currency and language are of feeling as much as fact, and that the mediator can display empathy without taking sides. This creates the conditions for problem-solving and negotiation, key goals of the mediation process.

The meeting usually ends with the decision to go ahead with mediation. This can be described as a form of 'situation selection',[196] where disputants agree to meet in a controlled environment. The mediation environment can also be considered 'situation modification',[197] in that the participants are regulating potentially negative emotions by choosing a prescribed process made secure by the presence of an empathic third party.

ii. Joint Session

When the parties finally meet up, the introduction is critical.[198] It can be understood as a form of 'priming': proposing that disputants listen without interruption and use respectful language, or alerting them to the possibility of 'time out' (a simple situation modification). The mediator reassures angry and fearful disputants that they will be heard but remain emotionally unharmed; implicit is the assurance that if either party is unable to regulate their emotions the mediator can be trusted to manage the situation. Some mediators talk of 'modelling' calmness by their tone of voice and posture, suggesting an important role for the physical dimensions of mediation practice.[199]

The session continues with each person hearing the other. Listening without interrupting resembles an act of empathy and helps regulate the speaker's emotions. True, the listening party is engaging in emotion suppression; in the long run this can be detrimental to wellbeing, cognitive capacity and memory.[200] However, here it is short-term and the listener can anticipate their own opportunity to speak.

At this initial stage disputants are often invited to address the mediator rather than engage directly with the other party. This can reinforce the sense of being empathised with; as Johnson says, 'Without agreeing with a party's story or appearing to take sides, an emotionally competent mediator can acknowledge the fundamental need to be heard'.[201] In addition, eye contact between parties can be confrontational and this strategy may help regulate anger and fear.

The mediator then summarises what the disputants have said, reflecting events and feelings as accurately as possible while simultaneously reframing and defusing provocative language.[202] By the end of this phase those involved will have had

---

[196] See above at section IV.A.
[197] Ibid.
[198] Folger and Bush, 'Ten Hallmarks' (n 72).
[199] See Beausoleil and LeBaron (n 130).
[200] Gross, 'Conceptual and Empirical Foundations' (n 181) 10–11.
[201] Johnson et al (n 115) 160.
[202] Depending on the mediation tradition. Bush and Folger, *The Promise of Mediation* (n 26), view reframing as disempowering to disputants, robbing them of the agency implicit in choosing their own words.

the opportunity, perhaps for the first time, to engage with the other's perspective in an emotionally-regulated environment. This brings new emotional and factual data into play.

As mediation progresses, parties may begin to address each other directly. Concessions made or reciprocated are examples of 'situation modification' where people contribute to each other's emotion regulation.[203] At this stage the mediator continues to provide extrinsic support, down-regulating negative and up-regulating positive emotion by giving and modelling empathy, asking relevant questions and deploying attention.

In short, mediation offers disputants opportunities to appreciate both events and emotions behind each other's perspective: in other words, to experience empathy. New data can be used to reassess judgements and reappraise stories, leading to a novel, mutually acceptable narrative. Mediation is rarely linear in progress. It can feel like 'one step forward, one step back'. The hope is for emotion regulation gradually to become intrinsic to the parties, accompanying a move into sustained empathy.

As parties give and receive empathy there may come a point where one party says: 'so what can we do?' and the other makes a positive response. While each wants a solution for herself it starts to make sense to accommodate the other. We see evidence of empathic concern and the surfacing of what Rosenberg describes as 'giving from the heart'.[204] There can be a tangible generation of positive emotions. The energy in the room may change dramatically, accompanied by a sense of gratitude, relief, release and even humour. With new emotional and cognitive understandings, the disputants are poised to reach agreement.

C. Emotion Regulation with 'High Conflict People'[205]

So far we have described a successful mediation experience. Most mediators, however, encounter situations in which one or both parties have little or no degree of empathy.[206] In spite of the support offered some disputants seem unable to adopt successful emotional regulation strategies or grasp the other's perspective. Such people struggle with emotion regulation.[207] This also applies to people with insecure attachment styles: who are either worried that an attachment figure will be unresponsive in times of need (anxious attachment) or distrusting of an attachment figure's goodwill and capacity to respond (attachment-related avoidance).[208]

---

[203] Part of Mayer's 'emotional dimension' of conflict resolution—Mayer (n 20).
[204] MB Rosenberg, *Nonviolent Communication: A Language of Life* (Encinitas, CA, Puddledancer Press, 2005) 1.
[205] For a fuller explanation of this term see: www.highconflictinstitute.com.
[206] Baron-Cohen (n 136).
[207] See: www.ncbi.nlm.nih.gov/pubmed/23327297.
[208] Anxious attachment is related to 'distress intensification': on the emotion grid (see section II.D above, Figures 1 and 2); we hypothesise that anxiously-attached people will be placed in the

In this connection Eddy proposes various techniques for dealing with what he terms 'high conflict people', including the EAR (Empathy, Attention and Respect) strategy.[209] Broadly, EAR affirms the need to make a conscious effort to communicate empathically with such people, who can often be extremely irritating and unpleasant. Attending through respectful listening is an important component of empathic communication. These techniques assist mediators to support emotion regulation in volatile circumstances and to secure agreement where perspective taking is unlikely to occur. Furthermore, they underline the fact that mediation can be challenging and that empathy is at the core of practice. Mediators must regulate their own emotions in order to relate empathically to these clients. We explain this more fully in the next section.

Eddy's approach offers mediators an opportunity to engage in their own anticipatory reappraisal.[210] They can reflect on what is likely to be their default response to a high conflict individual and prepare a more helpful alternative: essentially not taking it personally and focusing on problem-solving.[211] He highlights the need for both empathy and emotion regulation with high conflict people. Yet sometimes mediation can be successful even in cases of low mediator empathy and emotion regulation; for instance, some disputants may fortuitously possess sufficient resilience and emotional intelligence to achieve resolution for themselves within the parameters of the process. Nonetheless, we argue for the utility of both mediator empathy and emotion regulation in all conflict situations, even when their lack is masked in this way, and should be aspired to as a standard of good practice.

D. Emotion Regulation and Mediators

Emotion regulation is equally important for mediators, who must find ways of recognising and managing internal personal triggers alongside extrinsically challenging scenarios. Mediation organisations often support this process, for example, by providing training in aspects of self-development. A key aim is to improve the ability for self-reflection, enabling the mediator to understand her own response tendencies and develop skills for connecting with clients. Supervision sessions encourage cognitive reappraisal through disclosure; mindfulness practice has been found particularly useful by some mediators.[212]

---

high volume and high-intensity quadrant. Conversely, attachment-related avoidance is linked with 'emotional inhibition' (P Shaver and M Mikulincer, 'Adult Attachment and Emotion Regulation' in JJ Gross (ed), *Handbook of Emotion Regulation*, 2nd edn (New York, Guilford Press 2014)); such people will probably present at low volume, masking suppressed emotional intensity.

[209] See: www.highconflictinstitute.com. See also W Eddy, *What's Your Proposal? Shifting High Conflict People from Blaming to Problem Solving in 30 Seconds* (Scottsdale, AZ, Unhooked Books, 2014).

[210] See Maroney, 'Emotion Regulation and Judicial Behavior' (n 187).

[211] As expressed by the title 'What's Your Proposal?'—Eddy (n 209).

[212] T Fisher, 'Who's Minding the Mediator? Mindfulness in Mediation' (2003) 5 *ADR Bulletin* 1: epublications.bond.edu.au/adr/vol5/iss10/1.

In some professions, especially those where the culture of supervision and support is largely absent, professionalism can be used as a form of anticipatory cognitive reappraisal; effectively saying to oneself 'I am a professional carrying out my job' and thereby not experiencing distress.[213] However, over-reliance on this strategy risks a level of detachment akin to avoidance or suppression, which is ultimately counterproductive for professional and client. The same would apply to mediation.

McCluskey suggests that professional relationships with clients subject to stress and fear can result in potentially powerful dynamics in which the professional becomes the attachment figure. In this role, if she shows empathy, she supports emotion regulation to the point where the client's attachment needs are met, allowing the client to reconnect with cognitive problem-solving abilities and inner resourcefulness. McCluskey calls this 'goal corrected empathic attunement'.[214] Awareness of this dynamic may be helpful in mediation. It also underlines further the need for self-awareness and recognition of the 'pull' exerted by distressed clients.

V. Conclusion

Like lawyers, mediators faced with emotions have a range of options. On the one hand, they can ignore emotions in the hope that they will go away.[215] On the other hand, they can acknowledge them; they can enquire further about them (opening up emotion as a topic for discussion); and they can display empathy.

In our review of the mediation literature we find strong support for the latter option. A growing chorus of writers has called for mediators to become more emotionally literate, some drawing on the appraisal theorists for useful models.[216] In this chapter we have focused on the related concepts of empathy and emotion regulation, viewing mediation as a valuable opportunity to assist parties with both. Empathy could be seen as the oil in the machine of emotion regulation. Happily empathy is woven into everyday life. Humans seem programmed both to experience and generate it. This may be one reason for the common mediation training injunction to 'be yourself'.

A number of commentators have drawn attention to a growing urge for mediation to professionalise on legal lines.[217] Yet the wish for intellectual and

---

[213] Maroney, 'Emotion Regulation and Judicial Behavior' (n 187) 1517.
[214] U McCluskey, *To Be Met as a Person* (London, Karnac Books, 2005) 2.
[215] 'If [behavioural expressions of emotion] are inhibited, the emotion itself will be muted'—Gross, 'Emotion Regulation' (n 7) 504.
[216] See text at section II.D and accompanying footnotes.
[217] E Lieberman, Y Foux-Levy and P Segal, 'Beyond Basic Training: A Model for Developing Mediator Competence' (2005) 23 *Conflict Resolution Quarterly* 237, 240; Lande (n 74) 854.

commercial credibility can work against empathy and emotional literacy. The notion of professional distance; the commitment to neutrality; the privileging of rationality over emotion; all may lead mediators (like lawyers before them) to eschew emotions. Some do.[218] We counsel against this approach. To do so is potentially to lose a rich source of data; Lazarus calls emotions 'the wisdom of the ages'.[219]

Rather, we propose the opposite direction of travel, where those involved in the justice system 'peek over the fence' at mediation. While mediation is still at a relatively early stage in its understanding of emotion, many mediation practitioners have developed practical skills in the area; what Schon might describe as 'knowing in action'.[220] This may explain the popularity of mediation training among lawyers. Here is a world in which their clients' (and their own) emotions are accepted, worked with, learned from and regulated. A course in mediation is likely to enhance their tolerance for and comfort with emotional information, surely of value both in the courtroom and in face to face work with clients.

In this way, lawyers may come to view mediation as a key resource in developing their own emotional skills. This will enhance, not diminish, the cause of justice. As Benjamin Disraeli said: 'Never apologise for showing feeling; when you do so, you apologise for the truth'.[221]

---

[218] See section II.A above.

[219] RS Lazarus, 'Progress on a Cognitive-Motivational-Relational Theory of Emotion' (1991) 46 *American Psychologist* 819, 820.

[220] D Schon, *The Reflective Practitioner: How Professionals Think in Action* (Aldershot, Basic Books, 1983) 54.

[221] Quoted in B Curtis, *Classic Wisdom for the Good Life* (Nashville, TS, Thomas Nelson, 2006) 39.

11

Engaging with Emotions in the Legal Profession

EIMEAR SPAIN* AND TIMOTHY RITCHIE**

I. Introduction

Emotions are central to the human experience, and the legal arena provides fertile ground for the generation of emotion among participants including litigants, witnesses, legal professionals and observers. Legal professionals necessarily experience and manage emotions in many different contexts during their working lives, and yet they are taught to be suspicious of emotions and to value attributes such as reason, logic and rationality above all else.[1] In this chapter we explore the impact of the traditional paradigm of a calm and dispassionate law, unwilling to countenance the presence of unruly emotions, on key actors within the legal system. We focus on the impact of the traditional paradigm on shared norms that attempt to govern emotions and emotional expression in the legal workplace.[2] We explore the appropriate place for emotions in the practice of law and examine literature about the extent to which a variety of legal professionals engage in emotional labour, with a focus on the impact of emotional suppression and emotional dissonance on the health and wellbeing of lawyers. Attention is also given to the role of legal education in sustaining cultural norms around emotions, and to the emotional labour involved in meeting these norms. Given the ubiquitous nature of emotions and their prevalence within legal practice throughout the world, the

* Senior Lecturer in Law, School of Law, Centre for Understanding Emotions in Society, University of Limerick
** Chair, Department of Psychology, Saint Xavier University, Chicago

[1] J Stefancic and R Delgado, *How Lawyers Lose Their Way: A Profession Fails Its Creative Minds* (Durham, NC, Duke University Press, 2005).

[2] This will include a discussion of emotional display rules, described by Diefendorff, Erickson, Grandey and Dahling as 'shared norms governing the expression of emotions at work'. This concept is explained further below, but see generally JM Diefendorff, RJ Erickson, AA Grandey and JJ Dahling, 'Emotional Display Rules as Work Unit Norms: A Multilevel Analysis of Emotional Labor Among Nurses' (2011) 16 *Journal of Occupational Health Psychology* 170, 170.

chapter will draw on research emanating from a variety of jurisdictions including Australia, Sweden, the United States, and England and Wales, to explore these issues and illuminate our understanding of the challenges facing legal professionals in their professional lives.

II. Emotions in Legal Settings

There is growing recognition of the important role played by emotions in law and the legal system.[3] For instance, emotions have a central role in shaping the content of the criminal law, affecting decisions regarding what behaviour should be prohibited. Disgust, anger and repulsion each influence decisions on what actions should be stigmatised through the criminal process.[4] Fear has also played an important, and not always beneficial,[5] role in the creation of legislation[6]— themes which are also identified by McAlinden in her contribution to the current collection.[7] Emotion has also been observed to motivate criminal punishment; in the context of retributivist approaches to punishment in particular, emotions such as anger, outrage and sympathy are vital to normative judgements about the appropriate level of punishment.[8] Similarly, shame is viewed by some scholars as an integral part of the criminal sanction, with punishment serving at least in part to stigmatise the offender.[9] More recently, the role of empathy, remorse and guilt in restorative justice has been highlighted.[10] Emotions also play a vital part in the

---

[3] Something which is evidenced by the contributions in this volume. See also, TA Maroney, 'Law and Emotion: A Proposed Taxonomy of an Emerging Field' (2006) 30 *Law and Human Behavior* 119; K Abrams and H Keren, 'Who's Afraid of Law and the Emotions?' (2010) 94 *Minnesota Law Review* 1997; J Schweppe and JE Stannard, 'What is So "Special" About Law and Emotions?' (2013) 64 *Northern Ireland Legal Quarterly* 1; and R Grossi, 'Understanding Law and Emotion' (2015) 7 *Emotion Review* 55.

[4] E Spain, *The Role of Emotions in Criminal Law Defences: Duress, Necessity and Lesser Evils* (Cambridge, Cambridge University Press, 2011) 6.

[5] RE Freeman-Longo, 'Feel Good Legislation: Prevention or Calamity?' (1996) 20 *Child Abuse & Neglect* 95; RE Freeman-Longo, *Revisiting Megan's Law and Sex Offender Registration: Prevention or Problem?* (American Probation and Parole Association, 2001): www.appa-net.org/revisitingmegan.pdf.

[6] For example, legislative reactions to the 9/11 terrorist attacks or Megan's Law, the Sexual Offender (Jacob Wetterling) Act 1994.

[7] McAlinden, ch 7.

[8] Under the retributivist theory of punishment, a criminal should be punished because, and only because, he/she is deserving of punishment in retribution for the harm which he/she has inflicted. See generally, E Durkheim, *The Division of Labor in Society* (trans G Simpson, first published 1893, New York, Free Press, 1933) as well as SH Pillsbury, 'Moralizing the Passions of Criminal Punishment' (1989) 74 *Cornell Law Review* 655.

[9] J Braithwaite, *Crime, Shame and Reintegration* (Cambridge, Cambridge University Press, 1989). See also MC Nussbaum, *Hiding from Humanity: Disgust, Shame, and the Law* (Princeton, NJ, Princeton University Press, 2004).

[10] N Harris, L Walgrave and J Braithwaite, 'Emotional Dynamics in Restorative Conferences' (2004) 8 *Theoretical Criminology* 191.

commission of acts that contravene the law and strong emotions surround criminal trials.[11] Despite their obvious application in the criminal sphere, the central role of emotion in civil law must also be considered. Most obvious is the provision of compensation for the infliction of emotional distress in tort law. Family law is a challenging area of legal practice where emotions run high; from custody battles to divorce proceedings.[12] Indeed it is difficult to imagine a more emotional arena than a family law court. Similarly, medical negligence actions generate strong emotions in both the plaintiff and the defendant. Patients who have suffered harm as a result of a breach of duty by a doctor may feel distressed and angry while the doctors who treated them may experience shame, fear and sadness. While these emotions may have been generated by the initial clinical error, engagement with the legal system further heightens the emotional impact of the experience.[13] The rules of evidence are similarly shaped by this understanding of emotions posing a threat to our ability to reason with evidence excluded 'if it "stirs" or "inflames" the jury's emotions, or causes the jurors to abandon their mental processes and give expression to their emotions'.[14] In the same way, the inclusion of victim impact statements at the sentencing stage in criminal trials has gone some way to acknowledging the emotional experience of victims, something that in the past has often been marginalised during the trial process.[15]

While the importance of emotions in law and the legal system is gaining recognition, the idea that emotions are irrational and properly excluded from the law 'is deeply engrained' within the legal sector.[16] It has been suggested that it is a principle of law '[t]hat individuals ought at all times to control their actions and to conduct themselves in accordance with rational judgment'[17] as emotion 'undermines rationality and impinges upon moral responsibility'.[18] However, it is

---

[11] J Katz, *Seductions of Crime: Moral and Sensual Attractions in Doing Evil* (New York, Basic Books, 1988); Spain (n 4).

[12] K Abrams, 'Barriers and Boundaries: Exploring Emotion in the Law of the Family' (2009) 16 *Virginia Journal of Social Policy & the Law* 301.

[13] See CM Balch, MR Oreskovich and LN Dyrbye et al, 'Personal Consequences of Malpractice Lawsuits on American Surgeons' (2011) 213 *Journal of the American College of Surgeons* 657; as well as AD Waterman, J Garbutt and E Hazel et al, 'The Emotional Impact of Medical Errors on Practicing Physicians in the United States and Canada' (2007) 33 *Joint Commission Journal on Quality and Patient Safety* 467.

[14] SA Bandes, 'Centennial Address: Emotion, Reason and the Progress of Law' (2013) 62 *De Paul Law Review* 921, 922.

[15] SA Bandes, 'Empathy, Narrative, and Victim Impact Statements' (1996) 63 *University of Chicago Law Review* 361, 362. Booth recently explored the management and containment of victim participation in sentencing hearings—see T Booth, '"Cooling Out" Victims of Crime: Managing Victim Participation in the Sentencing Process in a Superior Sentencing Court' (2012) 45 *Australian & New Zealand Journal of Criminology* 214.

[16] Maroney, 'Law and Emotion' (n 3) 119. See also Grossi (n 3) 56; and Abrams (n 12) 306.

[17] A Ashworth, 'The Doctrine of Provocation' (1976) 35 *Cambridge Law Journal* 292, 317.

[18] Pillsbury (n 8) 674. Kahan and Nussbaum describe the 'mechanistic' conception of emotions as seeing 'emotions as forces that do not contain or respond to thought ... they are impulses or surges that lead the person to action without embodying beliefs, or any way of seeing the world that can be assessed as correct or incorrect, appropriate or inappropriate'—DM Kahan and MC Nussbaum, 'Two

suggested that the clear distrust of emotions and the persistent assumption that human beings generally lack control over their own emotions are erroneous, and contradict recent empirical evidence.[19] Indeed, emotions necessarily contain an element of rationality. We experience emotions based on our own assessment of particular situations, and how they affect us and our emotions are altered as our thoughts and beliefs change.[20] Rejecting the idea of emotions and reason as opposing forces, De Sousa states that

> [d]espite a common prejudice, reason and emotion are not natural antagonists. On the contrary ... when the calculi of reason have become sufficiently sophisticated, they would be powerless in their own terms, except for the contribution of emotion. What remains of the old opposition between reason and emotion is only this: emotions are not reducible to beliefs or wants.[21]

Moreover, emotions may be viewed not simply as rational, but as *vital* for rationality.[22] This is supported by empirical research which suggests that certain emotions result in more considered judgements than would be made ordinarily,[23] which has important implications for the quality of decision-making within a legal profession wherein individuals are expected to be detached and rarely acknowledge their emotions.[24] This is not to deny that emotions may be irrational in particular cases[25] and we need not accept all emotions as rational. Rather, in Nussbaum's view, emotions, like beliefs, 'can be true or false, and (an independent point) justified or unjustified, reasonable or unreasonable'.[26] Therefore, despite

---

Conceptions of Emotion in Criminal Law' (1996) 96 *Columbia Law Review* 269, 273. The second view of emotions they designate the 'evaluative conception', a conception which 'holds that emotions express cognitive appraisals ... that emotions do embody beliefs and ways of seeing, which include appraisals or evaluations of the importance or significance of objects and events. These appraisals can, in turn, be evaluated for their appropriateness or inappropriateness'—ibid, 278.

[19] Nussbaum, *Hiding from Humanity* (n 9) 10. See also RS Lazarus, *Emotion and Adaptation* (Oxford, Oxford University Press, 1991) 100.

[20] J Averill, 'Emotions Are Many Splendored Things' in P Ekman and R Davidson (eds), *The Nature of Emotions: Fundamental Quest* (Oxford, Oxford University Press, 1994) 99; R Solomon, *Not Passion's Slave, Emotions and Choice* (Oxford, Oxford University Press, 2003) 5; PM Salkovskis, DM Clark and A Hackmann, 'Treatment of Panic Attacks Using Cognitive Therapy Without Exposure or Breathing Retraining' (1991) 29 *Behaviour Research and Therapy* 161.

[21] R De Sousa, *The Rationality of Emotions* (Cambridge, MA, MIT Press, 1987) xv.

[22] Damasio states that 'certain aspects of the process of emotion and feeling are indispensable for rationality. At their best, feelings point us in the proper direction, take us to the appropriate place in a decision making space, where we may put the instruments of logic to good use'. He also goes so far as to suggest that a lack of emotion in the reasoning process is damaging to rationality—A Damasio, *Descartes' Error: Emotion, Reason, and the Human Brain* (New York, Avon Books, 1994) xii.

[23] LF Barrett and MG Seo, 'Being Emotional During Decision Making—Good Or Bad? An Empirical Investigation' (2007) 50 *Academy of Management Journal* 923, 923.

[24] This is discussed in the following section.

[25] For example, first, an individual may overestimate the personal relevance of the situation. Second, an individual may make a mistake of fact when appraising the situation, privately or publically. Third, emotions may be based on a flawed value system.

[26] M Nussbaum, *Upheavals of Thought: The Intelligence of Emotions* (Cambridge, Cambridge University Press, 2001) 46. See also Damasio (n 22) xii.

the fact that emotions may be irrational in some circumstances, such as when an individual feels fear believing a twig on the ground to be a snake or mistakenly believes a negative comment to be directed at him/her, we argue that emotions are not *inherently* irrational and devoid of reason, as traditionally conceived in legal discourse.[27] Indeed, there is a growing body of evidence which suggests that emotions play an important role in moral decision-making;[28] as Blumenthal points out, '[i]ncreasingly, moral, and ... legal, decisions are seen as depending heavily on emotion, as suggested by neurological studies that document the activation of specific emotion-related regions of the brain when individuals engage in moral decision-making'.[29] Here, rather than disrupting rational thought and moral judgement, emotions are seen as playing a vital role in these processes.[30]

Given the available evidence which links emotions and rationality, attempts to remove emotion from the legal system, and to require individuals working within the legal system to work in a manner which is devoid of emotions, must be challenged. This is particularly important in light of the ubiquitous nature of emotions within the legal system and the impact of this approach on the legal professionals such as judges, barristers, solicitors and legal executives.

III. Emotions in the Legal Workplace

While there is some evidence of a more nuanced understanding of emotions in isolated areas of Western legal practice (for example, in therapeutic and restorative justice practices),[31] legal professionals are often taught to be suspicious of

---

[27] Bandes, 'Centennial Address' (n 14).

[28] Feigenson and Park emphasise the 'centrality of moral emotions rather than moral reasoning to moral action'—N Feigenson and J Park, 'Emotions and Attributions of Legal Responsibility and Blame: A Research Review' (2006) 30 *Law and Human Behavior* 143, 145.

[29] JA Blumenthal, 'Does Mood Influence Moral Judgement?: An Empirical Test with Legal and Policy Implications' (2005) 29 *Law and Psychology Review* 1, 4. The author references the following studies: Jorge Moll et al, 'The Neural Correlates of Moral Sensitivity: A Functional Magnetic Resonance Imaging Investigation of Basic and Moral Emotions' (2002) 22 *Journal of Neuroscience* 2730; and JD Greene et al, 'An fMRI Investigation of Emotional Engagement in Moral Judgment' (2001) 293 *Science* 2105.

[30] Feigenson and Park (n 28) 145. Recent literature suggests that 'moral "reasoning" is in fact based on intuitive, emotion-based judgments, rather than more conscious, rational deductive reasoning'— Blumenthal (n 29) 4. This has been supported by research in the field of neuroscience where studies utilising neuroimaging have shown activation in parts of the brain associated with emotion rather than purely cognitive thought processes when participants are presented with moral dilemmas which require them to engage in moral reasoning—see J Moll, R De Olivierra-Souza and PJ Eslinger, 'Morals and the Human Brain: A Working Model' (2003) 14 *Neuroreport* 299. Perhaps the strongest defence of this thesis comes from Prinz who, following a review of psychology, cognitive neuroscience and psychopathology, proposes a 'sentimentalist' theory of moral concepts and concludes that '[e]motions co-occur with moral judgments, influence moral judgments, are sufficient for moral judgments, and are necessary for moral judgments, because moral judgments are constituted by emotional dispositions'—J Prinz, 'The Emotional Basis of Moral Judgments' (2006) 9 *Philosophical Explorations* 29, 36.

[31] Grossi (n 3) 57.

emotions. In particular, legal professionals, including judges, solicitors and barristers, are expected to be unemotional, rational and detached during their professional lives.[32] The value placed on attributes such as logic and rationality reflects a
'folk knowledge view of emotions as hot, chaotic, unpredictable flashes of feeling
that interfere with our ability to think coolly and rationally' and are therefore to
be viewed with suspicion.[33]

Despite this distrust of emotions, the practice of law forces one to encounter,
engage with and experience emotion, irrespective of the jurisdiction in which
one practises. Emotions pervade many legal disputes and strong feelings may be
invoked in the practice of any area of law—beyond the various criminal law and
criminal justice examples highlighted earlier in this chapter.[34] The circumstances
in which these emotions arise are also varied, such as when lawyers consider
emotional information in their assessment of a client, in cases which involve
distressing facts, or when hearing testimony. The extent to which one is exposed
to emotional stimuli will differ, depending on the type of legal work in which
one is engaged. For example, criminal defence lawyers are sometimes required
to defend individuals accused of terrible crimes and may be required to impugn
the character of victims and/or witnesses in the process.[35] They also have to
consider the impact of an acquittal, the potential for reoffending and cope with
'the public perception that they are engaged in a disreputable enterprise that
lies somewhere between pathological denial and out and out collaboration with
criminality'.[36] While tax lawyers, for instance, will be less likely to be emotionally
engaged than criminal or family lawyers, all lawyers will be exposed to emotion
to some extent. Indeed, even the tax lawyer may have to represent a client or take
a case which they have an objection to, or work on causes about which they are
passionate.[37]

Judges and magistrates will also encounter emotions in their daily working lives,
though the extent to which they do so depends on a number of variables, including the level and type of court over which they preside. An Australian magistrate
noted that 'when you see this passing parade of misery, day in, day out and folly
and stupidity and dishonesty and depravity, you know, it is truly emotionally

---

[32] Stefancic and Delgado (n 1). The nature of these expectations, particularly the expectations of
clients, will be explored in the next section.

[33] Bandes, 'Centennial Address' (n 14) 921. See also J Rosen, 'Sentimental Journey: The Emotional
Jurisprudence of Harry Blackmun' (New Republic, 1994): newrepublic.com/article/62712/sentimental-
journey (referenced in TA Maroney, 'The Persistent Cultural Script of Judicial Dispassion' (2011) 99
California Law Review 629, 631); and RA Posner 'The Role of the Judge in the Twenty-First Century'
(2006) 86 *Boston University Law Review* 1049).

[34] And illustrated by the range of subjects within the current collection.

[35] SA Bandes, 'Repression and Denial in Criminal Lawyering' (2006) 9 *Buffalo Criminal Law Review*
339, 346–47.

[36] Ibid, 347.

[37] D Luban, 'The Adversary System Excuse' in D Luban (ed), *The Good Lawyer: Lawyers' Roles and
Lawyers' Ethics* (Totowa, NJ, Rowman & Allenheld, 1988). See also S Yakren, 'Lawyer as Emotional
Laborer' (2008) 42 *University of Michigan Journal of Law Reform* 141, 148.

and psychologically abrasive and wearing'.[38] In courts at higher levels, lawyers may protect judges from emotional stimuli to some extent by filtering or managing the raw emotions felt by defendants, clients, victims and witnesses in the courtroom,[39] enabling judges to minimise their engagement with emotion and emotional labour.[40] Lawyers will use objective legal language, excised of emotion to the greatest extent possible,[41] and their presence in the courtroom protects the judiciary from direct contact with lay participants including victims, witnesses and defendants, creating a more emotionally sanitised environment.[42] However, while legal professionals insulate members of the judiciary from emotional stimuli to some extent, they are themselves engaging with lay participants and managing both their own and the participant's emotions. In the pages that follow we consider the norms which currently govern the experience and expression of emotions by legal professionals, before considering the extent to which such norms are beginning to change.

A. Norms Governing the Expression of Emotions

In line with the underlying assumption that emotion exists in opposition to reason, norms for emotional displays (known as 'display rules') have evolved within the legal profession, requiring professionals to limit their emotional experiences and expressions on the job.[43] Display (or feeling) rules are '[r]ules or standards of behavior indicating which emotions are appropriate in given situations and how they should be expressed publicly ... [and] guide emotion work'.[44] While in some occupations, such as in the service industry, employees receive explicit guidance on expected emotional displays and adherence is supervised by management,[45]

---

[38] S Roach Anleu and K Mack, 'Magistrates' Everyday Work and Emotional Labour' (2005) 32 *Journal of Law and Society* 590, 613.

[39] Ibid, 607.

[40] K Mack and S Roach Anleu, '"Getting Through the List": Judgecraft and Legitimacy in the Lower Courts' (2007) 16 *Social & Legal Studies* 341. See also S Roach Anleu and K Mack, 'Judicial Performance and Experiences of Judicial Work: Findings from Socio-legal Research' (2014) 4 *Oñati Socio-legal Series* 1015.

[41] Bandes, 'Repression and Denial in Criminal Lawyering' (n 35) 372–73.

[42] Roach Anleu and Mack, 'Magistrates' Everyday Work' (n 38) 607.

[43] Hochschild referred to feeling rules and referred to the 'rules or norms according to which feelings may be judged appropriate to accompanying events'—A Hochschild, *The Managed Heart. Commercialization of Human Feeling* (University of California Press, 1983) 59. This was subsequently refined, differentiating between emotions that ought to be displayed, rather than emotions which ought to be felt—see A Rafaeli and R Sutton, 'Expression of Emotion as Part of the Work Role' (1987) 12 *The Academy of Management Review* 23; and A Morris and D Feldman, 'The Dimensions, Antecedents and Consequences of Emotional Labour' (1996) 21 *The Academy of Management Review* 986.

[44] Yakren (n 37) 159. The concept of 'emotion work' or 'emotional labour' will be explored in greater detail below.

[45] Hochschild (n 43).

legal professionals are 'thought typically to supervise their own emotion work in light of informal professional norms and client expectations'.[46]

The rules which have developed within the legal professions across different jurisdictions are both implicit and explicit, drawn from ethical guidelines and observation of fellow professionals and professional norms.[47] Professional socialisation and training have been identified as key to the communication of dominant sectoral display rules. In the words of one barrister practising in England and Wales, 'Bar School teaches you little about the law, a fair bit about the process of law and a hell of a lot about what is expected from you; how to show respect, most of the unwritten rules'.[48] Similarly, evidence of norms for emotional displays by solicitors is provided 'through a traditional apprenticeship model'.[49] Harris has highlighted the importance of legal culture and tradition at the Bar in England and Wales:

> Whilst some organisational, societal and broader environmental issues were found to drive emotional display expectations, the centuries old, archaic traditions of the barristers' profession appear to exert a strong influence over the work roles of barristers. That is, the traditions and customs of the Bar have become manifested in a series of tangible acculturation rites and rituals as well as ingrained in the macroculture ... of the legal sector.[50]

Display rules have also been established through decided cases and are maintained through 'the risk of an appeal and denunciatory judicial comment'.[51] Linked to this is a fear of adverse media reporting which also perpetuates existing display rules.[52]

The role of legal education in creating or sustaining emotional display rules, which discourages engagement with emotion, must also be considered. The current paradigm in legal education is said to reflect the dominant view of emotions in law, in so far as the traditional method of 'classical legal education celebrates

---

[46] Yakren (n 37) 159–60.

[47] Display rules may differ across the legal professions, for example, the rules applying to paralegals will differ from those applying to lawyers—see Roach Anleu and Mack, 'Magistrates' Everyday Work' (n 38); LC Harris, 'The Emotional Labour of Barristers: An Exploration of Emotional Labour by Status Professionals' (2002) 39 *Journal of Management Studies* 553; J Rogers, 'Shadowing the Bar: Studying an English Professional Elite' (2010) 36 *Historical Reflections* 39; and C Westaby, '"Feeling Like a Sponge": The Emotional Labour Produced by Solicitors in their Interactions with Clients Seeking Asylum' (2010) 17 *International Journal of the Legal Profession* 153.

[48] Comments made by a barrister of three years' experience and reported in Harris, 'The Emotional Labour of Barristers' (n 47) 565. See also Rogers (n 47); and Westaby, '"Feeling Like a Sponge"' (n 47) 164–65. Westaby documents the gap between legal education and law in practice with socialisation and training on how to interact with clients occurring in the workplace rather than in law school—ibid, 165.

[49] Westaby, '"Feeling Like a Sponge"' (n 47) 166. Westaby notes that 'generally explicit references to emotional labour were not made, and so participants learnt to display appropriate emotions primarily through observation'—ibid, 66.

[50] Harris, 'The Emotional Labour of Barristers' (n 47) 576.

[51] Roach Anleu and Mack, 'Magistrates' Everyday Work' (n 38) 592 and 603.

[52] Ibid, 592.

reason and devalues emotions'.[53] Legal educators in the common law world focus on creating the ideal lawyer; that is, a calm, objective, rational and detached professional. Students are taught to think logically and rationally with no place for emotion: 'lawyers are taught to think and reason ... a way of thinking that values precedent and doctrine above all, exalting consistency over ambiguity, rationality over emotion, and rules over social context and narrative'.[54] One study conducted in England and Wales, involving 42 barristers and pupil barristers, nine solicitors and five barristers' clerks,[55] identified the role of legal education in exalting emotion among the profession as follows:

> Pupil barristers have to learn not only advocacy and negotiation skills but also about 'detachment'—[to] ensure that one acts as a rational voice for one's client. Learning to stay isolated is crucial to one's success. Involvement merely sullies the mind and excludes calm, professional logic.[56]

The display rules that have evolved within the legal professions reflect the underlying assumptions about emotion that prevail in that sector:

> In the conventional view the very acknowledgement of our work's emotional aspects—of the pain we cause, the pain we experience, the costs of the dissonance between role and conscience, the empathy or revulsion we may feel toward particular clients and how we ought to deal with it—seems at odds with law's essence as a rational and rigorous discipline. In short, acknowledging the role of emotion may brand one as not merely weak, but downright unlawyerlike.[57]

Much of the recent research on emotions in the legal system has focused on the judiciary, and it suggests that they are expected to exclude emotion from their professional lives, due to its perceived irrational nature.[58] Thus, Anleu and Mack note that '[t]he suppression of emotion and personal feelings is a key attribute of traditional conceptions of the profession'.[59] In the same way, Maroney noted that '[a] good judge should feel no emotion; if she does, she puts it aside. To call a judge emotional is a stinging insult, signifying a failure in discipline, impartiality and reason'.[60] The recent appointment of Justice Sonia Sotomayor to the US Supreme Court provides an interesting example of the public perception of the danger of

---

[53] AP Harris and MM Shultz, 'A(nother) Critique of Pure Reason: Toward Civic Virtue in Legal Education' (1993) 45 *Stanford Law Review* 1773, 1773.

[54] Stefancic and Delgado (n 1) abstract.

[55] The barristers and clerks were drawn from 15 different chambers, while each of the solicitors involved in the study worked in a separate partnership.

[56] Comments made by a barrister of nine years' experience and reported in Harris, 'The Emotional Labour of Barristers' (n 47) 575.

[57] Bandes, 'Repression and Denial in Criminal Lawyering' (n 35) 342.

[58] Maroney, 'The Persistent Cultural Script of Judicial Dispassion' (n 33). See also TA Maroney, 'Emotional Regulation and Judicial Behavior' (2011) 99 *California Law Review* 1485; as well as Roach Anleu and Mack, 'Judicial Performance and Experiences of Judicial Work' (n 40).

[59] Roach Anleu and Mack, 'Judicial Performance and Experiences of Judicial Work' (n 40) 599.

[60] Maroney, 'The Persistent Cultural Script of Judicial Dispassion' (n 33) 629. See also Roach Anleu and Mack, 'Judicial Performance and Experiences of Judicial Work' (n 40).

emotions in judging and the importance placed on reason and rationality within the profession.[61] Karl Rove, former White House Deputy Chief of Staff, suggested that Sotomayor was likely to 'discard the rule of law whenever emotion moves'.[62] At her confirmation hearing Justice Sotomayor was forced to address these concerns about her ability to judge without emotion and recognised that judges are 'not robots [who] listen to evidence and don't have feelings';[63] however, she emphasised that judges are under an obligation to 'recognize those feelings and put them aside'.[64] This example aptly illustrates two implicit assumptions about emotion in the legal sector: the assumption that emotions are irrational; and the assumption that emotions ought to be suppressed within the legal workplace. This is reflective of the findings of research conducted by Roach Anleu and Mack on the experiences and perceptions of Australian magistrates, where one magistrate described feelings of revulsion and sympathy but noted that 'you're not allowed to let that sympathy get in the way of what you do'.[65] In the words of Roach Anleu, Bergman Blix and Mack, the ability to be affectively neutral is 'thought to be essential to performing and communicating the central legal values of neutrality and impartiality'.[66]

However, members of the judiciary are not alone in their attempt to convey an impression of the legal system as unemotional and impartial. Thus, a recent study conducted by Bergman Blix and Wettergren in Sweden observed the 'subtle exchange of emotions between court professionals [as] a fundamental element in the joint effort to create an appearance of a rational (unemotional) procedure, constitutive of the judicial emotional regime'.[67] Similarly, in a study of the Bar in England and Wales published in 2002, 'it was consistently argued that the expression of genuine emotion was unprofessional and a sign of a loss of desired detachment'.[68] In a more recent study, conducted by the current authors in Ireland in 2014, the question of how emotions are conceptualised within the legal profession was explored, including the extent to which a variety of legal professionals adhered to a folk understanding of emotions as inferior, and even hostile, to reason.[69] Using qualitative and quantitative data, the study revealed that

---

[61] For full discussion see Maroney, 'Emotional Regulation and Judicial Behavior' (n 58); and Maroney, 'The Persistent Cultural Script of Judicial Dispassion' (n 33). The author also revisits this theme in the current collection—see Maroney, ch 12.

[62] K Rove, '"Empathy" is Code for Judicial Activism' *New York Times* (28 May 2009).

[63] Andrew Malcom, 'Sotomayor Hearings: The Complete Transcript, Part 1' (*Top of the Ticket*, 14 July 2009): latimesblogs.latimes.com/washington/2009/07/soniasotomayor-hearing-transcript.html.

[64] Ibid.

[65] Roach Anleu and Mack, 'Magistrates' Everyday Work' (n 38) 611.

[66] S Roach Anleu, S Bergman Blix and K Mack, 'Researching Emotion in Courts and the Judiciary: A Tale of Two Projects' (2015) 7 *Emotion Review* 145, 145.

[67] S Bergman Blix and Å Wettergren, 'A Sociological Perspective on Emotions in the Judiciary' (2015) *Emotion Review* 1, 5.

[68] Harris, 'The Emotional Labour of Barristers' (n 47) 570; and see also Rogers (n 47) 53.

[69] E Spain and T Ritchie, 'Engaging with Emotions in the Legal and Mental Health Professions' (Congress of the International Academy of Law and Mental Health, Amsterdam, July 2013). A total of

barristers and solicitors have a narrow conception of emotion with less content, nuance and complexity in their personal theories about emotion when compared with other professions.[70] Barristers have expressly linked the repression of emotion and emotional detachment with rational competence and the ability to represent their clients effectively.[71] The obligation to argue for clients in a rational manner, as explicitly highlighted in the relevant code of ethics, is considered to require emotional detachment.[72] Similarly, solicitors have identified the need to remain detached: as one solicitor said, 'you can't get emotionally involved with your client, to the extent that it will perhaps prejudice the objectivity you need to maintain when advising them'.[73]

B. A Changing Environment?

Despite the dominance of these rules, it is clear that as the professions have experienced change both from outside and within, the expectations of the public and of members of the legal profession have shifted to some degree.[74] In particular, there is a growing demand from clients for legal professionals to display emotions such as empathy, anger, disgust and sadness, when dealing with their clients or in the courtroom. In the courtroom, lawyers may appeal to the emotions of the jury or engage in an aggressive manner with witnesses.[75] Indeed, it is in the

---

352 individuals participated in the study, including 233 women, 105 men and 14 who did not indicate their gender. Participants included the 329 of 352 who reported their occupation. The sample included (a) students at universities ($n = 208$); (b) educators from all levels of teaching ($n = 26$); (c) caregivers from multiple disciplines ($n = 27$; eg, nurse, psychologist); (d) legal professionals from multiple disciplines ($n = 25$; eg, barrister, solicitor); and (e) those who work in an industry ($n = 43$; eg, media executive, accountant).

[70] Spain and Ritchie (n 69). The extant literature tends to focus on the highest profile group within the sector, the judiciary, even though this study explored how emotions were understood by both solicitors and barristers.

[71] Harris, 'The Emotional Labour of Barristers' (n 47) 571.

[72] Ibid.

[73] Solicitor with one year's experience, cited in Westaby, '"Feeling Like a Sponge"' (n 47) 161.

[74] For example, the changes brought about by the Courts and Legal Services Act 1990 and the Access to Justice Act 1999 in England and Wales, including changes in the way the professions were organised and regulated, and the loss of monopolies over conveyancing work held by solicitors, and by barristers over litigation work in the higher courts. The proposed Legal Services Regulation Bill 2011 in Ireland will introduce new business models including multidisciplinary practices and includes alterations to the regulation of the professions. Recent changes to legal aid procurement in England and Wales has further increased the financial challenges faced by some members of the professions. The large increase in the numbers of solicitors and barristers in recent decades and increasing diversity within the professions has also impacted on the membership—see Rogers (n 47) 45 who discusses the impact of the Bar having to 'sell itself to, select from, and then socialize an increasingly diverse group'. See also J Pierce, *Gender Trials: Emotional Lives in Contemporary Law Firms* (Berkeley, CA, University of California Press, 1995) 44–45.

[75] J Pierce, 'Rambo Litigators: Emotional Labor in a Male-Dominated Occupation' in C Cheng (ed), *Masculinities in Organizations* (Thousand Oaks, CA, Sage, 1996) 9, 16. See also Yakren (n 37) 164–65.

courtroom context that we see one of the exceptions to the general requirement of detachment: it is assumed that lawyers will deploy emotional narratives in making their client's case, since '[a]ny trial lawyer worth her salt knows that proving up a case through dry, deductive logic will rarely carry the day'.[76] Advocates, as 'rambo litigators',[77] are expected to display righteous anger or disgust when cross-examining witnesses, but to show empathy for vulnerable clients. Pierce describes these emotional tactics as 'intimidation'[78] and 'strategic friendliness'.[79] It is also normatively acceptable to be aggressive or strategically friendly when dealing with opposing counsel or case owners.[80]

Interestingly, even when displaying a particular emotion for a specific audience, such as clients or a jury, there is an expectation among fellow legal professionals that such displays are manufactured rather than real and that the individual remains professional and rational at all times.[81] In a study of the Bar in England and Wales published in 2002, evidence emerged which suggested that 'displays of "genuine" emotion were often viewed as "unprofessional", leading to a range of occupational coping mechanisms to suppress genuine emotional display'.[82] However, it has been suggested that expectations may differ between the various branches of the legal profession, with barristers in particular

[76] Bandes, 'Centennial Address' (n 14) 920.
[77] Pierce, *Gender Trials* (n 74) 50–82. The term is used to describe litigators with a tough, no-nonsense approach.
[78] Ibid, 59.
[79] Ibid, 71. Pierce also suggests that in the hierarchical legal professions, junior members engage in a further form of emotional labour, through the provision of emotional reinforcement to more senior members of the profession.
[80] For example, 'as a result of the perceived hostile behaviour of some case owners, intimidating or confrontational behaviour was deemed necessary either as a result of "emotional contagion" or as a way of connecting themselves to their status as legal professionals. By engaging in these types of emotional displays, it is maintained that these participants are also using emotional capital gained through their professional socialisation to display their authority as legal professionals'—C Westaby, 'What's Culture Got to do With It? The Emotional Labour of Immigration Solicitors in their Exchanges with United Kingdom Border Agency Case Workers' (2014) 20 *Web Journal of Current Legal Issues* [6]. The changing expectations of clients and the changing nature of legal work are also reflected in a new client-care ethos—see Rogers (n 47) 45–46. One empirical study involving solicitors identified 'detached concern', 'a deliberate attempt to identify with, and show concern for, the client's personal circumstances in order to develop mutual trust and confidence'—Westaby, '"Feeling Like a Sponge"' (n 47) 160–62. This is particularly difficult for solicitors who deal with very vulnerable clients; as one solicitor recounted, 'a lot of immigration clients have been to absolute hell and back, and they want a friendly face, who's going to listen to them, and hear what they're gonna say, and try and fight for them'– Westaby, '"Feeling Like a Sponge"' (n 47) 166–67. See also A Melville and K Laing, '"I Just Drifted Into It": Constraints Faced by Publicly Funded Family Lawyers' (2007) 14 *International Journal of the Legal Profession* 281; and H Sommerlad, '"I've Lost the Plot": An Everyday Story of the "Political" Legal Aid Lawyer' (2001) 28 *Journal of Law and Society* 335.
[81] Harris, 'The Emotional Labour of Barristers' (n 47).
[82] Ibid, 567. In a study of immigration solicitors, Westaby notes that the job involves the 'performance of diverging emotional displays. Intense emotional displays of empathy are expected to gain the trust of clients. However, these emotions have to be managed to maintain the perceived professional integrity of the solicitor'—Westaby, '"Feeling Like a Sponge"' (n 47) 153.

experiencing 'the need to suppress genuine emotional response in order to retain the "iron self-control" regarded as paramount within the profession'.[83] In contrast, solicitors will have direct contact with clients and are expected to engage with clients emotionally,[84] making it permissible for solicitors not to suppress all genuine emotions in England and Wales:

> Instead, mutual trust and confidence with the client is developed by engaging in deep acting or genuine emotional responses to produce authentic emotional displays of empathy and sympathy. Participants pointed to tension being created by having to produce empathic displays with such intensity, with the concern being of becoming too emotionally attached to the client. However, the solicitors interviewed relieve this tension by using the specialist elements of their profession to focus on the legal aspects of the case, resulting in the production of a form of 'detached concern'.[85]

C. Emotional Labour

Given the complex and varied nature of legal work, legal professionals cannot avoid emotional stimuli and associated responses,[86] and lawyers who encounter emotions regularly in the course of their work will have to deal with them in some way. This brings us on to the important issue of 'emotional labour'.[87] Emotional labour is a concept used to describe the efforts involved in dealing with and managing the feelings of others and regulating one's own emotions in line with organisationally defined rules and guidelines.[88] This field of research owes its origins to

---

[83] Westaby, "'Feeling Like a Sponge'" (n 47) 160.

[84] '[A]s barristers are not required to engage in direct contact with clients, the protection afforded by the use of surface acting in the production of emotional labour is more readily available'—Westaby, "'Feeling Like a Sponge'" (n 47) 160.

[85] Ibid, 170.

[86] Jacobsson has drawn a comparison between emotional labour and objectivity work which is 'carried out in a particular language and linguistic style with the aim to display a professional attitude'—K Jacobsson, "'We Can't Just Do It Any Which Way'—Objectivity Work among Swedish Prosecutors' (2008) 4 *Qualitative Sociology Review* 46, 49–50. In a study of Swedish prosecutors it was found that they 'cultivate objectivity by frequent appeals to (1) rules and regulation, (2) duty, and (3) professionalism'—ibid, 63. Jacobsson also notes that 'violations of objectivity are responded to or accounted for so that the major sense of objective decision making is nonetheless maintained', labelling these responses as '(4) incantations of objectivity, (5) corrections, (6) proclamation by contrast, and (7) appeals to human fallibility'—ibid.

[87] Despite not being required to perform emotional labour in a formal way, magistrates 'are conscious of feeling rules and presentation of self and express concern or the kind of experience and impression a person will take away from the magistrates court'—S Roach Anleu and K Mack, 'Emotional Labour in the Magistrates Court' (The Australian Sociological Association (TASA) 2003 Conference Proceedings) 6.

[88] Hochschild (n 43) 7. Hochschild describes this as regulating emotions 'in order to sustain the [organisationally desired] outward countenance that produces the proper state of mind in others'—ibid. See also N James, 'Emotional Labour: Skill and Work in the Social Regulation of Feelings' (1989) 37 *The Sociological Review* 15, 15.

the groundbreaking work of Arlie Hochschild which focused on emotional labour in frontline services jobs.[89] However, research 'has gradually expanded to consider interactive work in its broadest sense; this includes professionals' interactions with clients and coworkers'.[90] It has been suggested that there are four dimensions to emotional labour: '(a) frequency of appropriate emotional display, (b) attentiveness to required display rules, (c) variety of emotions required to be displayed, and (d) emotional dissonance generated as the result of having to express organizationally desired emotions not genuinely felt'.[91] Legal professionals engage in the various dimensions of emotional labour, driven by the complex display rules within the sector:

> The more attentiveness to display rules required, the more psychological energy and physical effort the service job will demand from employees—and hence the more 'labor' emotional displays will entail. Attentiveness to display rules required consists of both the duration of emotional display and the intensity of emotional display.[92]

As discussed, the predominant rule traditionally associated with the legal profession has required the various actors to remain detached and unemotional in their dealings with the clients, courts and colleagues. However, it is clear that legal professionals are now subject to diverging requirements and may be required to hide emotions (or display emotionlessness) in some circumstances and display emotions in others. Legal professionals respond to these emotional stimuli and expectations in a variety of ways.[93] In order to meet the predominant sectoral expectation of rationality and detachment, legal professionals are encouraged to deal with the emotional stimuli by detaching,[94] 'modifying feelings by "thinking good thoughts" or reappraising the event (deep acting), or modifying expression by faking or enhancing facial and bodily signs of emotion (surface acting)'.[95] So-called 'deep acting' involves an attempt to alter the emotion being experienced, for example, by imagining the event from the perspective of the difficult customer.[96] Individuals who succeed in this form of emotional labour will feel and display emotions in line with sectoral norms. In contrast, surface acting involves the simulation of feelings and displays to match those expected by the audience, resulting in emotional dissonance.[97] Emotional dissonance refers to the discordance between the emotions actually felt by the individual and the organisationally required emotions. For example, a lawyer discussing a complex custody case may display a rational and detached persona, despite inwardly feeling very irritated

---

[89] Hochschild (n 43).

[90] AS Wharton, 'The Sociology of Emotional Labor' (2009) 35 *Annual Review of Sociology* 147, 150.

[91] Morris and Feldman (n 43) 987.

[92] Ibid, 989.

[93] Westaby, '"Feeling Like a Sponge"' (n 47) 160.

[94] Yakren (n 37) 151.

[95] AA Grandey, 'Emotion Regulation in the Workplace: A New Way to Conceptualize Emotional Labor' (2000) 5 *Journal of Occupational Health Psychology* 95.

[96] Hochschild (n 43).

[97] Westaby, '"Feeling Like a Sponge"' (n 47) 153.

by the unreasonable behaviour of the parties involved. While all forms of emotional labour may have negative or dysfunctional consequences for workers, emotional dissonance is recognised as leading to decreased task efficiency,[98] stress,[99] lower job satisfaction[100] and 'personal and work related maladjustment, such as poor self-esteem, depression, cynicism, and alienation from work'.[101] Solicitors in England and Wales have reported struggling to detach sufficiently, with Westaby suggesting that this leads them to use 'coping strategies such as suppressing unwanted emotional responses, including care and concern and anxiety, and making use of surface acting to ensure a balanced emotional display'.[102] Interestingly, studies in the same jurisdiction have found that those who have been in practice for a shorter time are more likely to admit to being reliant on surface acting. More experienced professionals suggest that an ability to detach, and to balance this required detachment with required displays of concern, develops over time.[103]

It is clear that emotional labour, and emotional dissonance in particular, can have negative consequences for legal professionals on a variety of levels. Of particular concern to employers is the impact on productiveness and task efficiency. One study of solicitors highlighted an inability to organise workload as a potential consequence of over-identifying with a job.[104] Another consequence may be high staff turnover within the professions, and a significant number of individuals leaving the profession on a yearly basis, as highlighted by an Australian study.[105] There are also personal dangers associated with detachment, including a potentially negative 'effect on both job satisfaction and one's sense of personal accomplishment'.[106] The consequences of emotional labour on the mental and personal wellbeing of individuals are also well documented within the legal profession. In particular, Anleu and Mack report evidence from magistrates in Australia on the difficulty experienced in dealing with emotional labour:

> I have a problem walking away and just erasing everything I've heard … I just find it difficult to walk away from that and go home to my own children … Now, there's two things that can happen to you. Either you're going to remain a decent person and become terribly upset by it all … [or] you're going to grow a skin on you as thick as a rhino, in which case I believe you're going to become an inadequate judicial officer.[107]

---

[98] Ibid.

[99] Ibid.

[100] Morris and Feldman (n 43) 987.

[101] B Ashforth and R Humphrey, 'Emotional Labour in Service Roles: The Influence of Identity' (1993) 18 *Academy of Management Review* 88, 96–97. See also Westaby, '"Feeling Like a Sponge"' (n 47) 153.

[102] Westaby, '"Feeling Like a Sponge"' (n 47) 160–62.

[103] Ibid.

[104] Ibid, 168.

[105] C James, 'Seeing Things as We Are: Emotional Intelligence and Clinical Legal Education' (2005) *Journal of Clinical Legal Education* 123, 124.

[106] Roach Anleu and Mack, 'Magistrates' Everyday Work' (n 38) 613. See also Westaby, '"Feeling Like a Sponge"' (n 47) 168–69.

[107] Roach Anleu and Mack, 'Magistrates' Everyday Work' (n 38) 613. See also Roach Anleu and Mack (n 87) 7.

A similar sentiment was expressed by a paralegal in an American study who described engaging with clients when they are scared, needy and stressed as 'very traumatic'.[108] A male attorney working in personal bankruptcy described the stress of dealing with

> the unending sadness, [which] I think, is [actually] the hardest thing—just the unrelenting sadness of almost everyone that's sitting where you are. Because, naturally they are all in difficult situations—that's just the nature of this kind of practice ... But, I've found that very difficult to deal with—more than I would have anticipated.[109]

It seems that legal professionals are impacted upon, irrespective of the type of emotional labour in which they engage. Those legal professionals who engage too readily with clients report feeling 'devastated'[110] when their client's case is dismissed,[111] while emotional labour resulting in emotional dissonance and the maintenance of a detached persona can result in significant stress and depression. It is also important to note that, while there may be less effort required in expressing organisationally desired emotions when there is congruence between the organisationally desired and individually felt emotion, there remains an element of labour required to ensure that the emotion is displayed in an organisationally appropriate way.[112]

Emotional labour has also been associated with burnout and symptoms of depression. Pugliesi notes that '[e]motional labor can also be exhausting, it can be perceived as stressful, and it can increase psychological distress and symptoms of depression'.[113] While several studies have examined the prevalence of depressive symptoms in the professions, including the legal profession, these studies did not consider emotional work demands as predictors.[114] However, legal professionals have been shown to have higher levels of depression than any other profession: a study conducted by Eaton which studied 28 professions in America, found evidence that lawyers were 3.6 times more likely to suffer a major depressive disorder than other members of the population within the same social demographic.[115] A more recent study in carried out in Australia found that Australian solicitors and

---

[108] KJ Lively, 'Client Contact and Emotional Labor—Upsetting the Balance' (2002) 29 *Work and Occupations* 198, 208.

[109] Ibid, 209.

[110] Westaby, '"Feeling Like a Sponge"' (n 47) 168.

[111] Hochschild (n 43) suggests that identifying too wholeheartedly with the job may result in burnout.

[112] Morris and Feldman (n 43) 988.

[113] K Pugliesi, 'The Consequences of Emotional Labor: Effects on Work Stress, Job Satisfaction, and Well-Being' (1999) 23 *Motivation and Emotion* 125, 130. See also RJ Erickson and AS Wharton, 'Inauthenticity and Depression: Assessing the Consequences of Interactive Service Work' (1997) 24 *Work and Occupations* 188.

[114] See for example, A Elwork, G Andrew and H Benjamin, 'Lawyers in Distress' (1995) *Journal of Psychiatry & Law* 205; and J Hagan and F Kay, 'Even Lawyers Get the Blues: Gender, Depression and Job Satisfaction in Legal Practice' (2007) 41 *Law & Society Review* 51.

[115] WW Eaton et al, 'Occupations and the Prevalence of Major Depressive Disorder' (1990) 32 *Journal of Occupational Medicine* 1079, 1081–83.

barristers have much higher levels of psychological distress and depression than the general population, 'confirming the view, hitherto based largely on anecdotal evidence and the few available Australian studies, that there exists a connection between practising law in Australia and experiencing disproportionate levels of distress and depression'.[116] Within the profession, there may be a subset of practitioners who are more at risk, with criminal defence lawyers and prosecutors found to have 'suffered more vicarious trauma effects, depression, stress and adverse beliefs about the safety of themselves and others than did their colleagues (academics and conveyancers) who did not work with traumatised clients'.[117] This is an important finding, linking higher levels of vicarious trauma, stress and depression to a branch of the profession engaging with high levels of emotions. Bandes has also suggested that behaviours adopted to deal with emotions in the workplace by criminal defence lawyers 'may contribute to personal dysfunction, including an unbalanced approach to life, difficulties relating to peers, family, friends, and clients, stress-related physical problems, and far higher than average rates of depression and substance abuse'.[118] While these studies focused on one branch of the profession, it is clear that engagement with high levels of emotion is not unique to criminal lawyers, and that other branches of the profession, including family or property lawyers, may be exposed to high levels of emotion, with the attendant risks.

The causes of these negative effects must be multifaceted and result from a complex interplay of events and circumstances[119] including inflexible working conditions, heavy workloads and a struggle to achieve a satisfactory work–life balance.[120] The commercial realities of modern practice[121] linked to the pressures created by the significant challenges faced by the legal professions towards the end of the twentieth century and the start of the twenty-first century, including changes to regulation, legal aid and increasing numbers within the professions, may also play a role. However, it is suggested that we cannot continue to ignore the impact of emotional labour, and emotional dissonance in particular, on the mental health and wellbeing of legal professionals.

The impact of the current paradigm in legal education which 'celebrates reason and devalues emotions'[122] on students should also be evaluated. The removal

---

[116] S Medlow, N Kelk and I Hickie, 'Depression and the Law: Experiences of Australian Barristers and Solicitors' (2011) *Sydney Law Review* 771, 790.

[117] Ibid 790, 793 and referencing L Vrklevski and J Franklin, 'Vicarious Trauma: The Impact on Solicitors of Exposure to Traumatic Material' (2008) 14 *Traumatology* 106.

[118] Bandes, 'Repression and Denial in Criminal Lawyering' (n 35) 376.

[119] R Collier, '"Love Law, Love Life": Neoliberalism, Wellbeing and Gender in the Legal Profession—The Case of Law School' (2014) 17 *Legal Ethics* 202, 214.

[120] Collier has suggested that prudence and problem-solving are recognised as laudable attributes within the profession with the result that successful lawyers may also be more likely to be pessimistic—ibid, 210.

[121] Including the pressure to maximise billable hours and attract clients.

[122] Harris and Shultz (n 53) 1773.

of emotion from the classroom leads to less engaged students, truncates intellectual enquiry and leads to weaker reasoning among students. Students are asked
to learn and think in a way which is not reflective of their understanding of the
world and their reality, and results in them feeling alienated. Harris and Shultz
suggest that 'the attempt to stifle rather than utilise [emotions] exacerbates the felt
thinness and irrelevance of much discussion in the law school classroom'.[123] More
significantly, several studies in a number of jurisdictions suggest that law students
also suffer from higher rates of mental health problems than other student groups,
despite beginning law school with rates similar to the general population;[124]
according to one study carried out in the United States,

> by the spring of their 1L [first year in law school] year, 32% of law students are clinically
> depressed, despite being no more depressed than the general public (about 8%) when
> they entered law school. By graduation, this number had risen to 40%.[125]

In a further study, law students displayed 'higher levels of psychological dysfunction and illness at more intense levels than the general population, and more
often'.[126] Pritchard and McIntosh suggest that the research 'indicate[s] that what
causes the distress is something about the law school experience rather than law
students being atypical before entering law school'.[127]

In light of the above discussion, it is clear that there may something about the
culture of law and legal education which results in law being considered a 'dangerous profession'[128] and an important factor in this may be the impact of emotional

---

[123] Ibid.

[124] Including higher rates of depression and alcohol abuse—see ME Pritchard and DN McIntosh,
'What Predicts Adjustment Among Law Students? A Longitudinal Panel Study' (2003) 143 *Journal of
Social Psychology* 727, 728. It is important to note that there are significant differences between how
students are educated in various jurisdictions which may produce differing results in studies of this
nature. However, in response to concerns about the cross-jurisdictional applicability of research conducted in the United States on this topic, a study was conducted in Australia in 2009 which again found
that law students in Australia were more likely to experience high levels of psychological distress. The
research found that 35% of law students experience high levels of psychological distress, a rate 17%
higher than medical students and 20% higher than the general population—see N Kelk, G Luscombe,
S Medlow and I Hickie, *Courting the Blues: Attitudes Towards Depression in Australian Law Students
and Lawyers* (University of Sydney, Brain and Mind Research Institute, 2009): www.cald.asn.au/docs/
Law%20Report%20Website%20version%204%20May%2009.pdf.

[125] BS Clarke, 'Law Professors, Law Students and Depression ... A Story of Coming Out' (2014)
4 *Journal of Law* 219, 221. See also American Association of Law Schools Committee, 'Report of the
AALS Special Committee on Problems of Substance Abuse in the Law Schools' (1995) 44 *Journal of
Legal Education* 35, 40.

[126] JRP Ogloff, DR Lyons, KS Douglas and VG Rose, '"More Than 'Learning To Think Like
A Lawyer": The Empirical Research on Legal Education' (2000) 34 *Creighton Law Review* 73, 126 (citing
SB Shanfield, G Andrew and H Benjamin, 'Psychiatric Distress in Law Students' (1985) 35 *Journal of
Legal Education* 65, 68).

[127] Pritchard and McIntosh (n 124) 728.

[128] James (n 105) 124. James notes that: 'Law is a dangerous profession. Over the past two decades
studies in America have shown that lawyers suffer significant levels of depression, other mental
illnesses, alcoholism, drug abuse and poor physical health, in addition to high rates of divorce and
suicidal ideation'—ibid, 124.

labour on professionals and law students.[129] Studies to date have pointed primarily to factors such as heavy workload and inflexible working conditions, but it is important that the role of 'display rules' and emotional suppression should be explored in more depth at this time. As Bandes notes:

> [T]he traditional view tends to ensure that the emotional variables affecting legal practice will receive inadequate attention. There may be no other profession whose practitioners are required to deal with so much pain with so little support and guidance. And there is ample evidence that we could use the help: levels of alcoholism, drug abuse, depression, and other serious dysfunction that are well above those for other stressful professions.[130]

IV. Conclusion

Throughout this chapter we have attempted to convey the general importance of human emotions and how a variety of feelings are central to the legal profession. Indeed, as humans, legal professionals are as susceptible as anyone else to experience emotions in many different contexts, including when relating to clients and peers. As indicated by our review of the literature, emotional labour often entails a substantial energy expenditure on controlling one's emotions. Despite the factors that we have been discussing, lawyers continue to be taught to laud reason, logic and rationality, while the importance of feelings and emotions is ignored in legal education. Modern research suggests that emotions are not merely unthinking and primitive; instead, they become part of a person's cognitive processes and exist because of their contributions to survival. Throughout this chapter we have explored the costs of the prevalent view of emotions on members of the legal profession. While research suggests that legal professionals endorse a narrow conception of emotion and regard emotions as primitive and lacking value, it is possible to educate legal professionals and effect change. Just as Maroney and Gross put forward a 'new ideal of the "good judge"'[131] who seeks to manage emotion skilfully rather than eliminate it completely,[132] it is suggested that all legal professionals should also be encouraged in this endeavour and practical steps should be taken by educators and professional bodies in support.

Acknowledging the extent to which legal professionals themselves engage in emotional labour, and being aware of the deleterious impact of emotional suppression and emotional dissonance on their own mental health, may be a step in the right direction. Legal educators, employers and professional bodies should

---

[129] Ibid.

[130] Bandes, 'Repression and Denial in Criminal Lawyering' (n 35) 342.

[131] TA Maroney and JJ Gross, 'The Ideal of the Dispassionate Judge: An Emotion Regulation Perspective' (2014) 6 *Emotion Review* 142, 143.

[132] Ibid, 143.

recognise the need to support and educate legal professionals on how to manage their emotions and minimise the negative impacts of emotional labour. This could be achieved through ongoing educational initiatives offered by professional bodies on emotion, emotional labour and mental health. Given the important role played by ethical codes in perpetuating existing norms within the professions, a review of existing codes within the professions to reflect a more nuanced understanding of emotions would be beneficial. Special effort by legal educators to engage with emotions in the classroom and to promote a more rounded understanding of emotions, including the dangers of emotional suppression and dissonance, would reduce the risks associated with the practice of law for the next generation of legal professionals. The aim of this chapter has been to raise awareness of this need and argue for a less hostile view of emotions in the practice of law. While cultural norms about emotions within the legal system do not change overnight, nevertheless, the traditional paradigm of the calm and dispassionate lawyer has had its day.

12

Emotion and the Discourse of Judging

TERRY A MARONEY[*]

I. Introduction

Emotion typically is both banished from legal discourse *about* judging and presumed to be absent within the discourse *of* judging. Traditional legal discourse about judging presumes a standard of 'dispassion', reflecting a normative judgement that judges should not feel emotion or allow any such feelings to affect their decisions.[1] The discourse of judging has developed to satisfy that norm, such that judges often suppress or disguise the influence of emotion in their actions and words. Neither discourse creates adequate space for the reality of judicial emotion. Legal disputes operate within a territory shaped by the emotional experiences, commitments and dynamics of a large cast of characters—including judges. Further, legal disputes create emotional experiences, commitments and dynamics—including in judges. Our collective understanding of judicial decision-making therefore must openly account for emotion.

In this chapter I briefly explore two different angles on this theme: first, scholarly theory and commentary about the actual and proper role of emotion in judging; and second, evidence that emerges from the artifacts of judging, such as written decisions, media reports and personal accounts. The line between these two angles is not always sharp, as judges traditionally have been among the theorists promulgating the first level of discourse as well as those generating the second. It remains useful, though, in capturing the relationship between the ideas about the thing and the thing itself.

[*] Professor of Law, Professor of Medicine, Health and Society, Vanderbilt University
[1] TA Maroney, 'The Persistent Cultural Script of Judicial Dispassion' (2011) 99 *California Law Review* 629.

II. Emotion in Discourse About Judging

Traditionally, emotion has enjoyed two opposing characterisations in popular and scholarly discourse about judging. Either it is described as absent, which absence is a supposed marker of judicial competence, or its presence is noted as a supposed marker of judicial incompetence.

An early exemplar of the former characterisation may be found in *Leviathan*, in which Thomas Hobbes declared that the ideal judge is 'divested of all fear, anger, hatred, love, and compassion'.[2] His mid-1600s view was echoed some centuries later by the German scholar Karl Wurzel, who in the early 1900s classified 'dispassionateness of the judge' as a fundamental tenet of Western jurisprudence.[3] Indeed, Wurzel wrote, lawyers were 'the first and the most emphatic in insisting on the absence of emotional bias', because 'absence of emotion is a prerequisite of all scientific thinking', and judges, more so than other scientific thinkers, regularly are 'exposed ... to emotional influences'.[4] Even the decisional structures built into the US Constitution, such as the sharp separation of the judicial, executive and legislative branches, were meant to position judges as a bulwark against the perceived evils of emotion, particularly popular emotion.[5] I have called this remarkably stable narrative the 'persistent cultural script of judicial dispassion'.[6]

This script remains alive and well. It is true even today that to call a judge emotional is viewed as a sharp insult.[7] A prominent commentator, for example, harshly criticised the late US Supreme Court Justice Harry Blackmun for his 'legally unsophisticated and overly emotional ... jurisprudence of sentiment', characterised by 'over-ripe, self-dramatizing' and 'purple' prose. This jurisprudence, the author continued, rendered Blackmun a failure because 'feeling deeply is not a substitute for arguing rigorously', and because 'a big heart and the capacity to feel pain are not enough for success on the Supreme Court'. He compared Blackmun with the late Justice Frank Murphy, who in the author's view 'wrote emotional dissents' but 'whose tendency to let his heart get the better of his head deprived him of lasting influence'.[8]

The script of dispassion enjoyed a recent resurgence in the United States during the 2009 hearings to confirm Sonia Sotomayor as a Justice of the US Supreme Court. President Obama expressed his intent to favour a candidate with 'empathy'

---

[2] T Hobbes, *Leviathan* (first published 1651, AR Waller (ed), Cambridge University Press 1904) 203.

[3] KG Wurzel, 'Methods of Juridical Thinking' in E Bruncken and LB Register (eds), *Science of Legal Method: Select Essays by Various Authors* (trans Ernest Bruncken, The MacMillan Company, 1921) 298.

[4] Ibid, 298–99.

[5] D Gewirtzman, 'Our Founding Feelings' (2009) 43 *University of Richmond Law Review* 623, 679.

[6] Maroney, 'Persistent Cultural Script' (n 1).

[7] J Rosen, 'Sentimental Journey: The Emotional Jurisprudence of Harry Blackmun' *The New Republic* (2 May 1994) 13–14.

[8] Ibid, 13.

and listed among Sotomayor's qualifications her 'sense of compassion'.[9] The backlash was swift. Many senators (perhaps not coincidentally, those from the party opposed to President Obama) decried empathy as 'touchy-feely stuff',[10] warned that judges were being invited to ignore law and rule on the basis of 'personal … feelings'[11] and insisted that the most critical judicial quality is 'the capacity to set aside one's own feelings so he or she can blindly and dispassionately administer equal justice for all'.[12] This political response was strongly seconded in public discourse; a variety of commentators declared that 'emotive judges' are inclined to partiality,[13] led astray by 'passion' that, unlike rational argument, is 'inscrutable, idiosyncratic, and justified in and of itself'.[14] Even Sotomayor's defenders appeared to concede the point, as they defended empathy primarily on the grounds that it was a cognitive capacity to understand the experiences of others, not an emotion.[15] Summing up the apparent weight of popular opinion, one critic wrote that 'the compassionate, empathetic judge is very likely to be a bad judge'.[16]

Faced with this barrage of anti-emotion sentiment Sotomayor, too, largely conceded the point. 'Judges can't rely on what's in their heart[s]', she testified before the US Senate Judiciary Committee, because '[i]t's not the heart that compels conclusions in cases, it's the law'. Though she acknowledged that judges are 'not robots [who] listen to evidence and don't have feelings', the only acceptable response—as she explained it—is 'to recognize those feelings and put them aside'.[17] Sotomayor mouthed the script, and whether she believed it or not all were (more or less) mollified. In the wake of the Sotomayor incident the idea that emotion

---

[9] Obama nomination remarks, quoted in J Hasnas, 'The Unseen Deserve Empathy Too' *Wall Street Journal* (29 May 2009) A15; Barack Obama, Remarks to Planned Parenthood Action Fund (17 July 2007): perma.cc/YM5F-A48M: ('[W]e need somebody who's got the heart—the empathy—to recognize what it's like to be a young teenage mom, to be poor or African-American or gay or disabled or old—and that's the criteria by which I'll be selecting my judges'). See generally, SA Bandes, 'Empathetic Judging and the Rule of Law' (2009) *Cardozo Law Review De Novo* 133.

[10] 'Confirmation hearing on the nomination of Hon Sonia Sotomayor, to be an associate justice of the Supreme Court of the United States' (S Hrg 111-503, 14–16 July 2009): perma.cc/HCZ5-QY93 (statement of Senator Lindsay Graham) 135.

[11] J Sessions, 'Guest Commentary: "Empathy" no basis for judicial rulings' (*MLive*, Grand Rapids, 13 July 2009): perma.cc/B3P2-JXNC; see also 'Confirmation hearing' (n 10) (written statement of Senator Jeff Sessions) 1318–22.

[12] 'Confirmation hearing' (n 10) (statement of Senator Charles Grassley) 17.

[13] J Yoo, 'Closing Arguments: Obama Needs a Neutral Justice' *Philadelphia Inquirer* (10 May 2009).

[14] M Goldblatt, 'Against Judicial Empathy: Why the Supreme Court Must Be the Most Dispassionate of the Three Branches of Government' *National Review* (New York, 10 June 2009).

[15] R Just, 'The Empathy War' *The New Republic* (New York, 14 July 2009): perma.cc/5STU-SM6E; George Lakoff, 'Empathy, Sotomayor, and Democracy: The Conservative Stealth Strategy' *Huffington Post* (New York, 30 May 2009): perma.cc/YMM5-GLKR; K Greenfield, 'The Supreme Court, Empathy and the Science of Decision Making' *Huffington Post* (New York, 25 May 2009): perma.cc/HXG2-HPNZ; and Dahlia Lithwick, 'Once More, Without Feeling: The GOP's Misguided and Confused Campaign Against Judicial Empathy' *Slate* (New York, 11 May 2009).

[16] Hasnas (n 9).

[17] A Terkel, 'Sotomayor: "We're Not Robots"' *Think Progress* (Washington DC, 14 July 2009): perma.cc/9P9J-EWTM (statement of Sotomayor).

might influence judging was characterised as 'radioactive',[18] a must-to-avoid for subsequent judicial nominees.

The discourse lauding judicial dispassion has proven to be both persistent and culturally dominant. It has not, however, gone unchallenged. It has met with periodic dissents, some of which have altered the script and rendered it vulnerable to replacement.

Interestingly, from time to time legal systems have been structured so as to prefer, not suppress, certain manifestations of judicial emotion. While research on such script-defying moments is scarce, a few instances are worthy of mention. Looking to ancient times we may note the Babylonian Talmud's disqualification of childless men from judging capital cases—which, at that time, included most criminal cases. That case-driven disqualification from the Sanhedrin was justified on the ground that the childless are 'devoid of paternal tenderness' and therefore would lack a desired level of sympathetic care for the human interests at stake—not just for the defendant's life but also for the emotional lives of his parents.[19] More recently, we have seen the invention of an entirely new kind of judge, one who would populate the early-twentieth century juvenile courts in the United States. The institution of a separate court for juveniles accused of criminal offences was an innovation that began in Chicago and quickly spread throughout the nation and world.[20] One of the first juvenile court judges, Julian Mack, wrote movingly of the host of emotional qualities such a judge should possess, including a love of children and a 'sympathetic spirit'.[21] Such a judge, Mack wrote, would treat accused delinquents as would a 'wise and merciful father'.

Though they are separated by several centuries, these narratives have much in common. In both narratives judges were asked to have the capacity for empathy, which was believed to spark compassion, which in turn was predicted to manifest in mercy. In neither narrative, however, was this empathic arc seen as critical for judging in the ordinary case. Sanhedrin judges hearing property and commercial cases could be childless; adult criminal court judges could be heartless. Indeed, the preference for compassionate judges was deeply instrumental. Fathers serving on the Sanhedrin would, it was thought, minimise imposition of capital punishment, consistent with elites' preference to maintain the practice in name (believing themselves commanded by religious doctrine to do so) while eliminating it in practice. The fatherly juvenile court judge would protect young offenders from the harms regularly visited on adult offenders, and would instead deliver the rehabilitative product that the courts' advocates believed preferable as a matter of

---

[18] P Baker, 'In Court Nominees, is Obama Looking for Empathy by Another Name?' *New York Times* (26 April 2010) A12.

[19] TA Maroney and P Ackerman-Lieberman, '"As A Father Shows Compassion for His Children": Ancient and Contemporary Perspectives on Judicial Empathy' (2014) 3 *Journal of Law, Religion and State* 240.

[20] DS Tanenhaus, *Juvenile Justice in the Making* (New York, Oxford University Press, 2004).

[21] JW Mack, 'The Juvenile Court' (1909) *23 Harvard Law Review* 104, 107.

public policy and child development. While these structures preferring particular emotional commitments from their judges stand in sharp contrast to the script of dispassion, the fact that they were somewhat of a specialty product prevented them from challenging the script at its core.

A more frontal challenge to the script was raised by the early-twentieth century Legal Realists. The Realists—a major jurisprudential force in the United States— challenged a great multitude of ways in which they believed that legal theory misrepresented law as objective and certain.[22] One of the hidden contributors to law—both as written and as implemented—to which they called attention was emotion. As the great scholar and judge Benjamin Cardozo proposed, to engage fully with 'what judges really do' requires dialogue on the contrast between 'reason versus emotion'[23] and a more forthright acknowledgment of the latter. He wrote further that while most of judges' conscious decisions could be attributed to rec-ognised legal factors—such as respect for precedent and principles of statutory interpretation—that explanation was too shallow. Instead, he wrote: 'Deep below consciousness are other forces, the likes and the dislikes, the predilections and the prejudices, the complex of instincts and emotions and habits and convictions, which make the man, whether he be litigant or judge'.[24] Cardozo's was a particu-larly prominent voice in the Realist era, but it was far from the only one. A contem-porary wrote that judge-made law 'grows up in the semi-darkness of ignorance and emotion' rather than 'in the strong light of pure reason'.[25] Another noted that judges were influenced by 'sympathies they could not help but feel', based on their life experiences;[26] an example offered by yet another Realist thinker was a judge's 'known animosity' towards a lawyer, which might affect his rulings.[27]

To a modern-day ear these assertions may seem entirely obvious, perhaps even banal. For insight into just how contrarian they were at the time, how in ten-sion with acceptable discourse about judging, consider this account by Joseph Hutcheson, a federal trial judge. He wrote that he was prepared to be 'stoned in the street' for declaring that good judges, not just unavoidably human judges, rely on 'feelings' and 'hunch'. As a young lawyer, in contrast, Hutcheson was so invested in a formalist view of law that

> if anyone had suggested that the judge had a right to feel, or hunch out a new cat-
> egory into which to place relations under his investigation, I should have repudiated

---

[22] See eg, R Pound, 'The Call for a Realist Jurisprudence' (1931) 44 *Harvard Law Review* 697; K Llewellyn, 'Some Realism about Realism: Responding to Dean Pound' (1931) 44 *Harvard Law Review* 1222.

[23] BN Cardozo, 'Jurisprudence, Lecture before the Association of the Bar of the City of New York' in ME Hall (ed), *Selected Writings of Benjamin Nathan Cardozo* (Fallon Publications, 1941) 19.

[24] BN Cardozo, *The Nature of the Judicial Process* (New Haven, CT, Yale University Press, 1921) 167–68.

[25] AL Corbin, 'The Law and the Judges' (1914) 3 *Yale Review* 250.

[26] C Grove Haines, 'General Observations on the Effects of Personal, Political, and Economic Influences in the Decisions of Judges' (1922) 17 *University of Illinois Law Review* 96, 115.

[27] J Dickinson, 'Legal Rules: Their Function in the Process of Decision' (1931) 79 *University of Pennsylvania Law Review* 833, 838.

the suggestion as unscientific and unsound, while as to the judge who dared to do it, I should have cried, 'Away with him!'.[28]

A similarly evangelical note was sounded by Jerome Frank. His iconoclastic *Law and the Modern Mind*,[29] written a decade before he became a judge, made a particularly strong claim: in it he argued that lawyers and judges approached law with the '*emotional* attitudes of childhood', characterised by longings for a stable, authoritarian father.[30] This emotional drive fed a fantasy that certainty was possible and fuelled a concomitant need to insist on law's objectivity, with the result that law was treated as a father substitute.[31] Frank's ideal judge was one emotionally 'adult' enough to reject the fantasy.[32] Such a judge would not reject emotion itself, which Frank characterised as 'a large component of a trial judge's reaction' to cases.[33] Indeed, he disclaimed any 'naïve notion' that a judge without any 'emotional attitudes' exists, and declared bluntly that he had 'no desire to live in a society in which such sub-human or super-human judges exercised the power of judging'.[34]

Compared with the specialty-product model presented by the Sanhedrin and juvenile court visions of judging, certainly the Realist embrace was far broader. In the Realist account emotion potentially reached into every corner of judging, in every court, in every case. But what the Realist account gained in breadth it lost in specificity. The Realists were never able to specify precisely what they meant by emotion, often clustering the concept together with intuition, hunch, bias and the workings of the subconscious. Nor were they able to describe exactly what they thought emotion's influence to be. In Cardozo's words, '[h]ow much of the process is to be classified as reasoning and how much as mere emotion, the students of juristic method have been unable to agree'.[35] Finally, they seemed unable to decide whether that influence—whatever it might be—was a good or a bad thing. At one moment the Realists might enthusiastically embrace emotion and at others they might deride it as 'spasmodic'[36] or a 'perverting influence'.[37]

These theoretical stumbling blocks seriously limited the Realists' success in normalising dialogue about judicial emotion. Well into the post-Realist era the great Justice Felix Frankfurter echoed Hobbes in writing that a judge must 'submerge

---

[28] JC Hutcheson, 'The Judgment Intuitive: The Function of the 'Hunch' in Judicial Decision' (1929) 14 *Cornell Law Review* 274, 274.

[29] J Frank, *Law and the Modern Mind* (New York, Brentano's Inc, 1930) 143.

[30] Ibid, 89.

[31] Ibid.

[32] Ibid, 153, 177, 269–70.

[33] JN Frank, 'Say It With Music' (1948) 61 *Harvard Law Review* 921, 932.

[34] JN Frank, 'What Courts Do In Fact Part Two' (1932) 26 *University of Illinois Law Review* 761, 764, fn 55.

[35] Cardozo, *The Nature of the Judicial Process* (n 24) 44–45.

[36] Cardozo, 'Jurisprudence' (n 23) 141.

[37] Frank, *Law and the Modern Mind* (n 29) 148, 268.

private feeling on every aspect of a case'.[38] But the Realists certainly had *some* impact. By articulating something so thoroughly and obviously true—judges have emotions and they matter—they shifted the discourse in a subtle but important way. In the post-Realist era it has become possible, even commonplace, to acknowledge that truth. As Justice Robert Jackson wrote in 1944, truly 'dispassionate judges' are 'mythical beings' like 'Santa Claus or Uncle Sam or Easter bunnies'.[39] We now expect judges to manage their inevitable emotions. Even Frankfurter did not deny private feeling; he rather denied it any power. As Jerome Frank wrote:

> We cannot, if we would, get rid of emotions in the field of justice. The best we can hope for is that the emotions of the judge will become more sensitive, more nicely balanced, more subject to [the judge's] own scrutiny, more capable of detailed articulation.[40]

Certainly, the way in which we expect judges to manage emotion remains heavily tainted by the script of dispassion. If the pre-Realist vision of the 'good judge' was of one who felt no emotion, the contemporary vision is of one who recognises her emotions and firmly puts them aside. This is, of course, precisely the script that Sotomayor delivered.

After the Legal Realists' heyday the discourse on emotion in judging enjoyed a long slumber. It was reawakened by US Supreme Court Justice William J Brennan, who in a 1987 lecture praised Cardozo for having called attention to the 'complex interplay of forces—rational and emotional, conscious and unconscious—by which no judge could remain unaffected'. Brennan declared that it was time to answer Cardozo's largely-forgotten call for the vital 'dialogue of reason and passion' in judging.[41] Brennan argued that though the idea of dispassionate judges once served a useful role in fostering early American democracy, in the modern era 'the greatest threat to due process principles is formal reason severed from the insights of passion'.[42] Passion—which he defined as 'the range of emotional and intuitive responses to a given set of facts or arguments, responses which often speed into our consciousness far ahead of the lumbering syllogisms of reason'—does not 'taint the judicial process, but is in fact central to its vitality'.[43]

Brennan's vision, it appears, went a step further than Cardozo's, in that he more aggressively and consistently embraced a positive role for emotion. In some respects, however, his vision was also much like that of the Sanhedrin and juvenile court models. While Brennan's embrace of emotion had broad narrative sweep, his specific target was quite narrow; he advocated passion only in the context of judicial interpretation of due process claims made under the US Constitution. Further, he advocated passion in that domain for an instrumental purpose—avoiding a

---

[38] *Public Utilities Comm'n v Pollak*, 343 US 451, 466 (1952) (Frankfurter J mem).
[39] *United States v Ballard*, 322 US 78, 93–94 (1944) (Jackson J dissenting).
[40] Frank, *Law and the Modern Mind* (n 29) 153.
[41] WJ Brennan, 'Reason, Passion, and "The Progress of the Law"' (1988) 10 *Cardozo Law Review* 3.
[42] Ibid, 17.
[43] Ibid, 3, 9 (citing M Peterson (ed), *Thomas Jefferson: Writings* (New York, The Library of America, 1984) 874).

detached formalism that would tend to disfavour such claims—that he positioned against a disfavoured backdrop, a perceived trend towards an 'alien' and 'sterile' bureaucracy in which law was playing a part.[44] Brennan may in fact have imagined a much more expansive role for judicial emotion but he did not offer it. Even after Brennan's bold call, then, it remained unclear whether the claim was that emotion might offer something of value in judging generally.

Other scholars and judges have since more squarely made that claim. Judge Richard Posner, a prolific author on judicial decision-making, is perhaps the most prominent to have done so. Posner has sought to debunk the underlying fear of emotion as irrational by citing psychological and philosophical accounts; those accounts demonstrate that emotions are 'triggered by information', express 'an evaluation of that information' and motivate action.[45] Posner therefore rejects the notion that judges should 'be emotionless, like computers', and takes it as a given that emotion ought to 'enter into their judgments' in some way[46] and that good judging may even require emotion.[47] Here the Posnerian account thins considerably. He suggests that cases presenting a 'zone of reasonableness', within which one may articulate multiple correct answers, admit of more emotional engagement than others[48] and would benefit from judicial capacity to feel 'empathy or fellow feeling', particularly towards absent parties.[49] Posner further proposes that judges have different emotional propensities and profiles; that they are professionally motivated to avoid shame and guilt by doing a good job; that emotion may operate differently on the trial and appellate courts; and that the decisions of multi-judge courts (such as appellate panels in the United States) are influenced by emotional dynamics among the participants.[50] Most controversially—and most reminiscent of Brennan's vision—Posner asserts that emotion reveals legally relevant moral truths towards which judges cannot reason.[51] Thus, he claims, if a law sanctioning a moral violation with 'no plausible social-functional justification' were 'challenged before an emotionless judge' he would be unable to muster a rational justification for upholding it. In contrast, a judge 'with a normal emotional endowment would reject the challenge out of hand because his emotions told him to do so', which would be 'the correct response'.[52]

---

[44] Brennan (n 41) 18–19 (quoting Max Weber in G Roth and C Wittich (eds), *Economy and Society* (Berkeley, CA, University of California Press, 1978) 975).

[45] RA Posner, *Frontiers of Legal Theory* (Cambridge, MA, Harvard University Press, 2001) 226–28; RA Posner, *How Judges Think* (Cambridge, MA, Harvard University Press, 2008) 106.

[46] Posner, *Frontiers of Legal Theory* (n 45) 226.

[47] Ibid, 241–42.

[48] Posner, *How Judges Think* (n 45) 86–87, 102, 51.

[49] Posner, *Frontiers of Legal Theory* (n 45) 243, 245.

[50] Posner, *How Judges Think* (n 45) 39, 73–76, 132–35; Posner, *Frontiers of Legal Theory* (n 45) 228, 245.

[51] Posner, *Frontiers of Legal Theory* (n 45) 242–43.

[52] Ibid.

The contemporary philosopher of law, Martha Nussbaum, also has floated thought experiments about judicial emotion and has covered much of the same ground, at about the same level of generality. Her most focused treatment of the theme is a 1996 lecture responding to the criticism of Blackmun as having been overly emotional.[53] Like Posner, Nussbaum thoroughly debunks the idea that emotion is necessarily irrational—indeed, Posner later relied heavily on her work in making that point.[54] She asks, rather, whether the traditional objection might instead reflect a concern that emotion might lead judges towards what she colourfully called 'an inappropriate[ly] gushy way of proceeding'.[55] This she characterises as an 'interesting worry', one she appears not fully to share. Nussbaum draws on Adam Smith's *Theory of Moral Sentiments* to propose that a judge ought to engage with emotion as does a reader of literature or a concerned friend. That is, she muses, the judge should vividly imagine the emotions of the participants in any case before her but filter out 'that portion of anger, fear, and even compassion that focuses on the self in its cherished projects'.[56] Such a semi-distanced stance would allow the judge to share, for example, the participants' 'grief, but not its disabling and blinding excesses'.[57] Nussbaum's 'judicious spectator' would feel only such emotions as are 'tethered to the evidence'[58] and would work to avoid reactions stemming only from her 'personal goals and situation'.[59]

Though Nussbaum has not returned to this thought experiment, she elsewhere has introduced a tension within her theory by suggesting that a judge's personal reactions are sometimes both relevant and appropriate prompts to action. For example, she has defended legal decisions based on judges' 'outrage',[60] an emotion she characterises as a moral sentiment 'pertinent to legal judgment' and 'a reasoned judgment that can be publicly shared'.[61] Her positive assessment of outrage was, likely not coincidentally, made in the context of discussing a case with whose result she strongly agreed—preventing a convicted murderer from regaining possession of the instruments of his crime. In Nussbaum's work, then, we also find a critical indeterminacy. For most cases she appears to be advocating (if in a pensive, rather non-committal way) relative emotional distance, while she sees some subset of cases in which a more forthright emotional reaction as preferable in order to achieve a desired end.

Posner and Nussbaum thus have staked out the basics of the prevailing view among the script's growing number of contemporary dissenters: judicial emotion

---

[53] MC Nussbaum, 'Emotion in the Language of Judging' (1996) 70 *St John's Law Review* 25.
[54] Ibid, 25.
[55] Ibid.
[56] Ibid, 28.
[57] Ibid.
[58] Ibid, 30.
[59] Ibid, 28–30 (citing Adam Smith, *The Theory of Moral Sentiments* (London, Bell, 1880)).
[60] MC Nussbaum, *Hiding from Humanity: Disgust, Shame, and the Law* (Princeton, NJ, Princeton University Press, 2004) 169–70.
[61] Ibid, 170.

exists and in some way affects decisions, particularly in cases admitting of some discretion; further, emotion's influence should not be presumed to be deleterious and may in fact be beneficial.[62] We see much the same view echoed by Judge Irving Kaufman, who has written that when the law provides the judge 'with decisional leeway, we do well to recognize that our intuition, emotion and conscience are appropriate factors in the jurisprudential calculus'.[63] Accounts differ as to what sorts of cases fit these constraints—constitutional due process claims, for example, or cases resonating with strongly-held moral sentiments—and as to whether the emotions in question must be felt at a distance—with the judge as emotional proxy for others' interests—or can spring from the judge's own body, heart and mind.

Accounts differ, in part, because in a diverse society they must differ. The intellectual history makes clear that evaluation of judicial emotion is inescapably value-laden. It is difficult to imagine making judgements as to its propriety without some sort of normative guideposts tethered to an instrumental goal. We desire emotion, whether it be empathy or outrage, only if it will help judges take correct actions. Unfortunately, this necessary normativity tends to be buried or disclaimed even in contemporary accounts.

III. Emotion in the Discourse of Judging

Having looked to scholarly and popular discourse about judging, we now turn to an examination of the picture of emotion that emerges from judging itself. This picture is necessarily pointillist. Its dots of colour consist of judges' expressions of emotion in the written word, oral remarks, videotaped episodes and the like, with some outlines of structure provided by judges' first-person accounts.[64]

What emerges is a full range of emotions, as one would expect in a job that requires daily engagement with the human drama, whether in person (for the trial judge) or on paper (for the appellate judge). Not only must judges attend to, police

---

[62] SH Pillsbury, 'Harlan, Holmes, and the Passions of Justice' in SA Bandes (ed), *The Passions of Law* (New York, New York University Press, 2009) 333, 350; SA Bandes, 'Introduction' in SA Bandes (ed), *The Passions of Law* (New York, New York University Press, 1999) 1, 6–7; LE Little, 'Adjudication and Emotion' (2002) 3 *Florida Coastal Law Journal* 205, 218.

[63] IJ Kaufman, 'The Anatomy of Decisionmaking' (1984) 53 *Fordham Law Review* 1, 16.

[64] Like much of the analysis in this chapter, my focus here is on the United States. While the study of judicial emotion is not entirely limited to the United States—I also discuss some evidence from Northern Ireland, Australia and Sweden—the literature would be significantly enriched by a more international focus. Given how deeply rooted the notion of 'dispassion' is within Western jurisprudence it would be surprising in any contemporary Western legal system to find radical departures from the themes I explore. The same cannot be presupposed about the broader diverse swathe of legal cultures around the world, and even within Western democracies the likely impact of local culture should not be underestimated.

and channel the emotions of jurors, witnesses, lawyers and the public, but—as the Realists insisted—they clearly experience their own. Judges routinely encounter disturbing evidence that can trigger shock and disgust.[65] The parade of misery they must confront in their chambers and courtrooms—stemming from broken families, drug and alcohol addiction, carelessness, violence, greed, fraud and petty disputes, to name a few persistent triggers—can make judges angry and sad. Inability to fix all these ills can make them feel frustrated, even depressed.[66] Difficult colleagues and fierce intra-court personality clashes are not uncommon.[67] The pressure of decisional authority can weigh heavily.[68] Security concerns, backed by infrequent but salient episodes of retaliatory violence, weigh heavily as well. Fortunately, judges also experience pleasant emotions: joy when a needy child is placed with a family; hope when a drug-court defendant completes treatment; pride in crafting a tightly reasoned, well written opinion. A judge's emotions will be as varied as is his or her work.

As we seek to compile the evidence of this rich emotional palette some words of caution are in order. Finding emotion in judicial artifacts is not a straightforward enterprise. Not only do judges often mask emotion in order to project compliance with the script of dispassion,[69] but they may manufacture, manipulate, or exaggerate emotional expression in order to achieve their goals. As Lawrence Baum has elucidated, judicial behaviour is at least in part a performance aimed at a target audience.[70] Any regular observer in a juvenile court, for example, has witnessed judges 'ginning up' a stern demeanour, complete with displays of disappointment and anger, in an attempt to evoke fear or remorse in a young offender. Such emotional performativity is itself interesting and worthy of far greater study. For present purposes it is worth noting as a factor complicating an effort to use judges' behaviour as a true metric of their emotional experience.

Further, reading emotion into judicial observations is particularly suspect if undisciplined or grounded in faddish theory. One Realist writer, for example, regarded judicial opinions as 'confessions' from which, using 'the laws of

---

[65] McAlinden's chapter in the current collection highlights a number of judicial responses to this, in relation to child sex child offenders—see ch 7.

[66] *Carrington v United States*, 503 F 3d 888, 899 (9th Cir, 2007) (Pregerson J, dissenting) ('sometimes [the judge] has to just sit up there and watch justice fail right in front of him, right in his own courtroom, and he doesn't know what to do about it, and it makes him feel sad ... Sometimes he even gets angry about it') (quoting GH Spence, *Of Murder and Madness: A True Story* (New York, Doubleday, 1983) 490).

[67] 'One Federal Judge Does Battle with 19 Others' *New York Times* (1 May 1996) B6.

[68] A Liptak, 'Justice Thomas, 5 Years Silent: There's No Arguing with Him' *New York Times* (13 February 2011) A1 (quoting Thomas as saying that some cases 'will drive you to your knees' and can make him 'morose'). A delightful fictionalised account of the emotional toll of deciding may be found in P Calamandrei, *Eulogy of Judges, Written By A Lawyer* (first published 1942, trans J Clark Adams and C Abbott Phillips, New Jersey, The Lawbook Exchange, 2006).

[69] RA Posner, 'The Role of the Judge in the Twenty-First Century' (2006) 86 *Boston University Law Review* 1049, 1065.

[70] See generally, L Baum, *Judges and their Audiences: A Perspective on Judicial Behavior* (Princeton, NJ, Princeton University Press, 2006).

emotional behavior', one might diagnose deep psychoanalytic issues.[71] He then relied on an opinion in which the judge had expressed disgust about sexual matters to diagnose him as suffering from Puritanical shame; he further concluded that the judge had likely patronised prostitutes.[72] A rough contemporary examined more data points in diagnosing judges' 'emotional personalities', including their family lives, vocal habits, physical attributes and professional interactions, but came to similarly suspect conclusions—for example, by relying on one judge's 'exhibitionist and homosexual trends', evidenced by a 'florid' writing style, 'conspicuous' clothes and 'foppish' hats, and his habit of allowing 'his hands to hang limp at the wrist'.[73] That these conclusions now seem painfully off-base should remind us that some of our present assumptions someday will appear similarly dated. While modern-day efforts to tease out emotional motivators and influences appear far less suspect by virtue of being grounded in a more sophisticated emotion epistemology, the enterprise remains fraught.[74]

These cautions inform the discussion that follows. It gives disproportionate attention to evidence of judicial anger, not because anger is the most important judicial emotion—though it appears to be one of the most commonly experienced—but because it is relatively easy to recognise.[75] The discussion also privileges observations that have a sound methodological basis or that emerge from judges who are making a concerted effort to be candid.

A. Moments of Judicial Candour About Emotion

Candour is a nice place to start. It is not uncommon for judges to explicitly articulate the post-Realist script in emotionally challenging cases. Such articulations tend to follow a simple formula: acknowledge the emotion and then announce that it will have no impact on the proceedings. For example, in a non-injury armed robbery case a trial court judge struggled over whether to disregard a prior conviction that, because of California's harsh three-strikes law, greatly lengthened the sentence. Noting the defendant's troubled youth, grossly inadequate parenting and early gang involvement, the judge said into the record:

> [T]his is not easy for the court … It's sad [that the defendant] started out very young and God knows there was nobody there to tell him right from wrong, obviously. And he's locked himself into this position of being a dangerous bad guy. And it's sad and it makes

[71] T Schroeder, 'The Psychological Study of Judicial Opinions' (1918) 6 *California Law Review* 89, 96, 104, 107.

[72] Ibid.

[73] HD Lasswell, *Power and Personality* (New York, WW Norton & Company, 1948) 28–39.

[74] Pillsbury (n 62) 331; SA Bandes, 'Fear and Degradation in Alabama: The Emotional Subtext of University of Alabama v Garrett' (2003) 5 *University of Pennsylvania Journal of Constitutional Law* 520, 521; Posner, *How Judges Think* (n 45) 75; LK Ray, 'Judicial Personality: Rhetoric and Emotion in Supreme Court Opinions' (2002) 59 *Washington and Lee Law Review* 193, 223–33.

[75] TA Maroney, 'Angry Judges' (2012) 65 *Vanderbilt Law Review* 1207.

the court sad but ... the court cannot justify [striking the prior conviction] as much as I would like to see this young man have some hope of salvage. The court feels it has no choice but to deny the motion.[76]

Similar themes may be seen in a very different opinion, one written by a state-court appellate judge in a case involving the killing of a pregnant woman with whom the defendant had a small child. This judge agreed with one of the defence arguments on appeal. Cognisant of the intense publicity surrounding the case and his lonely status in dissent, he wrote a highly unusual 'preface' before explaining the legal basis for his opinion that the defendant was entitled to a new trial. Its rare level of raw emotional content makes the preface worthy of quoting at length:

I have never been involved with a case which has generated as much publicity, public interest and sharply defined opinions ... This is not unexpected given the extensive media coverage, the fact a police officer was the defendant, the attendant human emotions generated by the death of an expectant mother and her unborn child, and the extensive, protracted search for [the victim]. But justice does not and should not rush to judgment ... I confess being somewhat dismayed by public reaction after [a local newspaper reported on] the upcoming oral argument. In the article, the names and pictures of this panel's members were displayed, something I can never recall having been done before. While attending worship service that Sunday morning, I was engaged on two separate occasions by others quick to share their opinion the appeal was meritless and the death penalty should have been given. The next day as I drove to work, I was distraught to hear a local radio talk show host rant about what a waste of taxpayer money it was to even allow [defendant] an appeal and, if it were up to him, [the defendant] should be put to death—not by lethal injection, but the 'old fashioned way', using the gas chamber or electric chair ... I was further discouraged by both the volume and tenor of readers' comments to [newspaper articles before and after argument]. Judges are not insensitive to public sentiment nor shielded from such expressions of public outcry. We live and work in this community ... I have authored thousands of opinions and participated in many thousands more ... But often a judge is remembered only for one significant decision and his or her career is then defined by that decision. Perhaps [this] case will prove to be my legacy; albeit, an infamous one.

God has blessed me with two children and graciously spared me the loss of a child or grandchild. I am saddened by the tragic loss of life this case presents and sympathize with the families of all involved. But, when I put on the robe as judge, I must not let my feelings, my emotions, much less public opinion, influence my review and application of the law. I am mindful of the admonition: 'do not pervert justice by siding with the crowd'. I anticipate my dissent will be met with disfavor by many [though] few will read our actual words ... But the oath of office I have sworn charges me with the responsibility to administer justice without respect to persons, faithfully and impartially, to the best of my ability and understanding. Such responsibility feels, at times, burdensome. Yet, it is one I willingly chose to accept when I sought and assumed the bench.[77]

---

[76] *People v Cerda*, No B146553, 2002 WL 418156 (Cal Ct App, 19 March 2002). The defendant was sentenced from 33 years to life.

[77] See eg, *States v Cutts*, No 2008CA000079, 2009 WL 2170687 (Ohio App 5 Dist, 22 July 2009) (Delaney J concurring).

The juxtaposition of these two judicial narratives demonstrates that even in criminal cases a judge's emotional response will not necessarily tend in any particular direction; it might be felt for the defendant, a victim, victims' families, or all of the above. Both of these judges are conscious that they are being scrutinised; both feel the burden of decision-making; and both clearly feel the need to differentiate between their emotional response and their duty as judges.

This last commonality, strongly reflecting the standard post-Realist account, is shared in a great many other cases. In burial disputes, which easily can veer toward the distasteful and tawdry as long-standing family resentments are hauled into the public eye, judges often voice the 'dismay', 'sympathy' and 'difficulties and embarrassment' they experience before coming to a decision.[78] As one judge wrote in a rape and murder case involving the question of whether a trial judge could be trusted to disregard the defendant's incriminating statement, 'judges, being flesh and blood, are subject to the same emotions and human frailties as affect other members of the specie[s]', but—the judge went on—a trained judge can set those factors aside in evaluating the evidence.[79]

That this level of emotional separation is the expected—even required—script is made clear in a case involving a 13-year-old girl who was tried as an adult for a killing committed when she was 11. The trial judge had (among other things) openly expressed being 'angry' when an important psychological report was not prepared. She also had demonstrated sympathy and compassion for the girl in precisely the parental manner of which Judge Mack would have heartily approved had the court been a juvenile one. However, the Supreme Court of Pennsylvania ruled that the judge ought to have recused herself for partiality. In contrast, the court lauded the words of a different judge who, at an earlier stage in the same case, had said:

> I cannot exonerate Mariam just because I feel sorry for her. I cannot return Mariam to juvenile court just because her life story and her life circumstances make my heart weep. I can't do it. My oath as a judge requires that I decide this case on the basis of the facts that I heard in court, and that's what I have done.[80]

Such a distancing statement, the court made clear, would meet its approval; acting in accordance with the emotion would not.

Given the power that still attends the command that judicial emotion be made non-operational, one wonders why judges (at least at times) feel the need to express the emotion at all. They could avoid potential criticism by simply staying

---

[78] H Conway and J Stannard, 'The Honours of Hades: Death, Emotion and the Law of Burial Disputes' (2011) 34 *University of New South Wales Law Journal* 860.
[79] *State v Hutchinson*, 271 A2d 641, 644 (Md 1970). See also *United States v Beckham*, Nos H-05-484, H-08-3426, 2009 WL 2615817, at *8–9 (SD Tex, 24 August 2009) (sentencing judge, addressing defendant's parents, said 'it breaks my heart that their son is in this situation', and told defendant 'my heart goes out to you').
[80] *Commonwealth v White*, 589 Pa 642, 659 (PA 2006).

silent and ruling as, according to their assertions, they were planning to in any event. They also could deny the emotion entirely, as did this California judge:

> I learned a long time ago when I first became a judge, when there is a [plea] offer and it's not accepted and you go to trial ...,[and the] defendant is convicted, then I'm sitting here going to sentence the defendant, and all I hear is a lot of loud tear-jerking pleas. [Defense l]awyers ... try to get the Judge to feel sorry. [Prosecutors] try to get the Judge to be angry, and I'm past all that. I'm not moved by emotion one way or the other. I'm just kind of like an iceberg, but there is no heating. I'm just here.[81]

Perhaps it is testament to the Realists' influence that such a statement rings false. To a modern-day ear it sounds implausible that a judge would actually achieve emotional 'iceberg' status. More, the claim sounds not just suspect but alarming: we worry that the 'iceberg' judge is not really the judge we want, as he sounds like someone who has distanced himself from his own humanity. Rather than sounding appropriately neutral he sounds chillingly detached.

It seems likely, then, that judges who choose to acknowledge their emotions fear being misjudged as people. They fear being seen as the sort of people who are not sad when young people become violent after having been failed by their families and communities, or angry when pregnant women are killed by intimate partners, or dismayed when bereaved siblings devolve into petty rancour, or whatever other normal human reaction they fear others will conclude they lack. Baum's theory of performativity here seems particularly salient. Judges want to be perceived positively and 'engage in self-presentation to audiences whose esteem is important to them', such as social peers.[82] The choice to expose personal emotion but position it in opposition to professional obligation appears calculated to communicate with a potentially hostile or disappointed audience, both by educating that audience about a judge's allowed decisional parameters and by communicating a shared humanity.

Another, more countercultural, variation of judicial candour involves acknowledging the emotion and *not* overtly distancing oneself from it. Such moments are less common but indicate that not all judges accept the set-it-aside aspect of the post-Realist script. A federal trial judge, for example, wrote the following about criminal sentencing:

> Early in my second year as a judge I had a discussion about sentencing with a mentor judge ... I told him of the extraordinary difficulty and emotional toll I was encountering in sentencing. He said, 'Don't worry, Mark, it will get much easier'. Out of respect, I did not respond, but I said to myself, if it gets easy to deprive someone of their liberty please shoot me. I have not been shot, and it hasn't gotten any easier.[83]

---

[81] *People v Carter*, No C053369, 2009 WL 626113 (Cal App 3 Dist, 12 March 2009).

[82] Baum (n 70) 4.

[83] MW Bennett, 'Heartstrings or Heartburn: A Federal Judge's Musings on Defendants' Right and Rite of Allocution' *The Champion* (Washington DC, March 2011) 26, fn 1.

It has not got easier, as he further wrote, because some of the sentencing allocutions he hears from defendants 'have pulled at my heartstrings and even brought me to tears, while others'—such as 'infuriatingly insincere nonsense from sophisticated, highly educated white collar defendants'—have 'given me heartburn and elevated my already too high blood pressure'.[84]

Rather than disclaim the emotional challenge of sentencing, this judge has chosen to embrace it as part and parcel of the enterprise, an internal signal that he is still adequately in touch with exactly what is at stake. This perspective is echoed by a judge on a state court of appeals, also speaking to the dynamics of criminal sentencing:

> I see absolutely nothing wrong, and as a matter of fact I think it should be encouraged, in a judge speaking freely, openly and expansively to the defendant, [to] lecture, cajole, empathize, sympathize, show compassion, warmth, and comprehension, show anger, umbrage, ire and indignity. These are human emotions that are meaningful to the person before the court, emotions they understand and easily comprehend. To go by rote in an emotionless ritual loses its human values and is less effective ... [Sentencing is] a 'show-down' where society, as represented by the judge, confronts a defendant for his antisocial conduct ... The time of sentencing is a desirable place for the judge to let his feeling be known.[85]

It is not coincidental that the overt acceptance of emotion seen in these two narratives comes in the criminal sentencing context, as that is a place where emotion's influence is particularly hard to deny. As a prominent federal judge bluntly stated following his handling of the highly-publicised trial and sentencing of disgraced financier Bernard Madoff, '[e]motion comes into play in every sentencing decision'.[86] Not allowing that emotion to 'cloud your judgment' is different, he suggested, from allowing it to inform that judgement; a good judge 'has to care', and emotion is a sign of caring. Directly taking on the script of dispassion, when speaking at a public forum this judge rejected the notion that

> the law lacks a soul. The law lacks tenderness. The law is objective and cold and inhumane. The law abhors emotion. I don't think that's true. Every time I sentence a defendant, there is a lot of emotion ... I think there is a lot of humanity in the law.[87]

These moments of judicial candour provide a valuable window into the complexity of judges' emotional lives. That we are able to find such moments at all signals that the script of dispassion is not airtight. Nor can such moments be fully attributed to momentary lapses of self-control (though surely such lapses occur, as the following section shall make clear). Rather, judges appear sometimes to fear that acting in a dispassionate manner may make them look heartless, an image they cannot tolerate, or may make the law itself look heartless, an assessment they dispute.

---

[84] Ibid, 26.
[85] *State v Bragg*, 388 NW 2d 187, 194 (Donielson J specially concurring).
[86] B Weiser, 'A Judge's Education, One Time' *New York Times* (9 October 2011) MB1.
[87] Ibid.

B. Observational Evidence of Anger

Another window is opened by direct observation of judges' emotional experiences as they are externalised through contemporaneous verbal and physical behaviours. The most plentiful evidence here is of judicial anger. Anger is among the easiest emotions reliably to identify from external observation; its common triggers are plentiful in a litigation setting; and as it is an emotion of power, it is the one judges appear least restrained in displaying. Judges may sometimes wish they had been more restrained, as extreme expressions of anger can land them in disciplinary proceedings, which often are publicly reported. There is even a market for judicial anger displays: where cameras are allowed in courtrooms, videos of outbursts regularly are featured on local news and draw a large viewership on *YouTube*. The popular website *Above the Law* has dubbed such outbursts 'benchslaps' and regularly features them in a special column.[88] Examination of these artifacts demonstrates three main targets for judicial anger: lawyers, the first by a wide margin; litigants and witnesses; and each another.

As to lawyers, judges regularly are angered by perceived incompetence, particularly when it wastes the court's time and makes the judge's job harder. Add in a cocky attitude and judicial anger may be nearly impossible to avoid. As a state trial judge once quipped, nothing is more provocative than 'impertinence by the incompetent, a combination that persistently remains in fashion'.[89] Some judges express their anger in a planned and deliberate manner. For example, when a federal trial judge felt that lawyers in a civil case were handling the matter poorly he publicly issued a bitingly sarcastic order directing them to attend a 'kindergarten party' in his courtroom, at which they would learn such crucial skills as '[h]ow to telephone and communicate with a lawyer'. The judge went on to promise the lawyers:

> An advanced seminar on not wasting the time of a busy federal court and his staff because you are unable to practice law at the level of a first year law student.
>
> Invitation to this exclusive event is not RSVP. Please remember to bring a sack lunch! The United States Marshals have beds available if necessary, so you may wish to bring a toothbrush in case the party runs late.[90]

In another civil case, a judge struggling with persistently aggravating—one is tempted to say maddening—behaviour from a lawyer similarly and deliberately chose harsh words as a coping mechanism. Refusing a motion to disqualify himself, the judge in a written opinion admitted that he had 'expressed varying degrees of disapprobation, hostility, impatience, dissatisfaction, annoyance, and anger

---

[88] See *Above The Law*: abovethelaw.com.
[89] GC O'Brien, 'Confessions of an Angry Judge' (2004) 87 *Judicature* 251.
[90] *Morris v Coker*, Nos A–11–MC–712–SS, A–11–MC–713–SS, A–11–MC–714–SS, A–11–MC–715–SS, 2011 WL 3847590, at *1 (WD Tex, 26 August 2011).

with [the attorney's] antics', including by calling various of his statements '"baloney", "false", "fraud", "impossible", "incredible", and "a lie"'.[91] He refused, however, to apologise for his anger, for those statements, or for characterising the attorney's briefs as 'ejaculations'.[92]

That judge's refusal to apologise illustrates another interesting hole in the seamless web that the script of dispassion pretends to be: judicial anger (particularly at lawyers) is so common, and so often well justified, that reviewing courts and disciplinary bodies refuse to condemn it unless it is objectively extreme. As one reviewing court explained:

> [T]here is one form of professional predisposition all judges share that may be classified as a kind of bias: expressions of dissatisfaction with deficient lawyering, overbearing advocacy and deceptions that stretch judicial patience to its outer boundaries. These practices often arouse manifestations of frustration, annoyance and even anger on the part of judges. But, even if short-tempered, such reactions alone are not sufficient to disqualify a judge from a case because they are not necessarily wrongful or inappropriate; indeed, at times they may be called for or understandable.[93]

Sometimes, though, those reactions seem neither called for nor proportionate. In a *YouTube*-circulated courtroom video, for example, one can observe a judge blowing his top when a smug lawyer accuses him of condoning jury tampering and threatens an investigation. The judge's voice rises, he curses and becomes visibly agitated, and at one point he smashes the bench with his fist and declares, 'I'll yell all I want, this is my court'.[94]

Intervention is most likely in instances in which the judge's anger expression is unplanned and explosive. In a widely-followed 2014 case in Florida that became a veritable *YouTube* sensation, a judge became very angry at a public defender who was widely regarded by other judges in that jurisdiction as 'rude, disrespectful, incompetent' and 'highly unlikeable'.[95] After a contentious interaction over setting a case for trial, the judge stated: 'if I had a rock I would throw it at you right now. Stop pissing me off ... If you want to fight, let's go out back and I'll just beat your ass ... Alright you, you want to fuck with me'.[96] The judge then left the courtroom with the defender. A loud physical confrontation could

---

[91] *Fox Indus, Inc v Gurovich*, 323 F Supp 2d 386, 389 (EDNY 2004).

[92] About the term 'ejaculations', the Court wrote: '[T]he Court is at a loss as to how else to describe the sentences in [the lawyer's] brief that consist only of the words "How ridiculous!" and "How pathetic!" ... Surely [the lawyer] is aware of the alternate definition of "ejaculation": to wit, a "sudden short exclamation"'. *The American Heritage Dictionary of the English Language*, 4th edn (2000). The Court obviously did not intend an alternative available meaning—ibid, 388, fn 2.

[93] *Teachers4Action v Bloomberg*, 552 F Supp 2d 414, 416 (SDNY 2008).

[94] 'Prosecutor Makes Threats to a Judge?' (*YouTube*, 19 February 2009): perma.cc/8Q67-HHXG.

[95] Inquiry concerning Judge John C Murphy, before the hearing panel of the Judicial Qualifications Commission, State of Florida, Findings, Conclusions and Recommendations (19 May 2015) perma.cc/4SUB-8F7Z. As this chapter goes to press, the disciplinary case against the judge remains under appeal.

[96] Ibid.

be heard, during which the judge was heard to yell 'fuck': he then returned to the courtroom, appearing out of breath and dishevelled. He quieted spectators' applause and stated, 'not all public defenders are like that'.[97] The incident drew enormous public attention.[98] The judge was suspended, fined and ordered to continue therapy.[99]

Judges sometimes may be observed unleashing their anger on litigants and witnesses, not the lawyers. In a far less publicised case than the one described above, a judge was disciplined for an angry 'tirade' against a mother in a child visitation case, an episode he attributed to 'being "burned out" from his years in family court with its increased caseload and decreased staff'.[100] Consider, too, a case in which a judge who had been repeatedly sworn at by a defendant stated to the court reporter that the '[r]ecord should show that ... if I'd have had a shotgun I need to have shot him but I don't have it today'.[101]

Anger at litigants and witnesses is often far more controlled than these last episodes suggest, and not infrequently is regarded by observers and reviewing courts as both appropriate and proportionate. In response to harsh words spoken by a sentencing judge, for example, a reviewing court wrote that

> it should be recognized that a judge is only human, being ordinarily imbued with a strong sense of duty and responsibility to the community. In his or her conscientiousness, the judge will sometimes speak out in frustration and even anger.[102]

Similarly, several federal trial judges in New York reportedly were 'outraged' when they observed police officers telling blatant lies while under oath; no one complained about that well-placed ire.[103] Going beyond the bounds of appropriate

---

[97] Ibid.

[98] In contrast to earlier examples in which judges were deliberately exposing emotion to an audience as a sort of plea to be regarded as a decent human being, in this case the existence of a literal audience was a large part of the judge's problem. When he re-entered to applause after the altercation he sought to diffuse their reaction, perhaps realising even then the trouble he had just got into, and the audience he soon gained on the internet ensured that he would have to be disciplined in order to restore the Court's public image. Accidental performances of emotion, unlike strategic ones, may be more unpredictable in their effect.

[99] His therapist testified at the disciplinary hearing that he had in the weeks and days leading up to the incident experienced a series of events, including his father's death, that left him without 'the emotional energy' to cope with the difficult attorney—Inquiry concerning Judge John C Murphy (n 95). This testimony is reminiscent of another Florida case, in which a judge was removed from the bench after a series of abusive incidents that, according to his psychiatrist, were caused by a pathological inability to handle anger appropriately—see *In re Sloop*, 946 So 2d 1046 (S Ct Fla 2007) (per curiam). In the more recent case the anger explosion was deemed 'an anomaly' while in the Sloop case such incidents were typical of that judge.

[100] MA Spoto, 'NJ Court Punishes Judge for Yelling at Woman' (*New Jersey On-Line*, 17 June 2011, 6:00 am): perma.cc/9BFQ-2Z6G.

[101] *Johnson v State*, 642 A 2d 259, 262 (Md Ct Spec App 1994). No grammatical or stylistic changes have been made to the original quotation (the judge appears to be speaking in a somewhat odd regional vernacular).

[102] *Carr v Senkowski*, No 01-CV-689, 2007 WL 3124624 (WDNY, 23 October 2007).

[103] B Weiser, 'Police in Gun Searches Face Disbelief in Court' *New York Times* (12 May 2008).

anger, though, are occasional expressions of disgust and contempt, as when a judge at sentencing refers to the defendant as a 'lowlife', 'scumbag', or similarly insulting term.[104]

Finally, judges get angry at each other. The chief judge of a federal appellate court drew incredulous gasps and major media coverage when, during an oral argument, she slammed her hand on the bench, told a fellow judge to 'shut up', and suggested he leave the courtroom.[105] Similar public attention followed an incident in which a loud argument among a state's Supreme Court justices over a forth-coming opinion allegedly devolved into physical violence.[106]

The now plentiful observational evidence of judicial anger episodes dramati-cally illustrates that the script of dispassion is a fantasy. One could regard this bounty as nothing more than evidence of human failure, and clearly some of the described episodes are that. However, the frequency with which those who tend most aggressively to police the script—reviewing courts, disciplinary bodies and the public—endorse some anger expressions indicates that fealty to the script is not uniform.

C. Qualitative Research Projects on Judicial Emotion

Finally, a third window into the emotional discourse of judging may be found in a small handful of studies. The emergence of such studies is a positive move and one hopes that more such efforts will follow.

One series of relevant studies is being conducted by two Australian scholars,[107] whose work includes a highly informative survey of magistrate judges. These judges work in the shadow of a now familiar professional norm dictating that judges shall 'not be swayed' by 'irrational' emotion.[108] Nonetheless, they identi-fied management of their emotional responses as a key element of their work; substantively, they reported sympathy, revulsion, disgust and sadness, the experi-ence of which they find 'emotionally … wearing'.[109] One Australian magistrate characterised the work as 'seeing absolute misery passing in front of you day in,

---

[104] See *In re Merlo*, 34 A 3d 932, 972 (Pa Ct Jud Disc 2011) (judge 'in a tirade' called defendant a 'low life' and 'a scumbag'); *In re Lokuta*, 964 A 2d 988, 1054 (Pa Ct Jud Disc 2008) (judge screamed at the defendant that she was 'nothing but a fat pig, whore, lowlife'); *Milmir Constr v Jones*, 626 So 2d 985, 986 (Fla Ct App 1993) (judge called attorney a 'scumball').

[105] D Cassens Weiss, '5th Circuit Oral Arguments Turn Contentious When Chief Judge Tells Colleague to Shut Up' *ABA Journal* (26 September 2011). Jones later apologised for her 'intemperate language', ibid.

[106] C Stephenson, C Spivak and P Marley, 'Justices' Feud Gets Physical' *Milwaukee-Wisconsin Journal Sentinel* (25 June 2011).

[107] S Roach Anleu and K Mack, *Judicial Research Project*: perma.cc/DX9E-H26X.

[108] S Roach Anleu and K Mack, 'Magistrates' Everyday Work and Emotional Labour' (2005) 32 *Journal of Law and Society* 590, 601–02.

[109] Ibid.

day out, month in, month out, year in, year out'.[110] Another, reflecting on child welfare cases, said:

> I have a problem walking away and just erasing everything I've heard about families and the stress that they're under, the treatment children have been dished out, what will happen to them for the rest of their lives. I just find it difficult to walk away from that and go home to my own children and look at them and think 'Oh, God', you know. I usually find I try to be more patient with my own children when I go home after a day in the [family court]. So it's just the sadness; there is no good news.[111]

Yet another magistrate described a feeling of being stuck between poor options:

> Now, there's two things that can happen to you. Either you're going to remain a decent person and become terribly upset by it all because your emotions—because your feelings are being pricked by all of this constantly or you're going to become—you're going to grow a skin on you as thick as a rhino, in which case I believe you're going to become an inadequate judicial officer because once you lose the human—the feeling for humanity you can't really—I don't believe you can do the job.[112]

As just this small excerpt from the Australian project shows, those who experience judging first-hand rather than theorising about it paint a vivid emotional picture.

A smaller study from the United States also yielded rich narratives.[113] The study focused narrowly on judges' perspectives on 'victim impact statements', commonly offered in open court at sentencing by a victim or the victim's family members. The researchers described one interview thus:

> One judge ... recalled a DWI case in which a young child [had] almost lost his life. His mother delivered an impact statement in which she described how she thought her son was going to die. 'I remember thinking', the judge said, 'I am going to cry'. But he regained what he thought was necessary composure because 'you are not supposed to cry on the bench when you are a judge'.[114]

This narrative emerged from another interview:

> I said, 'Sir, you are going to prison, and that's where animals like you belong'. And I usually don't say that but, if you get called a MF [expletive abbreviated] ten times, and it was by someone who raped a step-daughter, and he's in your face ... And I felt bad later. I thought, 'OK, you lost your cool'. But I didn't feel that badly, but I try not to stoop to their level. I felt bad-good.[115]

Other judges reported frustration, anger and compassion.[116] Like their Australian counterparts these judges reported that the legal system aims 'to strip away

---

[110] Ibid, 611.
[111] Ibid, 613.
[112] Ibid, 612. No grammatical or stylistic changes have been made to the original quotation, which is a transcription of oral speech.
[113] M Lay Schuster and A Propen, 'Degrees of Emotion: Judicial Responses to Victim Impact Statements' (2010) 6 *Law, Culture and the Humanities* 75.
[114] Ibid, 89.
[115] Ibid, 93.
[116] Ibid.

emotions'. As a result, some indicated, they felt like they were 'working in a factory of sorts in which [they] are just grinding these cases out', and worried that they were becoming 'insulated and numb'.[117]

A third set of studies is currently underway in Sweden.[118] A pair of sociologists is combining courtroom observation, shadowing and semi-structured interviews to gain insight into the emotional dynamics of both judging and being a prosecutor. As they report, from 'a conventional perspective, which sees reason as the opposite of emotion, Swedish courts are *the* non-emotional arena par excellence'.[119] Nonetheless, they find evidence of emotion, albeit painted in shades far more muted than are the examples from the United States and Australia. One judge, immediately after exiting the courtroom following a proceeding in which she had forgotten an important procedural task, exclaimed 'I was so ashamed I could die'.[120] One judge, reflecting on an episode in which a prosecutor continued an inappropriate line of questioning after missing or disregarding a hint from the judge that he should stop, reported:

> I said: [hissing voice] You are not allowed to ask those questions, just be quiet ... I was so furious at [the prosecutor]. There were two things: one was what he did to [the victim], but the other thing was that he disobeyed. He questioned me, my authority.[121]

The researchers also came to realise that a very subtle signal—putting down the pen with which a judge usually takes notes—was a reliable sign of irritation.[122]

Each of these studies shines a light on the reality of emotion 'in a space where it is claimed to be absent'.[123] Together with the other observational evidence and moments of judicial candour they help us imagine the full range of judges' emotional experiences.

IV. Towards an Emotionally Intelligent Discourse About, and Of, Judging

The prior sections have shown the considerable distance between discourse about emotion in judging and the discourse of emotion in judging. The purest,

---

[117] Ibid, 89.

[118] S Roach Anleu, S Bergman Blix and K Mack, 'Researching Emotion in Courts and the Judiciary: A Tale of Two Projects' (2015) 7 *Emotion Review* 145; S Roach Anleu, S Bergman Blix, K Mack and Å Wettergren, 'Observing Judicial Work and Emotions: Using Two Researchers' (2016) 16 *Qualitative Research* 375.

[119] S Bergman Blix and Å Wettergren, 'The Emotional Labour of Gaining and Maintaining Access to the Field' (2015) 15 *Qualitative Research* 688.

[120] Anleu et al, 'Researching Emotion in Courts' (n 118) 4.

[121] S Bergman Blix and Å Wettergren, 'A Sociological Perspective on Emotions in the Judiciary' (2016) 8 *Emotion Review* 26.

[122] Anleu et al, 'Observing Judicial Work' (n 118) 9.

[123] Anleu et al, 'Researching Emotion in Courts' (n 118) 1.

pre-Realist account of judging is soundly belied by evidence that judges, including good judges, experience emotion in their professional lives. The conventional post-Realist account that acknowledges emotion but requires it to be set aside clearly retains prescriptive power, as many judges claim to be expending effort to do just that. However, that account, too, is suspect. It is challenged by evidence that judges often do not set emotion aside—not only as a matter of human failure, which certainly is present in abundance, but also because they believe it would be wrong to do so. Here the true dissenting strand of both Realist and post-Realist theory—suggesting that emotion can play a positive role in judging, the nature of which is not fully specified—gains traction. It also gains important detail. The words and actions of judges performing the acts of judging provide vital data points from which to construct a model of positive and negative iterations of emotion.

It is critical that we construct such models. Otherwise we risk being contented with broad, shallow assertions with a distinct 'Goldilocks' quality,[124] along these lines: judges should openly acknowledge and make use of their emotions to the extent it is legitimate and helpful to do so, and set emotions aside when they are unhelpful or destructive.[125] Emotion—Goldilocks might continue—should be deployed in just the right combination with cognition, logic and precedent, and that admixture will vary according to the particular case and its context.

These assertions are undoubtedly true; they are just not particularly helpful without being rooted in a deep set of grounded theories as to each element and their interaction. That is what is required to forge a space for an emotionally intelligent discourse about and of judging. Forging that space is no small endeavour, one about which I and others have written at greater length elsewhere and to which, I trust, many other scholars and judges will devote their talents in years to come. I here offer a few brief organising principles.

First, legal systems would do well to fully internalise the message that we need not—indeed, ought not—ask judges to 'strip away' their emotions. That we currently do so is revealed by accounts from the United States, Australia and Sweden, and in none of those places is the effort productive. Not only does the script of dispassion make it far more difficult to discern emotion's actual influence, but the effort to comply with it takes an enormous and unjustified toll on judges. The fact that we appear not even fully to endorse the script—in practice, we laud judicial expressions of emotion when we agree with the values and judgements they express, and deride them when we do not—adds a disingenuous wrinkle that from a judicial perspective can be unpredictable and confusing.

---

[124] As in the old fairytale of *Goldilocks and the Three Bears*, the concept of something being 'just right', with no way of specifying what this looks like or how to get there.

[125] See eg, Posner, *Frontiers of Legal Theory* (n 45) 228, 230–31, 245; Little (n 62) 211–12, 218; Pillsbury (n 62) 350–51; Kaufman (n 63) 16; J Soeharno, *The Integrity of the Judge: A Philosophical Inquiry* (Farnham, Ashgate, 2009) 67–68; E Ryan, 'The Discourse Beneath: Emotional Epistemology in Legal Deliberation and Negotiation' (2005) 10 *Harvard Negotiation Law Review* 231, 249.

The modifications of the post-Realist script help mitigate some of these harms, but it remains counterproductive to insist that emotion always be set aside. It often cannot, will not, or should not.

Second, we would do well to encourage judges in developing their skill at regulating emotion.[126] Regulation typically entails changing the emotion-eliciting situation, changing one's thoughts about that situation, or changing one's responses to that situation. Humans deploy a range of strategies to achieve these goals, some far more productive than others. The script of dispassion encourages the strategies that are least productive in the context of judging. For example, judges seeking to comply with that script may engage in suppression and denial of emotional experience, with negative impacts on their physical and mental health and on the quality of their decisions. Judges could instead be encouraged to practise—to single out one of the most promising strategies—cognitive reappraisal, which involves thoughtful examination of an emotion's underlying thoughts and judgements. Reappraisal entails none of the costs associated with suppression and usefully leverages the power of reason to shape emotion.

Competent judicial emotion regulation—a complicated enterprise of which the above account gives just a taste—may never be easy; it is a high-level skill with which all humans struggle. Some judges are naturally better at it than others. However, the skills are accessible to all and all can improve on their natural abilities. Further, given the abundance of relevant psychological research on emotion regulation its processes need not remain a mystery. The most critical regulatory capacities for a judge are sensitivity to one's experience, a deep bench of strategic options, and context-driven flexibility in how those options are employed. This combination allows a judge to exert far greater control over his or her emotions and how he or she chooses to express them. Such regulatory skill is far more likely to abound in a judge who rejects the script of dispassion than in one who accepts it.

Third, we should embrace rather than avoid the normative implications of judicial emotion. It makes little sense to say that emotion is important to judging but deny it operational significance. If empathy, for example, is merely an intellectual exercise it is pointless; why would we want a judge to be able to perceive the perspective of another unless we also want that judge to care and perhaps take action accordingly? Similarly, if we accept that anger, or sorrow, or any other emotion might be proper for a judge, we must believe that the emotion will help him or her take beneficial action. Simultaneously, however, it should be apparent that emotion is not *always* appropriate and *might* lead to detrimental action. The value

---

[126] For a far more detailed exploration of the mechanisms of emotion regulation and how judges can best make use of them, to which this short chapter cannot do justice, see TA Maroney, 'Emotional Regulation and Judicial Behavior' (2011) 99 *California Law Review* 1481.

of emotion is normatively variable.[127] No theorist or judge believes that emotion provides an infallible, indispensable guide to judicial action, and one would search in vain for a principled defence of that position when confronted with stories of judges belittling defendants or assaulting lawyers and one another. Cardozo put it nicely:

> Belief in the efficacy of mere emotion is not essential to the faith whereby a sinful idolizer of precedent may be transported into the beatitude of a renegade lover of reality ... there has been no thought to preach a doctrine of undisciplined surrender to the cardiac prompting of the moment, the visceral reactions of one judge or another ... [Instead,] the subjective creations of the mind must be constantly checked and restrained and reconsidered in the light of the tests and standards of objective or external verity.[128]

Rather than uniformly laud emotion or indulge a caricatured, emotionless version of reason, we must invest in defining the lines that separate positive and negative judicial experience—and expression—of emotion.

I have advocated, for example, a distinction between righteous and non-righteous anger, following the Aristotelean concept in which anger is virtuous if felt 'at the right times, with reference to the right objects, towards the right people, with the right motive, and in the right way'.[129] This is a highly context-specific enquiry, in which we must scrutinise the reasons underlying the anger and examine its behavioural impacts while holding in mind the fact that judges cannot 'have a sense of justice without the capacity and willingness to be personally outraged'.[130] The same approach—specific, detailed, grounded—is needed for every sort of emotion that judges experience.

These organising principles can help lessen the distance between the rhetoric and the reality of judging. The lesser the distance, the looser the grip of the script of dispassion. That is all to the good. Loosening the grip matters to judges as people: a judge whose professional identity is emotionally well-adjusted is likely to have better physical health, happier work–life balance and more functional personal relationships. But it also matters to judges as judges. An emotionally intelligent judge is more able to react appropriately to challenging stimuli, learn from experience and selectively integrate emotion into the varied tasks of judging.

---

[127] Maroney, 'Persistent Cultural Script' (n 1) 671.

[128] Cardozo, 'Jurisprudence' (n 23) 13.

[129] Aristotle, 'Nicomachean Ethics' 1106b20 in R McKeon (ed), *The Basic Works of Aristotle* (New York, Random House, 1941) 958.

[130] RC Solomon, *A Passion for Justice: Emotions and the Origins of the Social Contract* (Washington DC, Addison-Wesley Publishing Company, 1990) 42.

V. Conclusion

When Justice Brennan asserted that good judging flows from a 'dialogue of reason and passion'[131] he was urging us to embrace the model advocated decades earlier by Justice Cardozo. Cardozo, for his part, thus imagined how that dialogue ought to play out in any individual case:

> Justice reacted upon logic, sentiment upon reason, by guiding the choice to be made between one logic and another. Reason in its turn reacted upon sentiment by purging it of what is arbitrary, by checking it when it might otherwise have become extravagant, by relating it to method and order and coherence and tradition.[132]

A better discursive model we are unlikely to find. By embracing emotion as one— not the only—contributor to fine judicial decision-making we stand to rescue our discourse about judging from the realm of caricature, and to enable a discourse of judging that reflects and encourages emotional integrity and thoughtfulness.

---

[131] Brennan (n 41) 3.
[132] Cardozo, 'Jurisprudence' (n 23) 45.

13

Becoming Like Solomon: Towards an Emotionally Intelligent Legal System

JOHN STANNARD AND HEATHER CONWAY*

I. Introduction

One of the most famous stories in the Bible is the judgement of Solomon.[1] King Solomon, a man renowned for his wisdom, is faced by two women both claiming to be the mother of a certain child. The King announces his verdict—the child should be cut in two and half given to each claimant. One claimant agrees to this; the other says she would rather let her opponent have the child than see him die. Solomon then awards the child to the second claimant, as she is obviously the real mother. A classic illustration of emotionally intelligent judging—yet the traditional approach is to exclude such matters entirely from the legal sphere!

The present collection has thrown up numerous illustrations of the destructive potential of what might be termed 'emotional stupidity' in the legal context. Some of these involve the malign effect of inappropriate emotions, such as sibling rivalry in the context of inheritance disputes, or disintegrative shaming in relation to sex offenders, or the use of dehumanising narratives in end-of-life discourses. Others involve the misunderstandings that may occur when key actors in the legal process, such as lawyers, arbitrators and judges, fail to take proper account of the emotional dynamics of situations with which they are faced. In other situations the problem is not so much the total disregard of emotion as a failure to appreciate its nuances and subtleties, as in the context of the affective family, or the attachments that give rise to complaints of undue influence, or the appropriate response to victims. As against this, we have also seen the positive advantages of an emotionally informed approach, as in relation to the movement for immigrant justice in the United States. All of this suggests that nobody involved with the administration and

---

* School of Law, Queen's University Belfast
[1] 1 Kings 3: 16–28.

practice of the law can afford to ignore the need for emotional intelligence. As we shall see, this is an enormous field of study in itself, and there is much work that needs to be done in applying its insights to the realm of law and legal discourse. However, what we can do in this final chapter is to draw on some of the themes identified in previous pages and see if they can provide any pointers as to how this might be achieved. In doing so, we shall begin by looking more closely at the concept of emotional intelligence itself, before seeing how its insights can be applied in the legal context.

II. Emotional Intelligence

The concept of emotional intelligence is a relatively recent construct.[2] Its first appearance in the field of psychology seems to have been during the 1960s,[3] and it was another 25 years until it made its major impact. A groundbreaking article in 1990 by Peter Salovey and Jack Mayer in the journal *Imagination, Cognition and Personality*[4] was closely followed by Daniel Goleman's book on the subject,[5] and brought the concept of emotional intelligence to the forefront of popular psychology. Since then, the subject has been discussed extensively both at the academic and the popular levels, which in many ways has been both a help and a hindrance to understanding what it is all about.[6]

Emotional intelligence has been defined in terms of 'the capacity to reason about emotions, and of emotions [and] to enhance thinking', and to include 'the abilities to accurately perceive emotions, to access and generate emotions so as to assist thought, to understand emotions and emotional knowledge, and to reflectively regulate emotions so as to promote emotional and intellectual growth'.[7] Though as stated above the topic has spawned a vast amount of academic literature,[8] it is by no means an uncontroversial one in scientific terms; in particular, there have been problems in identifying its theoretical basis, in devising ways in which it may

---

[2] See generally, G Matthews, M Zeidner and RD Roberts, *Emotional Intelligence: Science and Myth* (Cambridge, MA, MIT Press, 2004) 10.

[3] Apparently the term first appeared in an unpublished doctoral thesis written by one Wayne Payne: see WL Payne, *A Study of Emotion: Developing Emotional Intelligence, Self-Integration, Relating to Pain, Fear, Desire* (Dissertation Abstracts International, 1986) cited by Matthews, Zeidner and Roberts (n 2).

[4] P Salovey and JD Mayer, 'Emotional Intelligence' (1990) 9 *Imagination, Cognition and Personality* 185.

[5] D Goleman, *Emotional Intelligence* (New York, Bantam Books, 1995).

[6] Matthews, Zeidner and Roberts (n 2) 10–15.

[7] JD Mayer, P Salovey and DR Caruso, 'Emotional Intelligence: Theory, Findings and Implications' (2004) 15 *Psychological Inquiry* 197.

[8] According to Google Scholar, the article by Salovey and Mayer (n 4) has been cited over 9,000 times to date: scholar.google.co.uk.

be measured, and in mapping it onto existing psychological constructs.[9] Nevertheless, it is at least a useful lens through which to view the field of law and legal discourse, and the rest of the chapter will attempt to sketch out ways in which this might be done.

Though there are a number of competing models of emotional intelligence in the field, one of the most influential is that proposed by Jack Mayer, Peter Salovey and David Caruso,[10] which identifies four key elements.[11] The first of these is the *perception* of emotion, both in oneself and others; this is said to be the most basic aspect, as it makes all other processing of emotional information possible. The second is the *understanding* of emotion, in particular the ability to understand the complex dynamics of emotion and the way emotions evolve over time. The third is the *use* of emotion, in which emotions are harnessed in order to facilitate various cognitive activities to achieve various goals. Finally, there is the *management* of emotion both in oneself and in others. Whatever one's views may be as to the usefulness of emotional intelligence as a scientific construct, it will be obvious that all of these factors are of great relevance in the field of law and legal discourse; but how can they best be applied? It is to this question that we must now turn.

III. Emotional Intelligence and the Law

How, then, can the law and the practice of the law be made more emotionally intelligent? Two problems come to mind in trying to answer this question. The first is that of applying a human characteristic such as emotional intelligence to non-human abstractions. This can only be countered by the realisation that this can only be done by analogy; when one speaks of 'law and the practice of the law' in this context one is thinking in particular of legal actors, in Maroney's taxonomy,[12] including not only judges and professional lawyers but the whole range of actors in the legal drama, including legislators, policymakers, pressure groups and those who seek to influence the development of the law. Second, when we speak of 'emotional intelligence' here we are thinking not in terms of an inherent characteristic such as IQ, which one is born with, but as a set of skills that can be honed and developed; were it otherwise, there would be no point in asking the question in the first place.

Bearing this in mind, we can now ask what lessons can be learned from the issues discussed in this collection. In doing so, we shall follow the model of emotional intelligence discussed in the previous section, by considering the four

---

[9] Matthews, Zeidner and Roberts (n 2) 514–16.
[10] Mayer, Salovey and Caruso (n 7).
[11] Ibid, 199–200.
[12] Ch 1, n 2.

aspects proposed by Mayer and others, namely the perception of emotion, the understanding of emotion, the use of emotion and the regulation of emotion. After this, we shall consider the ways in which these lessons can be applied before asking whether any broader conclusions can be drawn.

A. The Perception of Emotion

It goes without saying that before one can exercise emotional intelligence one has to recognise that there is an emotional dimension to the issue in the first place. In some branches of the law, as we have seen, the existence of that dimension is plain to see, for instance in relation to family law,[13] or victims of crime,[14] or the practice of mediation,[15] or public responses to sexual offences against children.[16] In others it is less obvious, for instance in relation to the law of property or the law of succession.[17] However, even where it is clear that emotion has some role to play, various problems arise.

The first is the need for those involved to recognise that *their own* emotions may be a relevant factor in the equation. Someone confronted with a highly emotionally charged situation, such as a family breakdown, may see the problem solely in terms of the emotions of others, without realising that they too may be part of the same problem. Thus, as we have seen decision-makers in these situations may have to navigate between the Scylla and Charybdis of emotional 'flooding' (in which too much account is given to the emotional factors)[18] and the opposing danger of vicarious traumatisation (in which a thick skin is cultivated in order to keep them at bay).[19] Another issue that we have identified is what might be called the emotional wolf in the clothing of the rational sheep. Thus, for instance we have seen how judges in succession disputes may seek to take refuge from the need to confront tricky emotional issues by using established legal doctrines to clothe their decisions in a false veneer of objectivity,[20] and how the assessment of risk in the case of sexual offenders may be coloured by emotional factors as much as by actuarial ones.[21] The very fact that those involved in these situations may deny the existence of these problems makes them all the more dangerous in the legal context.

---

[13] Ch 2.
[14] Ch 6.
[15] Ch 10.
[16] Ch 7.
[17] Ch 3.
[18] Ch 10, text accompanying n 104.
[19] Ch 8, text accompanying n 131.
[20] Ch 3, text accompanying n 120.
[21] Ch 7, text accompanying n 73.

B. The Understanding of Emotion

Recognising the presence of the emotional dynamics is of no use at all if those dynamics are not properly understood or taken into account. As we have argued in relation to such areas as family law and criminal law, the law has always been aware of the tendency of human beings to react in emotional ways, but this has often been accompanied by an attitude of suspicion, together with a perception that the law needs to 'rise above' these matters in the search for a sensible solution. Thus, for instance, relationships of trust and confidence are seen not as something of value to be encouraged, but merely as a potential source of exploitation;[22] the expression of emotions may be in order for clients, but not for lawyers,[23] still less judges.[24] In the same way, the law's understanding of emotions can often be superficial, unidimensional and lacking in nuance, with little appreciation of the complex and shifting emotional dynamics of such situations as family conflict,[25] sibling rivalry[26] and grieving for the loss of a loved one.[27] Indeed, as has been argued in previous pages in relation to the undocumented activist movement, the emotions to which law responds are not naturally occurring phenomena, but are themselves products of complex social formation.[28] In this sort of context, it is not surprising to find a plethora of common misconceptions: the punishment of the perpetrator will bring 'closure' to the victim and his or her family;[29] death brings families together;[30] what victims want above all is revenge;[31] those who have been traumatised will have a clear memory of their experiences;[32] restorative justice will not work in the context of sexual offences against children.[33] Closely allied to these is what can be described as the 'binary' myth,[34] in which issues are seen in black and white terms with no shade of grey in between; families are either loving or dysfunctional,[35] disputes must have a winner and a loser,[36] and there can be no tolerance of uncertainty in decision-making.[37] Needless to say, this is a failing to which an adversarial system of law is particularly prone.

---

[22] Ch 4, text accompanying n 77.
[23] Ch 11, text accompanying n 32.
[24] Ch 12, text accompanying n 6.
[25] Ch 2, text accompanying n 3.
[26] Ch 3, text accompanying n 28.
[27] Ibid, text accompanying n 21.
[28] Ch 9, 'Conclusion'.
[29] Ch 2, text accompanying n 36; ch 6, text accompanying n 108.
[30] Ch 3, text accompanying n 18.
[31] Ch 6, text accompanying n 5.
[32] Ch 8, text accompanying n 69.
[33] Ch 7, text accompanying n 190.
[34] Ch 2, section II.B.
[35] Ibid.
[36] Ch 2, text accompanying n 64.
[37] Ch 8, section V.B.

C. The Use of Emotion

One of the more interesting insights of emotional intelligence theory is the extent to which one's own emotions and the emotions of others can be harnessed towards the achievement of certain desired goals. One obvious application of this in the legal context is in relation to the practice of advocacy, in which emotional rhetoric has historically had as great a part to play as reasoned argument,[38] but the use of emotion in the legal context need not be merely performative;[39] on the contrary, it may be perfectly genuine, as where the emotion of guilt is used in the context of family disputes to promote reparation,[40] or where the emotion of shame is used in the context of reintegrative shaming processes.[41] Of course, just as emotions can be used, so they can be misused, as has been argued in relation to the emotional content of end-of-life discourses.[42] Similarly, we have seen how sympathy for victims can be harnessed to support hegemonic narratives in the sentencing context,[43] and how the notion of 'closure', often invoked in the interests of victims, can be essentially a reason for ignoring their interests where it no longer suits us.[44] Merely knowing how to recognise and harness emotions is not enough; rather it must be done in a constructive manner, though how this works out in practice is, as we shall see, not always easy to discern.

D. The Management of Emotion

Last but not least, emotional intelligence involves the ability to manage emotion. As we have seen in relation to the practice of mediation, there are numerous tried and tested techniques both for the management of the mediator's own emotions and for the encouragement of constructive emotional responses from each of the parties to the dispute,[45] and a moment's thought will demonstrate how similar insights can be relevant in other branches of the law. Thus, for instance, such practices as collaborative law, restorative justice and reintegrative shaming have emotional regulation at their very heart, and as we have seen these skills can be applied in a wide variety of contexts, ranging from the practice of adjudication to the drafting of wills. The key issue here is not *whether* emotional regulation has a part to play in legal discourse, but *how* it should be used. As we have seen from our discussion of emotion in relation to judges[46] and other members of the

---

[38] Ch 10, text accompanying n 76.
[39] Ibid, text accompanying n 81.
[40] Ch 2, text accompanying nn 58–59.
[41] Ch 7, text accompanying n 138.
[42] Ch 5.
[43] Ch 6, text accompanying n 20.
[44] Ibid, text accompanying n 108.
[45] Ch 10.
[46] Ch 12.

legal professions,[47] the emotional labour[48] involved in maintaining a facade of objectivity can lead to deleterious consequences for all those involved, and the same applies by extension to the other fields of legal discourse addressed in this book. So how can the insights provided by the concept of emotional intelligence best be applied? Obviously this is a distinct question in itself, which would require a lot more consideration than can be given in the present context, but some preliminary observations are worth making.

E. The Way Ahead?

There are two aspects to the question posed at the end of the previous paragraph, the first relating to *what* should be done, and the second as to *how* it can be done. In many ways the second of these questions is a lot easier to answer than the first, as there are various different levels at which those involved in the discourses of law can be more informed in their response to emotion, to be more sensitive to the emotions they generate, and to be more aware of their own emotions as they impact on legal practice. We have already seen how the insights of emotional intelligence can inform not only those areas of legal practice where the emotional dimension is clear to see, such as family law and mediation, but even such mundane tasks as the drafting of a will, and all those currently involved with the practice and administration of the law can be encouraged to be aware of emotion and the way it can impact on the decisions they make. At a more fundamental level, legal education has a key role to play both in the training of lawyers and in the evolution and development of professional norms; in particular, just as doctors are encouraged to develop a good 'bedside manner', emotional intelligence should be considered as important as intellectual ability in the selection and training of lawyers.

The more difficult question is determining the *appropriate* role of emotions in the legal context. As in the context of judging, so in emotions and law generally, it is simply not enough, as Terry Maroney has said in Chapter Twelve, to come up with a 'Goldilocks' aspiration which demands that something is 'just right' with no way of specifying what this looks like or how to get there.[49] In this connection some of the principles suggested by Maroney may be of broader application; thus, for instance, what she calls the 'script of dispassion' can be as unhelpful in the wider legal context as it is in that of judging, and other actors in the legal drama, no less than judges, should be encouraged to sharpen up their skills of emotion regulation and to embrace rather than avoid its normative implications. As well as this, attention needs to be paid to the ways in which emotional intelligence can be used to promote what might be called the communitarian or relational

[47] Ch 11.
[48] Ibid, section III.C.
[49] Ch 12, text accompanying n 124.

themes identified in this collection, including family reparation,[50] empathy,[51] communion,[52] reintegration[53] and relational autonomy.[54] To a certain extent this is already done in the context of practices such as mediation,[55] collaborative law[56] and restorative justice,[57] but there is surely scope for some of the insights provided by these practices to be applied in a broader context.

IV. Conclusion

In the opening sentence of this collection, we began with a reference to Daniel Goleman and his seminal work on emotional intelligence.[58] In the course of that work, the author quotes the famous aphorism by Aristotle to the effect that it is easy to become angry, but less easy to be angry with the right person, to the right degree, at the right time, for the right purpose, and in the right way.

The history of law and emotion scholarship in recent years can be divided into a number of phases. In the first phase the main task was essentially destructive: namely to demolish the traditional reason/emotion dichotomy and to show the way in which, in the words of Susan Bandes, 'emotions pervade the law'.[59] Since then, the focus has tended to be more descriptive, in the sense that writers on law and emotion have tried to explore different ways in which law and emotion interact, and what that can tell us about the law. However, as the present volume suggests, we are now perhaps moving towards a more normative phase, in which the interaction of law and emotion is taken for granted, but attention is paid to the ways in which these emotional dynamics can be used and misused. Bringing the insights of emotional intelligence to bear on the law and legal practice is one way in which this normative task can be approached, but there is a lot of work still to be done in this area. The task of formulating a sound theoretical basis for determining the appropriate role of emotion in legal discourse may be a daunting one, but it is one that promises to keep what might be called the law and emotion community well occupied in the years that lie ahead!

---

[50] Ch 2, section III.A.
[51] Ch 10, section III.G.
[52] Ch 6, text accompanying n 60.
[53] Ch 7, text accompanying n 126.
[54] Ch 4, text accompanying n 63.
[55] Ch 10.
[56] Ch 2, text accompanying n 46.
[57] Ch 7, section V.
[58] Ch 1, text accompanying n 1.
[59] SA Bandes (ed), *The Passions of Law* (New York, New York University Press, 1999) 2.

INDEX

society and emotion, 86–8
solicitors and emotion, 250–1, 253
Sotomayor, Sonia (judge), 250, 263, 267
  stasis in family law (US), 12–14
'strategic friendliness' (legal tactic), 252
stronger party, undue influence of, 68
'subsidiary protection', 158
substance and reparative model of family
  law, 23–4
support and accountability circles (Canada),
  147–8
  aim and focus of, 147
  evaluation of, 147–8
'surface acting', 254
survivors:
  rape, of, 174–5
  sexual offences, of, 159, 160–2
  sexual violence, of, 174–5
'suspicious circumstances' rule, 63, 65
sympathy, 230
  blame and, 124–5
  empathy and, 112–13

testamentary undue influence, 62–4
  description of, 62–3
therapeutic context and legal context compared,
  114–15
therapeutic jurisprudence:
  function of, 3
  movement of, 3–4
therapeutic relationships, adult and empathy, 229
torture, 156, 173, 181
transformative mediation, 217–19
  definition, 217
  emotion and, 218
transgression, (cycle of intimacy), 21
'trust and confidence' relationship and undue
  influence, 62
trust and undue influence, 75–8

uncertainty, tolerating, 180–2
undocumented activism, 187–98
  authorisation and, 206–8
  emotional transition in, 199–208
undocumented activists:
  civil disobedience acts, by, 193
  narratives of, 188–9
  political engagement and, 201–2
undocumented experience, emotion of
  and self-disclosure, 191–5
undocumented immigrants:
  alienation of supporters, 199
  educational prospects, 203
  identity and, 202–4
undue influence, 60–9
  'actual', 64
  'autonomy harms' and, 69
  'claimant-sided', 67

Classes of, 64, 74
Class cases, 64, 73, 74, 78, 79–80
coercion and, 61
consent or assent of weaker party and, 67
duties of (Atiyah), 67
emotion of, 73–9
emotional dynamics and, 59–82
fear and, 73–5
law and, 80–1
'presumption' and, 64
principle of, 65–6
proof of, 61–2
rationale of, 66–9
'relational autonomy' and, 68–9
stronger party, undue conduct of, 68
structure of, 79–80
trust and, 75–8
'trust and confidence' relationship and, 62
wills and, 64
unequal estate distribution and parental
  favouritism, 49
uneven estate distribution, discussion with
  children about, 47–8
United Nations High Commissioner for
  Refugees (UNHCR), 157
United States:
  American Bar Association decision on
    collaborative law, 20
  American Realist Movement, 3–4
  child welfare system, 13, 15, 23, 28
  criminal proceedings and capital cases, 114
  family law, 9–33
  immigration system, reform of, 185–6
  legal challenge to contested wills, 50–1
  research projects, 281–2
  'shame penalties', 138–40
  'signs and apologies' (sex offence penalty), 139

'Vicarious Traumatisation' (VT), 179–80
victim impact statements, 121
  empathy and, 108–15
  human dignity and, 113
  offender's perspective, 111
  victim narratives, in, 111
victim participation:
  emotion and, 123–6
  narrative issues, 123–6
victimisation:
  criminal justice process, 107–8
  experience, narrative of, 116–19
  secondary, 148–9
victimisation narratives and criminal justice,
  119–22
victims:
  accounts, belief in, 123–4
  criminal trials and, outcomes of, 119–20
  distress of, relieving, 124–5
  impact evidence at sentencing, 106–7